Cold Hit

D1451912

Cold
Hit

CHRISTOPHER G. MOORE

Heaven Lake Press

Distributed in Thailand by:
Asia Document Bureau Ltd.
P.O. Box 1029
Nana Post Office
Bangkok 10112 Thailand
Fax: (662) 260-4578
Website: www.heavenlakepress.com
email: editorial@heavenlakepress.com

First published in Thailand 1999
Trade paperback edition 2004

Jacket design: K. Jiamsomboon
Cover photograph: Ralf Tooten © 2010

ISBN 978-616-7503-05-9

Special thanks to Four's Studio Co., Ltd. for granting permission to use the lyrics to the song "Hello, Hia."

The song was popularized by the Tahi singer Yui during the time this story takes place.

Also special thanks to the following people:

Darrell K. Woolley was an excellent guide to the City of Los Angeles, California and assisted in making arrangements with LAPD on my behalf.

Pete Phermsangngam, LAPD Police Officer, was generous with his time and shared his knowledge about policing in Los Angeles.

Father Joe Maier, whose courage and compassion shows what one man dedicated to doing good can accomplish against all the odds.

Richard Diran's insight into expat life was helpful and he was a good guide to Washington Square.

Norman Smith and Fred Wunderlich acted as explosive and gun advisors.

INTRODUCTION

BIG MONEY, BIG CRIME

BIG MONEY AND crime have always been cozy bedfellows in literature. Writers long ago discovered that exploring the complexity in this connection yields a powerful combination of passion, adventure, intrigue, betrayal, and danger. Crime fiction is a literary form where the story revolves around the motives and intentions of the players in the big money dramas. Crime operates as it has always done: as another market force allocating resources.

What makes money and crime so beguiling is the interface between the police, judges, lawyers, private eyes, and others. On one side is the machinery of law enforcement and on the other are those who profit from breaking the law. Not all law-breakers are treated equally. Not all murderers are put behind bars. These are truths we know that exist. They are part of our history, part of our literature. We measure our progress by looking how well crime is contained to the margins.

Move the equation of big money and crime from the West to Southeast Asia and some of the fundamental premises change. The rule of law is fragile. Powerful forces operate above the law and the machinery of law enforcement is weaker, less developed and more easily intimidated in a showdown. There are many reasons to explain these cultural differences: the borders are less defined, less under the control of authorities allowing criminal elements to run guns, women, drugs, logs with less chance of getting caught. The pay of the police is low and this is one reason for corruption. Feudal structures composed of powerful clans and warlords continue to influence those will be punished and for what crimes. There is an absence of a large educated middle-class and instead one finds large gaps between the very rich and the mass of extremely poor landless farmers.

How do the very rich obtain that wealth, protect it, hold it, and defend themselves against forces seeking to ambush them? That is a question anywhere. In Southeast Asia, where the rich often have obtained their wealth from monopoly licenses, dubious deals, and from the illegal world of gambling, drugs, and prostitution, the crucial elements of crime fiction are found in abundance.

Prior to the launch of the Vincent Calvino private-eye series in 1992 with Spirit House, no writer had set an English language crime series in Southeast Asia. One obstacle to writing such a crime series has been to adjust the characters and stories to an environment where the shades of complexity between good and evil blurred beyond recognition. Also, there was a problem with the languagelearning Thai is not an easy task and there is the issue of access to the inside of the machinery of law enforcement. There were (and remain) many barriers to overcome. There is little history of crime literature in this part of the world (General Vasit Dejkhunjorn has written many outstanding books on crime but unfortunately his books are not translated into English). Thailand among all the countries in Southeast Asia is the one of the few countries (the Philippines being the other) with a tradition of freedom of expression, which allows a writer to undertake a series of books about big money and big crime. Other less tolerant regimes would have stopped the progress, pulled the plug on the computer, and asked the writer to leave or write something far less controversial or threatening. The thing about criminals is they fear exposure. In a culture where losing face is one of the most terrible of consequences, any crime writer walks a fine line between the truth of the fiction and bringing down a brick wall on his head.

As a former law professor, who has lived in Vancouver, New York and London before arriving in Thailand to live more than 15 years ago, I had spent time with law enforcement officers in big urban centers. I spent time in with NYPD officers in Manhattan, Harlem and Brooklyn and saw from the inside what that kind of life was. In Thailand through good friends I was able to meet a number of good, honest Thai cops who sought to enforce the law as professionally as any cops elsewhere in the world. If anything, the obstacles to law enforcement provided a far more interesting environment, as I was able to chronicle a particularly important decade of development in Thailand through the Calvino series.

Crime literature is more than recording basic elements of criminal activity. There should be a highly developed sense of place. One of the major characters in the Calvino series is the city of Bangkok. A geographically sprawl, with canals the color of dead batteries, traffic snarls where the roads turn into parking lots, motorcycle hit men, slums, Patpong, Nana Plaza, Soi Cowboythe comfort zone that many tourists already know. During the boom years of the 90s fast money was made. The crash of 1997 brought many changes. Hundreds of new buildings were left remain unoccupied if finished, and the work stopped on many others. Bangkok is a city of ten million. The renewal started in 2002 and gathered speed in 2003 only to find a new set of troubles looming large in 2004. The educated Thai-Chinese middle-class bought new luxury cars. The peasants from the Northeast again began arriving in buses and trains looking for work. The foreigners began to return. The old energy and vitality has gradually reemerged. But people are cautious along with increased fears of slipping back into old ways.

Bangkok is a place where cultures clash: urban and rural, urban and rural, Chinese and Thai, the second-class citizens like the hill tribe and illegal migrants and first-class Thai citizens, and the *farangs* and the Thais, the *farangs* are represented by many tribes English, Americans, Canadians, Germans, French, Italian, Dutch, Danish, Finnish and Russians. Also there are the non-*farang* foreigners such as the Chinese, Japanese, Koreans an others from Asia.

They are all living in Thailand. Some have been here for more than one generation. They are businessmen, diplomats, journalists, ex-military, chefs, hotel owners, engineers, lawyers, bankers, gangsters, felons, and retirees. Many find it difficult to leave Bangkok despite the drawbacks. Some fall into crime. Others are like the lotus-eaters of the past who were lulled by a siren song of strong desires.

In the eight Calvino novels I draw upon the diversity of these cultures, following the characters who attempt to retain a sense of their old identity as it slowly peels away like a snake s skin yielding a new expat identity underneath. In Cold Hit, the adversary is not the criminal; it is the City, the difference of cultural expectations, and surviving on a social terrain where personal conflicts flash quickly and understanding shatter into pieces, sometimes leaving a trail of blood. Readers often say they see themselves and their own experiences in the novels. The best crime novels, like the best of any kind of literature, raise a mirror to a world and make it more recognizable. In novels set in our own culture, most of the internal workings of inter-relationships, people s expectations, and their dreams come from a common base. Working in another culture as a fiction writer, it is wise not to make such assumptions. Part of the challenge of the Calvino series has been to create a sense of coherence in a number of sub-cultures: of crime, of expat life, of class, and of law enforcement.

At the end of the day, a crime novel is a reflection of the complexity of law enforcement. In the case of the Vincent Calvino novels, it is also a reflection of how these forces of law enforcement have developed over time; that is, finding the courage and means to apply the law to the untouchable class of the rich. This is happening. It is also a continuing story. There is yet no end, only a beginning but it is at the beginning of the universe that we learn so much about how everything ended up the way it did.

Christopher G. Moore
Bangkok
June 2004

ONE

THE RUSH WAS like an orgasm stretched out to infinity, gaining speed and altitude, like crashing through the sunset, spinning and coming out of the clouds into a perfectly blue sky. He had swallowed the pills. But only after watching his friend go first. Only then did he feel safe, confident in swallowing the blue tablets. His friend said that the pills were Viagra and the Goddess liked what that pill did to men. He wouldn't be disappointed. That had been thirty minutes ago, though he had lost track of the time. But the movement of time didn't seem to matter all that much inside the room. He was no longer afraid or anxious; he was more relaxed than he had ever been.

Closing his eyes, he saw shock waves of light, joining, uncoupling, exploding. It was hard to do so but he opened his eyes wide enough to find his friend's face. The friend winked and then smiled. Reassured, he closed his eyes once again. A brother whose cause-member nickname was Moondance.

He was a fellow member of the Cause. Sitting in the same room with Moondance made him feel that a miracle had happened; he felt how lucky he was to have someone waiting for him on his very first trip to Thailand. After all those months of planning, logging on, going through all the photographs, knowing he was about to enter a new, powerful, easier universe, his expectations had grown to enormous size.

The drugs were part of the experience, Moondance had said.

He watched as Moondance tapped the vein in his outstretched arm. At first he tried to pull his arm away but all resistance was gone. He kept thinking how beautiful the lights and colors and music were so he hardly noticed when Moondance slid the needle into the blue, blue vein. Moondance slowly pressed the plunger. *Funny*, he thought, *the needle is still in the vein*. He registered no panic over the needle. He had been punctured. This suddenly seemed perfectly normal. He laid his head back, listening to the music. Moondance had turned up some music on his portable CD player. It was New Age music. One of the song tracks from Enigma helped him go outside his body, let him drift, let him fly over the city at the speed of light.

Moondance had promised that she would be showing up at any moment. The Goddess. The one he had chosen from the web. Eighteen years old, doll-sized, long, dark hair and shy, soft eyes, and in the jpeg her hand was raised, combing her hair. Smiling one of those fifty-foot smiles, she was suspended on his computer screen, a screensaver, each day staring back with those eyes, that smile. Moondance had helped her send e-mails in English.

She was waiting for him, to please him, to love him and to be with him for as long as he wanted. This was his dream.

This was the turning point. This was the point of no return.

TWO

BANGKOK. A COAL black night, nine o'clock, with the rain blowing into a fine gray mist. Some of the smaller *sois* were filled ankle-deep in sludge water. Several cars had flooded and stalled near the Ding Daeng intersection. It was a miserable night to search for a birthday girl. She was an upscale hooker who worked in one of the Dead Artist bars on Soi 33. Her *farang* lover paid the freight, and he wanted her to—no, he demanded that she receive the birthday card, not tomorrow or the day after, but tonight, on her birthday. Hormones made a man in Bangkok hot, half-crazed, in a desperate hurry; and money made other men swim through sewers to find an angel who had vanished without a word.

Vincent Calvino wasn't on the streets just to find a woman gone missing in action, but to hand her a birthday card. Even in his world this added up to a twisted, strange assignment that he had taken against his best instincts, heading out into flooded streets with the card in his pocket. He drove through streets that had become sewer canals; all the underground filth rising to the surface, roaring out to the sea. Most of the world was lost or missing; only a small fraction ever had anyone looking for them, let alone someone with enough money for a private eye instructed to track them down on a rainy night. At any cost. The client obviously had the sickness— this wasn't to put him down—after all, *farangs* with the sickness had paid more than one private-eye bill.

Calvino glanced in the rear-view mirror to find it filled with a neon sign reading: HELL. Large, bold letters. The letters should have been backwards, thought Calvino. But there was a bright red HELL spelled out in the rear view the way *ambulance* gets properly spelled out for drivers checking their mirrors as they hear a siren and glance up at the mirror. Mirrors. All kinds of things were found on their surface. He turned, hooking an arm over the seat. Sure enough HELL on the building was LLEH. To the left of the main sign was a smaller cold blue neon with two words: THE CAUSE. This had been showing up on clubs, bars, and restaurants. The members of the Cause mostly confined their drinking and eating to the Causeway. Others wanted a cut of the market and started displaying the CAUSE sign. They were spreading out, advancing.

Net talk: the Cause, the Causeway, MF, GTF, and these *farangs* brought in a whole new line of business. The URL had become a legend in cyberspace—www.thecause. com—and the site was a powerful communication nerve center for members of the Cause. Members joined by paying a hundred bucks a year, got a password and a user-ID, and unlimited access to advice, comments, information, the basic tricks of where to find *yings*, *hongs*, bars—general advice on how things worked, how life was organized, and a one year subscription to *yingzines*— the ultimate *ying* insiders' guide to the Philippines, Cuba, Indonesia, Thailand. Each country had its own Causeway. But this hole-in-the-wall bar was off the beaten track. There was gold in Cause business. Calvino wondered if any *farang* had found this place. Had a member profiled it in his ten-day personal journal of conquest posted on the Cause bulletin board? He doubted it. HELL wasn't doing much business but then it was raining and early in the evening. HELL looked like the place people ended up in, having started somewhere else. The main parking lot was under water.

It was about breakfast time for the night stalkers who kept vampire hours. The people who lived in this kind of place.

He had several clients who were Cause members; they land at Don Muang, check into the Dynasty, Nana, Brandy, or one of dozens of other Causeway hotels, a base for drinking and playing at the Nana Entertainment Plaza, eating from food vendor carts or one of the hundreds of restaurants on the *sois* off Sukhumvit Road. They knew before they got off the plane where to get a massage, where the freelancers hung out, the full menu listing the price of every pleasure. The entire territory that the members traveled half way across the earth to find was only a few kilometres long: Soi 1 through 33, Sukhumvit Road. The members networked sharing their experiences, their pleasures, disappointments, heartaches, often in the form of a daily diary post. Most of the communication was about *yings*: descriptions, photographs in various stages of undress, dimensions, shapes, performances, positions, short-time or all-night, and the ever important economic factor of cost, sometimes broken down in bar-charts, colored graphics illustrating the math equations so dollar-to-minute performance ratios could be compared, analyzed, discussed, and debated along with betrayals and love and disappointment.

A member of the Cause had paid for this stakeout. A typical Calvino end-of-the-century client. A couple of decades ago the same guy would have sought magic in a different path; then it was the surfer who wandered the earth's surface in search of the perfect wave. Well, all of the surfers got old, fat, divorced, forced out of jobs at age fifty, so a new magic was invented, a new map for expression and experience which led the seekers to Bangkok, Manila, Angeles, Phnom Penh, Jakarta; a sexual circuit for adventurers in search of the Monster Fuck, or the Great Tsunami Fuck. Some used the initials "MF"; others liked to call the experience "GTF". Language was shifting, the landscape of meaning was up for grabs and there was no clear indication who would win the word war or who the men inventing the new language were. Of course, it wasn't only men; there were *yings*, too. The Cause was not actually one thing, one nationality or ethnic group, but many different factions seeking shelter in the same Monster Fuck dream: sex addicts, divorced, separated, widowed men, politically correct drop-outs, vegetarians, ex-cons, soldiers of fortune, homeopaths, psychopaths, warmongers, nerds, drunks, terrorists, scholars, skinheads, bankers, punks, men numbed from years at the front lines of women's liberation trench warfare, the obese, the bald, the rejected, bruised, abused, frustrated, disappointed, and bewildered in romance, Viagra reborn Jurassics—old guys, old women, the Dorian Grays, the Peter Pans, bikers, truckers, cripples, and thrill-seekers. That was the short-list. The agenda was never closed and no matter how much Calvino tried to imagine every class of member, the task was doomed to failure. The Cause was an open-ended, porous, ever-changing mass which no one could ever nail down.

Some of them were dying on the sexual front line.

Over the past ten months, five *farangs* had turned up dead. A couple of bodies had been found dumped in an isolated, dark *soi* a couple of miles away from Don Muang airport. The others had been discovered in a guesthouse and a short-time hotel. Calvino believed the murders were the work of a serial killer targeting foreigners coming into the country.

"Hey, I am from New York. I can *smell* a murder. A serial killer is doing these guys, Pratt."

Pratt wasn't moved by Calvino's olfactory facilities. "This isn't New York, Vincent. Each of the dead men died of a drug overdose. And each of them was found with their passports and their cash and their other valuables. Where's the motive? No motive, no smell."

Calvino cracked a smile, wondering if this was some Shakespeare paraphrase.

"I am working on motive. Give me some time." Pratt had him cold. Why would a Thai kill a *farang* unless it was about money or the *farang* had caused a major loss of face resulting in a fight? But there wasn't any sign of violence. There wasn't a bruise to be found on the dead men. Just the needle in the arm and a lethal dose of heroin in their blood. But there also had been a common thread: all of the victims were Americans, single men, and card-carrying Cause members who died somewhere between twenty-four and forty-eight hours after landing at the airport. Pratt's buddies in the police department shrugged off the serial killer theory. The police said they had no evidence of anyone being killed. There was no murder. These were junkies who overdosed.

Fact one: Each of the dead men had been American. Fact two: Each had died from a drug overdose. A syringe of heroin main-lined into the big fat blue vein that popped out of the crook of the arm. The needle still sticking out of the arm by the time the cops found the stone-cold body turned blue around the lips. Fact three:

Each was a member of a single male Internet travel club called the Cause.

The cases became a hobby after a relative of one of the victims paid Calvino to verify the police report and death certificate. The victim had been a middle-aged guy from San Francisco with no previous record of heroin. What had Pratt said? "So the *farang* hid his habit. Or your guy decided to walk on the wild side, didn't understand that heroin is a dangerous drug, and shot up an overdose first time out."

"I'm saying, Pratt, this tells me they got whacked," he touched his nose. "Some white-shoe guy from the 'burbs doesn't suddenly start sticking needles in his arm just because he takes a trip to Thailand."

They agreed to disagree. Stone-cold body and a stonewall. He verified the police report and death certificate but he had his doubts.

Calvino sat in his parked car, thinking how it could be that no one had robbed the dead *farang*. It bothered him in the way that the sign painted on the upper windowpane of a shop which read "Flowers" bothered him. This sign was a normal sign; none of the back-to-front lettering of HELL. He surveyed the inventory of the shop: stuffed toy bears and elephants and dogs, ceramic piggy banks, and streetwalker mini-skirts on plastic hangers. The essentials for people going to HELL, he thought. Calvino did not see a single flower. A flower shop that didn't sell flowers, not even a fake flower, was like murders without any money or passports being taken. Two hours into the stakeout and he was doing store inventory to pass the time, in between trying to find any other connection between the five dead *farangs* that would prove his New York nose had not failed him. The only flowers were hanging from his rear view mirror. The garland of flowers suspended from the end was two short strands threaded with *jampee* flowers: long, thin, elegant beige petals that had a languid, mellow fragrance. *Jampee noi* was what the Thais called this small twin tailing of flowers, which hung from the garland; it was also a phrase that was Thai slang for a man's penis. A small boy's penis. The *jampee* petals were faded, turning a burnished copper, dropping onto the dashboard. The smell of the *jampee* flower no longer shouted; it had become a faint whisper.

To the right of the flower shop that didn't sell flowers was a mini-mart. It did sell food so the world wasn't completely upside down. Hookers strolled in and out, thick, long black hair glimmering from the rain, buying beer, cigarettes and salted nuts, and on the other side was a hairdresser's with half a dozen chairs, a reception area with a TV. It was quiet inside. A hairdresser held a blow dryer above a customer's head; otherwise there wasn't much activity. The small village of shops was at one end of a parking square and serviced two towers of Grand Mansion. Like the flower shop with no flowers, this place would never be confused with a mansion in the real world. A dozen stories with few hundred *hongs*—which was Thai for rooms—occupied by students, clerical workers, and hookers. Three Thai men in flip-flops struggled with a queen-sized mattress in the light drizzle, stopping to catch their breath at the corner of the mini-mart. Another guy came behind them carrying a 25"TV set, and next to him were a couple of *yings* wearing the night-time gear sold in the flower shop. This was like a self-contained village where there was always something happening. And this was a transition hour at the end of the month. People moving in, getting their hair done, buying supplies, getting ready to go to work or coming home from work.

Calvino's assignment was simple—find Pao and give her a birthday card from Frank. Today was Pao's birthday; that is, if Calvino's client, an Australian named Frank Hogan, could be believed. Frank was a card-carrying member of the Cause. He had forked over six thousand baht for Calvino to make a personal delivery of the birthday card. Why not use a courier or EMS? Why not deliver it himself? These were legitimate questions and Hogan had some plausible answers. He wanted to receive a first-hand account of Pao's reaction to the card. That ruled out a courier or EMS. But he had had an argument with Pao and she wasn't speaking to him so that eliminated a personal delivery as well. Hogan was a guy with all the answers, and six thousand baht was not a bad deal in the rainy season during the middle of an economic depression. A hundred and fifty bucks got Calvino's attention. Pao had *gone walkabout*—Frank's Aussie expression—three days before her birthday; hadn't showed up for work at her Dead Artist bar, and she hadn't phoned him.

Calvino's secretary, Ratana, told him she had a bad feeling about Hogan. He nodded, thinking, *How bad can delivering a birthday card get?*

"That's a lot of money for delivering a card," she said. Deep in her Chinese genes was a built-in abacus that calculated the value of service or goods faster than a NASA mainframe computer.

"For some *farangs*, money is no object when it comes to *yings*."

She thought about this. "I thought *yings* were an object for some *farangs*."

He smiled; she was quick, bright, and on target. "It's ten minutes' work."

"Why doesn't he ask a friend to help him for five hundred baht?" Sipping her coffee she waited for Calvino to answer, knowing he had already made up his mind and was going to take the money because no one was knocking down the door to hire him as a private investigator.

"Men like Frank don't have friends. Or if they do, they don't trust them. At least not around their *yings*."

"Like I said, I don't have a good feeling about men who don't have friends."

"You aren't getting jaded?" he asked her.

She half-smiled, glancing down at her coffee. Calvino's Law: Being jaded meant the day had arrived when a person realized her cynicism about mankind had been fully justified.

"You look tired, Khun Vinee. Why don't you let me deliver the card? It will only take ten minutes."

The butt of his .38 calibre police special rode forward as he leaned over his desk to pick up the telephone. They both knew it was not a ten-minute job. "It might take more than ten minutes. And it looks like rain." He lifted the phone and dialled Frank Hogan's office.

"Frank. This is Vincent Calvino. I will deliver the birthday card tonight," he said, looking at Ratana the whole time. "Yeah, I will deliver it myself." He put down the phone and picked up a photo of the birthday girl from the pile of papers on his desk. Ratana turned and walked back to her side of the office, leaving him alone with the photo. Why a *farang* would be attracted to such a low-class, upcountry peasant girl, she could never understand.

Pao wore a green and black uniform, white shirt, and black bow tie; Calvino examined the frozen smile, the large eyes with painted eyebrows and the full lips. This was the uniform of a Dead Artist bar chick. The outfit looked like a Las Vegas blackjack dealer's uniform. Something was missing from the picture. Calvino studied her features. One distinguishing feature: a small brown mole on the right side of her chin. He was looking for whatever Frank Hogan saw in this woman which might explain the elaborate arrangements and cost of six thousand baht to deliver her a birthday card. He couldn't see it. There was nothing special about Pao. It didn't add up, he thought. Then he remembered what his father used to say to his mother, "Show me the place in the universe where everything adds up. I want to move my entire family to that place."

★★★★★★

CALVINO checked his watch. Time came to a standstill on stakeouts. Nine-fourteen. The guys were lifting the mattress like a lifeless thing pulled out of a shipwreck. A couple of taxis, windshield wipers slapping back and forth, windows fogged, crawled past looking for customers. Waiting and waiting. Then she appeared at the top of the staircase. The stakeout was over; the time for delivery had arrived and then he could go home. Pao stood alone. Dressed in a neon blue mini-skirt that looked like it was made out of plastic, matching vest, high heels. He quickly climbed out of the car and threaded his way through a couple of dozen motorcycles. By the time Calvino had started up the stairs, a friend had joined her dressed in standard hooker gear: tight black pants and a flimsy white top exposing her shoulders. Pao smoked a cigarette, flicking the ashes as she spoke to her friend. She was just standing there, talking, smoking her cigarette when Calvino called up to her.

"Happy birthday, Pao."

Her head jerked up and she stared straight at Calvino, her face clouded with one of those "Who the fuck are you?" looks.

"Do I know you?"

Calvino reached the top of the stairs, his hair and face wet with rain. "Frank Hogan wanted you to have this card on your birthday." He handed Pao a white envelope; one of those fat envelopes that promised a bundle of cash or drugs or dried flowers. Frank had written her name in English and had someone else write "Pao" in Thai script below the English spelling. She examined the envelope, her long red nails tapping the sides like scorpion legs, creating a mixture of dread and curiosity.

"Aren't you gonna open it?" asked her hooker friend, swaying easily from side to side in tight leather pants like a scorpion. Sting or get back in your hole.

She stepped back inside the lobby of the building and Calvino followed her inside.

"It's only a birthday card," said Calvino. "Frank wanted you to have it."

"Frank's a crazy sonofabitch," said Pao. "No girl can stay long with a man like him. Or she go crazy." She was buying some time, trying to decide whether she wanted to know what kind of craziness Hogan intended to inflict on her and whether his messenger was part of the conspiracy to drive her crazy. Hookers may not have invented suspicion but they had sublicensed the rights to use it after nine at night.

She pulled the card out of the envelope and slit it open with a long, red-varnished fingernail. The card was one of those corny musical cards that played Happy Birthday in a Donald Duck kind of half voice, half noise. She shook the card. Nothing fell out. She turned the envelope inside out. Nothing else was inside. No money, no check. Just one musical birthday card. "Cheap Charlie," said Pao. "Tell that crazy Cheap Charlie I never want to see him again. That I hate him."

Pao's hooker friend laughed. "No money?"

Pao's rage accelerated and her face flushed as she clenched her hands into fists. That was the reaction he would report to his client. His job was over; he could go home and dry off. Calvino started to turn around and, as he was off-balance, without time to react, a punch caught him nose-high, knuckles and ring finger smashing his right eye. A second punch hit him midsection, doubling him up; he slowly dropped to his knees. Two kicks to his ribs landed as Calvino tried to protect himself. He lay flat on his stomach, and as he tried to get up, his vision was obscured by blood. He was spitting blood as he tried to get a good look at the guy who had come out of nowhere. His first impression was that the guy was a *farang* with either Indian or Iranian blood. The kicks in the ribs had left Calvino gasping for air. As he finally struggled to his feet, Calvino saw the man moving in closer. His assailant had a moustache and a two-day growth of beard; he was wearing shorts, designer track shoes, and a Chicago Clubs T-shirt, and looked to be in his late twenties. Well muscled in the arms and shoulders, fit with a thick, tanned neck; the hair from the guy's chest curled like an unravelled rug against his throat.

"You motherfucking Cause creep, you come near my girlfriend again and I'll kill you," he said.

His face throbbing, bleeding, his guts aching from the blows, Calvino tried to focus on his attacker, who was dancing on his toes like a boxer. It looked like the man was coming in to do more damage, to finish him off. What had been entertainment for the hookers ended when they saw the blood on Calvino's face. Pao stepped in between them. Calvino wanted a piece of the guy. He was hurting—not the ego hurt like Pao finding no money in the birthday card but the pain of some serious physical damage. This young guy had put him on the floor with two punches, two solid, powerful blows. The worst thing wasn't the pain but feeling slow and old. Calvino was holding onto his forties like a dog onto a bone.

"Stop it, TJ. Don't you see you've hurt him enough? Besides, this isn't Frank. I don't even know who this guy is, okay." She looked at Calvino like a referee examing a beat-up fighter just before giving his opponent a technical knockout. "You better get out of here, Pa."

Calvino stared at TJ for a moment. *Pa*. She had called him dad, father, papa. Card delivered, nose broken, major mouse over the right eye, reminded of his age. It was time to move on; forget about the pride, own up to the fact that he was no longer in that awkward in-between age: too old for a boy toy, too young to answer to papa. He was old enough to be her father and the father of the guy who beat him up. Calvino nodded at Pao, wiped the blood away from his face and turned to walk away. Six thousand baht, he thought. Job done.

"If I ever catch you fucking around with old guys looking for a Monster Fuck, you can expect some of this."

TJ slapped her with the flat of his hand. Pao started to cry. Pao's hooker friend started to cry as well. This was her birthday, pissing down rain, a musical birthday card without any money inside delivered by a stranger, her boyfriend starting a fight, then slapping her around— things had shaped up on the ugly side of life, stacking the decks for a miserable year to come. Calvino closed his eyes for a second, thought, and before he knew what this thought was going to be he slammed his heel hard into TJ's right foot, and followed with a kick to his groin. TJ collapsed on the floor, blubbering, his face as tight as a fist. Calvino leaned down with his knee in TJ's back, pulled out a pair of handcuffs and slapped them around the right wrist and then the left.

"Apologize to Pao," said Calvino.

"What are you, a fucking cop?"

Calvino cuffed him on the ear. "I am not hearing an apology."

"Jesus, you are bleeding all over me."

Calvino's broken nose was leaking a trail of blood down TJ's neck. Calvino pressed his knee harder into TJ's spine. "Why don't I just call the Thai cops. Check your visa and your apartment for drugs."

"Okay, Pao. I am sorry. Okay?"

Pao was enjoying seeing TJ suffer some pain. Her hooker girlfriend giggled and lit a cigarette. Pao helped herself to a cigarette, taking her sweet time as Calvino's knee hit a nerve in her boyfriend's back. It wasn't turning out to be such a bad birthday after all.

"For fucksakes tell him it's okay. Please."

She liked that word. Please.

"She didn't hear you," said the hooker friend.

"Please," shouted the boyfriend.

"It's okay," said Pao, smiling, taking a drag on the cigarette.

Calvino removed the handcuffs. As he pulled back his jacket to clip the cuffs to his belt, TJ rolled over on his back, thinking his time had come for some revenge. He caught sight of the .38 police special in Calvino's shoulder holster. There was no more fight left in him. His fists unclenched. He must have realized Calvino could have shot him from the moment of the first punch. He backed off, backed way off, sliding towards Pao.

"She said it's okay," TJ said with anger, but the fire had gone out of his voice. He limped over to the couch in the foyer and sat down.

That was the way the birthday card night ended: Pao holding TJ's hand on the couch and kissing him on the cheek. Not so much a kiss as one of those smelling rituals Thai *yings* like to engage in from time to time; inhaling the smell of another human being the way a lioness smells her cub to make sure it is hers.

Most of the bleeding had stopped by the time Calvino got back to his car. He fished in his pocket for the keys, only to realize that he had locked them inside. He touched his nose; TJ's power punch had fractured it. He felt the rain on his face. The choices were not that great. Finding a *chang*—a kind of street handy-man whom the Thais sometimes called an "engineer"—to pry open the door would be an ordeal only one or two rungs below getting punched out by a stranger. The chang would demand a *farang* price, a rain premium, a flood bonus; and he would no doubt screw up the door, knocking off paint, bending the metal, tearing off the rubber around the glass. Calvino figured the other alternative would cost about the same and he would be inside his car immediately. Calvino unholstered his .38 police special, turned it around so the butt end faced the window, and with one swift blow shattered the window. A couple of hookers standing under the awning in front of the beauty shop saw him breaking the glass—*farang* with a gun and busted, bleeding face—and they quickly walked away, glancing back as they went. He opened the car door, swept the broken glass off the seat, slid in, and started the engine. All he had been hired to do was deliver a birthday card to a Dead Artist's bar chick . . . a ten-minute job.

★★★★★★

SIX thousand baht for a simple delivery. Ratana had had this bad feeling, and he had said to himself, *What can happen delivering a birthday card?* Two hours and four thousand baht later, he had his nose put back in place and was back at his apartment nursing an ice pack over his right eye. He was thinking all the time he should have seen that punch coming. He phoned Frank Hogan while waiting to get his stitches at the hospital.

"You didn't tell me this girl was involved with a Middle East terrorist," said Calvino.

"TJ's a dickhead Yank. Works freelance as muscle at the Hollywood."

"He broke my nose."

Frank laughed. "TJ was Golden Gloves champion in Chicago. A tough little dickhead."

"So that's why you sent me," said Calvino. A doctor walked towards him with a syringe that looked sharp, mean, and hard.

"Call the cops. Have his ass thrown in for assault. What do you think?"

The doctor stabbed the needle into the side of Calvino's face and slowly pushed the plunger down, injecting the drug that turned faces into numb putty.

"God, that hurts," shouted Calvino, clenching his teeth. He squeezed his mobile phone, closed his eyes, and remembered that he was talking to Frank Hogan.

"Are you getting a massage?"

The needle came out. His face was already going numb.

"Pao's right. You're crazy, Frank."

"You think I knew about TJ lurking around?"

"I think you had a good idea."

"But that doesn't mean that I knew for sure. I had heard rumors about her and dickhead TJ. Pao never told me that she had a boy toy American husband."

"And you figured the card was a way of finding out. Only you neglected to fill me in on a few details."

"Hey, you are the private eye, Vinee. You want to know something, all you have to do is ask."

Calvino's Law: Due diligence *always* on all clients and on all *yings*. No exceptions. Calvino had written this law down on a piece of paper and taped it to the mirror in his bedroom where the edges had turned up with age. He no longer read his own message.

"Frank, I have a message for you. I know why you don't have any friends."

He could hear Frank breathing on the other end. Only he didn't say anything.

"Because you're an asshole." By now Calvino's face had gone totally numb and the words came out like the singing of Happy Birthday on Pao's birthday card. Try telling a guy he's an asshole when your face is frozen. Calvino tried again, finally gave up, lay back and let the doctor finish the job of setting his nose.

★★★★★★

THE first thing Calvino's maid did when she saw him that night was cover her mouth and start to *wai*. And this set her half dozen dogs off howling. The water was so deep in the driveway that he had trouble opening his car door. Finally he stepped out and closed the door, sending a small wave splashing against his leg. He rolled his pant legs up to his knees, waded across the flooded driveway, leaving a wake that splashed against the staircase. He carried his shoes and socks and slowly edged forward, unsure what he might step on. Skin infections the Thais called Hong Kong foot were another hazard of Bangkok rainy season. The water covered the first step on the flight of stairs. Three steps up the stairs, his feet and legs were dripping, Mrs. Jamthong waited with a dry towel, dressed in an old faded nightgown, and four of her dogs, whining and shivering, sniffed around Calvino's feet as if the pieces of floating garbage that stuck to his ankles might contain some food.

She handed him the towel.

"The *khamoy* beat you bad. Too much crime. Break your car. Break your face. They steal your money, too?" She shone a flashlight on his car, keeping the beam on the broken window.

"This wasn't the work of *khamoys*," said Calvino. Local thieves were being spotted along every *soi* as the recession hit deep, and the only way to survive was to take something away from someone who had more than you, someone who would still have enough to eat after losing some cash, a TV, a fridge, a car. "This was a birthday card gone all wrong."

"You want me to call a doctor?"

"I already go to the hospital." He had meant to say "been" to the hospital. Sometimes he just lapsed into Thai-Ling with the maid.

"I so sorry Khun Vinee. It rained and rained. I never see so much rain. And your face."

By the time Calvino walked into his apartment and sat at the table to drink a Mekhong coke, the pain in his ribs, face and shoulders had shot back. He opened the bottle and popped one of the pain pills, washing it down with Mekhong and coke. The sound of the TV turned down low drifted across the sitting room of his apartment. He sipped from his glass. Holding up a mirror, he examined his face. The image in the mirror, had one eye swollen shut and a bloated, broken nose and looked somewhat like him, he thought. People with beaten-up faces were like the old: they all looked alike. A six thousand baht face, he thought. A ten-minute-job-for-easy-money face. He thought about his profit. Four thousand eight hundred for the hospital and doctor and eleven hundred baht to have the window repaired. He added it up. He had cleared one hundred baht. What was that in American money, he thought. Two and a half dollars. There was the non-money satisfaction of having taken TJ down, inflicted some pain on a man young enough to be his son, and with a well-placed knee in TJ's spine, even convinced him of the wisdom of paying respect to his elders. But another man's pain and humiliation wasn't going to pay the rent, Ratana's salary, or put gas in his 1987 Honda Accord. The previous car owner, Harold Jordan, an expat who had once been Calvino's client, had suffered the misfortune of the bad economic times: lost his job, ran out of money, lost hope, sold his car and mobile phone to Vincent Calvino, and fled back to North Carolina. Harold moved in with his parents. Forty-three years old and he moved back into basement of mom and dad's house where all his high- school stuff was still gathering dust and his closets smelled of mothballs and mildew.

He lay back on his bed feeling the Mekhong and painkillers doing their work. One eye was already swollen shut. He closed the other one and breathed in deep, listening to the rain outside.

★★★★★★

A stranger arrived in the village during the middle of the night. No one saw from which direction he came or whether he had his own ox and cart or had walked in. No one had been there at the moment of his arrival. He seemed just to have appeared out of nowhere. His presence was announced when a sleeping villager first heard a new sound never heard before. Filtering into his dreams there was a crackling noise and the smell of smoke. Soon a baby cried, then another. A dog in the distance barked. Soon a chorus of barking dogs could be heard throughout the village. Livestock made snorting sounds. Calvino opened his eyes as he sensed someone stirring nearby, then he heard many voices. They called for family and friends to join them, and soon everyone was outside of their bamboo huts, gathering around the stranger who stood a head taller than the tallest of the villagers. The stranger stood with his back towards them, warming his hands over a fire. No one in the village had ever seen a fire before. They wondered whether the stranger might be a god, a heavenly messenger who possessed secrets more powerful than their own magic man. Fingers of flames licked at the night sky. The stranger dressed in black robes, his head shaved, wearing sandals.

Then the stranger slowly turned around, his bright eyes meeting the eyes of each of the villagers. Neither surprise nor delight nor fear shone on his face.

"I thought you would come," said the stranger, nodding at Calvino.

Calvino looked to his side, then looked behind, then back at the stranger.

"You talking to me?"

The stranger pointed his long bony finger at Calvino. "You can help me explain to these people what fire is."

Calvino looked at the large pile of burning logs. A substantial fire roared, filling the sky with flames. Smoke and flames rose higher than the largest house in the village; this was a fire to cause awe, and as for the villagers' first ever fire, they witnessed a massive wall of liquid light quavering against the black sky. A stranger had turned darkness into light. The villagers were dancing around, laughing, drawing close to the flame, feeling the heat, then falling back.

"I think they have a picture already," said Calvino.

The festive mood ended abruptly as a village elder stepped forward, his sad eyes filled with suspicion.

"This is night. Who authorized you to make day from night with this trick?" He shook his finger at the burning mound of bamboo, dry elephant grass, and wood.

"They don't all have the full picture, do they?" the stranger said as the elder came closer.

"He's a village leader. What do you want me to do? This is not my village."

"Nor is it mine," said the stranger. "But like you I have come here to share knowledge. I have come to show them fire."

"You've showed them. You are offering me a job, and I am telling you, I am not taking the offer. This fire has nothing to do with me. I am just trying to get by. Bringing light isn't my business. Staying alive is. I am just trying to get through another night and not think too much."

The stranger shrugged off the rebuke and smiled at Calvino. Kneeling down, he removed objects from an old leather case. He carefully arranged each object on the ground like a teacher preparing a lesson. Three more elders now joined the village elder with the wagging finger and none of them was dancing, singing, or laughing. The men formed a semi-circle around the stranger, who studiously ignored them. No one in the village had ever danced in the dark with light to see themselves or others. The stranger reached back and threw more sticks onto the flames. They crackled and popped, a red ember shooting from the midst and striking one of the elder's robes, burning a hole through it. Calvino put out the flame. This was the elder's best ceremonial robe. The stranger could not have known it had special importance attached. The robe was the elder's rank, his face, his very self; it was worn on only the most important occasions or to receive a visiting dignitary. Now the robe was ruined. Destroyed in front of the entire village. The smell of smoke filled the elder's nostrils and ash fell on the robe, turning it from pure white into a smudged black.

The stranger held up the objects for making fire, picking up a piece of flint, a stone, displaying each for the villagers to see; he was teaching them the art of fire making. Telling them it wasn't magic, that any of them could do what he did. He did not speak their language and they understood nothing of what he said. Meanwhile, Calvino heard the elders exchanging whispers in angry, muted voices. They issued an edict for the stranger to cease and desist from his lecture, and to put out the fire at once, and to leave the village. The stranger continued speaking in his foreign tongue directly to the villagers.

What happened next came unexpectedly. Calvino had never known the elders to act so quickly, with such decisive force, such deliberation. This was as surprising as the fire. The small group of elders stepped forward as if the three men were one man on six legs, hoping to menace the stranger into silence. When that didn't work, the strongest of the elders in a fit of temper grabbed the stranger and tried to restrain him but there was a struggle. Calvino was one step away from coming between the elder and stranger. One step too late. Before Calvino could rescue the stranger, the elders acted in concert to throw this stranger into the flames. It happened so fast that at first the villagers thought this was part of a ritual or a game that the elders had invented on the spot. After

Christopher G. Moore

all, they had never seen fire or flames or smelled burning flesh. The man had appeared out of nowhere, and was now in the process of disappearing into nowhere. It was a perfect circle. This was an evening of marvels and experiences beyond all comprehension.

For what seemed to be an eternity the stranger stood in the center of the flames, arms stretched out, standing tall for one brief moment before collapsing. The villagers clapped with joy. They wanted to see this wonderful disappearing act again and again. But there would be no repeat. One moment a mysterious stranger had appeared in the village, a moment later they witnessed the lighting of the fire, and not longer thereafter they witnessed his disappearance into the flames. The elders egged on the villagers, clapping and dancing around the flames. Calvino sat back beside the blanket holding the objects to make fire. He watched until the dawn when the last ember died out and there was nothing but black ashes, charred bone, a piece of half-burnt sandal and smouldering robe. The stranger had vanished. The villagers waited and waited for him to reappear. They had no concept of someone being destroyed by fire. By noon they had begun peeling away from the ashes to find food. Calvino was left alone; he did not move from the base of the dead fire, the place of the stranger's death. That night the villagers and elders returned to the place of the fire, expecting more pyrotechnics. The elders held up the stranger's objects, showed them to the crowd, passed them amongst themselves. Everyone waited for the flames to appear. Only the darkness of night hid the disappointment on the faces of the villagers; on the faces of the elders were amusement, half-smiles. They fell on their knees and prayed to the objects. Still no flames rose from the ashes. Soon the villagers followed their elders and dropped to their knees. The elders told them a god had visited them, and that god had vested these objects in the elders. So long as the villagers obeyed the elders, then one day that god would return, and he would bring the flames from heaven once again so that they might sing, dance, and watch the pitch black night turn into a pocket of day.

Calvino finally rose to his feet and walked over to the spot where the fire had burned the night before. He picked up a charred bone and held it up. "The stranger was not a god. He was a man like any of you. He's dead. Burned by the flames. He cannot come back."

The elders laughed. "You see, like we told you, Calvino is not from this village. *Farang* does not understand our ways. He cannot think like us."

"You murdered him," said Calvino.

The villagers began laughing. "Nonsense. You cannot murder a god," said one of the elders. The others murmured their agreement.

"This bone is from the stranger's body," said Calvino. "He was a flesh-and-blood man and not a god. The fire killed him. He brought you the gift of fire. He was trying to teach you the art. Any man can make fire. You don't need to be a god."

"You see what a fool this *farang* is who has stayed in our village," said the elder whose best garment had been burned by the night before.

"Can you make fire?" asked another of the elders, holding out the objects of fire making.

Calvino took these objects.

Calvino looked at the elders, the villagers, and then out in the dark. There was not much to see. He stared up at the stars because it was a clear night. Stars cast some light but not enough to illuminate even the closest face.

But he knew already that he had a choice. Cry murder or make his peace with the village.

"Can do," said Calvino. A spark leaped out of his hands.

A stream of fire shot across the sky, circled around and came straight at Calvino.

As he smiled, the fire hit his face, then the blunt instrument to make fire struck his ribs, knocking him to the ground. Pain spread from his nose and eye and soon his entire body was in agony. Something inside his body had broken.

There was a loud banging on the door. Calvino opened his good eye; a sharp pain made his head throb. He reached over to the nightstand and looked at his wristwatch. It was ten in the morning. The pain pills had knocked him out, and now the pain was back. He climbed out of bed, pulled on a shirt, and slipped into his pants. He walked out of the bedroom through the sitting room.

Calvino stared at Pratt through the peephole.

"I have a bad cold," said Calvino. "You don't want to get it."

"Your maid said someone beat you up," said Pratt.

Maids were always the major security leak in every *farang* household.

"A small bruise is all. This cold is terrible." Calvino tried on his best fake cough, which caused his entire face to throb, and he moaned—that part was real.

"Vinee, I have a friend I want you to meet," said Pratt.

"I am in a contagious state. A virus like this could be dangerous."

"He has work for you. Well paid work."

Calvino unfastened the chain on the door and opened it. "The virus seems to have broken your nose and shut one eye," said Pratt.

"Close contact with a pig."

Pratt removed his shoes and waited to be invited inside Calvino's apartment. "Ratana said something about you delivering a birthday card," said Pratt. A secretary was the second major security leak. Another Thai followed Pratt inside.

Having talked to Calvino's maid and secretary, Pratt would have known the full story.

"Okay, I had a little birthday card surprise last night. It turned out different than I had planned. But that's life," said Calvino stepping back from the door.

"It must have been a lousy card?" asked Pratt. "No money inside, right?"

"How did you know?" He paused and looked at Pratt, his one good eye blinked. "You said something about work?"

Pratt nodded towards the tall, well built Thai in his late thirties wearing a sports jacket, blue shirt, and jeans. He stood just inside the doorway, looking around the messy apartment. It looked like a crime scene with only the yellow police tape missing.

"This is Jess Santisak," said Pratt.

"Jess as in Jessie James?" asked Calvino extending his hand.

"Jess as in Jessada," he said firmly, shaking Calvino's hand.

"Jess is Thai," said Pratt, beaming like he was introducing a member of the family.

"That's good, since this is Thailand." Calvino retained a small hope that they would turn around and leave. He let them stand in the doorway for a moment, assessing the situation.

"I never much liked birthdays. On my last birthday, I was stabbed, sir," said Jess, lifting his shirt and showing a long scar on his stomach.

"Stabbed? I am feeling better already." Did this guy just call him *sir*? This threw Calvino off a little, and he was about to say something but let it go.

Mrs. Jamthong had not cleaned Calvino's apartment for a couple of days as she bailed water out of her own room below the staircase, her dogs standing on shipping crates. In those few days of neglect, Calvino's newspapers, half-eaten fruit, socks, underwear, empty Mekhong bottles, dirty dishes and glasses, Domino pizza boxes, built up a certain level of mass as they were scattered across the room. Jess could see through the open bedroom door the far wall where a black lace bra hung over a poster of the 1968 New York Yankees team. A line of red ants streamed out of the empty Domino's pizza box, crossing the floor like an army on the march. Baby powder had been sprinkled across the floor of the bedroom and sitting room. A trail of small footprints ended in front of the black bra, then veered off towards the closet and bathroom. Calvino's Law: Never bar fine a *ying* who won't look you in the eye. If she will look you in the eye, pay the bar fine, but follow her footprints across the room to find out what she is really after.

Calvino made his way through the debris to the fridge. A rat ran across the carpet and disappeared into the bedroom. He threw a book at the rat. He missed.

"Make yourself at home," Calvino said, gesturing towards the sitting area. There was a sofa, a coffee table, and two old armchairs. "With the flooding, the housekeeping is a little behind."

He pulled a plastic bottle out of the fridge, nudged the door shut with his hip, and then poured two glasses of water. On top of the fridge were his painkillers. He opened the bottle, dumped two tablets into his hand, popped them into his mouth, and swallowed, drinking straight from the plastic bottle.

"Sorry, I don't normally drink from the bottle. These are my last two clean glasses. The doctor said to take the medicine, and in three days no more cold," Calvino said walking over to the sofa. He tried to put the glasses down on the coffee table but there was too much junk in the way, so he handed them each a glass and then sat down in his armchair. "Just push all that junk on the floor," said Calvino. "You won't hurt anything. I promise."

Jess carefully stacked up a pile of magazines on the floor and put a pile of unopened junk mail and books on top of the stack. He was the meticulous type, thought Calvino, as Jess sat down. Someone who never had anything in his office, his house, his life, out of place.

"Jess's been with LAPD nearly ten years," said Pratt. "He was LA County kick-boxing champion when he was fourteen years old." There was a note of considerable pride in Pratt's voice as he summed up this aspect of Jess's career.

Calvino cocked his head, thinking kick-boxing, LAPD. Yeah, that makes a lot of sense, so what is he doing in my apartment—looking for a sparring partner?

"You mean Los Angeles has Thai cops working for LAPD?"

"They have a few, sir."

There was that "sir" thing again.

"How many *farang* cops you got working in Bangkok?" Calvino looked at Pratt who raised his right hand and made a zero. Pratt, was a Colonel in the Royal Thai Police force and knew the impossibility of a *farang* ever becoming a police officer. Affirmative action would come about the same time that corruption would be wiped out of the system. "That many? So what's a Thai LA cop doing in Bangkok? Maybe transferring here and you're gonna sign on as Pratt's new partner," continued Calvino.

Jess shook his head. "Not exactly. I took leave for a private assignment, sir."

"Please don't call me, sir. It makes me nervous. And whatever you do, don't reply that you are sorry, sir. So you are here freelancing. Didn't know you guys could do that."

"It's a bodyguard assignment."

Pratt sat opposite Calvino. "And he asked who I would recommend for the assignment."

"What did you tell him?"

"Vincent Calvino grew up on the streets of New York City and put all that knowledge to work on the streets of Bangkok. And so far was still alive. Well, basically alive."

Calvino nodded, stared straight at Jess. "Do I look like someone who has mastered the streets? Last night that guy hit me so hard I thought I had landed in Wyoming."

"Pratt recommended you, Vincent Calvino. That's good enough for me," said Jess.

"Right now I am on the injured players list. Besides I don't do bodyguard work. I have to point that out to you. It doesn't pay and the people you end up guarding you mostly wish someone would whack them out."

"My principal is paying one thousand dollars a day."

"On the other hand, I didn't say that I never took bodyguard jobs," said Calvino. "So exactly who is your principal and why does he need a cop from LAPD and a *farang* to guard him in Bangkok? Who has threatened him? What are we bringing to this situation? What kind of deal are we making here?"

"That's a lot of questions," said Jess. Something was bothering him. It was all that powder on the floor. He looked at the ceiling as if this were the source. "What happened to your floor?"

Calvino wrinkled his nose. "Baby powder. When I bring a girl back, I head for the shower and afterwards I come back and do the due diligence. I follow her tracks to see where she's gone, and by knowing where she's gone I have a good idea what she is after. Money, a photo of another woman, passport, rings, gold, cameras, the usual stuff. For the past couple of nights I haven't felt like cleaning up. Then I wasn't expecting guests either." He shook his head, feeling the pain, winced, looked over at Pratt who had gone disturbingly quiet, then back at Jess. He tried to wipe the snot discharging from his nose, and groaned from the pain of touching it. He drew in a long breath, then slowly released it.

"When you roll over a couple of times, forgetting you have a broken nose and a stitched-up eye, you start getting inquisitive about the world again," Calvino continued. "How did I walk into this? Why didn't I see the tracks this guy was leaving before he punched me in the face? Simple, basic questions like that make you question yourself."

Betrayal laced with pain was humbling, as humbling as searching for answers, wishing for the right answers to emerge from a man's basic condition of confusion, indecision, and terror.

"It's good you have questions. But I am not certain I have all the answers, sir."

"Sir, sir. Cut the sir crap. Who does have all the answers?" Calvino slowly rose from the sofa and walked across the room back to the fridge, where he took out a fresh ice pack and put it against his face.

All the answers were stored in that place somewhere in the universe where all the numbers added up. One big vault and everyone living inside had a key. Only in Bangkok no one had a key, and no one knew what would or could happen next.

"If you can't do the job, then you can't do the job," said Jess.

Calvino closed his good eye as he pressed the ice pack against his nose.

"Who is the guy? Your *principal* as you call him."

"The principal is Dr. Nat. The asset's name is Wes Naylor. He's an LA lawyer. Naylor is assisting Dr. Nat on doing a deal here and there are some shareholders who don't want to see the deal done. He's had a couple of threats. His client is paying the costs. Paying in advance. We pick him up from the airport on Saturday and on Wednesday we take him back to the airport and put him on a plane to LA."

Jess pulled out an envelope and counted off forty Ben Franklin's, fanning them out near the pizza box like a fancy drawbridge for the ants. Calvino walked back and sat down, leaned forward and looked at the money.

"You walk into my place, see my condition, the condition of my house and you still want to put down four grand?"

Jess nodded.

"Life doesn't work like this. Ask Pratt. Tell him, Pratt; life doesn't come roaring up to your door with four grand and lay them on your table because someone thinks you know the streets of Bangkok."

Pratt listened to their exchange, wondering who had more of an edge in keeping someone alive in Bangkok: the Americanized Thai or the Thaified *farang*. They had been touched with a knowledge; they were the negative image of each other. Another self, a late in life learned different half, with all those new memories of events trying to make sense and come to terms with what they had been raised to believe and understand was real and true. Worlds independently occupied were about to join and they would be forced to work together, finding a common ground for four nights and days. Much could happen, or nothing, thought Pratt. And who was to say that mere necessity cannot create a bond of understanding. Pratt remembered the lines from *Macbeth*: "The attempt, and not the deed, confounds us. I have done the deed. Didst thou not hear a noise?"

He repeated the speech for Calvino.

"You see, you ask Pratt a question he doesn't want to answer and he goes all Thai, and what does he do when he goes all Thai? He quotes Shakespeare."

THREE

AS CALVINO OPENED the door to his office, Ratana was standing a foot away, waiting. She saw the damage that had been inflicted on Calvino's face—the broken nose, stitches, puffy, bruised skin around the eyes—and without any change of expression glanced down at papers on her desk. Inside, she wept. To make his appearance even worse, Vinee had worn his dead man's blue blazer, the one he had bought off a vendor's rack in Amarin Plaza for 199 baht. At least that was his story, but she was never sure when he was joking and when he was serious. And the blurry line between fact and fiction, Vinee had confided in her, was always moving; he didn't know himself most of the time what was true and what was false. Neither did any other *farangs* living inside the Comfort Zones of Thailand.

This much was fact: the blazer was second-hand. She could tell from the jacket's condition. For one thing, it was missing buttons—all the buttons were gone—one sleeve was frayed as if the previous owner had rubbed against sandpaper. Calvino had bought the jacket without noticing (or if he noticed, then he really didn't care) that all the buttons had been stripped off. Had they been put over the dead man's eyes? Sold separately in the Weekend market? Lost in an accident, a fight, or through a dry-cleaner's negligence? These thoughts sometimes entered her mind as she sat at her desk watching him on the days he wore the buttonless coat. Ratana's mind never stopped thinking of the possibilities of why things were the way they were. That was the way she was wired.

She wondered if he had noticed that she had sewn a set of buttons on his second-hand jacket a week ago. He had stepped out for a long lunch at Washington Square, leaving the jacket draped over the second-hand filing cabinet in his office.

"You had a call," she said. "The message is on your desk. Good news."

Calvino liked that she had not said anything about his damaged face. She had taken in the full extent of the wreckage but her self-restraint, her natural way of forcing herself to withhold what she was thinking meant there would be no drama. Her lack of reaction made Calvino respect her above everyone else in his life, other than a few people like Pratt and Father Andrew. No recrimination, no judgment, no asking about whether the injuries had hurt or were causing him pain now. That was not Ratana's style; she had been right about taking the birthday card delivery assignment. Nothing betrayed her feelings. He also liked that she didn't say who had left the message, which was waiting on his desk. She left these tiny discoveries for him to make, knowing men hated *yings* telling them what to do or spoiling some small, insignificant surprise. Her silence ensured that Calvino would read the message straight away. He was a curious man and she admired that about him. After all these years they had a way of working together; they knew each other's habits, what worked and what was best left unsaid. After she finished her law degree, she kept referring to herself as Khun Vinee's secretary. Whenever her parents—especially her mother—had demanded that she use her law degree and work for a law firm or at the very least start her own law firm, she told them she would think about it. She had been thinking about it for many years now and was no closer to leaving Vincent Calvino's life than the day on which she received her law degree.

"My luck has just turned around, Ratana. Forget about my face. I have some good news." He walked around his office, peeling off his jacket and throwing it over a filing cabinet. The metal buttons on the sleeve of his jacket struck the side of the filing cabinet with a thud. "First, you were right about that birthday card." She didn't say anything. He held up the sleeve of his jacket, then looked over at Ratana. "Seems like a fairy sewed buttons on my jacket. I guess you wouldn't know who that was?"

A few minutes later, she came into his office carrying a small black lacquer tray and set it down on the desk. There were several china bowls and a box of cotton balls. And some medicine in a strange jar.

"We have a new case. No birthday card this time. You might like to know, I got a four-day job. Big money. Legit, easy work." He laid out the forty Ben Franklins on the desk. "Paid in advance."

"Doing what?" she asked.

He leaned back in his chair and closed his one good eye. Ratana opened the black lacquer box with mother-of-pearl flowers inlaid in the top, took out a cotton ball, touched the edge of the ball in the bowl of water, then sprinkled a fine brown powder from the jar onto the ball.

"The money's for a bodyguard job. That makes the second case we've had out of LA this month." He half opened his one good eye, watching her prepare the cotton ball. He quickly closed it again. "The good news is that it pays a grand a day. Those are US dollars. Four days. Four grand. Forty times a hundred. And the bad news is the assignment is twenty-four hours a day. Still, I might clear enough to open a branch office in LA."

This was a bad time to try out some cheap humor.

He winced a little as the cold, wet cotton touched the eyelid of his damaged eye.

"Joking," he said, feeling the sting.

A branch office in LA, she thought. He was either joking or dreaming again; his face was broken and stitched and he kept on dreaming and cracking jokes like nothing had happened. The LA cases and the birthday card were the only two new cases he had this month. Ratana never lost track of the nature of the private investigation business—long stretches, weeks at a time with nothing but habit and hope to keep one going from one day to the next, then a flurry of cases would burst forth like spiders crawling out of rubbery wet eggs from a nest.

"What fairy sewed up your face, Khun Vinee?" she asked. "Hey, that stuff stings," Calvino said, squirming in his chair.

"Not much. Stinging means it probably is doing something good. And it wasn't a fairy, it was a doctor at Bumrungrad Hospital. At least I don't think he was a fairy. But then who really knows?"

The homemade medicine was made from ground-up mangosteen, ginseng, peach pit, and some other ingredients which Ratana's grandmother had kept as a family secret passed from mother-to-daughter—everything had been pounded into a fine powder.

"It is anti-fungal, anti-inflammatory. And it kills bacteria," said Ratana.

"Very New Age. Maybe very old age."

"This is your first bodyguard job," she said, throwing the first piece of cotton into the center of his wastepaper basket. Dead center hit. She picked out another ball, put it in water, squeezed it, and then touched the end in the powder.

"It kind of eats into the skin, doesn't it" he said. "So it's my first job. What's that supposed to mean? I am not worth four grand? Or that I won't know how to handle a situation if one comes up?"

"Sensitive," she said. "I mean the skin." "I know what you mean."

She ignored him as she wetted the second cotton ball in the water, squeezed out the excess liquid, then touched the ball to the powder. She slowly rubbed the cotton over the bridge of his nose, tracing a line up to his stitches. She pressed the cotton against the wound, held it for a couple of minutes, letting the medicine soak into the skin. Her grandmother believed there was a special technique to using Chinese herbs; her mother also believed that this powder prevented infections and healed wounds. The water was not ordinary water but *nam mon*, sacred temple water. The abbot had given this water to Ratana's mother, and because she had a good heart and loved her daughter, she gave it to Ratana with a pledge that she would use the water wisely. She thought about telling Calvino where the water came from but she figured he would not understand and wished to avoid hearing what she knew would be his point of view—no water was any more sacred than any other water. There were certain things they could never agree on. Next she would question herself, then her mother, and there would be no end to this inquiry; no good end could come from a debate with her boss.

Matters of faith were better left with the core material unexamined by analysis.

"You can open your eyes," she said. "If you can, that is."

One eye opened, no problem, the other half-opened, web-like frog skin hanging half-mooned. He found her staring intently at his wounds, assessing his condition. Smiling, he brought his head forward. "That feels better. Thanks. I want to read that good news message," he said.

"Four thousand to act as a bodyguard," she said, putting her things back on the tray. Looking at the money spread out on his desk. She had never seen so many one hundred dollar bills at one time. "Money like that means someone is very rich or in very serious trouble. Or both."

A Thai woman named Noi had left the phone message.

Calvino looked up at Ratana. "Is this the same Noi we've been trying to track down for the past two weeks?" She had left a contact phone number as well.

Ratana nodded. "The same woman."

An American named Gabe Holerstone had hired Vincent Calvino to find a missing woman. His missing woman. Noi's photograph was in the file opened on his desk. He looked at the photo. She had a white sheet wrapped around her, her thick long hair sprayed across the pillow, her eyes closed. Behind the bed was a bank of windows where one could see dozens of boats moored in the harbor. Pattaya, Calvino guessed, was where the photo had been taken. Noi appeared to be in her early thirties, slim, a soft, sensual face. In the shot her eyes were closed. He tried to imagine what she looked like awake. What kind of face had inspired Gabe's emotions that had been running the tightrope between desire and madness. She had been a singer in Gabe's LA nightclub until she disappeared for a pack of cigarettes and ended up back in Thailand.

That was Gabe's story.

He was crazy about her and he wanted her singing in his nightclub. That was the second part of the story.

There must have been a third part left out. Why hadn't Gabe sent him the head shots that singers have taken to hand out to agents, clubs, fans, and friends? He must have had dozens of pictures of Noi. It was the one of her sleeping that he had couriered to Thailand, the one he wanted Calvino showing around the pool tables of Patpong where Noi was most likely to be found. Every other day Gabe had been phoning long distance for an update, and every day Calvino had to tell Gabe that he was working on it but finding someone who didn't want to be found in Thailand was no easy thing.

"I thought that would make you happy," said Ratana.

"Get her on the phone."

A minute later Noi was on the phone.

"Noi, this is Vincent Calvino."

"You can call me Diane. Gabe calls me Diane. *Farangs* call me Diane. It is my stage name."

A healthy dose of attitude textured her voice.

"Okay, Noi, you want to be Diane, then you can be Diane or anyone else you want to be. But Gabe wants you to contact him. You can call him collect. You can call him now. Just talk to him."

"About what?" she asked.

"He likes your voice. He thinks you're a great singer. He wants you to go back to the nightclub and sing like before. So the man wants to hear from you. Why is that such a big problem? I don't get it. Is there something you would like to tell me about you and Gabe?"

"He wants me back in Los Angeles. But I am not going back. I don't want to talk to him. I don't want to argue with him. Tell him it's finished. Tell him to leave me alone."

She went silent. "Don't hang up," said Calvino. "Just chill out for a second. I've spent weeks trying to find you. Let's work this through and not get too excited. At least not all at once. No one is going to force you to do anything you don't want to do. You understand what I am saying, Diane?"

"I understand," she said.

"It's easy to just phone the guy. Phone him collect. That means Gabe pays."

"I am not a stupid country girl. I know what a collect call means."

"Sorry. Sometime people get confused about who pays for long-distance. I was just trying to make certain you were not afraid of getting stuck for the bill. If you don't want to go back to LA, then why not phone Gabe and tell him that you are finished? What's so hard about that?"

"I don't know. I am a little confused. I don't know you. But I know Gabe and the people around him. He's a bad man and has bad friends. And you don't know what he's capable of doing."

Ratana was on the other side of the partition, listening; she could not help but hear his side of the conversation. It was as if he were losing someone who was drowning. His arm was stretched out to a person who couldn't swim, but that drowning person was afraid of grabbing his hand and struggled against rescue as the tide pulled her out to sea. Life was never as one imagined. Noi (Ratana refused to think of her as "Diane") was feeling pain or guilt and convincing her over the phone to contact Gabe was never going to work. She knew how a woman thought. Calvino was going to have to meet her. Ratana went back to his office and handed him a note. It read: *Ask her to meet you. In person. In Bangkok.*

Calvino glanced at the note.

"Why don't we meet?" he asked Diane. "That way we can talk this problem through. I am not going to do anything you don't want. But I think a face-to-face might do some good. Where are you now?"

"In Roi Et."

He could hear a stereo playing in the background. The lyrics were from a popular *luuk tung* song *Hello, Hia*. The lyrics were about a *mia noi* who was trying to phone her husband but he won't take her call because his *mia luang* or major wife is sitting beside him. The singer asks, "Why don't you speak?" *Tammai mai phoot?* And her lover replies with a lie, "Because the line was cut." *Sai luut.*

"When do you return to Bangkok?"

"Tomorrow," she replied.

"Then we meet on Friday."

She paused as if she were thinking this over.

"Tomorrow's no good," she said. "I get into Bangkok on a late bus."

"What about Thursday." He was thinking the bodyguard assignment would be out of the way by then.

"I go to Hong Kong on Monday. I'm tied up on Saturday."

The private eye business always had a surprise or two, he thought. "That leaves Sunday," he said. "So we make it Sunday. Does that work for you, Diane?"

Calvino leaned forward and wrote down a time in his appointment diary that was otherwise filled with the words *bodyguard duty* in bold letters.

"Okay, Sunday, can," she said. "Come to my office," he added.

"I'd rather not. It's better if you meet me in a public place," she said.

"Where do you suggest?"

"The Emporium, first floor. I already tell your secretary how to get there." The "tell" rather than "told" was her first grammatical error. She had come a very long way from her *Isan* roots. But that was a matter of language; where was she in the other ways that mattered? Calvino looked at Ratana, cupping his hand over the phone. "She wants to meet me at a shopping mall."

"It's the best you are going to get out of her."

He held his hand over the phone, and thought about this piece of advice. No way did Noi or Diane, or whatever her name was, sound like she was open for much bargaining. It was take it or leave it time. The Emporium, then Hong Kong, then one very irate client in LA. He didn't need this.

"And when I meet you, you can tell me why you like *Hello, Hia*, and we can talk about calling Gabe."

"You know Thai music?" Her whole tone of voice changed.

"I love Thai music." Calvino was walking the rope between truth and fiction. He did like some of the music and found knowing even the lyrics to one *luuk tung* song would do more to gain the confidence of a Thai woman than sweet talk—which they distrusted instantly.

"No problem. We can talk," she said. "I've only seen a picture of you asleep."

"That bastard, Gabe."

"So how will I recognize you?"

"There is a UCLA button on my handbag. And how will I recognize you?"

"I will be carrying the video of *Hello, Hia*. A present for taking the time to meet me."

Calvino's office opened half days on Saturday and it was nearly noon as he put down the phone with Diane. Ratana was working a half day even though he told her this was not necessary; she was always at the office by nine on Saturday, checking the mail, waiting to see if there might be a new case. His head was throbbing as he looked at the *Bangkok Post*. There was a photograph of a woman walking through deep flood waters with her child beside her. The water hit the kid about chest high and she looked frightened. The mother wore lipstick, jewelry, and an expensive dress; she was smiling into the camera. Go figure life, he thought. If she picks up the kid, she ruins her dress. Let the kid walk.

"Why didn't you tell me she wasn't going to phone Gabe?" asked Calvino, looking up from the newspaper.

"I thought you should talk with her first. And that you'd get her to change her mind."

"But you knew she wouldn't phone Gabe." "I had that feeling," said Ratana.

"Like with the birthday card."

"Something like that."

Noi's missing person case had been in his office for a couple of weeks and like a dead fish smelling up the place he had been about to throw it out. Gabe's deposit of five hundred dollars had been chewed up trying to find her and what did the client have for his money? The client had nothing and that made Calvino feel like he had ripped the client off. Most of the money had gone to so-called informers, people who worked the edges of the Comfort Zone, including those in Pattaya where the photo had obviously been shot. They had taken the money and made promises. Promises came easy, performance came hard. Think of a pack of dogs when a bone is thrown into the *soi*. The dogs scramble and do what they need to do in order to be the first dog on the bone. Informers were like a pack of mangy *soi* dogs; they fought over and devoured bones Calvino threw to them. And found new ways to get more bones.

The fact was that Calvino had been unable to turn her up. It didn't do any good to explain that trying to find a Thai named "Diane" based on a photo of her sleeping on a pillow was not that easy. If it was, then the client wouldn't have needed a private investigator. Gabe had been bitching at him on the phone every other day from LA, asking for a status report. Then out of nowhere, she appears. Like a broad in a magic act. Puff of smoke and there she is. Well, not that she exactly made her appearance but the phone call was the next best thing, and she had made a promise to appear on Sunday. Which led Calvino back to where he had started, thinking about how meaningless most promises were unless someone had a real incentive, a personal interest which meant they would follow through. Most of the time the only incentive was to get rid of the person wanting the promise to be made.

Why couldn't she be available some other time? he thought to himself. Noi choses today to phone, and not from Bangkok—or so she says—but from some dive in Roi Et; Noi, calling herself Diane, of Roi Et who suddenly had learnt that he was looking for her and she couldn't meet him until Sunday. He was on bodyguard assignment on Sunday. He had made a promise. Now he had a conflict. A full-time bodyguard assignment. Around the clock. He bargained to meet her on a day that he had already sold. He wanted Wednesday afternoon so bad that he could taste that day. "No can do," she said. "On Monday I fly to Hong Kong."

He did not need to ask what that trip was about. It would be a new nightclub. Maybe she would even do some singing; mainly it would be a fresh start at making money in the flesh trade far away from Gabe's organization. Why not cut the *ying* loose? He asked himself why he was wasting time over a bimbo for this asshole in LA when he had a real job, one paying a grand a day? Because it didn't matter that the *ying* was a bimbo and the client a low-life; he had already given his word to find her. Now that he had, it was a question of honor to follow through and not just walk away because someone had thrown some big bucks at him. The next item on the agenda was figuring out how to wedge an appointment to meet Noi or Diane into the schedule on late Sunday morning, and how to square his point of honor with Jess who believed no doubt his honor was already on the line.

★★★★★★

MUCH to the surprise of the regular customers, the Thai cook had talked Black Hawk, who was the head American cook (on the advice of a fortune teller who promised this would work), into making chicken pot pie on Friday. Chicken pot pie had never been served on a Friday; everyone knew it was Tuesday's Special. This was new and untested territory. Calvino closed the door behind him as he walked into the bar and found the place nearly empty. All those sixty-baht chicken pies and there were only a couple of takers. Black Hawk stood in the doorway with a frown on his face.

"Fucking fortune teller, what do any of them know?" he asked as Calvino strolled past a couple of empty booths.

"Someone gives you a bum lottery number?" asked Calvino.

"Man, I got thirty fucking pies and only a couple of takers," said Black Hawk. "I'd settle for a bad lottery number. Fat Ralph's pissed off at me over these pies."

"Twenty-nine," said Calvino. "Bring me one of the pies."

At the counter, most of the barstools were unoccupied. One middle-aged man with his gut hanging six inches over his belt hunched forward, his face in his chicken pie, only looking up to take a swig from his Singha beer bottle. Another regular named Ricky slumped forward, head resting on his folded arms, weeping over the Vietnamese he had killed during the war. He hit his forehead against the counter. Once, twice, as if to recreate the dull thud of distant mortar shell striking the ground. A friend sitting on the next barstool put an arm around Ricky's shoulder and tried to comfort him. Ricky didn't look like he was in any chicken pot pie mood. A couple of waitresses sat in the booths watching the TV mounted on the wall and two more waitresses sat on stools staring at the ceiling. Something they normally did on their back. One waitress shuffled out of the kitchen with a steaming pie on tray. She walked past Calvino and set the pie down on the table in front of Fat Ralph.

"Goddamit, who kicked you in the face?" Fat Ralph asked, sitting under the enormous horned head which had at some distant time belonged to a water buffalo. Flared nostrils, glassy-eyed, its ears half-erect. Like the Vietnamese that Ricky had killed, this trophy had had a place on the land, a desire to live, eat, drink, fuck, sleep. And instead would spend eternity in Fat Ralph's bar—or until the lease ended, whichever happened first.

"Just a scratch," said Calvino. He looked over at Ricky, his face all red and wet from crying. Some wounds were a whole lot more nasty than others. He wouldn't trade Ricky's psyche damage for what had happened to him the night before.

"At least you can talk. I had a guy in here the other day that had his jaw wired in four places. Try eating a chicken pie with your jaw wired. This is my third goddamn pie.

The fucking cook made all these fucking pies on a Saturday. I need money. And what do I have? All these goddamn fucking pot pies that no one wants to eat."

One of the waitresses who hustled drinks was twenty-eight years old, under five-foot and weighed about eighty pounds. Ewok was the nickname given to her by some Star Wars freak boyfriend from Austin, Texas that no one could remember. She tossed her long hair out of her face.

"Buy me a drink," Ewok said to Calvino.

"Special effect creatures like Ewoks shouldn't be drinking this early in the day," said someone from the bar.

Ewok flipped him the finger. "Fuck you, McPhail," she said.

She turned her attention back to Calvino. "Drink, okay?"

This was a sure-fire request. Calvino always bought Ewok a drink. Any eighty-pounder who could knock back five Mekhong shooters and still carry a chicken pie out of the kitchen had his admiration. She ran over to the bar and ordered her Mekhong with a side glass of water.

"Hey, Daddy-O, are you contributing to the delinquency of someone who wishes she were still a minor? Ain't that right, Ewok? You're an old special effect trying to pass for eighteen," said McPhail from an end booth, an imported Marlboro cigarette burning in an ashtray and a club sandwich on a plate. McPhail was the only guy at Lonesome Hawk bar who never ordered the chicken pot pie even on chicken pot pie day. And sometimes tried to order it on a non-chicken pot pie day. McPhail wore a black T-shirt with Kalashnikov in both English and Russian lettering. An image of an AK-47 ran from one side of his ribs to the other. Basic information also had been printed on the front and read: *7.62mm calibre, length: 880/645 mm and mass: 3.8 kg.*

"Fuck you, McPhail," said Ewok, flipping him the finger.

"You already said. You got to increase your vocabulary. You can't go through life saying, 'Fuck you, McPhail,' and pretend you know more than three words of English. Giving the finger is a nice gesture, but you use it all the time so it loses its meaning. Besides, you don't usually start talking dirty before you've had at least three early afternoon shooters."

Calvino sat down across from McPhail, staring at his T-shirt. "It looks like you're having a Kalashnikov kind of day."

"Man, you look like hell, Calvino. Like someone's been beating the shit out of your face with an assault rifle," McPhail said, putting down a wedge of toast with tomato, lettuce, ham, and chicken inside. He retrieved the cigarette and took a long puff. His bottle of Singha beer was nearly empty and he held it up and motioned to the bar for another one.

"I was delivering a birthday card," said Calvino. "And the next thing I know there is a fist in my face."

"Working the Thai postal service in a rough neighborhood is a bummer. I didn't know you had gone into that line of work. I didn't know a *farang* could get a work permit for mail delivery. Isn't that one of those restricted professions like making amulets and planting rice? In any event, man, I'd say that you ain't cut out for the delivery business. Jesus, your face is even more fucked up looking at it close up." McPhail sucked in the smoke, put down the cigarette, and picked up the sandwich.

"Thanks for the advice, McPhail. I'll keep it in mind as I plan my career." He had gone to the bar half hoping that McPhail would be there (as he often was), thinking this might be a solution to the meeting problem Noi's appointment had caused.

"No problem." He took a bite out of the sandwich, then waved at Ewok. "Send another Singha to Fat Ralph, will you sweetheart? He's having a bad day."

"Remember I was telling you about the problem I had tracking down a woman named Noi?" asked Calvino.

McPhail was still chewing his sandwich. "You found her and she did this?"

"No, I haven't met her. Not yet. She phoned from Roi Et and we arranged to meet on Tuesday at the Emporium."

"I knew you'd find her. The way you were throwing money around you must have had a hundred Noi's falling out of the bushes. Maybe you ought to hire a bodyguard when you go after these *yings*."

Ewok delivered the Singha to McPhail, giving him an evil, nasty glare, then slid into the booth next to Calvino. She raised the double shot glass of Mekhong and toasted him. Touching the glass to her lips, she closed her eyes and swallowed the double-shot in one gulp. She winced, made a face, and swallowed some water, refusing to smile as if she had got religion.

"You ever notice how Mekhong almost makes a human being out of Ewok?"

A waitress brought Calvino vegetable soup and a chicken pot pie. The Lonesome Hawk bar was the kind of place where there was no need for him to order; they knew on Monday through Friday when he came through the door to just bring whatever the special was and he would eat it without much comment or complaint. But this was Saturday.

His waitress spread a plastic mat on the table in front of Calvino. Ewok had gone to the bar and ordered a second Mekhong shooter. She knew Calvino was good for it and after the first shooter she was already forgetting how bad his face looked and how bad she was feeling about herself, her kid, her mother, her friends, about the hopelessness of her life. She looked over at Ricky hitting his head against the bar and knew exactly how he felt.

"You may have got tagged on the snout, but I almost ended up in jail last night, man. It was a close call," said McPhail, exhaling smoke from his nostrils.

"Did you get caught swimming without a permit in the street?" asked Calvino, pushing aside the soup and cutting straight into the chicken pie, steam pouring out of the vent. McPhail, an antiques dealer, found those rare 12th century Khmer pieces, but before he could sell them to a collector, there were all kinds of obstacles: the military, the police, custom officials, NGOs, a chorus line of officials claiming McPhail was doing something illegal, wrong, like selling off the national treasure.

"You think you're being funny but you're almost right. I was at Patpong. I got into a cab on Silom just opposite McDonalds. We take off. I say to the driver, 'Do you mind if I smoke a joint?' It's pissing down rain. I always like to smoke in the rain. The driver turns around and says, 'I am a cop.' I mean he's got the badge and all that shit. The old windscreen wipers are beating back and forth. And he's looking real happy. He says, 'Five thousand baht.' I look at him, and say, 'Hey, man, you gotta be kidding, man. I will eat it.'"

Calvino smiled. "You said you were going to eat the joint?"

"You got it, man. Then he's got no evidence. I say to him, 'Man, you see this? It's your evidence. I eat it, you got nothing.' The cop looks in the rear view mirror and he says, 'Okay, one thousand baht.' I say, 'I am still gonna eat the sucker. Tell you what, I am gonna give you a hundred baht. The fare ain't gonna be more than fifty baht. You make out; I get stoned.' The cop thinks about this, and he says, 'You mind if I turn off the air-conditioner and roll down the window?' It's pissing down rain and I say, 'Fine, man, do it.' I light up the joint, and am smoking away. Of course the fucking rain is coming in on me. This is his revenge. Get that fucking *farang* wet. I ask him, 'How long you been a cop?' He says, 'Five years.' I say, 'You ever catch someone high on pot robbing a bank?' He said, 'No.' I said, 'You ever catch a crook killing someone on pot?' He says, 'No.' I say, 'You ever catch someone raping someone on pot?' He says, 'No.' I say, 'Doesn't that tell you something? Pot isn't causing any crime wave. It's reducing crime. You guys ought to ease off.' When we got to where I was going, I was totally wet from the rain coming through the open window, but his car was fucked up too. I figured I'd dry out before his car did. I gave him the hundred baht, and made certain he let me off in a dark spot, and I slipped away. Man, no way he could identify me. We all look alike to them in the light. In the dark and rain? No way that cop could finger me. What I am saying is this, before you ask a cab driver if it's okay to smoke a joint, find out what his day job is first. Otherwise you could end up shitting yourself."

"I had two cops in my apartment today."

"They busted up your face for what?"

"I got a new job. A bodyguard assignment."

"No shit? They're hiring you after they saw your face? That's something."

Fat Ralph was shouting at the help. "Put on some goddamn country music. Why isn't there any music? And goddamn, will someone buy these fucking chicken pies? I need money." A redneck bar not having country music playing was as close to sin as anyone could ever get in

Bangkok. This wasn't what motivated Fat Ralph; a failed chicken pot pie special was something that only a country music record could put right.

"What are they paying?" asked McPhail.

"One grand a day."

McPhail puffed hard on his cigarette. "That's some real money for a change. Who are you protecting, Hun Sen?"

"An American lawyer."

"Man, that's even worse than guarding Hun Sen. No need to ask why someone wants to kill a lawyer."

"I need a favor, McPhail."

"What can I do? Guns, bullets, broads?"

"I want you to meet Noi for me on Sunday." He laid the photo of her on the table and slid it over to McPhail.

McPhail eyed the woman in the photo, pouring his fresh beer into a glass, then taking a long sip.

"She's not bad looking. But someone sleeping looks better than when she wakes up and is flying around the room trying to hammer you or rip off whatever isn't nailed down." He was thinking about Calvino asking him to meet this woman. What was this about and why was he asking McPhail to make his appointment? This was the woman he was looking to find and now he wanted him, McPhail, to take the prize of the meeting? It didn't make sense. The Ewok nuzzled against Calvino's shoulder, sticking her tongue out at McPhail.

"It doesn't make sense," said McPhail. "Why don't you go out and meet her yourself? Ain't you getting paid to do that?"

"I have a conflict. She's only available on Sunday. This Sunday. That's it. Monday she's on a plane to Hong Kong. So it's Sunday or never. And on Sunday, I am on bodyguard duty."

With a column of smoke rising from his cigarette, McPhail squinted and looked at Ewok through the haze; for the first time a dim, faint smile appeared at the very edges of Ewok's mouth. It was a smile the way that planet earth was a cloud of dust on its way to being a planet four billion years ago. "And it would be just your luck that someone would whack out your lawyer while you were meeting with sleeping beauty."

"That would be my luck."

"Okay, but what do you want me to do with Noi? Buy her a couple of shooters and put her back to bed?"

Calvino did not have much of an appetite. His chicken pot pie was largely untouched. Ewok leaned over and felt his forehead, then pressed her head gently against his shoulder. "I want her to make a telephone call. One call, McPhail. That's it."

"This is about making a telephone call? Man, this private-eye business is strictly low rent. Delivering birthday cards, getting prostitutes to make phone calls. Maybe you ought to add driver's training for newly arrived *farangs*."

"So you will do it?"

"Of course I will do it." "You got some time now?"

"Does it look like I have an appointment with the Prime Minister?"

"Good, let's go do some shopping."

FOUR

FAT RALPH THREATENED that he was gonna throw each of the twenty-nine fucking unsold chicken pot pies one at a time into the street and watch the dogs get sick stuffing themselves and he then was going to put out a goddam contract to whack that fucker of a fortune teller. McPhail was one step behind Calvino as they left the Lonesome Hawk and the ravings of Fat Ralph. They walked along the road; the pavement was all broken and the parking spaces blocked with junk and laundry hung out to dry on metal gates. Calvino made a mental note to buy a lotto ticket which had the number twenty-nine. It was one of those Thai things; whenever someone died or some shit came down, the number with luck attached was found on the wall, door, car license of the victim. He saw no reason why the same principle shouldn't apply to chicken pies flung into the snapping jaws of the *soi* dogs. One man's bad luck brought another good fortune. That was how the universe kept itself in balance.

Calvino had parked his car in front of the wine store that never seemed to have any customers. McPhail lit another cigarette from the one he had smoked to the far end and threw the old one in the street, stepped on it with his shoes, ground it into the hot cement like he was making a statement. McPhail was always making statements. He blew out a lungful of smoke. McPhail gave a long, hard, mean look at a Thai male in his early thirties. Calvino knew the guy McPhail was giving the evil eye to was an undercover cop. McPhail had some bad jazz channel with the volume turned up inside his head and he looked like he might square off on the cop. Whatever had triggered this reaction in McPhail didn't seem all that important as they paused under the baking hot sun. Calvino looked at the sky for clouds. Would it rain again? Would the night bring more floods sweeping down Sukhumvit Road? He hated to think about it as he fished in his jacket for the car keys. He smiled as he pulled out the key chain. Acting out of habit, he looked at the keys. What good were they? The window was busted; there was nothing to lock. Besides locks made no sense in Bangkok. Any fool could open a locked door in under two minutes unless of course they were being paid to open a locked door for a *farang* and then it would take about an hour so the fee the *farang* had to pay could be justified. Stealing direct as opposed to stealing in your face were two different time zones where money was minted. It was just the way it was. Calvino reached inside the broken window and opened the door.

Then McPhail climbed in on the other side, slammed the door, pushed his seat back to gain some leg room, and adjusted his sunglasses so that they fit snug straight on his nose. McPhail had that grim, faraway look—a look that said he wanted to take a nap, suck on his cigarette and dream about making a big score in some jungle village deep inside Burma.

"You've gone all quiet," said Calvino.

"You see that guy back there?"

"The one you were staring at?"

"Yeah, that's the asshole."

"He's a cop. His name is Surat." Calvino saw this surprised him.

But it was uncool to show his surprise. McPhail blew out some smoke.

"I know he's a fucking cop. But I didn't know when I shouldn't have known it. You know what I mean?"

Surat worked the Square as plainclothes cop. He often hung around one of the massage parlors. He leaned inside a doorway a couple of feet away from Calvino's car. He fit into the background, and for the casual visitor or the regular with too much to drink, Surat could've been just about anyone hanging out in the Square. Another meaningless face amongst the security guards, touts, bouncers, messengers, waiters, merchants, traders, pimps, gangsters, or he might have been someone's driver waiting outside the massage parlor while his boss was inside getting a blow job. Calvino remembered him straight away. The first time he laid eyes on Surat, Calvino made him as a cop; his traditional shirt with the Nehru collar was worn on the outside of his trousers, showing the bulge of a .357 magnum concealed in his belt. His hair was short like he'd been out of the monkhood for a month. His eyes were hard and always moving, following *farangs* coming and going from the bars. The Square was home to all types of locals, and they had a sameness, allowing them to blend in. Only Calvino's nose told him this guy was a cop and he asked Pratt about him. Pratt confirmed his suspicion. Several weeks later, Calvino had been at the firing range with Pratt and they watched Surat draw and shoot a .357 magnum. The man was a good shot.

"Well, Sir Rat," said McPhail twisting up Surat's name into something ugly in English. "The bastard caught me with a roach. I saw him coming at me and I tried to throw it down the drain. But I fucking missed. What a time to be a lousy shot. So Sir Rat leaned over and picked it up, and said, 'I am a cop. You're busted.' I looked at him, and I thought, *Man, this ain't a cop. It's some asshole trying to shake me down.* He was holding onto my arms. I made one of my moves and broke his hold. It wasn't all that hard. And I started to walk away. Big fucking mistake. He came after me, I mean really pissed off, and he pulled a big motherfucker of a .357 and put it against my head. 'Okay, you're a cop,' I said. But he was too pissed to settle for two thousand baht. He gets on his walkie-talkie and they send a police car to the Square. I am in deep, deep shit. They book me, fingerprint me and haul my ass down to jail. I had to call in favors from people I don't like to bother. These Thai friends came down and handled the negotiations. I was shaking like a leaf. It took my friends two hours to buy my ass out of there. I was shitting bricks. Forty thousand baht. They asked for a hundred thousand. Two hours later I was back in the Square nursing a Singha, and thinking to myself I am starting to understand what makes Ricky hit his head against the fucking counter. It ain't because he killed all those Vietnamese, it is because he fucking miscalculated the most important decision of his life. It's because he got sucker punched into going to 'Nam in the first place."

McPhail sighed long and hard.

"I've seen Surat on the firing range. He's got a knack with the .357," said Calvino.

"Fuck, Calvino, where were you when I needed you?"

Calvino stopped for traffic at the mouth of Rama IV. "Some place else. We are always some place other than where we ought to be."

McPhail sucked on his cigarette. "Where I ought to be is looking over twenty thousand jade beads and two Burmese *yings* who are waiting for me to book my next trip to Rangoon."

Calvino turned his car into Rama IV and found himself behind a dump truck disgorging clouds of dust and gravel and building site debris. A gust of hot, dusty wind passed like a firestorm through the broken window. Choking and hacking, McPhail covered his nose and mouth. "What's that guy hauling, toxic waste?" asked McPhail.

The cloud of foul air was thick. Calvino watched the road through the fog of dust. Finally he left the dump truck on Rama IV as he turned into Soi 22. Driving in Bangkok was like going through one of those FBI urban terrorist training ranges where they gave a guy a gun and walked him down a specially built city block. In one window a dusky guy with a moustache popped up with an Uzi and in the doorway a pop-up target of a nine-year girl holding school books. There was never any warning. And you couldn't trust anyone. Motorcycles cut in and out of the lanes, coming off sidewalks, going the wrong way down the road. Pickup trucks parked wherever the driver's brain had cut out. Buses screaming down the outside lane, unloading passengers in the middle of traffic. A normal Bangkok traffic day. After a couple of near misses, Calvino took the short cut past the President Park connecting to Soi 24. McPhail leaned forward, his jaw dropped open, he stared at the broken window, the ragged edge of glass still hanging loose.

"No wonder I can't fucking breathe in here. There's no window. Don't tell me, not only did you get beat up, but someone burgled your car," said McPhail.

"I locked my keys inside last night." The light changed but the traffic had not yet started to move.

"You broke your window? In that rain. You broke your own fucking window? And I thought I'd done some dumb things in my life."

"It was flooding and I had to get to the hospital. I was bleeding all over the place. A broken window was the last of my worries."

McPhail threw out the cigarette and lit a joint, closed his eyes, rolled down his window, and smiled. "Jesus, Calvino, you are running a streak of some really mean bad karma. What did you do in your last life to have all this shit come down on you?"

Calvino smiled as they reached a four way stop, one of those Bangkok intersections where any self-respecting driver bluffed that he wouldn't stop. Playing chicken made Calvino think of all those wasted pies Fat Ralph was crying about. On Bangkok streets, whoever had the better, more expensive car and could intimidate others, make them fearful, could force them to give him the right of way. In Thailand, stop and yield signs were roadside decorations; the real rule of the road was what one could get away with. "We've just turned the corner, McPhail. I see the beginning of a wonderful day."

He drove down the ramp and into the basement parking lot of the Emporium. Calvino parked close to the elevators on Level B1. He got out and slammed the door. Some loose pieces of glass fell onto the cement floor, turning the head of a guard. It was just glass breaking into finer pieces.

"Guess it makes no sense to lock the door," said McPhail, nodding at the broken window. "Besides what Thai would want to steal it? Where's the face in driving a wreck?"

★★★★★★

ONCE they entered the shopping mall, Thailand disappeared—no smoke, no pollution, and no chaos. On the ground floor hall was the world of Louis Vuitton, Celine, Christain Dior, Hermes, Espada, and Versace. Calvino kept on his sunglasses; he felt conscious of how bad he looked and thought hiding under the glasses might help. But that was bullshit. Even without the beaten-up face, he would have kept them on. Why? He hated shopping malls; the whole idea was repulsive. He didn't want to see anyone he knew in such a place. It was as if the displays in the windows had been shot out of the belly of a spacecraft hovering over the city. Alien names, alien fashion, and alien prices. A father pushed a stroller past Celine. A fat Chinese boy with dirty knees raced around in his designer shorts; he jumped on and off the first step of the escalator.

"Piss off, you little bastard," said McPhail, as the boy brushed against him.

A central atrium rose five stories. Calvino leaned forward over the railing and stared up at the ceiling. Webbing had been draped over the arched windows and outside it was overcast, threatening to rain again, and the interior lights were turned down, casting a soft, mellow burnished light as if in this designer-made world it never rained. But even the management couldn't erase all storm clouds. There had been jumpers. Despondent Thais climbing over the railing and falling headfirst in someone's Caesar salad or hitting the polished white and black marble floor. News of the jumpers had been kept quiet to stop copycat suicides.

Classical music filtered up from the floor below. Presumably this was to soothe people, make them feel good, want to live, want to shop, not think about their problems or want to die.

McPhail had followed Calvino's eyeline. "No jumpers so far today," he said.

"I saw one last week," said Calvino.

"God, they make a mess. It is incredible how fast Security cleans up the bones. I mean you've got teeth and blood splattered twenty feet. You don't bounce when you hit this marble from the fifth floor."

McPhail *would* have those details, thought Calvino. There was a Calvino's law that a hardcore was someone who had witnessed so much death, violent death, that all the normal emotions had been peeled away to be replaced by statistics like the ones recited by baseball freaks who remembered every player and every game.

Most of the shoppers could have been exchanged for shoppers from anywhere else in the world. Caught in the soft lights and music, they walked the corridors looking for things to spend money on. The mall had succeeded in stripping Thailand clean of the peasants, construction workers, tuk-tuk drivers, the louts; none of them had sun-wrinkled, raisin faces with blood-red betel nut mouths. And it was quiet like the inside of a church in the suburbs. No constant buzz of fluorescent lights with swarms of insects bouncing off the bulbs. No traffic noises, no vendor carts, no blind lotto sellers, no limbless beggars with runny-nosed kids, no hilltribe mothers smelling of wood fires, holding a jaundiced baby in one hand and the other held out for donations.

McPhail followed Calvino up the escalator and they got off where a fashion walkway was being set up. A sign called this the Fashion Floor. This was the spot Noi had pre-arranged for the meeting. "If she's a fashion model, I think I am going to like this assignment," said McPhail.

"She's a singer and has worked in LA."

"Singer. Fuck that. Worked in LA, maybe. I can buy into that."

"You don't have to buy into anything, McPhail. My client wants her to call him. Nothing complicated," said Calvino as he turned to look at the workers putting up the ramp. At the far end another crew was working on the entrance to the ramp.

"And what? Sing him a song?"

"Does it really matter?" asked Calvino.

"Well this ain't LA. And in Bangkok everything is complicated. Just look in the mirror at your face and you will get a reminder."

He ignored McPhail's remark, walking around the perimeter, wondering whether McPhail might be right and this was something weird after all and that he, Vincent

Calvino, was asking someone else to step into a trap that was being set for him. This made him edgy.

"This is where she will be waiting." Calvino pointed at the door off the main stage.

"How am I supposed to recognize her?"

"I already showed you her photo."

"She was sleeping. I presume she'll be awake here."

"Look for a UCLA button pinned to her handbag."

"You got to be joking?"

"No joke."

"What if there are two broads with UCLA buttons?"

"Ask which one is Diane. And sings. If there is more than one singer named Diane wearing a UCLA button, I'll buy you lunch at the Lonesome Hawk."

"You never know, big spender," said McPhail.

McPhail was right. One never knew. Calvino's mobile phone rang, and he pulled it out of his jacket pocket and pressed against his ear.

"Look up. At the top of the up escalator," said the voice. Calvino turned, looked up, lowered his sunglasses and saw Jess leaning over the railing one floor up, waving down at him.

"What a coincidence," said Calvino, sliding the sunglasses back snug against his nose.

"Let me buy you a coffee. Say, the fifth floor in five minutes?" It was a question but before Calvino could answer the call had ended.

Calvino put down the phone. "Got to go McPhail. You're sure you can handle this on Sunday?" He handed him a piece of paper. "This is the guy's number. Take her to a pay phone and put through a collect call. Then put her on the line. Once she says hello, you're done. They've

connected. I've done my job, and I owe you a big one."
Calvino folded a thousand baht note into McPhail's hand.

"Piece of cake. I get her to phone this guy in LA. End of story. How can anyone fuck that up?"

★★★★★★

JESS sat alone at a Burger King table demonstrating another one of Calvino's laws: that it is better to be alone and lonely than lost in a crowd one can't escape. It was hard to know whether he was lonely and lost in some escape no one could understand but himself. One table away two old Chinese ladies chomped down on Whoppers. Grease and ketchup bleeding between their fingers, they stopped only to put a straw between their lips and suck from huge cola cups. The burgers were larger than their heads. Jess had chosen fast food alley for a coffee—one of those LAPD habits. Bunched together side by side was the unholy trinity of junk food— Dairy Queen, Burger King, and KFC. Bloated teenagers sat around tables in their school uniforms looking like they had stepped out of an American TV series set in an Americanized ethnic community.

"We could be in LA," said Calvino as he pulled up a chair.

"What are you drinking?" asked Jess.

"Coffee. I'll get it myself," Calvino said pushing the chair back. "Nice ambience."

No reply from the LAPD cop.

Calvino glanced at the escalator carrying people up to the cinemas on the sixth floor. Kids with greasy food patches on their faces, pumped up with coke, shot like fleshy flames up the escalator to the cinemas. Calvino edged his way back through the burger eaters and escalator runners. As he approached the counter, he looked back and saw Jess waiting in silence, his hands wrapped around his paper cup of coffee. Turning back around, Calvino watched the fry cook lowering a wire basket of French fries into a boiling vat of oil. A moment later he was back at the table. Funny that Jess would be here, funnier still that he would be asking Calvino for coffee in the Emporium, but the funniest line was this LA cop's silence. Calvino decided to let it go, wait until Jess had something to say. Whatever was on his chest was taking a while to work its way up to his throat and to form into words.

Calvino sat sipping his coffee. The two old Chinese women had finished their Whoppers, looking glassy eyed from a major grease injection as they stared silently into their cokes.

"Colonel Prachai says you know your way around. I was glad to hear that," said Jess, stopping to sip from his coffee for the first time. He looked over at Calvino, betraying no clear expression.

"Call him Pratt. It's okay. I've called him Pratt for more than twenty years. You know that even his wife calls him Pratt?"

"I didn't know that."

"But you've got some doubts about hiring me for this job."

Jess pressed his lips tight and nodded. "You could say that. I couldn't quite understand why the principal had insisted that I team with you."

Calvino drank some coffee. He was a little surprised. "I thought Pratt had got me the job."

Jess grinned. "He is a major fan of yours. But the job came from someone in LA. My principal mentioned a friend named Gabe who had recommended you. When I learned you had never heard of my principal, I became . . ." His voice trailed off.

"Suspicious. Doubtful. Uncertain. You're thinking, what is going down here. I am being ordered to work in Bangkok, my hometown, with a *farang*. Why a *farang*? Why this *farang*? What gives? And why doesn't this *farang* know him?"

"Something like that."

"Gabe I know, though I can't imagine why he would recommend me to your principal. I haven't exactly come through for him," Calvino said. He paused, watching the steam rise from his coffee, collecting his thoughts. "And I am thinking, why does a Thai who works for LAPD come knocking on my door, looking to put a grand a day into my pocket. No one hands over that kind of money without a reason. The guy we are guarding, Wes Naylor, is just another low-life LA lawyer who has probably never earned a grand a day in his life. It seems out of proportion to the circumstances. Unless someone is trying to make a statement. Someone trying to give us some advice through the kind of money they are throwing around, and if you're smart, if I am smart, then we should listen to what they are saying."

"Naylor only has a limited law practice. He's mainly a businessman."

"Yeah, what kind of business?"

"He's got something to do with e-commerce—you know selling stuff on the Internet."

"*Stuff* covers a big category of things."

"He has one of those single male traveler websites."

The light went on for Calvino. He knew about these sites. "He sells information on where to find *yings*," said Calvino.

"That's one way of looking at it. The hotel deal is an extension of his business. That's what Kowit has told me. I think he has been pretty honest about this. He didn't need to tell me this background about Naylor. But he is coming here as a lawyer," said Jess. "Kowit confirmed that."

"Who's Kowit?"

"He's a personal friend of Dr. Nat."

"And Dr. Nat figures in how?"

"There is a hotel in Bangkok he's buying."

Jess took another sip of his coffee and smiled; not a broad grin, but one of those smiles that indicate that some kind of reality had registered, logged into the ledger as valid.

"None of this is adding up, Jess. Think about it."

"I am listening," said Jess.

LAPD Jess wasn't stupid enough to fully accept the situation as presented to him, or was he? His willingness to listen was an encouraging sign, thought Calvino, who liked the idea that just maybe the set-up disturbed him. It damn well should have given him some restless nights. What needed to be understood was that neither of them was going to be blinded by the money. But money had that blinding light function for a lot of people.

"Okay, you're an LA guy. Let's put it in film terms. Do you remember the film where the Internal Affairs cops frame the black cop by planting offshore bank account files in his house?"

"*The Negotiator.* Yeah, I liked that movie," said Jess.

"Like it or not, you gotta believe that those files prove the black cop has been ripping off the police pension fund for years, otherwise the Internal Affairs Department case falls apart. Am I right?"

"You're right," said Jess.

"There is no way that offshore rip-off could work the way Internal Affairs said it worked. You just don't open an offshore account over the telephone. This is not like ordering take-out pizza. There are forms to fill out. Copies of passports to be sent in. Bank officers who know your name and send you letters. So they got a file with papers in it. If the cop is innocent, then how is his name on any of those papers? Evidence is a chain. One bad link and it breaks. If the bad guys forged the papers, then his lawyer phones the bank and gets copies of the originals. His client's name isn't on any of the originals. So how is he dirty? He ain't. That's the point. The cop should have walked. Internal Affairs had nothing. Jess, banks don't go around transferring millions of dollars without a paper chain a mile long to document what they are doing. You don't change a couple of years of fraud overnight by doctoring a file. Real life doesn't work that way."

"You're saying Naylor or my principal is lying?"

"I don't know if they are lying. But they might be acting on some misinformation," said Calvino.

"Remember that Grisham novel *The Firm* where the plot turns on a limited partnership formed in Hong Kong for tax purposes? Hong Kong is a tax haven. Why would you form a limited partnership there? The answer is, you wouldn't. What I am trying to say is that most of the time Americans get international connections and deals dead wrong. They don't understand the process:

how things work, the system, the tracks left by messages, letters, statements, records. Take bodyguarding. This is a big deal in America. Thai gangsters have bodyguards, too. But the guy actually funding this deal is Thai. Does he come to Thailand? No. He sends a part-time lawyer who is in the sleaze business to negotiate his deal. He stays home and pays eight grand and expenses for bodyguards. One he doesn't know. Jess, it doesn't add up except in an American movie or novel where no one seems to care that things don't add up. They just follow the action and don't think too much. I live here; you were born here, Jess. And we have some heavy thinking to do. What we are being asked to do is something no one who has ever lived here would ever believe. Not for a moment. So we have to ask ourselves who these people are who hired us and what they *really* want? And why are they throwing around all of this money? No client has ever peeled off four grand in advance and not wanted something more than he says he wants."

"What's your theory, Vincent?"

"These people are selling a set-up that is tailored for American consumption."

"Wes Naylor doesn't need to arrive tomorrow. If we think we can't handle it, then all I have to do is make a phone call. Cancel out the arrangement and we walk away from the job."

Calvino watched a couple strolling past sharing a Diary Queen peanut and chocolate sundae. Each digging into the side with their tiny red plastic spoons. "You wouldn't have come all the way here if you were going to walk away."

"And I don't see you reaching in your pocket and handing back the four grand," said Jess.

"How do you want to play it?" asked Calvino, watching the female member of the couple stick the red spoon in her mouth, her eyelids half-closed in ice cream pleasure. He wondered if she had that same look in bed.

"As it comes." "That is very Thai.

"I am Thai and I know what I am doing."

Here comes the right-wing nationalist bullshit, thought Calvino. Part protest, part threat, part a show stopper. Meaning, not only am I Thai but you are a *farang* and no *farang* can ever make the right call in Thailand; *farangs* don't know enough. They don't have Thai blood.

"So where do you want to take it, Jess?" asked Calvino. Some serious tension was heating up. Calvino was halfway to throwing the four grand on the table and walking away from the junk food, this junk case. He could smooth it over with Pratt; tell him the truth, that he had a conflict— this meeting with a singer named Noi, the sleeping broad who called herself Diane. The appointment came out of the blue, and he owed it to Gabe to follow through, otherwise where would his reputation be? Gabe would never recommend him again. The way Jess was fingering the paper coffee cup, it wouldn't be long until leaks started to appear. He didn't look happy; Calvino didn't look all that happy either. The assignment was shaping up to be something like the Emporium itself—a fake world with controlled temperature and light. Inside Jess's own self-contained world of LA, it made sense, but once outside into the real stink of Bangkok, it began to fall apart, like a movie or novel that asked someone to believe in a premise which they knew rang false because they lived in the real world. So where were they? Inside another cartoon scripted by those looking to make fast money.

"If you pull out, I can phone LA and tell them the situation."

"In other words, you want me to make the decision for you."

"Then you are in?"

There were defining moments in everyone's life and Calvino felt this was one of them. Fish or cut bait time. He stared at Jess, wondering if this cop had leveled or was still holding back. Pratt's recommendation had to count for something.

"I don't have anything else on this weekend." Calvino rose from the table.

"See you tomorrow at the airport," said Jess.

"We will meet Mr. Naylor's flight at noon."

"Exactly what kind of cop are you?"

Jess pushed back the coffee cup.

"Narcotics. Undercover narcotics."

"Putting drug dealers in jail?"

"Sometimes," said Jess.

"Then bodyguard duty should be a piece of cake."

Jess laid a small plastic bag on the table."That's your first mistake." He opened the parcel as he talked, never losing eye contact with Calvino. "If someone really intends to take someone out, it's difficult to stop the shooter." Jess removed a radio transceiver from the bag, connected a mini-mic and then a control switch. "But if he's simply intimidating for business reasons, then that's a different story. But either way, I promise you one thing, it won't be a piece of cake."

The last item he took out was the flesh-colored wireless earphone that was shaped like the nose cone of a rocket. He allowed the earphone to roll back and forth in the palm of his hand before handing it to Calvino.

"You ever use one of these before?" Jess asked. "It's called an earphone inductor."

Calvino picked the earphone out of Jess's hand. "No wires. The signal transmits from the induction coil."

"The main rule in surveillance is to stay in communication with your partner. You see or hear anything I should know about, you push the talk toggle on the control switch. And I will do the same thing. We work together by being in different locations around the asset. I go ahead and you follow. The radio transceiver goes on your belt, the induction coil and mini-mic concealed in your jacket."

"Let me guess? This goes in my ear," said Calvino.

Jess didn't smile. He was into toys.

Let Jess take point, Calvino thought. He was beginning to understand that Jess wasn't much of a follower. This was more than just who led and who followed at the dance but who became the prime target if a shooter appeared. Something told Calvino all those years in the States had changed some core value in Jess, or was he simply trying to prove something to Calvino or to himself? Or it may have been even simpler than that: he didn't trust Calvino to be on point.

FIVE

LEK WORKED BEHIND the bar, her arms wet to the elbows, washing and stacking cocktail glasses and beer mugs. Steam from the coffee machine fogged the mirror. With her usual line of vision clouded, it was difficult to do the washing up and manage the bar. She stood with her back to the dance floor and the door. She'd half turn from the sink, hands dripping, take in the action, before washing another glass. She spotted Calvino on a stool tapping his fingers against the side of his glass.

"What happened to you, Khun Vinee?" asked Lek, wiping her hands on a towel.

"I fell off a motorcycle," he said in Thai. She smiled at him.

A motorcycle accident was an old bar *ying* stand-by lie.

"Or maybe someone get angry with you. Want a drink, Khun Vinee?"

"When you have time."

"Just washing glasses. It never ends. So I just stop. Say finished. Look at my hands. They look like an old woman's hands," she poured him another Mekhong, put more ice into his glass and topped it off with an ounce of cola.

"Get one of the *yings* to help."

She laughed. "They don't know clean from dirty. Give a customer a dirty glass and unless he's drunk, he's gonna complain and not come back. No, I wash the glasses. Besides, I've got lots of time. And I go to see the doctor today. He check everything. Stomach, chests, down there. Take my blood. Everything okay. No HIV, no problem. He say I can have kid. I think it is time."

"Jack and you are long overdue," said Calvino. Jack Mellows, a fifty-eight year old American from Alaska, was Lek's old man. He'd financed the bar from the sale of his fishing boat which had been called "Lovejoy". He called the bar by the same name. From a commercial point of view the Lovejoy was probably less seaworthy than Lovejoy the boat, but he managed to keep the business afloat by doing odd jobs. Being single didn't mean that one lacked attachments; it meant that you slept alone in your own bed at least five nights a week. Any other arrangement was a kind of putative marriage. Many gray-area marriages existed; men who were neither single nor married, somewhat like the living dead or a Benz station wagon—odd, strange compromises that seemed to deliver the worst of both worlds. But Jack and Lek were "married" not in the way most *farangs* were married to a Thai woman. These two had actually registered their marriage in the district office and that made the union as official as any marriage could be under Thai law. There was no ambiguity in the legalities of their relationship; but the actual practice of being married was riddled with many contradictions for both of them.

"Jack can not make baby."

"Yeah," said Calvino arching an eyebrow. "What's his problem?"

"He shoots blanks," said Lek, making her index finger into a gun barrel, her middle finger the trigger and her thumb the hammer. No question she'd picked up the expression and gesture from Jack. Calvino raised his glass and touched her index finger.

"Don't shoot," he said, smiling. "I am in bad enough shape without getting shot."

"Do you know what a blank is?" she asked him.

"A fake bullet."

She shook her head. "Wrong. Blank means sperm is no good."

This was how English was absorbed in the bar. He wasn't going to argue with her.

"So who is the lucky father going to be?"

"Not sure who I want. You want baby, Khun Vinee?"

"I am a solo act. And look at me, do I look like Darwin selected my genes for another generation?" said Calvino, glancing at his watch and gesturing for another drink.

"You mean Dwayne?" She had never heard of Darwin. Dwayne she had slept with.

"Where is Jack, by the way?"

"Upstairs watching Larry and eating pizza. Why do you Americans all eat pizza?"

"Because Larry and pizza go together."

She laughed, an easy laugh. Lek was about twenty-three, twenty-four, easing into a career shift from *mamasan* to motherhood. Running a bar was on-the-job training in how to discipline children. And after all, Motherhood (with a capital "M") with a *farang* was a good direction to head after the younger *yings* made competition in the bar more and more difficult. Not that a married woman like Lek was competing in the bar for customers . . . but there had been Dwayne, and a couple of other chances for romance and income, actually several others.

"Who's on your short-list? The guys you'd consider for father material?"

A puzzled look crossed her face. "A short what?"

"The top three guys you want to father your child."

"Only three? Not enough."

"I figured your short-list might turn out to be a long list. You thought it through, right? You have a *luk-krueng* and you take her straight from the hospital to the TV studio to do a Johnson and Johnson baby powder commercial, pick up a fat paycheck on the way out the door. Then when she's older, she gets a huge contract from Grammy Records. You never have to work again."

The TV had lots of air-time about the paycheck the parents had pocketed after their *luk-krueng* scored a major commercial, increasing the birthrate overnight among *yings* who got the message that having a *luk-krueng* was the fast track way to pick-up truck, motorcycle, condo, and a new wardrobe. No one mentioned all the ugly half-breed kids that no advertising agency would put on camera to push baby powder or dog food.

"*Farang* stay in Thailand too long, know too much about Thai girl. No good."

Early on a Friday evening, Lovejoy was subdued, *yings* shuffling like their legs were numb. A few regulars sat in the back keeping to themselves, ignoring the *yings*. Or were the *yings* ignoring them? Some were tourists— they had the look of someone who had strapped on roller-skates for the first time—off-balance, wobbly, awkwardly moving around the half-dark interior, their Dobie Gillis/Forrest Gump smiles setting them apart. What Lek was saying is that this kind of *farangs* they wanted in the bar; *yings* could draw down some real cash from such *farangs*. Like taking money from the IMF but without all those reporting and spending conditions and paperwork.

Two offs had been chalked on the white board.

"Two *yings* out early. Business must be good," said Calvino, looking at black numbers 31 and 45 on the white board.

"Not really."

"Maybe the numbers are from last night. With all the washing up you haven't had time to clean the board," said Calvino. Sometimes the *mamasan* wrote the numbers on the board on the same theory that a beggar puts some coins in the hat. Seeing someone had gone first inspired confidence, thinking that it is okay to bar fine a girl. One of those great comforts of life is that someone else has been there, done that. One of the great fears is, if you don't act now, who knows, there might not be any *yings* left.

"You thinking I'm joking about a baby?"

The *yings* on stage in bikinis looked like a warm-up act for superstars that had yet to arrive. The real talent didn't show until nine or so if they showed at all, and that depended on whether some Dobie character had dragged her deep into some domestic fantasy about getting married and going back to Portland with him. Lovejoy pulled most of its talent from a couple of *Isan* villages and this created a family-like environment where *yings* shared their problems and fried grasshoppers, but all that good feeling didn't stop the *yings* trying to scratch out the eyes of someone who had poached another girl's customers.

"No, but I think you need to work on your pitch. It needs a polish."

"What a pitch?"

"Your story line is rusty. You've been out of circulation."

"Just married to Jack."

"Whatever. If you want stud service, then you need a good pitch."

"Pitch. What do you know about pitching?" asked Jack Mellows.

He appeared at the bottom of the stairs wearing sandals, overalls, and a carefully ironed red shirt. Jack walked behind the bar, picked up a freshly washed glass, put it under the Johnny Walker Black bottle dispenser and pressed the plastic button, releasing a shot. He hit the dispenser one more time. It wasn't clear how long Jack had been standing at the foot of the stairs listening. With the fogged mirror, he was outside of Lek's field of vision and Calvino sat with his back turned away from the stairs.

"Some of the world's greatest major league pitchers are from the Plaza."

Jack thought about this, wondering if Calvino was fucking with him. He decided the smart move would be to forget it since Calvino owed him money and Jack owed him some photos of dead *farangs* and getting into some extended con- versation about pitching was going to lead nowhere he wanted to go. But the booze told him to forget the smart move and push this asshole who had the full attention of his wife.

"Why didn't you come upstairs?"

"And interrupt 'Larry King Live'?" Calvino knew that Jack was a TV freak, and that this show was one he always watched. "Larry interviewed a guy who heads Sex Addicts Anonymous, California branch. The guy is belly-aching that he was a total addict, has screwed eighty-four *yings* in the last twelve months, and I am thinking to myself, eighty-four in twelve months? Has he got an impotence problem? Eighty-four isn't even a good start. The guy doesn't know fucking addiction. And what in God's name is wrong with screwing? I kept asking myself, this guy has started a support group for Sex Addicts Anonymous. Anonymous? I say to myself this guy's on national television talking about all the *yings* he's fucked. That's not exactly anonymous, that's bragging. Support? Support for what, I ask myself. Do these guys sit around crying about how ashamed they are of themselves, handing each other tissues? How has America got itself so fucked up? It don't make sense, Vinee. Then I remind myself, hey, this is from the U.S. of A. And I remember the reason I pay for sex in Thailand is because free sex is too fucking expensive in America. No wonder this guy is on Larry telling his story. If he doesn't cut back on sex, he will end up in the poorhouse. Half-fucked and totally broke. Ain't that right, honey?" He looked over at Lek, toasted her with his glass. He was rambling, and Calvino was thinking that Jack had been into the Johnny Black upstairs watching Larry King.

"Lek told you she wants to have a kid," said Jack. He sipped from his glass, leaning forward on his elbows close enough for Calvino to see some cracker crumbs in Jack's white beard. "And that I shoot blanks?"

He had been listening for a while, thought Calvino.

"Jack, I didn't come around to talk about Larry King or your fertility problem. I came on business."

"Excuse me. I was trying to explain about how fucked up Americans are and how lucky we are that we don't live in that Nazi-feminist state." He punched back the double shot.

After the long sigh, Calvino hit him with the question that had brought him to Lovejoy in the first place: "What did you find out for me in Phuket?"

Jack, a big boned man, his nose puffy and lined with blue veins, his jowls saggy, reached into his overalls and pulled out a brown whisky-stained envelope and tossed it on the bar. Calvino had no trouble seeing him pulling in nets filled with salmon over the side of Lovejoy the boat.

"The photos are inside. I don't know if your man is there or not. Some of those bodies had been in those drawers for going on two weeks. Some are pretty ripe as well. They had two or three stacked inside each drawer."

Calvino opened the envelope and flipped through the photos, looking at faces of dead *farangs*. Bloated, twisted, discolored death masks of *farang* men in their twenties. Their naked, dead bodies in an apparent embrace with the other bodies in the drawer, limbs tangled together, hair matted onto the chest of another body. The face he was looking for belonged to Dale Macdonald, a young Canadian back-packer from Toronto. Dale'd gone missing during the Full Moon party. Every month on Koh Pha Ngan thousands of young travelers slept on the beach, did drugs, fucked each other, and watched the full moon over the sea. Each month some of them died of an overdose. It was the law of averages. Drugs and booze culled the weak members of any herd. Calvino had been paid to find Dale, twenty-one years old, just graduated from the University of Toronto and gone to Thailand after he had read on the Internet about the Full Moon party every month on Koh Pha Ngan. Dale's father, a newspaper editor, hired Calvino to find his son, comb the beaches, talk to people, find someone who had been on the local scene and might have information about Dale. Calvino had done that but no one had any information about Dale and either they were lying or Dale wasn't on Koh Pha Ngan.

Ratana had suggested the morgue in Phuket. Good idea, only Calvino wasn't going to the South to check out any morgues. So he sub-contracted Jack to do the job.

Calvino laid out photos of stiffs on the bar counter. Like playing cards. Thirty-seven jokers inside Phuket hospital morgues. The bodies had come from Koh Pha

Ngan and been shipped to Phuket. There was no place to keep bodies on the island. Phuket had the facilities for handling and disposal.

A good business? Not really. No one was claiming the bodies and they were piling up, becoming a health problem, a public relations problem. The image of all those young dead *farangs* wasn't good for tourism. But it would have been worse to bury the bodies on the beach or tie some weights around the legs and dump them in the sea. And it sure wasn't any good for anyone to keep them decomposing in half-assed facilities in local hospitals.

Calvino found Dale among the photos; Dale looked like he was in a deep sleep. His body was in a lot better shape than most of the others. What had Dale been looking for? Adventure, enlightenment, sex, love, and friendship? The search had ended in the morgue. The family would be notified and arrangements would be made to ship Dale back to Canada for burial.

"That's him," said Calvino, turning the photo around. Jack looked at the photo in a detached way like he wasn't thinking about what he was looking at. Calvino had been half-hoping the kid wouldn't be in any of the photos. Now he had the unpleasant job of phoning Toronto and breaking the news to the family.

"I mean what is a sex addict?" asked Jack. "Think about it. These assholes hate sex. It's not a drug or cigarettes or picking your nose. Getting laid is about the best thing you can do."

Soon a half-dozen bar *yings* edged around Calvino, elbows on the bar, handing each other the photos.

"Jack, this is my guy. I don't want to talk about Larry King. I want to deal with this. Are you with me?"

"You'd better phone the hospital. A doctor said they were thinking about tossing dead *farangs* into the hospital incinerator. They've got unclaimed bodies coming out of their ears and no place to bury them. No money to pay the wats to burn them. They are pretty pissed off. The cemeteries want money. Everyone has their fucking hand out. So the doctor says they will burn the bodies with the garbage. Kind of makes you think, Calvino."

"Jack, don't you think Khun Vinee's baby would be *nah-lak dee*?" asked Lek.

"I've got pictures of dead people on the bar that look in better condition than Vinee."

Calvino took out a hundred-dollar note and pushed it over to Jack.

"Who are you bar fining, my wife?" He blinked at the note, then looked at Calvino.

"That's for bringing back these." Calvino slipped the photos back in the envelope.

Jack held the C-note up to the light, one of the new ones where the engravers had made Ben Franklin look like the man in the moon. Having cleared up two missing persons within the space of twenty-four hours (and only getting beat up once), combined with the grand a day bodyguard assignment had Calvino thinking that he was coming out of some dark tunnel; the place of that nightmare where the locals were burning up *farangs*. He watched Jack fold the C-note in half and stick it inside his shirt pocket. Then Jack leaned over and slapped Lek on the ass. "You're pushing the edge of the envelope, Lek."

She extended two fingers like a double-barreled handgun, tapping her thumb as the hammer rapidly several times.

"Bang, bang," she laughed.

"Not dangerous. It only shoots blanks."

"I catch you fucking around, I won't be shooting blanks," said Jack.

Calvino was thinking that would make an interesting Larry King: owner of Lovejoy goes postal in Bangkok. She wrapped her arms around Jack's thick fisherman's neck, kissed him on his bearded cheek, and looking past her husband, she locked Calvino in the cross-hairs of her sight and squeezed off a wink. If a picture is worth ten thousand words, then Lek's wink was running the length of the Encyclopedia Britannica. Calvino's mobile phone rang, giving him an excuse to pick up the photos and step outside to answer it.

"This is Father Andrew, and I have an extra bottle of a pretty good French wine and no one who can appreciate it. So I thought about you. And I am putting together some dinner. Say you come to my place in about an hour?"

"Tonight is Friday. You never go out on Friday nights."

"That's right. That's why I am asking you to come in."

"You're not flooded in?" asked Calvino.

Father Andrew laughed.

"What's this? Vincent Calvino's afraid of getting wet?"

Calvino watched the passing *farangs*. Mostly middle-aged men fingering a Viagra in their pocket, eyeing the bars, trying to decide which bar to try next. The blue pill was like the hoola hoop or bell-bottom trousers, a time lock forever freezing the takers as creatures of the late nineties.

"Dinner?"

"Dinner. And it is a very good Bordeaux."

"You've got a deal. And I'll pick up another bottle. God's been good to me."

"He must have time on his hands if he has been good to you, Vincent Calvino."

The good father liked drinking wine and breaking bread with a Jew whose father was a Roman Catholic.

★★★★★★

CALVINO killed the ignition and turned off the headlights. He got out of his car, slammed the door, and stood in the darkness for a moment, looking at the outline of the old slaughterhouse in the distance. More cars than usual were parked in the lot between large flatbed trucks. The place had been quiet ever since the municipal authorities had closed it down. The flood water had gone down. A couple of wooden planks provided a bridge to the main slum. He crossed through a maze of small walkways that ran between the shanty houses built of wood, structures without glass or screens on the windows. Inside, old people and small children watched TV. The sixteen to thirty-five age group didn't register on the radar screen. Gone. Vanished until the early hours of the morning. Laundry hung on lines to dry. Dogs sniffed around the edges of the walkway scavenging for food. He passed a shop selling the basics—rice, candy, soda, water—displayed on a couple of shelves, and, for those who knew the vendor well, a selection of drugs under the counter. Calvino knew the way to Father Andrew's house, walking along the narrow alleyways built of wood. The slum was built on stilts over swampy ground. Most of Bangkok had been built on swamp land. The water was always deeper in the slums after the rain, an evil deep black. Half-submerged bottles, cans, shoes, paper not so much floated on the top but looked like the trash dropped on long strips of tar. Mosquitoes bounced off neon lights. After a few minutes, Calvino stopped in front of Father Andrew's wooden house. The lights were out and it was very quiet. He didn't like the feel of the stillness. No radios, shouting, talking, or laughter, or the sound of people cooking or rattling around tin-roofed houses. The slum was a rough and tumble place that no one looking for peace and quiet would want to be in for five minutes. Funny, what was in his head was how Father Andrew had been talking with foreign journalists about the injustices the cops and officials had caused in the slums. Had someone been sent to silence him? Calvino looked for someone to ask if they had seen Father Andrew but the gangway was empty. Nothing was moving. Calvino slowly reached for his .38 police special and just as he was about to kick down the door, the lights came on inside. Someone was blowing a horn. And everyone was singing Happy Birthday. Father Andrew stepped outside and put his arm around Calvino.

"We were going to wait until you walked inside. But someone said, 'He's pulled his gun.' So I thought it best to move things up a little. Vincent, you can put that thing away for now," said Father Andrew. "Some bad people are selling drugs about a hundred meters from here. What if I pay you five hundred baht and take you and your gun over there. Just wave it around to scare them away. There will be another time. Happy Birthday."

Calvino holstered his handgun, removed his shoes and entered into the kitchen. Grouped inside Father Andrew's small shanty were many familiar faces. He locked eyes with Father Andrew, then smiled at Ratana, who looked away. No doubt, he thought, she had played a major role in organizing the surprise party. Pratt and his wife, Manee. McPhail, Black Hawk, Fat Ralph, Ricky, and a few other old hands, long-term *farangs* from Washington Square, the Foreign Correspondents' Club, an office on Silom Road, business people. McPhail stood beside Ewok, the top of her head reaching the middle of McPhail's ribcage. This crew was what substituted for family, thought Calvino. They had driven out to Father Andrew's Klong Toey slum dwelling not knowing if it was going to rain and flood again to say happy birthday. He spotted Jess standing slightly behind Pratt and Manee.

"Your fourth cycle, Vincent," said Pratt. In New York City two cycles earlier, when Pratt had still been a student, he had explained how every twelve years from the date of birth was a separate cycle, and how the Thais and Chinese and other Asians put great significance by the passage of one cycle and the entry into a new one.

"Where did the last two cycles go?" asked Calvino.

"Stolen by the *khamoy*," Father Andrew used the Thai word for thief, never passing up the chance for a pun.

Ewok ran up and gave Calvino a red rose. "McPhail pay bar. Say we go to a party. Happy Birthday Khun Vinee."

McPhail shook his head. "I told Ewok not to say I paid the bar in front of Father Andrew."

"I know. I forgot, okay?" said Ewok.

"It's okay," said Father Andrew. "I'm certain Edward's motives are pure."

Jess had been near the window and saw Calvino draw his .38.

"You missed an important clue," said Jess. "What wasn't outside?"

"And what would that have been?" asked Calvino.

"Shoes. There were no shoes. There are always shoes outside a Thai house," said Jess, smiling like he was happy with himself. "Father Andrew had us keep our shoes inside."

"Vincent might tell you that my guests always take their shoes inside. Otherwise their shoes might disappear," said Father Andrew. "Most of people in the slum are very poor. Not your middle class Bangkok or LA crowd. But there are millionaires living here as well. They mainly operate the drug cartels. People steal shoes to pay their runner for drugs."

"Good thinking," said Jess, swallowing hard, looking away like he had lost some major face.

"I missed enough other clues," said Calvino quickly. "I have been sleepwalking all day."

The surprise birthday was starting to register. Calvino was holding onto his forties like a drunken chef holding onto the wrong end of a greasy spoon. Friends were gathering around to watch him let go. His face bruised, the stitches still fresh, pale and tired, he suddenly looked miserable. What he had missed was Father Andrew's timing.

"Wait an hour," Father Andrew had said on the phone. He missed the definite tip-off. And, of course, there were the extra cars in the parking lot. Cars that didn't belong there.

Across the room, he watched as Ratana and Ewok, who stood on her tiptoes, leaned over a table and lit the candles. The others joined in. Everyone seemed to have a lighter or match; taking their turn to lean over and light a candle. Soon the horror of all those tiny flames ignited on the cakes on Father Andrew's kitchen table began to sink in. For a brief moment no one said anything, looking at all of the lit candles. One candle on each of the forty-eight small cakes. And there was a large cake with forty-eight more candles. McPhail started singing "Happy Birthday" and Fat Ralph joined in and then the others. Someone turned out the lights and the only illumination in Father Andrew's sitting room came from the candles on Calvino's birthday cakes. Calvino listened to them singing, thinking that this was the passage of another year, the beginning of the fifth cycle; a new period of twelve years. Jess was right. He had missed something. Like an entire cycle of his life. This cycle he promised himself to be more observant, not to let the years slip away and next thing he would be sixty. There were no sixty-year-old private eyes. In the next twelve years he had to get it right or it would never be right.

"Make a wish and blow out the candles," Manee said. "If you can."

He made the wish to get it right. The way his nose was stitched up, trying to blow out the candles was not all that easy.

He leaned forward and blew out one candle, then another, and another; his friends joined in until there was one candle left burning. He moved forward and looked at the solitary candle on the big cake. Calvino smiled, leaned forward, puffed up his lips and blew it out. And for a long moment, everyone stood silently in the darkness. When Father Andrew switched on the light, the door was open and outside dozens of children crowded around; they lived in the surrounding shacks. Dressed in T-shirts and shorts, they pushed forward for a cake.

"Khun Vinee, now you can make merit," said Ratana.

This was her way of ensuring that he would be around for the fifth cycle. And as a way of making merit, he had to admit it was better than releasing sparrows from small wooden cages a wat into polluted air or turtles into a dirty *klong*.

Calvino held a small cake in each hand. He squatted down in the doorway and passed out the small cakes to the first two children. Ratana handed him two more, and he held them out to the next set of children, and five minutes later all of the cakes had gone out the door and most of the children had disappeared into the darkness. Forty-eight cakes in five minutes. Not all that different than the passage of the years themselves, he thought, rising to his feet.

Father Andrew gave Calvino a glass of red wine.

"Like I promised, we are going to drink some fine wine."

Calvino took the glass and raised it to Father Andrew, then Pratt, Manee, Ratana, his friends, and then turned and touched the rim of Father Andrew's glass to make a toast.

"In my line of work, I've been set up a lot of times. Most of the time it means I get a trip to the hospital. This time something good came out of it. I don't really know what else to say. I mean, I didn't have time to write anything down or think I was going to have to say anything. What I am trying to say is that the fact that you came to Father Andrew's house after the flooding yesterday means something. It means a lot. No one would have blamed you for staying home. You didn't. You came around to make a point. Friendship counts for something."

"We came because Father Andrew threatened us with hell if we didn't," said someone in the back. Everyone laughed.

"My birthday wish is that Father Andrew gets his school finished this year." Because that would make things right in the world. And it would be a chance to square accounts with Father Andrew.

"You're not supposed to tell your wish or it won't come true," said Jess.

"I'll take my chances, Jess."

Father Andrew refilled Calvino's glass. It was a good wine, Calvino thought. As Father Andrew poured, he recognized one of the children who had taken one of the small cakes. She looked about eight years old; large, watchful, questioning eyes with huge black pupils, looking down at the cake that Calvino had handed to her. She had moved in next to Calvino.

"Something wrong with the cake?" he asked.

She nodded her head.

"This is Dew," said Father Andrew. "She showed up last night with her two brothers. Younger brothers. Since Dew's parents are both dead, she's now head of the household."

Dew stared down at the small cake cupped in her tiny hands.

"Mee nong chai song kon. Mee khnom cake nueng chin." Two younger brothers. But only one cake. What should she do?

Calvino looked at her, then over his shoulder at the dining room table. He walked over, picked up the large cake with *Happy Birthday Vincent Calvino* in pink icing with the forty-eight candles still smoking. He handed it to her. "Give them this," said Calvino. Like a shadow, the large cake in her hands, she left without another word.

Thank you was not a word used in the slum. There wasn't much time for politeness; the more urgent necessities of living intervened, like hunger and fear.

Jess said, "There is more to you than I thought."

He handed him a present wrapped in green paper with a red bow.

Calvino shrugged, taking the gift. "Now you're missing something. I hate cake. I would have thrown it to the dogs. So giving it to the kid is no big deal. Getting all sentimental is the worst thing you can do in Bangkok. All the years I've been coming out, there is almost never a happy ending. You can guarantee what you hear is nothing remotely touching reality. The kid was probably lying. The odds are five to eight she's on some corner selling the cake. She'll use the money to buy drugs for herself and her brothers. So do you still think there is more to me than you thought?"

"Open it," said Jess.

Calvino tore off the paper and held up an official LAPD T-shirt.

"Thought you might like," continued Jess.

"Nice. Is it bullet-proof?" Calvino asked.

"What a practical man you've become, Mr. Calvino," said Father Andrew.

"Impractical men aren't around to celebrate four cycles," he said.

"That they aren't," said Father Andrew. "Not in Bangkok."

"Why did you come here?" asked Calvino, turning to face Jess.

"Pratt thought I would learn something about you, seeing you here." He had started to call him Pratt, thought Calvino.

Calvino could see that play. Pratt giving Jess a talk about seeing Calvino in Klong Toey would tell him about his partner on this assignment. A slum was a better place to judge the cut of a man working in Bangkok than the junk food court of the Emporium. Anyone could look good, walk tall in the Emporium; but in the walkways over the swamp land of Klong Toey, there were no designers or gunmen, but just a lot of poor people trying to make it to the next day with food in their belly.

Also Jess had his own reasons for coming, which he left right to the end.

"I spoke with Wes Naylor. He's had another death threat. A more serious one. Someone shot up his car and left a message: *Go to Bangkok and you end up like your car. Full of holes.*"

"He cancelled?" asked Calvino, feeling the four grand slipping out of his pocket.

Jess shook his head. "I told him to stay in LA. Getting shot over a hotel deal is stupid. Is the hotel deal worth dying for?"

It was the way Jess said this that made it clear Naylor hadn't listened to him.

"Meaning we're on schedule. We pick him up at Don Muang tomorrow," said Calvino.

"Right." He walked off as Father Andrew drained the last of the wine into Calvino's glass.

Another wine bottle was opened, and the glasses refilled. And before long the friends began to drift out of Father Andrew's zinc corrugated house, with kids from the slums guiding them with flashlights along the narrow walkway into the night. After everyone had left, Father Andrew and Calvino sat at the dining room table and talked about the problems the priest was having getting the school built. Afterwards, Father Andrew walked with Calvino back to his car. A few feet from the parking lot, Calvino saw the girl with the large birthday cake and stopped.

"That's the girl you gave the big cake to," said Father Andrew.

"Dew. Her name's Dew. She's part of the new breed of eight-year-old single mothers."

"You were listening," said Father Andrew.

"I bet Jess she would sell the cake."

"You lost the bet."

"Maybe I won." He smiled and leaned down to look at the brother in the beam of the flashlight. Two little boys squatted on the gravel. Lit candles illuminated their faces. They were maybe four, five years old. They didn't have plates or forks or spoons. All they had were outstretched hands as their sister cut the cake with a pocket-knife. She handed one piece to the first brother, then cut a second piece for the other brother. They ate like kids who had not eaten all day. Dogs watched motionless from the shadows. Some other kids hovered nearby, saying nothing as they watched her cut the cake. As they walked on Dew looked up.

"*Khob khun ka,*" she said. Thank you, sir.

He turned, walked back, reached into his pocket and gave her a five-hundred baht note. She looked at the note, then at Father Andrew, her eyes filled with a combination of suspicion and surprise.

"It's okay," said Father Andrew. "You can keep the money."

"I always pay my bets, Father Andrew. And I am certain Jess would like to see the money go to a good cause."

Father Andrew took some liberties with the translation into perfect *Isan*, saying that Calvino wanted her to use this money to buy food for her brothers and herself over the next few weeks, and she was to keep it hidden and not show it to any of the bigger kids or adults, and if anyone tried to steal the money she should tell them the *farang* named Calvino would come back and give them a really big problem.

They reached his car, and Calvino offered his hand.

"What happens to her next?"

"What happens to most street kids like her? They don't make it. But I have a strange feeling this kid just might beat the odds. Something strange has happened in the slums. The family has disappeared. Fathers and mothers living under the same roof taking care of their kids. Most of that is gone. Mothers sell drugs, sell their bodies. There's no time or interest in raising kids. Now kids raise kids. So they turn to speed. If you can't have love, or comfort, or a mother or a father. Then what do you do, Vincent? There is only one way out of the slum. Swallow a pill that makes you feel good. That destroys the pain. There isn't a household that doesn't have someone taking or selling drugs."

"She didn't sell the cake."

"No, she showed something we all could relearn now and again. It's called a lesson in humanity. Being your brother's keeper. There's one eight-year-old slum kid doing that right now in Klong Toey. You see anyone else doing that lately?"

Under the starlit night, Calvino shook his head and figured he got the only birthday wish he had ever wanted. The one, he thought, if he were a better man, he would have wished for before blowing out the candles.

It was called "hope."

SIX

COLONEL PRATT WORE his uniform to the airport. And he looked impressive in a uniform as well. He was the first person to greet Wes Naylor as he walked down the long, wide corridor towards Immigration. Unshaved, his eyes far too close together, squinting as Pratt approached him. The front of Naylor's shirt hung over his wrinkled trousers and his suit coat had the look of being slept in. On the lapel was a crescent-shaped blue pin—like a Turkish military officer or a Shriner might wear. A white Panama hat was pushed forward, touching his eyebrows; he carried a carry-on bag and a briefcase. Pratt's first impression was that Naylor could have passed for a homeless burnt out man who ate at the City Mission and slept on park benches with the LA Times covering his face. He didn't look remotely like an LA lawyer— or what Pratt thought an LA lawyer ought to look like. Naylor instead looked like a mid-forties Truman Capote, risen from the grave, soft around the midsection, thick lips forming a rubbery mouth; a strangely hopeless and disoriented man, blinking as if his light blue eyes hurt under the glare of the interior airport lights.

It would be easy to kill such a man, since he looked already on his journey into the next life. Anyone who had received as many death threats as Naylor should possess a certain bearing, an edge, a *jao poh* demeanour of automatic authority, the ability to strike terror simply by looking straight into another man's eyes. While he fell short of *jao poh* material, Naylor was not by appearances just another ordinary *farang*. He had a certain style, like one of those child actors who forty years later gets invited to appear on a late night TV talk show.

"Mr. Naylor," said Pratt in perfect, official English as he was no more than two feet away.

Wes Naylor stopped dead in his tracks as if someone had pressed a gun barrel into the back of his neck. Colonel Pratt walked up to him.

"Is there a problem, officer?" asked Naylor in a stressed -out, reed-thin voice. He knew of the stories of the Americans, his web site members, who had gone home in body bags having been befriended by strangers at Don Muang.

"Welcome to Thailand. I am Colonel Prachai. A friend of LAPD Officer Jessada. Follow me, I will help you clear Immigration and Customs."

Naylor loaded his carry-on bags onto a trolley. "I don't know any Jessada. Do you mind if I see some ID?" His right hand started to shake.

Pratt showed him a police ID card.

"His nickname is Jess. Maybe you know him as Jess," said Pratt.

Naylor looked at Pratt's photo on the card, turned it over, not being able to read a word of what was on the card and handed it, hand shaking, to Pratt. "Was it Jessie's idea to give me the red carpet treatment?"

Pratt nodded. "There's no red carpet. We want to see that you have no problem from the airport to your hotel."

That was the Thai way, cast the situation as a "problem" because powerful people helped less powerful people avoid "problems"; that was their function, the nature of relationships was premised on keeping one another problem free. Putting out the small brush fires before they burnt down the forest.

"You mean you are here to keep me alive. I've lost some friends in this town. So-called heroin addicts. I think they were killed. And what are the police doing to find the killers?" He asked, turning his feeble joke into a demand for action. That was putting a precise spin on a particular kind of problem.

Pratt preferred that any "problem" be kept vague and imprecise. Putting a name to a problem was a "problem" itself. He passed on Naylor's invitation to discuss the nature of these deaths. He had been through the cases dozens of times with Calvino. Standing in the airport, Pratt had no appetite to debate the fine points of homicide theories versus overdose with this stranger.

Naylor was looking for reassurance, expecting Pratt to say something like, "There is no killer. These guys stuffed themselves with drugs and checked out. It happens every day in every big city right around the world. And, in any event, even if they were murdered, you are totally safe in our hands."

Instead what he got from Pratt was a cold stare.

"Jess is waiting. If you please," said Pratt pointing the way.

"I know. You are the government and you are here to protect me," said Naylor.

Pratt responded, "Life is uncertain, Mr. Naylor."

"You don't instill a lot of confidence, Colonel Prachai. Life is uncertain. What does that mean? Is that ancient Asian wisdom? If something happens, it is my tough luck?" But this police colonel in brown dress uniform walked alongside silently. "You don't say much, do you?" Wes Naylor continued, eyes peering out from under the hat.

Other passengers rushed past as Naylor trundled along, slowly pushing his trolley. Pratt escorted him to a special clearance area. The Immigration officer on the desk looked up at Naylor, a flicker of a smile on his lips, and then he saw Pratt and his colonel rank on the uniform. "VIP," said Pratt. The letters stuck a little in his throat as he spoke but Pratt managed to get them out, slow, one at a time. "VIP." The Immigration officer took Naylor's passport and processed the paperwork, stamped the passport, pushed it back over the desk to Naylor, and nodded towards Pratt. It was over in a couple of minutes.

"We can go," said Pratt. No other passengers were around. Naylor seemed nervous. "I said we can go."

They walked down a short corridor, turned left and right, and came to an unmarked door. Pratt spoke to an armed guard who took out a key and opened it. Naylor walked out into the hot Bangkok early afternoon air. Jess and Calvino waited on the other side of the door, and spotted Naylor huffing under the weight of his suitcases as he came out of the door.

"He's all yours," said Pratt, giving Calvino one raised eyebrow before he disappeared. "We will be out front with a police escort."

Naylor blinked, screwed his eyes against the sun. He was pulling cash out of his wallet.

"Thanks," said Jess as Colonel Pratt walked away towards a waiting police car.

"Hey, I want to give you a tip," Naylor said, calling after Pratt.

Jess turned and held his hand out and started shaking Naylor's hand, the one holding the cash. "Not you. Him."

Pratt had half-turned around as Calvino stepped in front of Naylor and Jess, blocking Pratt's line of sight. "See you out front." Calvino flashed a left-eye wink, meaning Jess was a crazy.

Naylor stood on the pavement, his luggage on the pavement, attracting a crowd with his fistful of American dollar bills.

"Glad to see you, Wes. Good flight?" asked Jess. He saw the money. "And put away the cash."

"Boy, am I glad to see you. That cop's a strange bird. Wouldn't take cash. What has happened? Reform?" He gestured at Pratt who was standing beside the police car with the blue light on top flashing. Two police motorcycles were parked in front of Pratt's BMW, and two officers mounted their bikes, strapped on their helmets, as Pratt opened the car door.

"Not strange at all," said Jess. "There are a lot of good, honest cops you never hear about."

Naylor's lower lip shot out in a mock pout. "Sure, and you're gonna introduce them to me."

Jess shook his head. Arguing with Naylor wasn't going to change his mind. What was foremost on Naylor's mind was the intense fear he had felt. "For a moment, I thought I was being set up. I really thought, *yeah, this is it, I am gonna die.* Right here in the airport. No one would even know that I arrived. This cop leads me down a series of small hallways, through hidden doors. I thought it was a trap. Baam, baam. They would never find my body." Naylor held his fingers out like smoking guns, looking at the police car, as he spoke.

When he turned back around, he saw Calvino staring at him.

"You have an active imagination," said Calvino.

"Who are you?" asked Wes Naylor. "And what the fuck happened to your face?"

"This is Vincent Calvino, and he's working with me. Vincent is a pro. His job is to help me watch over you for the next few days."

"Calvino looks more like an unsuccessful tour guide than a bodyguard," said Naylor. "And, Jesus, have you had a doctor look at your face? Your girlfriend put in those stitches? Crude stuff. You want us to take you to the hospital? Get you patched up right?" Beads of sweat dripped down from the rim of his hat.

"Get rid of the hat," said Calvino.

"What's wrong with my hat? This hat is my signature in LA."

It seemed like a good time to avoid a pissing contest with the client, so Calvino decided to ease up, not challenge the man; to try one more time to establish a connection with Naylor. Then he thought, *what the hell. Give Naylor a taste of reality and see how he swallows.* "It's not that the hat makes you look more like a pimp than a lawyer. And it may be your John Hancock in LA. But in Bangkok, that what makes you an easy target. If someone is trying to whack you, all they have to do is look for a white Panama hat. No one but bald guys wears a fucking hat in Bangkok," said Calvino.

"*Jai yen,* bro!" said Jess.

"Have a cool heart," said Naylor. "You see, I know my Thai."

Naylor and Calvino had just met and already hated each other. This wasn't a good start. Why was the initial reaction of the two *farangs* so hostile? Jess asked himself. Not that it mattered; it wasn't in the job description that Calvino had to like Naylor, only that he would work to keep him alive. Thais prided themselves on civility and cool heart. Why couldn't the *farangs* be more like the Thais? Jess asked himself. Naylor might know some Thai but did he understand the Thais?

Wes Naylor smiled, took off his hat, found a handkerchief and wiped his brow, then his face before blowing his nose. He was bald with a fringe of blond hair running in a monk-like ring around his head. "A pimp? I like that. It sounds like the punch line to one of those terrible lawyer jokes." His voice had a hollow, echo quality, now that he'd cleared a half-mile of snot out of his head.

"That's my car over there," said Calvino, nodding to the beat-up Honda.

"Now that is a good disguise for a car," said Naylor. "In LA no one would be caught dead in that car."

"I had a minor accident," said Calvino.

"Several accidents, I would say. Remind me to give you one of my cards."

The tension eased. "We booked you at the Oriental Hotel," said Jess, as he got into the back with Naylor, leaving Calvino up front to drive. "All the arrangements have been made. It is the best hotel in Bangkok."

The two police motorcycles pulled in front of Calvino's car, and Colonel Pratt's car pulled in behind. They left the airport with lights flashing.

"Whoa, my friend. Who asked you to put me in the Oriental? I've made my own hotel arrangements," said Naylor.

Calvino looked at him in the rear view mirror. "Which hotel?"

"The Brandy Hotel of course. That's where I always stay."

"But the Oriental is the best hotel in Bangkok. Maybe in the world. Security will be far less of a problem. In fact there will be no security problem."

Calvino wasn't surprised that Naylor wanted to stay at the Brandy; he picked out the crescent-shaped blue pin on Naylor's lapel. These guys displaying their blue www. causemember.com pins booked into a dozen different "Cause friendly" hotels on Sukhumvit Road. The Brandy Hotel was a haven for the single male tourist, and the Cause had given the hotel a full five starlet rating. In terms of security, the Brandy would be a total nightmare. Working *yings* were in and out of *hongs*—rooms—all night long; a disco downstairs attracted hundreds of people. There was no question Wes Naylor hadn't made a mistake by booking himself into the Brandy—he had stayed there before. Only he had forgotten people weren't trying to kill him before. Calvino had a pretty good idea by the time he had pulled away from the curb that this was not going to be any ordinary assignment.

"You two guys were hired by Nat to babysit me. It wasn't my idea. I think it's a fucking waste of money. You know what I could do in this town with that kind of money? But Nat wants to spend the money out of his pocket. Who am I to complain? But remember one thing, I am not a baby. I know Bangkok. I am perfectly capable of choosing where I am going to stay. And I am staying at the Brandy Hotel. End of story."

"This must be a new five-star hotel," said Jess.

"It has at least five stars," said Calvino. "And most of them go short-time for a gray."

Jess had left Thailand at age thirteen and on his trips back had stayed with relatives far away from Sukhumvit Road. He had not been back since there had been a thousand-baht note in circulation. It bothered him slightly to have to ask Calvino to translate what he was saying.

"The Brandy's a 'Cause friendly' hotel on the Causeway," continued Calvino. "Am I right, Mr. Naylor?"

Now he had the man's attention. He leaned forward, patted Calvino on the shoulder.

"You know about the Cause? Maybe you're a member?"

"I saw your blue pin. And I've seen the website. But mostly I know about your club from a number of clients who have crashed and burnt along the Causeway. They thought there was no speed limit in the Zone. Until they hit the wall."

"Jesus, you are full of gloom. Must have something to do with what happened to your face."

Calvino dialed through to Pratt on his mobile phone. "Slight change of plans. Mr. Naylor is not staying at the Oriental. He's booked himself into the Brandy."

There was a moment of dead silence. "Pratt, are you there?"

"In that case, we have a slight change of plans. His escort has ended. He makes his decision; we make ours. And, Vincent, watch yourself. Phone me when you get him checked in."

As Pratt's car pulled along Calvino's, he nodded, then his car shot ahead, his two motorcycle escorts following behind.

"Where is he going?" asked Naylor. "And I still can't believe he didn't take the cash."

"Fighter escort decided not to follow this bomber to the new target destination," said Calvino. "Meaning, no way are the cops giving a VIP escort to the Brandy Hotel. It would be less embarrassing if they shot you, Wes. No offence. But face matters."

"Would someone mind telling me what the Causeway is?" asked Jess.

The traffic was moving on the expressway; their car passed the Thai International Building on the left. Calvino noted they had reached the half way mark to Sukhumvit Road and the Brandy Hotel.

"I keep a map of the Causeway in my head," said Wes Naylor. "I'm the financial backer of www.causemember. com. We have about ten thousand members from all over the world clicking in twenty-four hours a day, and the membership keeps growing and growing. In two years, I can see us taking the company public. This is the IPO everybody has been waiting for."

"I thought you were a lawyer," said Jess.

"Been there, done that. Still keep a hand in. Like on this deal with Nat. But the Internet's where it's happening, and our Causeway in Bangkok runs from Buckskin Joe Village under the expressway ramp all the way down Sukhumvit Road to Soi 33."

"So?" said Jess, more confused than ever. "On the Causeway you are looking for what?"

"The Monster Fuck," said Calvino. "Am I right, Wes?"

"Bull's-eye." Naylor clapped his hands.

"My instructions were that you came here to negotiate a contract for Dr. Nat."

"That's right. With the cash from our membership, we are looking to buy into suitable hotels. So Nat comes to me with a possible deal. I said, 'Okay, I'll think about it.' Then Nat says, 'We have a deal. A couple of things need to be worked out. Nothing serious. Go close the deal. We are partners.' So here I am. But I don't work like my website twenty-four hours a day," said Wes Naylor. "Besides, this bullshit of a hit squad doesn't wash with me. I know you're a Thai and all of that but Nat is really Thai and a pretty weird guy. A control freak. He's the nervous type. He's never done deals. Just practiced medicine. So there's a little friction and he starts to fall apart. I've seen it a thousand times. That's why he wants me in the deal. I've got street smarts, common sense, and a business that can help the hotel business. One hand washing the other hand."

What he didn't have was modesty.

Naylor had laid it out. He was no newbie to Bangkok and he was hell-bent on heading straight for the Causeway. Calvino figured Jess had a reasonably good idea that the asset they were hired to protect was as much interested in Monster Fucking as in closing any deal on behalf of Dr. Nat, who suddenly was a partner and not just a client. And if they were smart, Calvino was thinking, they would dump this asshole at the Brandy Hotel, call Dr. Nat and tell him there was no way they were going to guard this lunatic from LA.

"What's your name on www.causemember.com?" asked Calvino.

"Tail-gunner7," said Wes Naylor with a squeaky glee in his voice, as if revealing a deep secret. "And what is yours?"

"Pickup the Pieces for Hire," said Calvino as a ripple of anger rolled over him.

"Hey, that's too long for a name."

"That's why I never joined," said Calvino. "Every time I see the word *member* on any door, even one in cyberspace, I get nervous. In the old days it usually meant Jews were excluded. My mother was a Jew. So I avoid membership places. And I never found a cause that was naturally right that needed to recruit members to keep it going."

"Very noble of you, Mr. Calvino. But you have been given some bad information about the Cause." He clearly had had enough of Calvino and focused his attention on Jess. "There is very good information on where to stay, eat, the best bars, short-time hotels, the price of short-times, experiences from real life from men who have fallen in love. From people who have been there. These men know what they are talking about. They share with each other. Bangkok is the 'Show' and everywhere else is the minors. That's why many of our members save all year so they can make a pilgrimage to Bangkok."

Jess, hands rested on his knees, looked straight ahead, catching Calvino's eyes in the mirror.

"My only cause is to get you back to Los Angeles alive," said Jess.

Wes Naylor smiled a wounded smile and put his white Panama hat back on.

"Now you have made me a happy man."

That was more than Calvino could say for himself. The truck behind him was following too close; it was bothering him, getting on his nerves. Minutes after Pratt's car sped away, lights flashing, with the motorcycle escort, he had picked it up in his rearview mirror. Pratt and the boys had shot out of sight in an instant. Calvino moved over into the far left lane, letting the faster traffic pass him. He kept the truck in his mirrors, switching to the center lane and saw that the ten-wheel truck stayed on his tail. He braked, then switched back to the slow lane. The truck driver eased off the accelerator until the truck could fall behind Calvino's Honda once again. The truck was riding his back bumper hard. No question he was coming in for contact.

"We have a situation," said Calvino.

"I've made myself clear, I am staying at the Brandy."

"Jess, get his head down."

Jess reacted instantly, jamming Naylor's head down with the flat palm of his hand, crushing his Panama hat. He kept on pushing until he had Naylor below the window level, face in the seat. "What the fuck are you doing?"

"Stay down."

Jess turned around just as the truck hit Calvino's car. The truck rammed the car hard. Jess drew a .9 mm automatic out of a holster concealed under his jacket and swung the gun around.

"Get on the shoulder," Jess said.

Calvino punched the accelerator and tried to pull away from the truck. The truck caught up in a couple of seconds. Backseat driver, thought Calvino.

"The engine's souped up," said Calvino. He was driving on the shoulder.

"Or this piece of junk has no power," said Naylor. The truck nudged the back bumper, a kiss, then a hard ram. "This isn't real," said Naylor, his head jerked from the impact. Jess no longer had to push him down.

"I thought Thais weren't supposed to touch another person's head in Thailand," said Naylor.

"The exception to the rule is a *farang* someone's trying to kill," said Jess.

"Here it comes again," said Calvino. "Big mama of a truck."

A Thai male in his early twenties, a full head of thick black hair flying in the wind, leaned out of the passenger's side of the truck and squeezed off several shots from a handgun he held with both hands. He was a bad shot. And the cabin of the truck was too high, forcing the shooter to aim and shoot downward at the moving target. One shot hit the door, and another shot hit the headrest on the passenger's seat next to Calvino. Another shot blew out Calvino's rear window. "Can you get a shot?" shouted Calvino from the front seat.

"I can't get a clear shot," Jess was looking up at the grille of the huge truck. There was no shot to be had.

"Can't you go any faster?" screamed Naylor from the back-seat.

Calvino switched from the shoulder to the slow lanes, then switched lanes again, the truck in hot pursuit, and as he doubled back onto the shoulder, the truck shifted gears and at the last moment, Calvino made a hard right turn. The truck slammed head on into a Thai motorcycle cop gunning his bike at high speed, going the wrong way on the shoulder. Since he was one of the "boys" he apparently didn't feel he had to follow the normal rules: like obeying the prohibition of motorcycles on the expressway or going in the right direction. No one would ever know for sure what was in that cop's head in the nanosecond he had between seeing the huge fucking truck and getting himself smashed against the grille like a bug. He didn't leave a skid mark. Head on straight into the truck. His motorcycle, crumpled like a cheap toy and slid underneath the truck, sending sparks of metal against cement across the expressway. As Calvino slowed, he looked back and saw the truck veer off to the left, dragging the motorcycle, which had caught on the undercarriage of the truck with the cop slammed against the grille, the truck exiting the expressway on the off-ramp to the Suttisan.

"Jesus, they killed that cop," said Naylor, looking out the window. "Mangled him. Have you ever seen people drive like that? That driver had to be nuts or on speed."

Calvino dialed his mobile and Pratt came on the line. He explained what had happened. Pratt said he would take care of it.

The incident was over in less than five minutes.

"Anyone hurt?" Calvino asked, while he still had Pratt on the line. "Everyone's okay," he said, dropping the mobile phone on the seat. He leaned forward and brushed some of broken glass off the dashboard.

"Do you still want to stay at the Brandy?" asked Jess.

Wes Naylor sat up straight, his hat in his hands, assessing the damage.

"I can't wait to post this airport-ride-to-hell story. *Don Muang Death Ride*."

Calvino shook his head. "Brandy Hotel it is." He stopped at the tollbooth, paid the fare and headed for the Sukhumvit Road off ramp. There was enough loose glass on the floor that every time he switched lanes the glass shifted, making a soft distant sound like ice striking an empty glass at the end of bar counter.

"You're not taking this seriously enough," said Jess.

Naylor's eyes suddenly got big. "Seriously? Are you joking. Those guys were high on drugs. Calvino dissed them. They got angry. Road rage is how I read this. We get this all the time in America; you know what it's like, Jess. This happens five times a day in LA. They weren't trying to shoot me. They were trying to kill you." A strange laugh came out of his throat like he had gone insane.

"That's an interesting theory," said Calvino. "But it is totally fucking wrong."

"Yeah?"

"No question about it."

Naylor was looking angry. "I can prove it. I am still fucking alive. If they had wanted to kill me, I would be dead."

Arguing with a reductionist asshole was a waste of time.

Calvino was trying to make sense of this LA lawyer and Cause-member website owner/operator/member— what he was and what he did. Calvino still hadn't decided as Naylor's story kept shifting. Even in the worst neighborhoods of the Bronx or Brooklyn, Calvino had never met anyone who had been shot at and showed so little emotion. Was Naylor some kind of California fruitcake and this was really the way Americans on the coast dealt with an ambush? It was starting to bother him that whoever this Naylor guy was, nothing about him fit together. The puzzle was scattered pieces without any design emerging. The whole set-up was as crazy as a betrayed wife. Calvino just drove, keeping his thoughts to himself, letting Jess keep up the conversation with Naylor.

When they finally reached Sukhumvit Road, Calvino turned left, then at Soi 1 he made another left-hand turn, taking the short-cut through the grounds of Bumrungrad Hospital which came out on Soi 3—Nana Nua—a one-way *soi* which became Soi 4—Nana Tai—on the other side of Sukhumvit Road. Security guards stopped them as they entered, looked in and saw that two of them were *farang* and one of them looked in need of medical attention, and then waved them in, directing them to the parking lot. Calvino accelerated past the parking lot, weaving through the narrow lanes until he came to Soi 3.

"Those guards thought you were going to see a doctor about your face?" asked Wes Naylor in a joking voice.

"You can't make a right off Sukhumvit onto Soi 4 so I am cutting through the hospital lot rather than going halfway to Cambodia before I can make a U-turn."

"You ought to be driving a cab," said Wes Naylor.

"Driving a cab is safer. You just don't get what happened on the expressway. And because you don't, I feel we could be in for major trouble," said Calvino.

"I don't think so."

This was one of those stupid, throwaway lines that one can never believe someone says but somehow in real life people say such things all the time. Calvino stayed silent, looking at Naylor in the mirror, the clinical way an adult looks at a child who has asked if there are chrome poles on Mars with beautiful *yings* swinging around them dressed in bikinis.

Jess looked at the steady stream of six lanes of traffic that barely moved one-way along Soi 3. Calvino edged into the flow. Every time Calvino braked, more pieces of broken glass spilled from the rear window, raining down on Jess and Wes. Jess picked a small piece of glass off his collar, rolled it between his finger and thumb. "Fucking glass," said Naylor, brushing a shard off his hat.

Jess was also thinking about how close they had come to being shot. How the truck had hit the car, then killed the cop and fled the scene rather than coming in for the kill.

Fifteen minutes later, Calvino pulled into the parking lot of the Brandy Hotel. It was an old R&R hotel built in the Vietnam war era; eleven floors high, and memories stretching from rice paddies and foot patrols to the peace time generation of the Cause-members. In the background, the contour of the new Marriott looked like an alien spacecraft hovering, closing in from the horizon, threatening to dwarf the Brandy, swallow it whole. As Calvino got out of the car, he reached back and opened the back door and Naylor climbed out, kicking broken glass onto the pavement. "You are like a fucking bull in a china shop," said Naylor, grabbing his hat and putting it on.

A row of small stunted trees—lacking water and oxygen and poisoned by the traffic fumes—somehow survived in the center of the parking lot at the entrance to the Brandy Hotel. Along the side of the hotel, an open-air bar had already drawn a few customers and *yings* who were perched—the *yings* with bare legs crossed—on high bar stools drinking Singha beer or soda water. Jess pulled

Naylor's bags out of the trunk of the car. He made a point of walking around the back of the car and putting them down at Naylor's feet. "Your bags." He didn't need to say any more. Naylor could see that there was no way Jess was going to carry his bags for a grand a day or ten grand a day. Jess still didn't much like Naylor's crack about not touching his head because this was Thailand. He was trying to save the man's life. Calvino was probably right: this guy was a total asshole. It was hard putting one's heart into keeping a complete asshole alive.

"This is great," said Naylor, reaching down for his carry-on bag, leaving the heavy one on the pavement. "Just like I remembered it. The really good things in the world never change. You come back to Bangkok in a hundred years and the Brandy will still be here."

"What's to like?" asked Calvino. As far as he was concerned the place was a box, a dump, a sterile concrete bunker made of too much sand and not enough cement and there was no way it would be still be standing in a hundred years.

"You don't get it. This place occupies a time warp from the sixties universe. This could be 1968."

"If you don't mind, Captain Kirk, let's check you in," said Calvino.

"Don't forget your other bag," said Jess. His toe touched the heavy bag.

Naylor grunted and leaned over and picked it up.

Walking in single file, they entered the large, open hotel lobby. On the right was the main reception counter and a wall of small safety deposit boxes. Naylor marched straight to the counter, put down his bags, and asked the clerk to check for his reservation. His name came up on the computer screen, as Naylor craned forward to see. "That's me. Naylor, Wes. I've stayed here before. Do you remember me?" The clerk handed Naylor a form to complete. He looked at Naylor like he had never seen him in his life. Naylor looked far more startled at not being recognized than he had been during the shooting on the expressway. Jess stood to Naylor's right facing the door, checking the guests in the lobby. It was pretty quiet in the lobby.

"What do you think?" asked Jess.

"From a security point of view the place is hopeless," said Calvino. "One of us should phone Dr. Nat and let him know that Naylor's made a change of plans. Here, use my mobile phone."

Jess took the phone and started to dial. "He's not going to be happy about this."

"If he wants the four grand back, tell him that's no problem. I can wire it to him tomorrow or give it to you now. However he wants it."

This was the last thing Jess wanted. He held up his hand. "Keep the cash. And don't get in a rush."

"The guy's stupid or he has a death wish," said Calvino.

"Or he's both." The phone was ringing in LA and a moment later Jess was speaking in rapid Thai to Dr. Nat who was on the other end.

The Brandy wasn't exactly the hotel that people came to looking to be protected against corporate take-over death threats. Running from the entrance to the coffee shop were large windows. Chairs were scattered around the lobby. Groupings of chairs with tall straight backs were situated near the windows. A half-dozen old geezers in their sixties and seventies slouched down in the overstuffed chairs with blonde fake leather coverings, which had that early Thermae look. They looked like what the Cause-members called a Pfizer Gang. The *yings* called them Jurassics. After the dinosaur movie. A packaged tour of pensioners was being arranged on-line by retirees; Cause-members, fellow-travelers (though in need of that afternoon nap) in search of the Monster Fuck at an age when their cocks should have stayed flaccid. Instead with a drug boost, fifteen, thirty minutes into an erection they still had an erection that a dog couldn't chew off. They wore the now classic Causeway "V" T-shirts. One of the old guys turned and Calvino spotted the blue "V's" stitched over his heart. Most of the others in the lobby wore the blue crescent-shaped lapel pin. One little blue pill stretched out the wrinkles from one organ but left its toll in the exhaustion etched onto their faces. The old men in the lobby looked dead tired. Some of them dozed, mouths open, and if they hadn't been snoring, they could have passed for the dead. Pfizer heads never took naps in their *hongs*; it was part of the code, saying you were old and had to go to bed, but catching forty winks in a stuffed chair, that was inside the line of acceptable behavior because the moment one's eyes popped open there was a selection waiting, signaling, promising, and propositioning.

At that moment, they were better off sleeping, as there were few *yings* in the lobby. Behind the Pfizer Gang were a couple of fake Christmas trees set up on tables. Red bows and blue balls covered both trees. Four or five *yings* wore evening dresses and pancake make-up. They sat in a circle at a table drinking orange juice; they leaned forward in Chinese chairs hand-carved with scrolls, flowers, fancy whorls, glancing over at the Pfizer Gang wondering when one might wake up, pop a pill, stagger over to their group, and take one of them up to his *hong*. One of the *ying* brushed back her long flowing black hair to reveal a pair of blue "V" earrings. A gift from a Cause-member.

Calvino leaned over the counter and addressed the woman working the counter. "We will need three adjoining rooms," he said in Thai.

The woman at the desk didn't even blink. "Cash or credit card."

"Put the *hongs* on Mr. Naylor's credit card," said Calvino. "All three rooms."

"Wait a minute, Calvino."

"The *hongs* at the Oriental are paid for. We're talking rack-rate about three times your hourly billing rate. So I think under the circumstances you might be generous enough to your client to spring for the *hongs* at your choice of hotels."

"I am not going to argue with you." But he wasn't paying any attention to Calvino and walked straight past him and over to the Pfizer Gang. "Boys, how are you? I am Tail-gunner." He winked.

One of the old guys sat up in his chair, his eyes popped open. "I've read your stuff on the web. It's great. And I hope you can settle the conflict between Weasel and Mucus."

The Cause-members had online names that made ham operator names elegant.

"I am certainly gonna try. I am here to hold a peace council. Glad to see you boys are in town and having a good time. If you need anything, I am in *hong* 501."

Calvino exchanged glances with Jess. "Peace council," mouthed Calvino. Jess shrugged his shoulders.

"Dr. Nat told me you were here on a hotel deal," said Jess.

"Yes, I am. But I am also a man with many missions," replied Naylor.

A bellboy picked up Wes Naylor's bags. Two more bellboys sniffed around, looking for Jess and Calvino's bags, and getting the hint quickly that there were no more bags, they peeled off formation and shuffled back to the entrance like cranky wind-up toys with rundown batteries.

With Naylor walking between his two bodyguards, they passed a bank of telephones where three or four hookers thumbed little black books, phones cradled between their necks and shoulders like brokers selling swamp land in a boiler room set-up. The hookers were trying to get early bird short-time bookings. The *yings* eyed Naylor, ignoring Calvino and Jess; they seemed to have a sixth sense about who was new, who was on the make, and who might be another black book entry. Naylor returned their smiles. That was first contact, thought Calvino. Captain Kirk and alien creatures exchanged facial gestures that were a prelude to earthly breeding.

"Love those smiles," Naylor said. "They melt you right down to the core."

"The Pfizers in the lobby make me look like a kid," said Calvino.

Naylor glanced at his watch. "I have an appointment at the Plaza in two hours."

"Don't you have an important meeting tomorrow?" asked Jess.

"I am prepared. Over-prepared. I need to unwind. I've had a long day. I've been shot at. Seen life pass before my eyes as that cop called my name at the airport. And now I want to have some fun."

Calvino and Jess exchanged glances as if to say someone would be waiting to unwind his main action, ripping off the hour, minute and second hands, leaving him outside of time. Leaving him dead.

They waited at the elevator and a bellboy pushed the up button. A security guard in a blue shirt sat at an old-fashioned wooden office desk reading a black and white comic book. He didn't bother looking up as he turned the page.

Not more than two minutes after they entered their *hongs*, Jess knocked on Calvino's door. "Come in. It's open."

Jess walked in and closed the door behind him. Calvino stood with his back to the door, looking out the window. "What did Dr. Nat decide?"

"Stick with him. I know this is crazy, Vincent, but Dr. Nat thinks that Naylor can pull off the hotel deal and get back to LA alive."

"Are you a betting man?" Calvino turned around and faced Jess.

Jess shrugged. "I am Thai. I believe in karma."

"I would bet that Wes Naylor knows something he's not telling us."

"Like what?"

"Like why he didn't shit his pants on the expressway."

"What are you saying?"

"Something's not right about any of this. I don't know what is wrong, but I am saying that we ought to be asking a few more questions. With your friend Dr. Nat for a start. Why didn't he tell you Naylor had part of the action and had something to do with the Cause-members website?"

"Dr. Nat's of the generation before TV. Forget about computers and websites. He wouldn't know about that. And Naylor's not going to tell us anything we don't already know," said Jess.

"But I can tell you where this is going. He's likely been online with his Cause buddies and a dozen guys know exactly where he's planning to go, who he's planning to see, not to mention that he's staying at the Brandy. He announced his *hong* number in the lobby.

Someone who is trying to maintain a low profile doesn't go broadcasting this information to the world. And we find out he's settling a personal conflict between a couple of Cause-members. The guy is trying to get himself killed."

"What are you trying to say, that you want off the assignment?"

Calvino stared at him. "I think you better tell me a little bit more about Dr. Nat's business in LA and the deal that is attracting the death threats."

SEVEN

DOCTOR NAT WAS a slight, smallish Thai man with a moon-shaped face. He weighed about 130 pounds and measured no more than 5'6". Dr. Nat looked like he had made up his mind to stop growing around fourteen years old; that he had had enough with childhood and decided it was time to become an adult. After finishing medical school, he went to LA to visit an uncle. He never came back. After finishing an internship, he opened a small-time medical practice on the fourth floor of a rundown office building in downtown LA. For Dr. Nat, time had stopped twenty-two years ago. Posters of Krabi and Phuket were thumbnailed to the walls of his sparely furnished waiting room. A Thai receptionist who had turned forty sat leafing through magazines behind a window inside the entrance. On a good day there would be one or two patients waiting in the lobby for appointments with Dr. Nat. Most of the time there was no waiting; it was straight in to see the doctor. Almost all of Dr. Nat's patients were first-generation Thais, who took off their shoes and sat barefoot—on that rare day when they had to wait—thumbing old copies of Thai magazines, waiting for the doctor to call out their name. Confiding in each other how much they missed Thailand. *Khit tueng muang Thai mak.* Nat had been Jess's doctor ever since he was a teenager. Nat had harboured a secret that one day he confided to Jess, "As soon as my last son finishes college next year, I am going home." He meant Thailand.

From the way that Dr. Nat delivered his confidential speech, he gave every indication that he had been waiting to buy his return ticket for the last twenty-two years and had been telling every patient the same confidential story for the last twenty-two years. To the same patients, in the same office. Dr. Nat had spent his time in LA like the patients in the waiting room, waiting for an appointment and returning to their real life on the other side of the doctor's office door. He had lived in LA most of his adult life but his true life, his inner secret life, remained firmly rooted in Thailand. Sundays he took his family out to the Valley and walked around Wat Thai, walking down the ramp to the basement, buying noodles with green curry. Dr. Nat after all those years had become something of an institution in the Thai community. But his practice never took off. His office was shabby and in a low-rent part of LA. He made enough money for a modest house, for two new cars, to send his two sons to university and to set aside money for resuming his life in Thailand. His wife did not work; she stayed at home, cooking, tending the garden, and looking after the children. They were decent, hard-working, frugal people and very conservative with their money.

Then Viagra came out and suddenly Dr. Nat had a new class of patients: *farangs* going to Thailand. Money started to accumulate for the first time in his life and he started to feel like he was secure enough to make a financial investment back home. His patients, old and new, gave him advice about investment opportunities in

Thailand in real estate, stocks, rice mills, petrochemical plants, fisheries. Everyone had a brother, sister-in-law, or uncle who had the inside track on a sure deal. Dr. Nat heard each of them out, took down the details and phoned Dr. Damrong, his younger brother, who was a doctor at Bumrungrad Hospital. And Dr. Damrong would check out each tip, only to phone back a week later with evidence of fraud, incompetence, non-existent inventory, big shareholders' loans, and other defects in the usual structure of family-run Thai companies, not to mention the almost universal absence of any business plan. Sure they were ready to unload the rotten stuff at a high price. Only Dr. Nat and his brothers were buying. Sometimes a patient with the hot tip phoned him and asked if the good doctor wanted to put money in a surefire deal, one that only he and his mother and father were investing in personally, it was that certain, and Dr. Nat told them kindly—having heard this line before—that his funds were locked up. He was, in other words, someone who was not a soft touch; he was conservative, cautious, and skeptical during the boom years when everyone else lost their heads, throwing all their logs into the fire of greed. Those people ended with a heap of ashes to show for their efforts, but not Dr. Nat. A year into the recession, a deal came to him not from a patient but from his younger brother, who was even more cautious than he was about investing with strangers.

There was a small hotel in a reasonably good part of the Sukhumvit Road that had been chronically mismanaged by a Chinese-Thai family and after the father died—a tragic accidental death—the children were at each other's throat over who would win control of the hotel. With all the time spent fighting amongst the brothers and sisters, the management became distracted and the hotel had become rundown and squalid and was running at a considerable loss. The eldest brother, Kitti, had been one of Dr. Damrong's patients, and had confided in the good doctor the family story of how much revenue the hotel was losing since the old man's strange, unexpected death and how the conflict and struggle over ownership and division of the spoils was ripping apart his family. One brother had been wounded by a gunman. A sister-in-law had received death threats. The family was at war with itself. Kitti's second youngest brother, Prapat, had hinted his vote was for the family to sell the company which owned the hotel. He also hinted that his vote was for sale.

Prapat said, "Sell the hotel. Talk with Dr. Damrong."

The plan made sense to Kitti. Why not sell the hotel and divide up the proceeds of the sale between the brothers and sisters? What better way for the family to reconcile? Cash was, after all, a great healer of all wounds. Well, almost all wounds—exceptions were many, including the self-inflicted wound of their father's, a mortal wound which all the family wealth, nor had it prevented their father's terrible, bitter end. Why not sell the hotel for a good price to Dr. Nat and Dr. Damrong? It would be good karma for the family to have sold the hotel to two good doctors that everyone respected and admired.

Dr. Damrong was invited by Kitti to come around to inspect the hotel. Later that afternoon, he drove over to the hotel, walked through the large lobby with dead plants and broken furniture, an empty coffee shop with cockroaches scuttling across the floor. He was taken up to see some of the *hongs*. The elevator was out of action so they walked up the stairs to the fourth floor. The first three floors had been closed off due to an "electrical wiring" problem, Dr. Damrong was told by the elderly receptionist. Meaning it was a death trap with enough code violations that it should have been closed down as a public safety threat years ago. Only nothing in Bangkok had ever been shut down for that reason in her memory. After she unlocked the door, he stepped into a cell-like *hong* with a musky, closed up smell; the walls were damp, the blue wallpaper peeling off in sheets. "We have a little water problem upstairs. It only affects this *hong*," said Kitti. The old woman lit a cheroot and smiled, leaning against the unpainted, open door. The toilet had not been cleaned in months and had a yellow filmy scum over the water thick enough to pass for custard. Maybe it was custard. A thick layer of dust forming itself into balls covered the window sill behind the toilet. The pillows smelled of mildew. If there was ever a place that appeared doomed, ready for a mid-night insurance fire or the wrecker's ball, it was this hotel. Neglect, hatred, distraction had laid waste to the structure; the hotel, if this *hong* was any indication (Dr. Damrong suspected they had showed him one of the better *hongs*), was in a state of ruin. But in that ruined condition, he saw an opportunity. When God served up a miserable, doomed piece of rubble, one looked at the small but quiet, nice, efficient hotel being held captive inside. It was the tiny woman inside the fat, bloated patient who pleaded for redemption, hands in a *wai*, asking for the magic pill to strip away the fat. Here was the perfect chance to start to free the hostage from the crazed family. He knew what prescription was needed. Dr. Damrong couldn't wait to phone his brother.

On the way down the stairs to the lobby, the receptionist stopped in the stairwell and blew out a cloud of smoke, her old yellow eyes smiling as she said there were one hundred and twenty *hongs* but only eight *hongs* were occupied. On the other hand, only eight *hongs* might have been habitable. "We have renovation plans which will be included in the purchase price," said Kitti, giving the old woman a dirty look. Even the minimal amount of loyalty expected of hotel staff had evaporated. How old was she, wondered Dr. Damrong. And who was she?

Dr. Nat had never heard his brother so excited about an investment. Not ever. For a million and a half dollars they could own a one-hundred twenty room hotel in the heart of *farang* ghetto section of Sukhumvit Road. This was the deal they had been waiting for; this was the deal that would give Dr. Nat the face he needed to leave LA and to return to Thailand. Kitti wanted a quick sale. Paperwork was dispatched to Dr. Nat, and he telephoned Prapat, who had flown into LA, and they had lunch. Another patient and investment advisor, Kowit was also at lunch. Kowit, a Thai who had been in LA for longer than Dr. Nat, owned a funeral home, a golf course, a night club, and several minimarts. It was Kowit who suggested that the doctor might cut a lawyer by the name of Wes Naylor into a part of the action, say five percent, for a premium payment and use the *farang* to look over the documents, negotiate the details, and draft the contracts as well as to deal with the family in Bangkok and help bring in the *farang* customers. "Say five percent of five million dollars. That's closer to the real value. Why give the *farang* a break?" This seemed like a good idea: a *farang* front man who could put the whole deal together and pay money for a small interest in the hotel and fill up the *hongs* with rich *farangs*. The deal was looking better by the day. Until, two days after Dr. Nat had offered Wes Naylor a minority partnership arrangement and plans were already made for Naylor's trip to Bangkok, Naylor received his first death threat at three in the morning. Naylor was sleeping, rolled over, picked up the phone, and as in a dream, heard a male with foreign accent telling him that he was dead meat if he came to Bangkok. He phoned Dr. Nat, who phoned his brother, who phoned Kitti, who phoned Prapat, who then phoned Dr. Nat to tell him that a faction involving one younger brother and one older sister were against the sale but didn't have sufficient power in the family to stop the sale from going through.

★★★★★★

"THE kid brother and dragon lady sister are making death threats?" asked Calvino, coming out of the bathroom having splashed water on his face. He was dripping on the carpet.

"We don't know for sure. But it looks that way," said Jess. "Once the deal is signed, the danger is over. Their fight is lost. Only if they can scare away Wes Naylor they can win." He looked away from the window where he had been watching the parking lot below. From Calvino's *hong* there was a line of vision that allowed one to watch who came and left the hotel.

"Or if they kill him, they win. Someone in the family has already been shot. Another threatened. Sounds convincing enough to me."

Calvino picked up the towel from the end of his bed and dried his face.

"That's where we come in," said Jess. "Our job is to keep Naylor alive."

"If they kill him after the deal's done?" Calvino left the question hanging.

"Then that's his problem." Jess smiled and gave Calvino the thumbs up.

"Good. We are thinking along the same lines," said Calvino. "After all, he's only in for five percent."

"The real threat ends in the next couple of days. Meanwhile, we have to expect more of what happened on the expressway." Jess backed out of the window of Calvino's *hong*, watching men leaving for Nana Plaza.

"Whoever is stalking Naylor knows they can threaten him with no problem," said Calvino. "You get a free pass to threaten a *farang*."

Calvino's Law: Never threaten anyone wearing a uniform, or who has more influence or packs a gun with higher velocity. The last part can be omitted if one is a better, faster shot than the gunman.

"I think I understand why Naylor wanted part of this hotel."

"He's branching out from the website. Adding on value for his members. The hotel is a clubhouse for the Cause. What else?" Calvino was pulling on his jacket.

"Dr. Nat would never have heard of the Cause."

"Dispensing all the Viagra to *farangs*, it had to cross his mind, 'Hey, why are all these guys wearing the same blue pin?' "

Jess nodded. "California's full of cults. No one notices."

"Had you?" asked Calvino.

Jess shook his head.

"Come on, let's get Naylor and see if we can keep him alive tonight."

★★★★★★

JESS looked on as Calvino rapped his knuckles on the door, forgetting his hand was still bruised and tender from his fight. That hurt. He shook his hand, thinking a fist was nothing more than a hand shaped by fear and anger, a hand that could be offered in friendship or as a weapon. As a damaged weapon, this hand was swollen, throbbing. "Fuck, it's still sore," he said, shaking his hand. He was also thinking he was cursing more than he used to; his tolerance was fraying. Drawing in a big breath, he waited a moment before trying the door knob. He stood back, waiting for Naylor to come to the door. But he wasn't in his *hong* or if he was in his *hong*, he wasn't answering the door.

"He's gone," said Jess.

No question about that. Naylor had already left. Calvino turned around and said to Jess, "Let's go find him."

In the lobby they found him sitting at a table with three hookers. The Pfizer Gang had vanished—wandered off to their *hong* with their first-round choice in search of the Monster Fuck, or to the bars for an early-bird special before younger guys showed up and hogged all the attention from the best looking dancers. Naylor had already changed out of his long- haul flight clothes and into his boogie night-time gear; his hair was still wet from the shower. He had gone for the all black look: trousers, boots, and a black shirt buttoned to the neck with a green and red serpent necktie. Over the collar was a fifteen-baht gold chain as thick as a gangster's pinky finger, hanging down over the tie. From Truman Capote to Johnny Cash. He rolled up his shirt to his elbows and explained his tattoos to the *yings*.

"My bodyguards," he called out. "Yings, meet my guardians."

The jet lag and speed pills had turned his eyes bloodshot over a yellowish color. His eyes immediately registered that neither of the men standing over him had come to the table to learn about his tattoos. He pushed down his shirt sleeves and buttoned them. The hookers looked disappointed. Most hookers loved looking at tattoos. It was close to interest in reading palms. Though fondling Naylor's fifteen-baht gold chain would have given them the most pleasure. But the fun had ended.

"You should have waited for us, Wes," said Jess.

"I know, I know. But I figured coming down the lobby was no big deal."

"Like driving on the expressway was no big deal," said Calvino.

One of the *yings* unbuttoned his cuff and rolled the sleeve back up.

"What's that?" she asked, tracing the image with her finger.

"Now that is something you don't wanna ever see in real life," said Naylor, as he pointed at the tattoos on his right arm—a "snake" (the word uttered by Calvino in a low whisper) ran from the elbow to his wrist and had an uncanny resemblance to the decorations on his necktie. More of a serpent-like creature than a snake since it was breathing red flames and the two-prong tongue licked at the palm of his hand.

"And this dragon here is a big warning sign. It's from a Southern China triad. And it means I am Chinese Mafia. So don't fuck with me or you are in big, big trouble. Whatever you do, don't call this animal a snake." He switched to his left arm, "And you see this writing in Chinese here? You know what it means? I am to be feared."

"With arms like that, you don't need bodyguards," said Calvino.

"That's what I tried to tell Doc Nat. We talked about it, and I said, 'Okay, doc, we do it your way. Two bodyguards. You pay for them. They don't come out of my five percent. And I think you're wasting your money. Nobody is going to fuck with the Chinese Mafia.'"

His blue eyes were a little too close together and he squinted at Calvino like somehow he could bring him into focus. Blond-haired, blue-eyed Chinese Mafia, sure, thought Calvino.

"I think we should stick close to the hotel," said Jess.

"No goddamn way," Naylor was on his feet. "I am heading to the Plaza. I also have a delivery to make. A letter and some pictures a member wants me to deliver to his girlfriend. Apparently she was a Monster Fuck. And I have a peace council to hold."

He stood up in his Judge Dredd outfit looking like the kind of judge Cause-members would expect to arrive to settle their disputes. Naylor headed straight for the door.

★★★★★★

THE Plaza was nearly invisible from the Brandy Hotel parking lot. This was Mecca for those with a new religion. The narrow entrance was jammed with tuk-tuks, motorcycles, vans, vendor carts and cars—a two-car-wide esophagus leading into a U-shape gut that had swallowed more than it could digest; a gut roiling with juices, dense from a huge banquet of neon-lit beer bars, go-go bars, restaurants, food stalls, massage parlors, short-time *hongs*, and discos. Three stories of esoteric possibilities, a buffet feast for members of the Cause, Pfizer gangs (who had their own chapter in the Cause), and thousands of unaffiliated others, who, squeezing through this tiny obstructed passage to the growling stomach of the night, knew the most important ingredients were the *yings* who lined the edges, crowding the slopes, talking in the stairwells, hanging over the balconies, smoking cigarettes in their short bar robes.

Jess stood frozen in his tracks, in a state of shock. He had no idea such a place existed. His jaw hung open. No idea at all. How many middle-class Thais had stood where he stood and peered inside this *farang* place? Not many. He hung back for a moment, gathering his wits, deciding where to look and what to do. He turned back and saw Calvino following behind Naylor, "This place isn't for real, is it?" he said into the mini-mic.

Jess's voice inside Calvino's earphone was crystal clear. He pushed the control switch. "It's for real."

"Keep directly behind him. Watch the hands of anyone close to the asset. Look for anything that might be a weapon," said Jess. Then he went silent.

The question inside Jess's brain was simpler: What were they doing here? Then he saw Naylor five feet behind him and knew the answer. They—meaning the *yings*—were marking time, waiting for the arrival of *them*. The *farangs*. Hundreds of bar *yings* were like a colorless, odorless, volatile compound, a chemical Eros, lurking in the shadows, finding the right moment to attach themselves for as long as it took until the cash leached out of the john's wallet. Spilling onto Soi Nana, tuk-tuk drivers ran along holding up laminated photos of massage parlor *yings*, and the next wall they hit were Plaza touts. "Come see, free show. Beautiful *yings*. No cover charge."

"You can close your mouth, Jess," said Calvino into the mic. "Don't worry, I've got him covered."

"I will stay at eleven o'clock. I will stay in a covering position until you can get him to move forward," said Jess.

"You don't have to watch him. Just everyone near him."

"His biggest danger is himself," said Calvino.

He looked over at Jess, who was trying to pretend he fitted into the crowd. But he stood out like a pimple on an unblemished face. A man talking to himself in the crowd. Jess looked awkward, uneasy. Not an uncommon experience for guys arriving from America, after years of sexual repression, all ideas of sexual pleasure purged as wrong and sinful. They arrived as refugees from history's most massive sexual witch hunt. And for the first time in their lives they looked inside the Plaza and realized they had escaped, climbed over the wall separating them from sex. Jess now found himself inside a re-education camp for these escapees.

The clarity of police training started to break up with the static line of all those years of politically correct training jamming his senses; he lapsed into an embarrassed silence and shock of someone who believed such a thing did not exist in his country. Such things were not discussed or admitted except in a vague, abstract way. This way it had been kept as part rumor, part myth. But there was an actual physical place—the Plaza—and the place and the *yings* were real. All the time he kept pushing the message of the medium away, looking for the threat, scanning for danger, trying to ignore where he was and what these *yings* were really doing in this place.

"I'm losing him," said Calvino into the mic.

"I've got him." Jess was moving forward through the crowd.

Between Calvino and Naylor was a firewall of children selling packets of chewing gum, food vendors hawking everything from fried shrimp to fried grasshoppers, blind lottery ticket salesmen, *yings* on their way from and into the Great Stomach. Bar-fined *yings* edged past arm-in-arm with their customers circum-navigating troupes of ass-grabbing tourists, leading their johns out of the Plaza. Candidates for a short-time, partying, boozing, screwing, and candidates for acute, exotic diseases— all moving, seeping, leaking as a single movement like follicle cells of ovaries excited by a chance encounter.

Every other step as they edged forward into this concrete canyon of the Plaza someone in the throng of humanity recognized Calvino.

"Khun Vinee, *sabai dee?*"

And there were the *wais*, the hands folding together, palms touching, fingers touching, raised to the forehead. Calvino recognized the faces, remembered the names.

Jess, who walked ahead, saw the reaction. "You know some people."

"Like you in LA, you know some people," whispered Calvino into the mic.

"But you're a *farang*," said Jess, stunned by the presence of all the foreigners compressed into the small area. "And you know Thai people. The Thai people who come to this place."

"Amazing isn't it? And in LA, do you know any Americans, Jess?"

"Don't get distracted. Keep your eyes moving on people's hands," said Jess as he caught sight of Calvino making his way through the crowd.

"There isn't any such place like this in LA," said Naylor as Calvino caught up with him. "The fucking ABC would close them down, throw their asses in jail. Sometimes, in America, don't you just hate the rule of law?"

Wes Naylor worked his way, Jess on point, and Calvino following behind. They squeezed through the crowd and the dozens of motorcycles parked in the path. A young girl with a huge front porch under a thin cotton T-shirt which had "Size Does Matter" printed in bold letters on the front, flicked her lighter and touched the flame to some incense sticks. She bowed her head at the large spirit house in front of the Spirit House bar.

Two vendors were hot on Naylor's trail. "Nah, I don't want any gum or fried bugs or fucking flowers or a massage. Get out of my face," he said, bulling ahead.

"Did you spend much time with Naylor in LA?" Calvino spoke in the mic to Jess. One of the touts caught Calvino's eye, nodded in recognition. A vendor smiled and called out his name, but Calvino never took his eyes off Naylor.

"He acted different in LA. More like a lawyer. He never showed his tattoos or mentioned the Cause." Jess's voice was coming clearly through Calvino's earphone. Jess had already witnessed that Calvino was hard-wired into the electrical grid of the Plaza.

"Maybe he thinks the Cause is a *farang* thing," said Calvino.

"You think that?" asked Jess.

"What?"

"That I don't understand *farang* things?"

"It doesn't really matter what I think," said Calvino.

Naylor pushed ahead of them, stopping to buy a shwarma from a middle-eastern looking vendor with sad eyes and a droopy moustache that covered his upper lip. "You guys want one?" asked Naylor. Calvino shook his head. Jess had a smirk on his face. An underweight middle-aged *farang* in a black biker's jacket, thick glasses and a shaved head who carried a crash helmet tucked under his arm walked up and shook Calvino's hand.

"How's it going, Larry?" Calvino asked.

Jess's voice boomed in his ear. "Watch that guy. He looks like trouble."

"It's okay, I know him."

"Calvino, do you always talk to your jacket?" asked Larry.

"Only when I hear voices," said Calvino.

"I'm off to Cambodia tomorrow. Doing a feature on Deuch, one of those look backs at Tuol Sleng as Cambodia's first born-again Christian mass murderer," said Larry as he slipped back into the crowd. Larry had left Australia years ago. He had written many stories on regional wars, but it was the sustained cruelty of the Cambodians that repelled him, much like the large capacity of the Thais for *sanuk* attracted him to Thailand.

"Nice angle," said Calvino.

As Naylor bit into the shwarma, Jess stepped closer to Calvino. "I am sorry I brought you into this assignment. If you want to go, I wouldn't blame you. It's clear there is no way I can control him. He won't listen to anything you or I say. I know you didn't sign on for this. No hard feelings. Keep the money. I'll work it out with Dr. Nat."

Calvino smiled, watching Naylor finish off the last of the Shwarma. "I don't work that way. I signed on for the job. So let's do it the best way we can, given we are protecting an asshole."

Naylor stopped at the staircase, wiping his hands on a napkin, which he balled up and threw on the ground. He waited at the bottom as Jess ran ahead, taking the steps two at a time.

"I know you were talking about me. But that's okay. I've got thick skin."

"Where do you want to go, Wes?" asked Calvino.

"Lovejoy. You know it?" asked Naylor.

"Yeah, I know it," said Calvino. He informed Jess of the location of the bar.

Jess was ten feet ahead watching them approach. "Maybe I don't understand *farangs*," said Jess.

"Maybe not," said Calvino.

"From the reception you get in the Plaza, you'd think you were some kind of celebrity rather than one of my bodyguards," said Naylor. "A celebrity bodyguard. That's a twist."

As they stepped inside Lovejoy, Calvino saw Jess in the far corner. The DJ was playing Pink Floyd's "Another Brick in the Wall." At the bar a dancer who was about eighteen years old squirmed inside a micro-bikini, her thin arms and legs twisted in knots around a customer's neck and waist, as if she were some alien life form seeking a partal to enter his body. Naylor walked straight up to the bar and ordered a double Stoly on the rocks.

"These your friends, Khun Vinee?" asked Lek, as she looked around Naylor.

"Business associates," said Naylor. "And that guy in the corner, he's another business associate." He nodded down the bar at Jess, who slowly shook his head.

This didn't stop Naylor from continuing. "Jess is my main LA man. He's *khon Thai* and I am Wes Naylor, an American."

"Lek and her husband own the bar," Calvino said, more for Jess's benefit than Naylor's.

She *waied* Jess and extended her hand to Naylor. "Glad to meet you."

"So where's your husband?" asked Naylor. "Jack." He waited to see if she were surprised that he knew his name; but Lek's face showed no reaction. She was cool all of the time.

"Jack's upstairs watching TV." She blew Calvino a kiss, mouthing the word "later."

The words to the song—*you are all just bricks in the wall*—blared from the loudspeakers in the ceiling. On stage, three dancers, looking bored, shuffled their feet, hands grasping chrome poles like straphangers on the E train in New York, going home after a long day working in a department store.

The high-pitched roar of rotating helicopter blades sweeping in low drowned out the conversation for a moment.

As the choppers disappeared into the sound system, Naylor gestured at the bar. "How can you watch TV with beautiful *yings* dancing downstairs?"

"How do you know Jack doesn't have his private dancers upstairs?" asked Calvino.

"Because Mrs. Jack standing right here would cut off his dick and feed it to the ducks," said Naylor. "Ain't that right, Jess? You Thai guys have ducks quacking all night long inside your nightmares."

Jess shifted his weight on the stool, watching the door, watching customers. He was totally alert. One of the dancers tentatively approached Jess and asked him to buy a lady's drink. She automatically spoke to Jess in Thai. Just another brick in the wall . . . as the lyrics said. Jess at first ignored her; she asked again, and this time he nodded his approval and she *waied* him. So far he had not exchanged a word with her and the dancer hadn't decided whether Jess understood her Thai or whether he was from some other part of Asia.

"Wes wants to deliver a letter to one of your *yings*," said Calvino.

"What's her name?" asked Lek.

"Jep," said Naylor. "Number 17. I've been looking around but I don't see any dancer wearing number 17."

Lek laughed and pointed to a slender beautiful young girl in blue jeans and a long-sleeved shirt sitting alone in a dark corner, her arms folded, staring ahead as if lost in a dream. "That's Jep against the wall. She's *mai sabai*," said Lek, pushing a fresh glass of orange juice in front of Calvino.

"What the fuck does that mean? *Mai sabai.*"

"She's ill," said Jess.

Naylor eyed her, sipping from his glass and crushing the ice between his teeth. He had a look that passed for the process of thinking going on inside his head. But one might be mistaken about that conclusion.

"What's wrong with her? I mean she looks okay from here." He tensed the muscles in his jaw, the hair stood up on the back of his neck. "She ain't got AIDS or something like that?"

Jess's dancer returned with a drink chit which she slipped into the bamboo chit box holding her lady's drink in the other hand—a cola with one ice cube—and clicked her glass against Jess's, wishing him luck. "*Chok dee,*" he said. For the first time he had spoken Thai to her and she responded by cradling her body between his legs; she relaxed, smiled, and leaned her head against his chest as if they had known each other for months if not years. Instant bar intimacy went with the territory of language proficiency. Comfort came from sleeping with someone the girl could understand: what he wanted, what he expected, what he was prepared to give in return. Someone who could count money in Thai. The comfort lasted less than ten seconds as he peeled her off his lap and lifted her onto the stool next to his and told her to stay very still.

"No, not AIDS. No *yings* here have HIV. Jep's sick because she got more than two hundred and fifty mosquito bites," said Lek. "You never seen anything like what happened to her. Her legs, her ass, her arms, her stomach covered with red bumps."

"How did that happen?" asked Naylor.

"She go out drinking with her friends last night after we close, and she very sad so she drink half a bottle of Mekhong, and then she is walking back to her *hong* alone. She walks into an empty lot because she has to piss. She pulls down her jeans and panties, squats down and passes out. She wake up. Three hours later in the weeds. Millions of mosquitoes all around and they eat her body for three hours."

"You ever hear anything like it?" Wes Naylor asked, glancing at Calvino.

"Give her the letter and let's go back to the hotel," said Calvino.

"You are a barrel of laughs," said Naylor. He called over to Jep. "Hey, sweetheart, come over here. I got a letter from Eric Hull for you. And there are some pictures inside, too." Naylor looked like he was directing traffic, waving her over with both arms in motion. She sat motionless, ignoring him.

"*Dtoo yen, ma nii,*" said Lek.

Calvino smiled, "Did you just tell the Fridge to get its ass over here?"

"Fridge is her real name," said Lek. "Jep is her nickname."

"A fucking redneck name. Fridge," said Naylor.

Jep slowly got off the stool, but not after first looking behind her, thinking Naylor had been gesturing to someone else. Not until Lek had yelled at her from the bar that the *farang* wanted to buy her a cola did she slowly walk over. The fat envelope with her name written in big letters lay on the counter. She leaned against the empty stool beside Naylor and Lek pushed the letter towards her. Jep saw her name, turned it over, saw Eric's name on the other side, then dropped the envelope down on the counter.

"Eric asked me to give you this letter. But you don't seem all that excited."

Calvino was thinking, I hope it's not a fucking musical birthday card without money inside. At the same time, he motioned to Lek that a lady's drink was in order; a cola appeared on the bar next to the envelope. Another chit stuffed into the bamboo chit box. The lady drink gesture perked Jep up. She managed a smile. Bar *ying* lethargy was an occupational hazard. Any bar *ying* with a couple hundred mosquito bites had the added problem of not only being in a weakened condition but being asked to spend what little energy was left for the luxury of self-pity on the price of a lady's drink. Jep was lost in a deep mosquito funk.

"Eric have a wife in America," Jep said, sipping her cola. "I no like butterfly."

"But you have no objection to other bugs like mosquitoes," said Naylor.

"You've delivered the letter, now we can go back to the hotel," said Jess.

"Hold on, Jess. I am not finished. She's not opened the letter."

"Maybe she doesn't want to open it," said Calvino. "Let her open it in her *hong*."

"Bullshit, there might be money inside."

And, again, there might not be money inside, thought Calvino.

A Mexican stand-off was developing. A customer in a muscle shirt and short-clipped beard several stools down the bar had begun to pull down the bikini top of a dancer, peering at her breasts as he worked the top down. Mr. Biceps leaned over and shouted down the bar to Naylor. "Her tits seem smaller."

"Or her body shrank," said Naylor.

The guy with large biceps closed in on Naylor, carrying the topless bar *ying* under one arm.

"Get between him and Naylor. Now," said Jess, who was already off his seat.

As he arrived, Calvino had wedged himself between Naylor and the customer and Jess was directly behind him.

"Hey, what's going on? Have I done something to piss someone off? Does one of these belong to you?" he asked, blinking down at the girls under each arm and then up at Calvino.

"You're a Cause-member, aren't you?" asked Naylor.

The man nodded. "Okay, let him alone. He's one of us."

Jess had patted the customer down. He was clean. Lek stood up and he moved next to Naylor. He reached over and pushed his finger against Naylor's Cause pin. "You a Cause-member?"

"The causemember is my website," said Naylor. "Tail gunner's my nickname."

"No shit?"

"Swear to God."

"Hey, glad to meet you. I love your site. I am on it every day in the States, downloading JPEG's and stories that guys post. I read about this place on your site. I didn't know you traveled with bodyguards. Let me buy you and your two friends a round."

"What's your online name?"

There was a toothy grin. "Weasel." The girl looked like she was sleeping nestled in his armpit. This was the guy who had bar-fined another Cause-member's girlfriend, violating one of the central tenets of the unwritten, informal code of ethics: don't fuck your Cause brothers' wives, girlfriends or steadies. The Cause brotherhood swore to uphold this code of ethics, which was nicknamed YINGS—your informal normal guidelines for sex. *Ying* was short for *poo-ying* or "girl" in Thai. The only sin recognized by Cause-members was a violation of YINGS. Such violations were strongly discouraged.

Naylor looked around the bar for Mucus. "I know you've come to patch things up between me and Mucus. But he's too pissed off to show. I got word an hour ago. He doesn't want the peace council. Thought you should know."

Naylor looked disappointed.

"Maybe tomorrow." Calvino motioned to Lek and waved off the drink.

"Nah, we gotta go. But next time," said Naylor, catching the gesture.

"Jerry's my real name," said Mr. Biceps. "If it wasn't for the Internet, most guys would have no idea they don't have to put up with all that shit with American women." Weasel clearly didn't want to talk about what had happened between him and Mucus. Naylor couldn't help wondering if the girl under his arm was the evidence to be presented to the peace council.

"You got that right," said Naylor. "Next time, I buy you a drink, Jerry."

Weasel disappeared back to the other end of the bar, carrying his catch. She hadn't said a word the entire time.

Naylor nodded towards Calvino before turning his attention to Jep as he moved his face close to hers, his nose touching hers. "What if the mosquito bites never happened? If you drop your pants and there are more than a dozen bites on your ass, I will pay your bar fine. How's that for a deal?" Naylor took a five-hundred-baht note from his wallet and slammed it on the bar.

"And if she loses, then what?" Lek asked from behind the bar.

"She buys me a drink."

"Drop your pants," Lek said in Thai to Jep. "Show this *farang* your ass."

She unfastened her belt and slipped the jeans over her hips. Turning around, she slid the jeans and underwear down and bent forward. "Jesus Christ, you ever seen anything like that?"

Calvino glanced at Jep's bare cheeks, all red, puffy, and raw from the mosquito bites and the scratching. "She wins, Naylor. Give her the money."

The girl cuddling against Jess shivered, turned her face, and buried it in his chest.

"Look at those bites," murmured Naylor.

"Good one, Tailgunner," said Jerry, shouting down the bar.

"*Sai kang-keng,*" Calvino said to her. Put your pants on.

Jerry cupped his hand and shouted a crack about Jep having AIDS. Then two more customers were laughing at her, making crude jokes about her having AIDS. Calvino was off the stool and over to table where he lifted one of the customers up by his shirt. "It is the worse kind of scum that laughs at a girl trying to make a living the best way she can. What makes you think you're better than her? When you laugh at someone else's misery you stop being a human being. Why don't you and your buddy get out?"

"Don't get involved with them," said Jess's voice in his ear. "It's not the job."

But it was too late. The music had already stopped and the bar went into a deathly silent mode. One moment everyone in the bar is thinking about getting laid; a moment later, they are thinking about going to a hospital with their head split open. Eyeing Calvino with his bruised and stitched face in the half-darkness of the *hong*, his jaw hardened with anger, the two punters paid up their bill and left. The three *farangs* shifted nervously in their seats and also discreetly paid their bills, slipped out into the night through the beaded curtain entrance. Suddenly the bar was empty except for the dancers, the *dek serve,* Naylor, Jess and Calvino. And Weasel, who had been necking with his girl in such a way that it looked like he was kissing his own armpit, also paid up and joined the others who had left.

"We were just having some fun, Tailgunner. You ought to get your friends to lighten up," said Jerry, flexing his biceps on the way out.

"You're great for business, Vinee," said Lek.

"Jesus, Calvino, are you trying to destroy my reputation?" asked Naylor. "These men look up to me. How can I hold a peace council if I have no respect?"

Calvino pulled a five-hundred-baht note out of his wallet and bought a round of lady's drinks for the bar. He also bought a gin and tonic for Lek and asked her to send a Johnny Walker Black upstairs to Jack.

"No respect? You have a reputation for what?" asked Calvino as he finished ordering the drinks.

"Now we go back," said Jess, gently uncoiling the girl from his lap as the *farangs* left the bar.

Jep slumped forward on the bar counter, resting her head on her folded arms. Tears spilled down her face, splashing on her bare arms and onto the counter. She was crying softly.

"Why are you crying, sweetheart? It's all these problems Mr. Calvino is causing, isn't it?" asked Naylor. He had his arm around her waist.

She lifted her head, blew her nose on a bar napkin. "No one ever help me before," she said.

Naylor thought she meant him.

"Anyone picks on you and my bodyguards will take care of that punk," said Naylor, his face full of sympathy. He patted her on the shoulder.

She did nothing to correct his confusion. "I think you good man." Why turn away an opportunity?

"Wes Naylor is a good man."

"You know in my life, only Jep help herself. Last night you know why I get drunk?"

"I have no idea. Maybe your boyfriend broke your heart," said Naylor.

She shook her head. "My sister die. Boyfriend's motorcycle crash. She die. He's fine. I think too much. Remember everything. Like when I was eleven years old. Just a young girl. I go to the river with my sister. My friends, my sister, and me. We want to play in the water. We can't swim so we stay close. Laughing together. Splashing each other. I laugh and laugh so hard and feel so good. When I get out of the river, I have a big shock. I feel something down there," she touches between her legs. "And I look. It is terrible."

"What was it?" asked Naylor. She hesitates. "Not important."

"You can tell me. What was there?" asked Naylor.

"A *pling*," Jep said. "I forget the English word."

"Leech," said Jess, who was listening to her story. "The English word for *pling* is a leech."

"The *pling* is inside me. Part in, part out. I start screaming. I don't know what to do. My friends run away. My sister run away, too. They are too scared to help. I run around after them, this thing hanging around, hitting me on my thighs. It's like I want to run away from the *pling*. But I can't; it's stuck inside me, sucking my blood. I cry so hard. I think I will die. I fall down on my knees. I can see myself in the river. Like a mirror. I am very afraid. But I reach down and I pull it out. This *pling* is in my hand and I throw it down. There is blood everywhere. On my legs, on my hands and arms. I look at the *pling* on the ground. It is big and fat with my blood. Sucked from inside here. I find a stick and I hit the *pling* until it is in small pieces. My blood is on the grass, and I sit there still and wait. Twenty, thirty minutes, maybe longer, I wait until my friends and sister come back. And they see all that blood and how pale I look, and they think I am ghost. That the *pling* has killed me and I come back for revenge. Now they are screaming and running away. They stop laughing. They are scared. Scared of me. And I know that I am alone. No one will ever help me. Not in this life. And now my sister, she die. And I want to think it is all mistake. That she's sitting on the grass all pale and she will come running after me like I go after her. I know she won't come. I know I can't help her. She die jing jing. And my father, he say, 'I name you dtoo yen. I am a poor man. You are the only dtoo yen I ever have. The *pling* go up you. It is my fault. I bring bad luck on you. On our family.' Then my sister die, he say the same thing. '*Dtoo yen*, I do the wrong thing in my life,' my father say. 'I am sorry.' It was the only time he ever say sorry to me." Tears dropped down her cheeks.

"Why don't you let me help you?" said Naylor.

"You have a wife?" asked Jep, fastening her belt. It was as if she had already shifted channels as if she surfed on remote control. She was now back to the standard bar question. The Fridge had gone ice cold.

Naylor laughed, one of those loud thunderclouds of a laugh. "Me, a wife? You've got to be joking. I am a confirmed bachelor. A free-range rider. Mr. Tailgunner."

Calvino translated this into Thai. "*Mai mee mia.*" He has no wife. Jep understood without the translation.

Jess was pacing back and forth, watching the door for any new customers, stopping to check out Naylor—doing his job in other words.

"Okay, okay. We'll go back to the hotel. These guys are staying with me. But don't worry, they have their own *hongs*."

"Where are you staying?" asked Lek, wiping the bar counter.

"The Brandy. All three of us. This Thai and this Italian." He points a finger at Jess, then punches the air at Calvino. Lek smiled at Calvino; the kind of smile that registers a plan, a threat, an appointment in the making.

Jep squeezed his hand. "I come back with you. You already pay bar fine."

"That was a bet. You won it fair and square. But if you wanna come back, I mean, you can come back. What I am saying is Eric said you were really nice and cute and it's not far. The Brandy's just across the street." He was also thinking about the Cause brotherhood code of conduct and how this was Eric's girl, and how Weasel, whose own reputation was under a cloud for poaching Mucus' girl, had seen him in the bar. She was so goddamn tempting. Weasel was gone. So were the others. He would sneak her back, Naylor thought. He could always claim Jep had gone with Calvino or Jess.

Jep knew where the Brandy was; probably knew the inside of most of the *hongs*.

"Not a good idea," Jess said to Naylor, looking Jep over.

"I don't think I asked you whether it was a good idea," said Naylor.

"Thank you for helping me," Jep said to Calvino, as she touched the edge of his hand. A quick, soft movement.

"I like this girl. So she's coming with me whether you like it or not."

"Jep, do me a favor," said Calvino in Thai. "Anything you want," she replied.

"Keep him off the street tonight. Make certain he stays in the *hong*," said Calvino in Thai. Since Naylor's bar-fining was likely at a minimum a technical breach of the YINGS, the odds were in their favor that Naylor wouldn't venture out of his *hong* with Jep. Being disgraced by his Cause-members would be terrible for his Internet business.

She nodded slowly, taking in Calvino's instruction, trying to decide if this was his way of asking for re-payment.

"Hey, what are you telling her about me?" asked Naylor.

"That you are kind and generous man."

"Like hell you did."

Jess wasn't so sure he liked Calvino intervening in this way, taking the lead when he should have known it was his place to stay one step behind and let Jess make the decisions. Their asset had paid for a bar *ying* and was taking her back to the hotel. Jess clearly understood why Pratt had declined to escort Naylor once it became clear the Brandy Hotel was the destination. To make a stand would be pointless; one Thai against the two *farangs*, they would win. So Jess remembered his police training and remained calm; he did not raise his voice, show emotion.

"For tonight," said Jess. "I can go along with it."

"Tonight, tomorrow night. Let's just get through the moment. You guys need to get a life. Better yet, take back a girl. I'll pay the bar fines."

"We're on duty," said Jess. "No drinking, no *yings*."

"I've got to hand it to Doc Nat, he found the last two men in Thailand to take this job seriously." He picked up the drink slips from the chit cup and added them up in his head. "Don't forget the ten percent discount you give to Cause-members."

Calvino exchanged a look with Lek. She leaned forward, the palms of her hand flat on the counter, her fingers splayed out. All those many hours of working on her nails on full display.

"The discount was Jack's idea," she said. "See you after closing."

"I am working." Calvino watched as she raised her index finger snakelike and pointed it at him.

"I won't get in the way," she said.

All the while Calvino thought that nothing he would say would keep Lek from coming around to his *hong*. That he would just have to deal with the situation when she came knocking on the door. Jack had once said of his wife, "She's a time rat. She would eat the hands of the clock face of any man." Then he had grinned that terrible fisherman's grin of pulling in an empty net and said, "All *yings* are time rats, time bandits. Open their guts and what you find inside their digestive tract are the seconds and minutes of a hundred men's lives. Time cannibals. All those broken minute and hour hands just lying undigested in her stomach. It makes me want to drink."

And on the way out of the bar, Naylor walked ahead holding Jep's tiny hand inside his huge fist. He was more than double her size. She looked like the eleven-year-old who had climbed out of the river and onto the soft, wet bank and discovered the ultimate facts of life as a *pling* dangled from her vagina—that you are basically alone in the universe, and come that moment of perfect terror, no one can save you but yourself. If you are lucky.

Back in his *hong*, Calvino stretched out on the bed, hands folded behind his head. The only light came from the neon lights below and CNN flickering across the TV screen. He turned the volume off. There was nothing from the outside world that he wanted to hear. He was thinking that he had been too hard on the *farang* at Lovejoy. He tried to figure out why he had done what he did in the bar. Most guys like them arrived in a bewildered, lonely state—middle-aged men who had the look of men who had been in a guarded camp for many years, living in a police state with twenty-four hour surveillance. Sex, like politics, had always been local. Wars had always globalized sex. But the Internet globalized sex for the vast civilian population. No one forced them to wear uniforms, carry a gun, or get shot at. They could concentrate on hunting *yings* as a full-time occupation. And a generation of men were trying to understand what had happened to their lives and how their maturity had not prepared them for places like the Plaza. They were pumped from all the posting on the Internet but it never occurred to them that nowhere in all those postings was there ever one from one of the *yings* who actually worked the scene. Her voice was always absent. Punters always spoke for her. Attributed words to her, gave her motives and desires and expectations. Painted her any color they wanted. But none of the Cause-members ever asked if in that silence there were decent human beings, *yings* who were not on the con, *yings* looking for a way out. Not that Jep was necessarily that woman. But what was it in the hunters, what hunger or need was in them that made them accept the presumption that she couldn't be? It was that presumption which was the creed of the Cause; one voice which said, presume guilt, presume the con, presume the rip-off. Calvino's Law: Put the baby powder on the floor and take a shower but don't assume the footprints of the girl you brought back will always lead to the cash box. And that was the worst part of thinking; one looked into the mirror of another's hypocrisy and saw oneself.

It had been McPhail who had once said, "Sex with a beautiful *ying*. What else is there worth rolling out of bed for in the morning and rolling back into bed for? Think about it. There ain't anything else."

★★★★★★

PRATT had lightly knocked on Calvino's *hong* as he was about to turn up the volume and find a way out of all the troubled thoughts Naylor had caused him. Calvino hit the remote and the sound came on. There was a major snowstorm in the Midwest and cars were skidding all over some Chicago highway. Pratt knocked again, this time his knuckles banging hard, a cop's way of getting attention.

"Lek, I don't sleep with married *yings*. Go home," said Calvino.

The knock came again. He rolled off the bed, muttering under his breath as he unfastened the chain on the door and shouted through the crack. "Jesus, don't you take no for an answer?"

He checked the peephole. Pratt stood relaxed, his hands at his side. He was dressed in civilian clothes. His gun was in a shoulder holster. Calvino opened the door.

"Expecting someone named Lek?" His smile kept on getting wider as he waited for an answer.

"Someone who wants my body."

"A pound of a *farang* private eye's flesh?" asked Pratt, turning and flashing a smile. "Therefore prepare thee to cut off the flesh. Shed thou no blood; nor cut thou less, nor more, but just a pound of flesh; if thou tak'st more, or less, than just a pound, be it but so much as makes it light or heavy in substance, or division of the twentieth part of one scruple, nay, if the scale do turn but in the estimation of a hair, thoudiest and all thy goods are confiscate."

Pratt walked across the *hong* and sat down as Calvino locked the door, thinking of the *Merchant of Venice.* Calvino ignored Pratt's recital of Portia's speech, knowing there was some message inside that would only distract him from his mission.

"I just came away after having a long talk with Jess."

Why a long talk, wondered Calvino. What was hatching? Only he didn't want to get distracted over the word "long" and so he kept to business. "The Plaza blew Jessada away. And it didn't help his view of the world to find out about Naylor's other business interest on the Internet. A website for single guys traveling to Bangkok. About peace councils and holding court for YINGS violations."

Pratt nodded. This he understood. "He might be Thai but he's from LA."

"Did he tell you that I started something in a bar? Something that was stupid."

Pratt did that little shrug of his. The one he did with his kids when they were telling him a half-truth and it was something that annoyed him. "Jess said you did something he hadn't ever thought a *farang* would do. You defended a bar *ying*. You showed compassion. That was his word."

"Jess got it all wrong. I didn't like the way the guy was looking at me. That's all. It had nothing to do with the girl. Some asshole in a muscle shirt."

"Sure, Vincent," said Pratt, opening his briefcase. "I brought you something that might be useful in keeping

Wes Naylor alive. After he leaves Bangkok, he can die in any way and any place he pleases. But I don't want him dying in Bangkok."

He tossed a folder onto the bed. Calvino slowly opened it and saw that there was an auditor's report about the hotel Dr. Nat, his brother, Dr. Damrong, and Wes Naylor were preparing to buy. *Confidential and private* was stamped all over the report. Calvino looked at the words, which meant one thing in the States—meaning privacy and confidentiality—but repack- aged and imported into Bangkok, the ideas floated in the air, bursting like bubbles. Calvino leafed through the report, then flipped back to the executive summary. Company bank accounts were in the individual names of directors and not of the hotel company. The company had received millions of baht but no official company receipts had ever been issued. There had been all kinds of advance cash payments and no documents or explanations as to who made the payments or what they were made for. The depreciation expenses were totally screwed up. There had been overpayments to creditors by millions of baht. There were millions of baht more for maintenance of the elevators and hotel premises but the transactions were unrecorded. Receipts were not attached to payment vouchers. Seven BMW's had been bought with company funds and registered in family members' names. Forty-three employees with *Isan* family names and upcountry addresses were listed on a "ghost" payroll. In other words, a family-run business operation where the family pocket and the company pocket were in the same pair of pants and everyone's fingers were dirty from grabbing whatever could be hauled away.

"Not what I would call a clean bill of health," said Calvino. "All those sticky fingers in the rice bowl."

"With one finger on a trigger aiming at Wes Naylor."

"He's a pretty reckless guy. And not all that sane. That's not a good combination, Pratt."

"You signed on to keep him alive."

"I have been making mistakes all week. The Naylor job is not my first mistake." Calvino put down the report. "You show this to Jess yet?"

"I gave him a copy."

"What did he say?"

"That Dr. Nat had already sent him a copy of the report."

"No surprises, in other words."

"Something like that."

"If I thought someone was trying to kill me, I mean really had a contract out, I wouldn't be delivering letters to bar *yings*. I wouldn't be in Thailand. You know what I am saying?"

"You're right. Naylor's not afraid. Meaning, as you said, he is very stupid or very clever or crazy," said Pratt.

"I don't take Wes Naylor to be a stupid man. He's a greedy and careless man and that makes him dangerous. I was joking about the crazy part. Well, maybe kidding a little."

On Pratt's way out of the *hong*, Calvino spotted Lek sauntering down the corridor as if she were a *ying* on a low-flying Brandy mission. She had changed out of her work clothes, putting on a tight, slinky red dress. A different line of work clothes. There was no underwear line under that dress either. No nylons. Hips swinging as she walked; long, thin legs in black high heels with the strap over the ankle. She had Monster Fuck written all over her. Pratt blocked the doorway as Lek stopped, her hand resting on one hip, eyes bright in the corridor light, her full lips parted in a smile. The curve of her breasts revealed under the red fabric. This time-rat had never looked so good, thought Calvino. And her husband Jack ran around on her as if he didn't know or care what he had waiting for him at home. Now she had gone on her own DNA run to the Brandy Hotel. Calvino wasn't sure whether he knew what to say or had anything worth saying to her. Pratt understood the situation from the moment Lek smiled at Calvino.

"As I was saying, I think your infection should clear up in a couple of days," said Pratt. "Just take the pills like I told you."

"Doc, what about sex?" asked Calvino.

"You don't want to pass this one on to anyone. No sex."

"But the pills you gave me, they will work, right?"

Pratt shrugged. "For your sake, let's hope so. I'll have the full lab report tomorrow. Stop at my office tomorrow afternoon. And hope for the best, Mr. Calvino. Hope for the best." Pratt winked, then pushed ahead from the door and walked down the corridor. He pressed the button and before the elevator arrived, the lady in the red dress was standing beside him, looking grim, smoking a cigarette and shaking her head.

"You just saved my life," she said to Pratt. "*Farang mai dee.*" The foreigners are bad. She was waiting for the normal Thai co-conspirator agreement on this point.

Not tonight, not with this cop pretending to be a doctor. The elevator arrived. "When I cut a foreigner open, you know he or she looks exactly the same inside as you or me. So I can't say they are bad and we are good. Under the knife, we all look the same. Same heart, liver, lungs, and kidneys. There is no difference."

On the way down in silence Pratt wondered if he believed that.

EIGHT

WHEN PRATT HAD disappeared into the elevator with Lek it was about 3:00 a.m. The *ying* time-rat had gone home without fulfilling her carefully planned insemination session. Calvino sat back in a chair outside of Naylor's door. He nodded off, his chin on his chest. A few minutes later he was out, watching the stranger walk into the village. The tall, thin man was teaching the villagers the art of making fire. Villagers danced naked around the flames. The stranger removed the black hood obscuring his face. It was Naylor's face and Calvino watched as the village elders lifted him up and threw him into the flames. A loud bang echoed down the corridor and Calvino lifted his head, rubbed his eyes and looked around. A few feet away a working *ying* had slammed the door on the way out. She walked uneasily down the corridor in her highheels, swaying as if she had too much to drink or had done drugs. Not long afterwards, other *yings* emerged like bees out of a honeycomb and headed for the elevator at the end of the corridor. He couldn't sleep any longer. All the activity of *yings* coming and going from the *hongs* along with the sound of moaning and screaming penetrating the walls spilled into the corridor. It was as if a special-effects sound track were playing in the background; the sound track that came packaged as part of the price of a short-time.

Passionate doorway kisses and hugs, then money changed hands, the door closed, the *ying* lighting a cigarette, collecting herself, breathing out a long sigh, then pushing off with just enough steam to reach the elevator. Calvino heard the angry American voice shouting into the phone inside the *hong* across corridor.

"Tim. I want to speak to Tim. No, not Kim. It's Tim. I just told you it's Tim and not Kim. I want to speak to him. Tim that is T for Thailand and not K for knife. You know knife, right? Okay, I will spell Tim. It's T for Thailand. I for India. And M for moron. Tim."

The tourists were *different* from the old Asian hands, he thought. The *yings* turned a lot of tourists into moody, screaming, middle-aged teenagers. What gave old hands their edge was life spent in the proximity of surplus of beautiful, available *yings*; there wasn't any rationing. These Goddess-like creatures had opened a door into a world where suddenly a man's class, age, nationality, education, and accent no longer counted. They had no way of judging such *farang* matters, so they counted for nothing. A surplus of *yings* created a level playing field with enough supply to accommodate every guy so long as he spoke two or three words of Thai and had some cash ready to spend. Jealousy was wasted as the supply was constant. Competition among men was viewed as adolescent behavior. With the never ending flow of *yings*, hoarding, even competition, made no sense. The old hands—or at least most of them—checked their egos at the bar door; they cultivated a mellow, detached attitude about sex. Calvino's surplus/ rationing law of sex translated into those who rationed time with men they didn't love for money. Once she loved the guy, then she wanted not only his money but all of his time. Money-rat turned into time-rat. When a *ying* fell in love, then a man had only one choice: he rationed his time or he lost it altogether. Rationing time made her attentive, kind, considerate, interested, and always available. Once she moved in, life was over, like Jack's life. Lek had created surplus time with her man, turning her affection for him into indifference, her kindness into contempt, her attention into boredom. She was out hunting for another man.

About four in the morning, Naylor opened the door wide enough to ask Calvino to go out of the hotel and buy something for Jep's mosquito bites; she was scratching herself until the blood spilled onto the sheets. Calvino knocked on Jess's door, they had a short exchange in the doorway; Calvino looked inside. Jess opened the door wider. He saw Colonel Pratt inside the room.

"Come in for a moment," said Pratt.

"What's going on?" He exchanged a long look with Pratt.

"Come in and shut the door," said Pratt.

Jess sat back at the table covered with computer print-outs, photographs, and a laptop with an Excel file showing some kind of a graph. "As you know, I work undercover narcotics in LA," said Jess. "Pratt and I are comparing notes."

Calvino looked over at Pratt. "We think one of the men Jess busted with one kilo of heroin is connected to one of the major players in the North. They are refining the heroin in factories over the border in Burma and then it transits through Thailand."

"We've already figured out that a lot of heroin is on the street in LA. We are pretty certain it is coming through Thailand," said Jess.

"What we can't figure out is what happens to it between Burma and LA."

"The heroin from the Burmese border just disappears," said Pratt. "We are trying to track it and we think the guy Jess arrested can help."

"What you're saying is the bodyguard assignment for Naylor is cover for an LAPD drug investigation," said Calvino.

"I can't believe that I've been set up. And to run cover for a drug case. Someone might have let me know."

He stared straight at Pratt. They had an understanding, going back many years: honesty and loyalty above everything else. The pact was never to hide the ball from the other. And Pratt knew what Calvino was thinking, that he had let him down, drawn him into a situation without really explaining what the situation was.

"No one has conned you, Vincent. This is a legitimate bodyguard job," said Pratt.

"Colonel Pratt's right about that. It was my idea to try and work a new angle on the drug case while I am here," said Jess, turning around the computer screen so that Calvino could see it. "See the graph. That's the amount of heroin increase on the streets of LA in the last two years." The line shot up like the graph of an Internet IPO.

"I still haven't got a straight answer. Is Naylor being used as a decoy in a drug investigation?" asked Calvino.

Jess bit his lower lip and slowly shook his head. "Not exactly."

"That's what I figured. Yes and no. Not exactly. Maybe. One of those Thai answers that means nothing. Christ, I should've known, four grand for four days has to involve something like drugs," said Calvino, sitting down at the table in front of the computer.

"No one knows that I am in Thailand. Not even my wife," said Jess.

"Like you have taken advantage of me," said Calvino. Not even his wife, thought Calvino. Something was starting to add up; weren't the DEA and the Embassy supposed to be involved in drug suppression? If LAPD was doing an end run, there had to be some question as to whether those assets in Bangkok had been compromised.

"Naylor's not been set up. Let's say we have taken advantage of the situation."

"You could make a call to the DEA at the Embassy, but you have done that. Meaning there is a trust issue. Someone taking advantage of their position and the situation."

He went out of the room without waiting for any reply.

Nothing was straightforward in Thailand: there was always another agenda. And thinking no agenda existed behind the scenes was the mistake of a greenhorn. Like delivering a birthday card and thinking it was only a birthday card. On the way to Bumrungrad Hospital, Calvino thought about quitting the job; going home, sleeping in his own bed, and letting Pratt and Jess sort out whatever play they had in motion. Instead, he went to the hospital and saw a doctor, picked up a prescription for pain pills and cream for the bites, and returned to the Brandy. He passed the cream through the half-opened door to Naylor. By the time he had returned, Pratt had gone and Jess was asleep. At 5:30 a.m. Jess relieved Calvino on the watch. Calvino hadn't fallen asleep but sat, his arms folded, thinking about what he should do, when Jess tapped him on the shoulder.

"Get some sleep," said Jess as he held a small metal detector the size of a pack of cigarettes out, pointing it towards Naylor's room.

Calvino looked up slowly. "Are you beaming yourself up to the Starship Enterprise or is that a video game?"

"It scans for open circuits, polarity reversals, possible transmitting devices up to one thousand feet away. See the LED? If it flashes, then it detects a change. Someone has bugged Naylor's room. It picks up the radiation of any transmitting device."

"Sorry I asked," said Calvino as he rose from the chair and walked to his room without saying anything further.

In the morning they were to take Naylor to his appointment with the hotel owners. Calvino knocked on Naylor's door. A few minutes later he opened the door and Calvino saw Jep curled up in the bed. Against all expectations, she hadn't gone short time—the rationed commercial time of no more than two hours allotted to customers like Wes Naylor. Instead, she had stayed all night, which meant a different rate applied and altogether different *ying* methods of emotional calculation were in motion. She was still sleeping in Naylor's bed when Naylor opened the door and found Calvino and Jess standing outside in the corridor.

"Time to go, Wes," said Jess.

"Yeah, I know. I am behind schedule." He held a jar of cream in one hand; the cream smeared on the fingers of the other hand. It had taken him less than twenty-four hours to switch from hunting for the Monster Fuck to fulfilling the role of an emotional NGO. Jep's mosquito-mutilated body lay motionless under the sheets. Another explanation for her presence was that the pain pills had knocked her out; she was outside of time, outside of pain, dancing in the shadows of the flames of the stranger.

"You did plan to close the deal today?" asked Calvino.

"Don't be a wise guy. That's why I am in Bangkok. You guys look like shit," Naylor said.

"You don't look so good yourself," said Calvino.

"Soon you'll be on a plane back to Los Angeles," said Jess. "And we can all catch up on our sleep."

"I will be here as long as it takes. If you signed on for four days, that is your business with Dr. Nat. It's got nothing to do with me," said Naylor

Naylor slammed the door, locked it from the inside.

Calvino turned and started to walk away from the door, then stopped and turned and looked at Jess. "I am not going to talk about your drug bust. Whatever that is, I don't know. And to tell you the truth I don't want to know. I am not a cop. And I've been thinking about what you said, that no one knows you are here, not even your wife. After I had a look at the auditor's report on the company that owns the hotel last night," said Calvino. "It is clear that someone in that Chinese family might want to kill the deal. And kill the messenger as well."

"Colonel Pratt said you would come around."

"Come around what? You mean blind corners with no one telling me what is waiting."

"My investigation in LA has nothing to do with you or what you've been asked to do. They are separate matters."

Nothing is ever separate in this life or in this world, thought Calvino. "And no doubt you will be the first to tell me when they come together," said Calvino.

"What I can tell you is to expect some problems this morning at the hotel," said Jess.

"Guaranteed."

"Nothing money can't fix," said Jess. He smiled, arms folded, leaning back against the door to Naylor's *hong*.

"Does Doc Nat know that he's financing an LAPD drug investigation? Or was that just another separate kind of deal?" asked Calvino.

Jess smiled, put an arm on Calvino's shoulder. "It is separate. Dr. Nat's getting what he paid for. I don't see how my investigation causes him any problem. As for the deal itself? He didn't hire us to review the deal. That's his business. So we leave it alone. Keep it simple. We don't get involved in their deal. We only do what Dr. Nat hired us to do. Guard the asset." Every time he referred to Naylor as the capital "A" asset, Calvino shook his head in disbelief. The quality of assets had depreciated substantially in Thailand but calling Naylor an asset was like calling a non-performing loan an asset. One could call Naylor an asset or whatever one wanted, but Calvino wasn't yet convinced that Naylor was adding real value to Dr. Nat's deal.

"Maybe it's not our problem directly. But why send Naylor? Why didn't he come himself? Why does he need a *farang* to deal with a dysfunctional Chinese family? The members of this family have committed every possible commercial crime anyone has ever thought of and then added a couple more."

"You don't understand how Thai people think. If there is a problem, send another person. And why not a *farang*? They are more expensive to have killed. I thought you would have learned that during all your years here."

★★★★★★

EVERYONE was quiet during the ride to the Grand Rose Hotel. Calvino concentrated on driving; this made it easier to ignore his concerns about Jess networking an LAPD heroin case with Pratt. His thoughts turned to the BMWs the Chinese family had bought themselves out of the hotel revenues and the *Isan* ghost workers who never showed up for work and drew checks that they never received. Naylor fingered the fifteen-baht gold chain around his neck like the links were worry beads, thinking about whether Jep would be waiting for him when he returned. Wondering whether Weasel was posting on the Cause-members, site that Tailgunner had clearly violated the YINGS in front of witnesses. Jess was thinking about his first kick-boxing teacher, who had lived in a small wooden house in Sukhumvit Road years before there were any apartments or office buildings there, and how the teacher had been killed a few years ago by gunmen who had ambushed him as he got out of his car. The hit was connected to fixing a kick-boxing match and gambling and misunderstandings over turf and face.

The Grand Rose Hotel was located on an even numbered *soi*. Sukhumvit Road had even and odd numbered *sois* on different sides of the road but adjacent numbers rarely were opposite one another so that Soi 38 was opposite Soi 55 and so on. This mismatching was a perfect metaphor for mismatching between the *yings* and their johns on the Causeway. As Calvino turned into the *soi*, the road passed through empty overgrown fields. Five minutes later, he entered the driveway of the hotel, set back at the end of a small sub-*soi*. On the left was an open-air noodle shop where a half a dozen locals in shorts and flip-flops, seated on plastic stools, slurped down bowls of noodles. On the right of the hotel, a new office block with a tall, ornate gate with a guard box had been constructed. Food vendors had staked out the front entrance of the Grand Rose, setting up folding tables and plastic stools and colorful beach umbrellas to provide shade, and these acted as unofficial boundary markers. Location, location, location, thought Calvino. The place was a three-time loser.

"Looks more like a hotel that has been converted into a guest house than a hotel," said Naylor, craning his neck to get a closer look.

"Not like the hotel in the color brochures the owners Fed Ex'ed to California," said Calvino. The accountant's report said money had been diverted from maintenance. What it didn't say was that all of the money had been diverted, thought Calvino. He tried swallowing the laughter building up in his throat. He coughed into his hand, and turned away.

"I am shocked," said Jess, taking off his sunglasses. He was smiling.

The hotel grounds were overgrown with weeds and hundreds of rose bushes that had been allowed to grow wild. Deep red, pale pink, pure white roses grew in thick clumps, the stems bending over to touch the dirt. Tall weeds everywhere. It looked like an evil garden. A place haunted by spirits. Plants were dead or dying, brown stumps dotted the grounds. Chickens scratched in the dirt, others ran under the rose bushes in one corner of the garden. A goat tied to a tree, head down, eyed them as it chewed some very dry looking grass. A couple of dogs with pink sores on their bellies slept on their backs under a cement table with stone benches and ignored them altogether.

"This place is a fucking dump. Someone is trying to kill me so Dr. Nat doesn't buy this place? Getting shot at for a five-star hotel is one thing, but getting shot in a language I can't even understand, for this? I can't fucking believe it."

"Want to go back to the Brandy?" asked Jess.

"We're here now. Let's at least talk to them. I mean the land has to be worth something. Maybe if we bulldozed all the weeds and bushes, got rid of the chickens and

goats and, you know, fucking started from scratch."
Naylor stayed in the car until Calvino and Jess were out,
and they had a look around. The purpose was to make
certain the immediate perimeter had no threats before
letting Naylor out of the car. When he finally crawled
out of the backseat, Naylor almost tripped over a one-
legged beggar sprawled out on the curb holding a tin
cup and ringing a small temple bell. The sound of the
bell filled the air as a kind of warning, clear as a prayer
to the Almighty.

"The Grand Rose has a certain native charm," said
Calvino. He dropped a few coins into the cup.

"Isn't that the credo of the Cause? Buying native
charm?"

"Rub salt in the wound. If that makes you feel any
fucking better," said Naylor.

Jess, who had been leaning on the door of Calvino's
car, slammed it shut. The three men stood at the foot of
the stairs, each waiting for the other to make the first
move. No one had to hammer home the obvious: the
Grand Rose Hotel was no longer a functioning hotel. All
one could say was that a number of the wild rose bushes
had flourished as a by-product of the neglect but there
was nothing grand or flourishing about the garden, the
grounds, or the hotel.

"I'll go ahead and check it out first," said Calvino.
He climbed to the top of stairs and opened the door
to the lobby. Or what had once been a lobby. The open
space had been converted into a series of small wooden
stalls with vendors selling an odd assortment of items:
carry-on luggage, back-packs, headless dummies in one-
piece swimming suits, dusty metal kitchen cupboards
stacked with tablecloths, linens, towels, swimming suits,
wood carvings, hot tubs, and kitchen appliances. It

seemed that everyone in the Chinese family had their own pet project, their sure-fire scheme to sell goods to the people who had once stayed at the hotel. Though the hot tubs and kitchen appliances catered to another market—*farangs* living in the general area. Since *farangs* couldn't own houses, the venture, like the hotel, appeared doomed. What struck Calvino as he walked past the stalls was the absence of customers. Not even one Australian-packbacker. Beyond the stalls, they found the front desk, with a tiny, ancient Chinese woman with black teeth, her silver hair tied in a bun on the back of her head, wearing green brocade silk pyjamas.

Calvino spoke into his mic. "It's clear. Bring Naylor up." Clear wasn't exactly the right word, he thought.

A moment later Naylor and Jess entered the lobby. The old woman looked up from a Chinese language newspaper and stared without blinking at the two *farangs*. Then she stared at Jess and asked him how much commission he was asking to bring the *farang* to the hotel. She frowned when he said he didn't want a commission and that Naylor had a business meeting with the owners.

"I am Wes Naylor and I have a meeting with Mr. Kitti." He had not followed Jess's explanation in Thai.

The old woman blinked for the first time as she stared at Naylor's huge gold chain and looked away at Jess, her eyes laughing the way the smug, the insane laugh, someone with the knowledge that she had them walking into a trap. *I know what these farangs want,* her eyes were saying. *But they are wasting their time.*

"I have an appointment with the owner of the hotel," he said slowly. "I am buying this hotel. Treat me well. I am about to become your new boss. So be nice to me or you'll be on rose pruning detail for the next six months. Is that clear, Private?"

Jess translated into Thai (minus the military allusion and the irony—neither of which translated well into Thai) as the old woman lazily picked up a telephone and started speaking in Chinese dialect to someone on the other end. A couple of minutes later a Thai in his late thirties appeared at the reception desk. He wore a white shirt open at the neck with a gold chain and amulets that rattled as he walked.

"I am Kitti," he said looking over the two *farangs* and one Thai, rocking back on his heels.

"And you have already met my aunt. I am afraid her English is not very good."

"I think she understands more than you think," said Naylor, introducing himself as Wes Naylor. He offered his hand to Kitti, who shook it. "I am Doc Nat's lawyer. Partner, whatever. I am here from LA to close the deal."

"Yes, I know who you are and why you are here." Kitti had one of those nervous laughs. But his eyes were dead like a fish in the market. He obviously did not take after his aunt. "My brothers and sisters are running a little late. Bangkok traffic. But of course I am glad that you are on time." Meaning by being on time they had arrived early.

"Please follow me." Kitti led them through the lobby area to a stairwell. A sign on the elevator read in English, Out of Service. It was an old hand-lettered yellowing paper sign, the edges curling up as the tape had turned brown with age. Neglect. The entire place reeked of a terrible, awful neglect like one of those German corpses someone found five years after some loner died in his Berlin apartment. The conference carpet smelled of mildew and a rat ran across the floor and between Naylor's parted feet. They entered a conference room.

"Please take a chair," said Kitti gesturing at the table.

"What kind of dog was that?" Naylor asked, pulling back an armless wooden chair and sitting down.

"An urban legend breed," said Calvino.

Jess stayed at the entrance, his right hand raised, palming the scanning device, keeping Kitti in sight at all times. Calvino watched him scanning the room. Through the earphone he heard Jess whisper. "Clear."

Kitti walked around to the head of the table, pulled out the chairman of the board's chair, one of those chairs with armrests done up in expensive leather that looks like a throne, and sat down. Papers were spread out neatly in front of his place. A few minutes later a couple of young *Isan yings* appeared with trays of water and coffee. They served the guests first and then Kitti, before silently disappearing from the room. At least two of the *Isan* employees on the payroll seemed to be found and accounted for, thought Calvino.

"You do have electricity?" asked Naylor, squinting at his coffee.

Kitti pushed his chair back and it made the sound of chalk going the wrong way over the blackboard—a high-pitched squeal. Then Kitti rose and walked over and turned on the lights. The carpet had been peeled back from under the table, leaving bare wooden planks. Several long overhead neon lights started to twitch to life.

"Is that better?" asked Khun Kitti with a nervous laugh.

"Yeah, I can see, if that's what you mean." Rats had gnawed on the curtain, leaving the ends in tatters. A line of scum like a bathtub ring from an offshore oil rigger stretched across the windows. Dust balls were stacked against cobwebs in the corners. An empty fish tank was in one corner; the glass of the tank was yellowish and inside were pieces of rock and what looked like dead weeds. It could have been a rat's nest. A line of red ants marched across the far end of the table. The conference room made Calvino homesick for his apartment.

On the wall directly behind where Kitti sat was a framed painting of an old Chinese man wearing a gray shirt with a Mao collar; his ears were huge and he wore scholarly gold-rimmed glasses. The skin was pocked and hung loose around his neck. Hundreds of roses dotted the foreground and background. The artist was much better at painting flowers than portraits.

"That's a painting of my late father," said Khun Kitti.

"Heart attack or cancer?" asked Naylor.

Kitti bit his lip and ignored the question, shifting his papers. "A highly unfortunate accident," Kitti whispered from the top of the table.

A small altar had been erected in front of the painting—a couple of Chinese blue and white vases holding fresh roses, a glass of water, a cup of tea, and cups filled with sand holding several burning incense sticks. The conference room smelled of stale incense; and the old man's eyes in the painting followed them around the room in an intrusive, suspicious fashion. Calvino had the feeling that members of the family didn't like coming into this room except for very important affairs where the authority and stature of the dead father was called for. The old man looked like a menace and he wondered if his accident might have been planned.

"And Jess and Vincent are my bodyguards. I have had several death threats. Seems someone didn't want me coming here. Didn't want me coming to close this deal. You wouldn't happen to have any idea who that might be?"

Kitti's laugh became a rattle-like noise in the back of his throat.

"What I just said doesn't strike me as being all that funny. What I said was someone doesn't want the deal to go through. And I thought you might share with us your thoughts on that subject. Since we have a little time until the others arrive, we might want to cut straight to the chase. Exactly who would want to kill me because Doc Nat and Doc Damrong and me are buying this fine hotel?"

"No, no. Nothing like that. I think you don't understand us. My brothers and sisters have some conflict. This is normal. What family doesn't have their differences? Is everyone in America happy with each other? I don't think so. Always there will be someone who says, 'I don't agree.' You persuade that person with reason. Our family doesn't use threats."

Calvino glanced over at Jess. Did Kitti believe this bullshit? Members of the family had already established a history of shooting and knifing each other. And they wouldn't threaten a *farang*? Does a bear shit in the woods?

"Then let's call it a big misunderstanding," said Naylor. "Obviously you have persuaded your family and they agree with you that this is a good deal. That will make things simple."

Naylor seemed to be handling himself okay. He tapped his fingers on the table as Kitti closed his eyes, collecting his thoughts.

"Simple and complex." Kitti grinned without laughing this time.

"Which is it? It can't be both."

"Gray is both white and black. Many things in the world have more than one color or texture or meaning."

Other members of the family slowly started to filter into the room, walking past Jess, who cupped his metal detector, checking each of them out as they filed inside. None of them had any concealed weapons, or weapons the metal detector would have picked up. Finally they all had taken chairs at the table. Five men and three *yings*. They came to the meeting dressed in casual clothes. The *yings* wore all their jewelry, wore a lot of make-up and had their hair done in those helmet-like *khunying* styles. Kitti rattled on to the guests in English and from the expression on the faces of the newly arrived it was clear they were not taking on board what he was saying, and that the absence of understanding didn't seem to bother any of them. They left Kitti to talk in English, letting him take on his powerful role of the family's English language spokesman. That was easy, since nothing said or promised in English mattered. English had performance value but it had no value beyond the show.

"Doc Nat showed me your power of attorney. It says that you can sign for all the shareholders. Your signature binds all of them. They can't even revoke the power of attorney without giving Dr. Nat two weeks' notice. So there shouldn't be any gray or black. Just pure white all the way." Wes Naylor looked across the table at what he assumed were all the other family shareholders.

"I can sign but before I sign I must consult with my brothers and sisters." Kitti then went around the table and introduced all of them. "Our family does things by consensus. We don't like pressure."

Wes Naylor immediately forgot which names went with which faces across the table as he tapped the table with the knuckle of his thumb. He looked totally pissed off. Jess leaned against the door and Calvino stood opposite him in the far corner of the conference room; each closely watched the members of the family.

"Ask them if they want this." Naylor pulled an envelope out of his briefcase and opened it. Inside was a check. He laid it on the table, turned it around and slid it down the table in front of the family. "One and a half million dollars. That was your price for the hotel. Let's sign the contract."

"What about our employees?" asked one of the brothers in halting English.

"Except for the old lady at reception, and the two tea *yings*, I didn't see any employees," said Naylor.

"We have seventy-three employees on the payroll," said the brother with a small moustache. He looked like a bad carbon copy of the old man in the painting. "You must guarantee them a job for five years."

"That's not part of the deal," said Naylor, his eyes narrowed to slits.

"And my sister and her family live on the fourth floor in three rooms. We want them to have the right to live there for the next ten years."

Naylor sat down, the check on the table, shook his head, which he cradled in his hands, elbows resting on the table.

"Does anyone else have a request?" asked Naylor. "Please raise your hand. I am taking notes. Say, a pension plan for the receptionist?"

No one understood Naylor's attempt at irony.

"My younger brother Viravat wants a five year extension on the maintenance contract between the hotel and his company."

"Maintenance of what?" asked Naylor.

"The grounds, the hotel, and the elevator."

"Keeping them in the their current five-star condition. Look, the purpose of this meeting was for Kitti to sign the contract. And for me to deliver the check and to witness your signatures on the agreement. Not to renegotiate the deal. Doc Nat and his brother Damrong have already signed. Look. Those are their signatures. I have the money.

Now you are telling me you want to rewrite the deal?" Naylor sat back in the chair, his face flushed red with anger. "I can't fucking believe it."

"We want you to be flexible. To understand us."

"This place is a third-world slum. The elevators don't work. The lobby is filled with hawkers. You have ten guests for one-hundred and fifty rooms. And now you want us to make concessions. Now. At the closing. We should be knocking a million off the purchase price."

"My brothers and sisters have raised very minor changes, Mr. Naylor," said Kitti. "You have a power of attorney. You can just write down a few words and amend the contract. Then everything will be fine. We don't want to make problems. Our father built this hotel. He loved roses. He loved gardens. We must do nothing to tarnish father's memory. You have to understand the decision to sell is hard for us. Our father spent his whole life building this hotel for his family."

All the time that Kitti was talking, the brother who chain-smoked was cracking his knuckles one by one, then bending his fingers all the way back so that the nails touched the wrist.

"Exactly what do you and your brothers and sisters want?" asked Naylor.

"We were thinking a joint venture might suit every-one much better."

"A joint venture?" asked Naylor, his jaw clenched as he pushed the check back into his briefcase. The knuckle cruncher had pushed all of his fingers back so they touched his wrist.

"A fifty-one percent, forty-nine percent joint venture. Of course, we will adjust the purchase price. Only one million two."

"And you keep fifty-one percent of the hotel?"

The nervous laugh accompanied the nodding of Kitti's head. In an oddball way, Kitti, like his brother with the moustache, bore a striking likeness to the dead father: same big ears and bad skin. "Yes, of course." Roses off the same dead branch.

"Over my dead body," said Naylor. He rolled up his sleeves, leaned over the table as if he were about to stick a needle in his arm, and showed the family his Chinese triad tattoos. They stared at the blue dragons, and from the way one of the sisters was moving her lips, she appeared to be reading the Chinese tattooed scroll. "You know what these mean?"

No one said anything.

"They mean I am connected with the Chinese Mafia. My Chinese family is much bigger and meaner than all of you."

Kitti, the grin never leaving his face, translated as Naylor spoke. The other family members sat stone-faced staring at the tattoos. Then they stared at Naylor. One yawned and rubbed his eyes. Another lit a cigarette. One peeled an orange and sucked on a slice, showing long, yellow ratlike teeth, spitting the seeds on the floor. Another took hard candy from a large ornate bowl in the center of the table, unwrapped it, and popped it into his mouth. Soon the entire family was eating, smoking, yawning, and talking. Calvino could imagine them watching a public execution in a football stadium with fifty thousand other people. Bullshitting, eating, watery eyes, detached, as if the sound of a rifle recoiling was no different from a two-stroke motorcycle being started. So much for Naylor's secret weapon, his ultimate threat. He had no idea of such people.

"I don't think you are taking this seriously," shouted Naylor.

He was getting angry and one thing that was taboo in Thailand was showing anger or, even worse, forcing people into a corner and confronting them with gangster tattoos. Threatening them with Chinese dragon tattoos. This was not a good start and could not have a good ending.

"It is nearly lunch time. We have arranged lunch for you and your friends," said Kitti. A face-saving suggestion, and a way to defuse the tense situation. A wise move, thought Calvino. Before the family started choosing lots to see who would reach across the table and put a knife in Naylor's neck.

"They aren't my friends. And I am eating my lunch back at the Brandy where sometime in the last six months someone in the kitchen attempted to wash the spoons and plates."

"Have a good lunch," said Kitti.

If irony was ever a weapon, the entire family had been dipped in Kevlar.

Jess and Calvino exchanged glances. This was the first they had heard of Naylor's lunch plans. Naylor gave almost no resistance to the lunch break idea. It was already in his head to get back and rub more cream onto Jep's ass. A combination of greed and the desire to rub the mosquito bites on a teenage *ying*'s ass conspired to bring a halt to the meeting without any resolution on the contract. As the family began leaving the conference room as quietly and secretly as they had arrived, Calvino's mobile phone rang. McPhail was on the other line.

"Man, this is some fucked up woman you've lined me up to meet, Calvino."

"What's the problem? She didn't show?"

"No, she showed all right. But she ain't making the phone call to LA."

"Why?"

"She wants you at the Emporium, Big Daddy, when she phones this guy Gabe. Apparently she's afraid of him big time. I said I would break his jaw in five places. But no way, Jose. She says either Vincent Calvino gets his ass down to the Emporium or she's going off to Hong Kong tomorrow morning and she doesn't give a flying fuck if she ever talks with that asshole again. Those are her exact words."

"I've got a problem here."

"Man, you've got a problem right here where I am standing, too. It's up to you. What do you want me to do? Cut her loose or tell her that you are on the way?"

Calvino paused, looking over at Jess, who caught his eye. "Tell her that I will be there in fifteen minutes. If she leaves the building, follow her. Better yet find a way to keep her in the building."

"Don't worry, I will pin her down to the floor. Sit on her. She's right here. You want to talk to her?"

"What's the point?" asked Calvino. "You might try and persuade her."

"Fifteen, twenty minutes. Stay on the second floor. Where I told you to meet her and wait for me."

Kitti stood up from his chair.

"I propose we start again at 2:00 p.m.," he said.

Naylor sneered. "Let me think about that." He thought for a moment. "Yeah, I can live with two."

NINE

NAYLOR'S MOOD TURNED vile and nasty. "I pay for sex in Thailand because free sex is too fucking expensive in America." He pushed his floppy Truman Capote hat forward, maximum attitude position, just over his eyebrows as he stood in front of the hotel, his bare, tattooed arms raised palms up like a country preacher. His eyes surveyed the gnarled rose bushes, the chickens, the goat, the sleeping dogs, the peasant burning garbage at the end of the driveway. "But the hotels in America are better," he said. The Grand Rose Hotel had been his dream; his chance to set up a business that dovetailed with the Cause, his own private escape penthouse on top, a *pied-a-terre*, the ultimate *hong* to impress *yings*. As he surveyed the grounds, Naylor couldn't help but wonder who in their right mind among the Cause-members would come for a Monster Fuck in a hotel occupied by the Adams family. They had patents pending on greed, stupidity, sloth, and corruption.

"They want a joint venture? Are they out of their fucking minds?" He turned away from the garden. "Did you see that guy do that bending thing with his fingers? The whole family is weird."

Jess held the rear door open. Calvino was already inside the car. He switched on the engine and checked his rear view mirror. He rolled down his window and gestured at Naylor to get in.

"I suspect they will want to keep the roses," said Calvino. "Let's go." Not doing due diligence on a deal ran the same level of risk as not doing due diligence on a *ying* only to find out down the road that what she had promised bore no relationship to what she was prepared or able to deliver. Blinded by the beauty of the rose, the buyer had forgotten about the hidden treasure of thorns ready to draw blood.

Naylor kicked the toe of his boot in the dirt, sending up a small cloud of red dust. He waved his fist at the hotel, huffed and muttered, and then climbed into the back of the car. Jess shut Naylor's door, walked around to the opposite side and got in. Chickens flew in all directions as Calvino gunned the engine, peeling out of the Grand Rose Hotel grounds. Calvino's car looked like it belonged to the hotel; it fit into the overall ambience of broken objects, things gone to ruin, the rewards of neglect and accident. Naylor stuck his arm out the window and gave everyone in sight the finger, only no one in particular noticed. None of this acting up had improved Naylor's mood; if anything he was more agitated, slamming his hand against the seat. Calvino said nothing as he felt the muffled blow. After all, Naylor's Hollywood show of anger was more for Jess and him than for the family of owners who were nowhere to be seen.

"I don't think you gained anything by showing your tattoos," said Jess. "Or giving the street vendors the finger."

"Fuck them. I felt like a monkey in a bag hung on a shit-house door."

Calvino caught Naylor's flash of anger in the rear view mirror. Where the hell did he get that expression?

"Monkey in a bag? Or was it money in a bag? How's that feel, Wes?"

"It's monkey in a bag. Monkey is money with a "k" jammed in the middle. I had this *ying* last year. Fon was her name. You know, 'Rain' in Thai. She gave the best blow jobs in the entire fucking world. Rain would just keep at it. Three, four times in one day she would go down. I mean again and again. She was relentless in her desire to go down. Fon had a pet monkey she called 'Lucky Luke'—a guy had given it to her along with the usual gold and fridge—and that goddamn monkey went everywhere with her. It thought the world of her, Luke was crazy about her. And she loved the monkey like it was her kid. It put me off with Lucky Luke watching her going down on me. Her moaning and Lucky Luke looking like he had some strange rain forest disease. She said it was just an ear infection. But I couldn't keep an erection. So I made her put the monkey in the bag she used to cart it around in. But Lucky Luke wasn't stupid. He knew how to get out of the bag. There I would be with my pants around my ankles with Rain falling down and that monkey would jump on her shoulder and fucking stare. Those big monkey eyes, and Lucky Luke's upper lip riding up slowly and showing razor sharp teeth. Fon couldn't understand why I made such a big deal about her goddamn monkey. I told her Lucky Luke was jealous and one day he was going to take a run at me. I finally figured out that after putting Lucky Luke inside the cloth bag, if I pulled the string tight at the top of the bag and hung it on the back of the bathroom door, he couldn't get out. Then I could get down to concentrating on business with Fon. All the time, I could hear Lucky Luke struggling inside the bag on the shithouse door. This dull thump, thump against the wooden door. Lucky

Luke screaming in total monkey rage. There I was in the bedroom with Fon on her knees and her goddamn monkey banging the bathroom door, trying to find a way out of the bag, knowing it was stuck in the dark, shut out, cut off from the world, and for the life of that monkey Luke had absolutely no fucking idea why he had been tied into a bag and suspended in mid-air on the back of a door. Afterwards Rain would say, 'Lucky Luke *pai nai?*' Where did Lucky Luke go? This was one of those *ying* questions that ring false. She knew full well that Lucky Luke was in the bag hanging on the door. She pretended not to know. That way she didn't have to take any responsibility. Today, I understand exactly how that poor bastard monkey felt. Kitti was doing the same thing as Fon. He was pretending not to know how I got in the bag. And he just let me bang my fucking head on his shithouse door while he and his crazy family were jerking off."

Halfway through the telling of his Lucky Luke story, Naylor had started to unwind, grow calm, his voice smoothed out with the rough, hard edges sanded down by the memory of all those blow jobs. Like a lot of angry people without someone to fuel the fires of rage, and left alone to think about what had happened, he put the experience in the context of what he knew. Getting a blow job with a monkey kicking up a storm in a bag. Naylor looked contemplative as he stared out the car window. Thinking about Kitti, thinking about Lucky Luke, and remembering Rain on her knees, eyes looking up, making those sucking noises as her monkey screamed bloody murder from the bathroom.

"She left you for the monkey," said Calvino. He was thinking: what goes around comes around. He liked the idea of Naylor being the monkey in the bag. There was some justice in the world after all.

Naylor nodded his head. "I hate to admit it but she did. I trust Rain and Luke are happy in some upcountry jungle hovel. Enough of monkey business, tell me again," he said. "Why are we stopping at this shopping mall? After meeting these assholes, you want to go shopping? Dr. Nat's four grand is burning a hole in your pocket, right?"

Before they had got into the car, Calvino had laid the groundwork for the diversion, casually saying he had to meet someone for a few minutes at the Emporium. As they left the conference room, Naylor was still too upset with the hotel owners and had not focused on Calvino's request and certainly had been in no state to respond to this request. It took a monkey story for him to remember Calvino had been leading up to something.

"I have a personal problem I need to fix. It will take ten minutes and then I buy lunch," said Calvino. After looking over the family, the threat to Naylor had diminished in Calvino's eyes. Not that he was easing off—someone had taken a shot at them on the expressway—but right up close none of them seem capable to doing much of anything but argue over their share of the family pie.

"Yeah? I thought you were working for me. Now you have a problem and I am supposed to approve your plan to ruin my lunch with Jep."

"Let's say I've got a monkey on my back," said Calvino.

"We pass the Emporium on the way to the hotel," said Jess.

Out of the blue, back-up was coming from LAPD; something that Calvino had not expected. Maybe Jess had tired of babysitting this asset, with Naylor's attitude, the tattoos, his murky business connections, his degrading *ying* stories, so any excuse to shove back had to make Jess feel as good as landing a foot into the jaw of a kick-boxing opponent. "I need to buy a new battery." He was playing with the device that picked up transmitting devices.

"Ten minutes, Wes," said Calvino.

Ten minutes should be more than enough time, thought Calvino. But nothing in Bangkok ever happened in ten minutes. It was a way of speaking, a time span that meant a short-time, not that other short-time where a *ying* was selling her sabai time. Calvino had planned out what he was going to do—he would first find McPhail and Noi, and even before finding them, he would have Gabe on his mobile phone ready to talk to Noi. He planned it out in his head—he'd walk straight up to Noi, and say. "How's it going Noi? Glad to see you. Gabe's on the phone from LA. Just tell him hello. That's it. No other commitment." Then he would put the phone to her ear. She'd say a few meaningless words and listen to him plead to come back, she'd refuse and then it would be over. Some *yings* were mistresses of the quick brush off.

Naylor was about to say something when Jess cut him off. "And you can buy something nice for Jep at one of the shops."

Calvino smiled to himself, exchanged a glance with Jess in the rear view mirror. "You don't want to go back to the room with nothing in your hands and only tattoos on your forearms," said Calvino.

"Do I have any choice?" asked Naylor as Calvino pulled into the underground parking lot of the Emporium.

Choice and purpose were the two elements missing from the known universe that no scientist would ever locate. They were not permanently lost, they had never existed, thought Calvino.

He followed the down ramp into the underground parking lot, slowing to take the ticket from the uniformed security guard. No place to park, he turned right, taking the ramp down to B2, pulling into a parking spot within sight of the entrance for the elevators. The B2 parking lot level was half-full. The recession had cut the power on their aircraft, turning most of them into glider pilots. Naylor was out of the car last. He slammed the door hard. "I could use a drink. You think that is going to be a problem here?"

"I am buying," said Calvino.

"Goddamn right you are buying," said Naylor.

Jess was out the other side of the car; he closed the door and he leaned against the side of the Honda. "I'll stay with the car. Pick me up a new battery, will you?"

"Forget it," said Naylor. "This Italian is buying both of us a beer."

Jess smiled. "I don't drink on duty."

"Then I'll drink your fucking beer if that makes you feel any better."

"It won't take long," said Calvino. "Come along, Jess. No one's going to bother the car."

Jess tapped his fingers on the roof of the Honda, then broke into a smile. The car was a write-off, a wreck. Who would bother with such a car? "Okay."

They crossed the parking lot; Jess taking point, then Naylor with Calvino following behind. Jess pushed open the glass door, looking around before waving Naylor to move forward.

"You buy the Lucky Luke story?" Jess asked through the mic. He was scanning the area for transmitting devices. There was always the possibility someone was intercepting their radio transmissions.

"Monkeys are jealous," replied Calvino, looking over the parking lot. "And they are curious. And on the whole much better companions than someone like Naylor. The girl made the right choice."

193

Jess watched as Naylor came through the door. "I am feeling better already," Jess whispered into the mic.

Naylor breathed deeply, waiting for Calvino to catch up. He was smiling. The recovery had been rapid. He had already shaken off the meeting with Kitti and his nutty and dangerous brothers and sisters. For a moment he had stopped wishing that he had never met Dr. Nat and invested in a hotel venture in Thailand. Fon had reminded him of why he had come in the first place—to buy *hongs* and to hunt *yings*.

They rode the elevator to the second floor. As the door opened, Calvino dialed the country code and LA city code and Gabe's home number. All he had to do was press the 'yes' button and the call would connect. As they walked out of the elevator, a *farang* in a cowboy hat, late twenties, muscle shirt and no gut, swung at Naylor, landing the punch smack on the side of his jaw, sending him reeling against the wall. Naylor hit the wall, looking like a stunned prize-fighter. Calvino moved in front of Naylor, waiting for the *farang* to come in. He didn't have to wait long. Jess reacted with a kicking-box maneuver, coming off the floor, his right leg hitting the cowboy as he moved in to hit Naylor again. The *farang* absorbed the blow, which caught him in the chest. He threw a series of punches at Jess, who easily ducked away from the blows, waiting for the precise moment when the *farang* was off balance, and then Jess nailed him three, four times on the neck and head with his fists, and, spinning him around, brought his foot up hard under the *farang*'s jaw. The sound of the jaw cracking echoed off the walls and windows of the lobby near the elevator. The *farang* hit the marble floor and he wasn't moving. Unconscious.

Calvino knelt down in front of Naylor. "You all right?"

A crowd of shoppers gathered around.

"Who was that sonofabitch?" asked Naylor, gasping to catch his breath.

"He doesn't look Chinese to me," said Calvino.

"What I am saying he's not part of Kitti's family. These people don't hire *farangs* to whack *farangs*."

"I had a gut feeling that coming here was a mistake," said Naylor.

Jess helped Naylor to his feet. "Here's your hat."

"Let's get out of here," said Calvino. The crowd swelled as the *farang* started to move his head on the floor.

"I've never seen anyone hit someone so fast and so hard," Naylor said as he took the hat. "Where'd you learn that fancy shit?"

Jess had won the kick-boxing championship of LA county at age fourteen. He had learned the art by the time he was twelve. His dad had built shelves to proudly display all of Jess's trophies. But none of this mattered at that moment.

"You don't know this guy?" asked Jess, deflecting the "fancy shit" comment.

"Never seen him before. He must have confused me with someone else."

"He went straight for you," said Calvino. "It didn't look much like a mistake."

Naylor fingered his hat, looking for damage, smoothing it out and then carefully putting it on, he smiled, using his hand to work his jaw from side to side. He stepped forward and kicked the *farang* in the groin. A huff sound like air going out of a tire came out of the man's mouth. When it looked like Naylor might have one more shot, Calvino took his arm and pulled him back.

"Enough already." The *farang* was coiled up on the polished marble floor in front of the ATM machine. He looked like he had passed out or was sleeping.

"The bastard tried to mug me," said Naylor. "Just one more little kick."

This time Jess came alongside with Calvino and together they ushered him away from the unconscious *farang*. Calvino knew this was not a stalker, a mugger, a crazy, no, this was a deliberate planned assault and, like the truck on the expressway, the intent was to intimidate, throw them off-balance, lead them to make conclusions that others wanted them to make.

Calvino waited until they were clearing away until he said anything to Jess. "You're good."

"I don't think we should be here, Vincent. Someone doesn't come swinging at Naylor without a reason. You know how that *farang* knew we would be here now?" Jess held out a small device that looked like a remote control. "He was picking up the GHz from this." He held out his own anti-transmitting device. "They were tracking us the whole time."

"The road from Damascus to Tel Aviv also goes from Tel Aviv to Damascus," said Calvino.

"Are you guys protecting me or holding a committee meeting?" asked Naylor.

They walked past the imported designer shops: tall walls of glass and inside the robes and gowns for the priestesses of fashion. As they entered the fashion hall, McPhail spotted them and shouted Calvino's name. "Vinee, over here, man."

"That's my guy. We'll be out of here in a minute."

McPhail stood next to a *ying* who was dressed to kill: black tight-fitting slacks, high heels and a halter top, bare smooth shoulders showing. She looked like an entertainer backstage, distracted, smoking a cigarette, looking at her watch. Long red fingernails set off her hands. She looked like she could be a singer or a model with her fresh, shiny black long hair touching half way down her back. In the advertising business such *yings* were called "Pretties," the good-looking *yings* who were hired for car shows, conferences, conventions. Pretties attracted crowds, and crowds wanted to be around beautiful *yings* and the things Pretties were selling. Calvino recognized Noi from Gabe Holerstone's photo. Calvino hit the dial button as he approached. The phone was ringing and Gabe picked up the phone on the third ring, answering with a slow, husky voice dulled by sleep.

"It's one in the fucking morning, who are you, asshole?"

"Vincent Calvino. I have Noi here and she wants to talk to you."

"Noi? Where did you say you are?" He sounded like he was drugged.

"In Bangkok."

"I know in Bangkok, but where?"

"I am at a shopping mall," said Calvino.

"So talk to her. That was our deal. Find the girl, put her on the phone. That was the assignment. Now the case is closed."

Calvino held out the phone and she stared at it and then at Calvino, slowly sucking in a long hit from her cigarette, one arm folded around her waist, her elbow resting on her folded forearm. Smoke coiled out of each nostril like she was the Queen in *Alice in Wonderland*.

"It's Gabe, he's in LA and he wants to talk to you."

"What's he want from me? I don't work for Gabe anymore." A bored look crossed Noi's face like a late afternoon shadow. As if a group of fans had hassled her an autograph. Her voice broke slightly as she uttered the word "me"; the amount of gravity attached to that simple two letter word was enough to pluck the moon from the night sky. She said it in a way that seemed to indicate there was no room for anyone else in the world but her.

"Ask him yourself." He stood beside her, his arm outstretched but she made no effort to reach for the phone.

"See what I mean," said McPhail.

"This is one awkward fucking *ying.*"

Calvino put the phone to his ear. "She wants to know what you want from her?"

"I want to talk to her."

Calvino stared directly at her. "He says that he wants to talk to you."

"If the *ying* doesn't want to talk, she doesn't want to talk," said Naylor.

"Who is this asshole?" asked McPhail.

"His fucking boss. What fucking rock do you live under?"

The situation was becoming complicated beyond Calvino's wildest expectations. McPhail and Naylor had taken an instant dislike to one another. Calvino swiftly moved between Noi and McPhail as if he were back in New York on a Sunday afternoon and happened upon a pick-up baseball game and people were choosing sides.

"Your friend is right," said Noi. "I don't have to talk to anyone."

Gabe screamed in Calvino's ear, "Put that goddamn Vine Street bitch on the phone."

"That approach isn't working, Gabe. Maybe you ought to come up with a reason to talk to her," said Calvino. "What's the message?"

"I want her to come back to LA. I'll give her a raise. Tell her that."

Calvino watched Noi light another cigarette from the one she was just finishing. A flicker of recognition appeared to pass between Noi and Naylor. It was also the look of two pros sizing each other up. Calvino's Law: The line between who a *ying* knew and who she wanted to know was as blurred as a cross from a double-cross in back of a dark alley. "He wants you back in LA and you get a raise."

She thought about this. "How much of a raise?"

Gabe heard her response and shouted in the phone at Calvino. "Two-hundred and fifty a week."

"Two fifty a week," repeated Calvino.

Calvino edged in with the phone until a moment later it was against her ear and she was talking to Gabe. McPhail rolled his eyes. "Jesus Christ, she's entering into collective bargaining on your dime. Can you believe it?"

"Three hundred," said Noi. "Otherwise I am on the plane to Hong Kong. I can make more than three hundred a day in Hong Kong."

"You heard that?" asked Calvino.

Of course he had heard it. "Noi, okay, just come back to LA, honey."

Calvino motioned for her to hand back his mobile phone. She pretended to ignore him. "There was nothing in my deal with Gabe for you to carry on a long distance salary negotiation. Phone him back collect."

"I'm almost finished," she said.

"Good bye, Gabe," said McPhail, taking a swipe at the phone, but he missed as Noi stepped to one side.

"I don't like the way you treated me." She spoke into the phone.

McPhail rolled his eyes. "How are you going to make that kind of money in Bangkok?"

"It's finished. We can go now," said Calvino. "Let's get back to the car."

Naylor was watching *yings* in short skirts ride the escalator.

"You were buying us a beer," said Naylor, looking away from the two *yings* riding the escalator. "Forget the beer, let's go back to the Brandy."

Meaning that he wanted to check on Jep. He was still on compassion alert, and telling himself that technically he hadn't really breached the YINGS, as he had administered care. There had been no sex.

This suited Calvino fine and he nodded, turned to Noi, gesturing for his phone, as a loud boom echoed through the second floor. An explosion that shattered glass. Calvino immediately pushed Naylor down. The force of the blast sucked a massive volume of dust and debris through the main shaft of the atrium. The explosion knocked out the electrical supply and the emergency lights came on, flickered, and then cut out as well. The air was dirty and the light like near dusk; darkness had descended inside the mall.

"What the fuck was that?" asked Naylor.

"That was no fucking electrical transformer exploding," said Calvino. "That was a bomb."

"Let's get Naylor out of here. Now," said Jess, pulling Naylor by the arm.

Calvino reached to take his phone from Noi. "I am not finished talking to him."

"Noi, time to go. Give me the phone. Don't make a problem," said Calvino. He grabbed at the phone but missed.

McPhail laughed. "You're right, that was no transformer. Someone has set off the heavy shit. Look at the shoppers run like rabbits. Where the fuck do they think they are going?" He shook his head, pulled out his pack of cigarettes and offered one to Noi. "Anything else you need, just give me a call. If you can get your phone back." With a quick flick of his wrist, McPhail snatched the phone from Noi's hand and tossed it to Calvino. "See you around."

As Calvino's mobile phone spun in the air, Jess was already in a half run holding onto Naylor's arm, directing him back to the emergency stairs next to the elevators. The elevators had already been shut down. As Calvino caught up they ran into a wall of customers and staff pushing and shoving to get down the stairs. Security guards tried to maintain order with the crowd; *yings* were crying and screaming, clutching children, and shop clerks were pushing against each other to get to the stairs. A strong herd mentality pushed the shoppers into a crowd— it was difficult to bring any order or provide direction to the people. They ignored orders from a whistle-blowing twenty-year-old security guard. The guard waved his hands, trying to control the flow of people, and they ran around him. The smell of Bakelite, dust, of stuff burning—plastic, upholstery, electrical wiring—filled the air in the staircase. People choked on the debris they inhaled; coughing, they staggered forward, their eyes and throats burning from the smoke.

"There has been an explosion," said a voice over a loudspeaker system. The disembodied voice echoed up and down the five floors of the shopping mall.

"The second bomb this week," said Calvino. He had followed the recent history of bombings: an explosion at Democracy Monument, another inside a police station, someone had bombed a bar. No one knew exactly what combination of dark forces were setting off the bombs, how they were selecting their targets, their demands, or what concession would be required to stop the terror. The motive for the attack remained murky; any number of candidates might have had reason to plant a bomb to settle a power struggle. Calvino took some comfort from this history of bombings as strong evidence that the blast was unrelated to Wes Naylor and his business activities in Thailand.

"Nothing personal," Calvino said to Naylor. "We just happened to be in the wrong place at the wrong time."

"What about the detector Jess found on the guy at the elevator?"

Jess had picked up the conversation off Calvino's mic. "Naylor's right, Vinee. That guy could have been one of the bombers."

"Let's get out of here," said Calvino.

The crush of frightened people all pushing and shoving each other down the same narrow escape route made it nearly impossible to move. It seemed as if most of the fashion show audience had headed for the same exit. Timing was everything. And now was the time to shift direction, find a different way back to the parking lot, thought Calvino. Jess wanted to believe Calvino's assessment of the situation. Yet there was a Calvino's law that said there were no coincidences when two unrelated events occurred at the same time. In Thailand there was always, underneath the surface, a thin coil connecting the events, an aggressive hard-wired connection that only the people directly involved understood. Reach back far enough or dig deep enough and original hatreds, jealousies, rivalries were embedded in the original DOS system of Thai government and society and all the modern updates had done nothing but patch the old flaws, and the old flaws were what made the system crash.

It was Jess who had a bad feeling. Someone had set off the bomb to do a job. But had they finished what they set out to do?

"I don't think we should take any chances," said Jess. "We need to get Naylor out of this crowd."

"I know a short-cut," said Calvino.

Naylor followed him, "Then let's take the short-cut. I hate fucking crowds. Get me out of here."

Calvino ran ahead, taking two steps at a time climbing up the stalled escalator.

"Christ, we want to go down, not up," said Naylor following, choking on the dust. "Jesus, I can hardly breathe."

"You want to keep breathing? Then get your ass going now," said Calvino. Like the universe, Naylor's middle-aged body was expanding, and if he didn't keep moving he would die.

Jess followed right behind Naylor. He wasn't so sure that going away from the crowd was the right thing. Sometimes it was easier to protect an asset in a crowd than in an empty place that one did not know. Calvino had already committed them and he had no other plan.

By the time they reached the fifth floor, the fast food area was deserted—no shoppers, no clerks, no lighting except a dim shaft of dusty light from the atrium. The lights had likely been cut, thought Calvino. The distant sound of people screaming, crying, and yelling filtered up the atrium. Sounds of people running on the escalator, their feet hitting the cleated metal steps. Calvino stopped, knelt down, and Jess and Naylor knelt down, beside him. Naylor started to say something and Calvino put his hand over the big man's mouth, and with his other hand, he pressed his index finger against his lips. Slowly he took his hand away from Naylor's mouth, reached in under his sport's jacket and pulled out his .38 police special. They took refuge in Burger King, moving quickly, passing through tables, and ducking behind the counter. Naylor reached up and grabbed a hamburger out of the bin, opened the wrapper and started to eat. "I guess it would be too much to ask for a beer," he whispered to Calvino.

"Yeah, it would," replied Calvino. They stayed together, securing a position with the best view of the two escalators.

A couple of moments later, the sound of male voices came from the direction of Dairy Queen. Three men spoke Thai using short, clipped sentences. They stood near the escalator that led to the sixth floor and cinemas. One of them was making a command decision how to sweep the floor and who should go where next. The three men fanned out with automatic weapons. CAR-15s. The short version of the M-16 assault rifle, easy to sweep inside confined spaces, the barrels didn't get snagged on weeds, branches, or on the electrical cords hooked to Coke and coffee dispensing machines.

Jess looked around the corner of the counter, leaned back and showed Calvino and Naylor three fingers. Naylor kept chewing the burger. They had moved into the kitchen. Then Jess crooked his fingers into the shape of a weapon; he moved his hands up and down his chest, signaling they were wearing bullet-proof vests. They were armed, protected, and fanned out from the escalator. One went left towards the elevators and restrooms, another member of the team swept through the tables in front of Burger King, while the third guy moved quickly to the right and down towards the Food Hall. Calvino was pretty sure that the hit squad must have followed them from the second level, taking the escalator, knowing they had gone exactly where they wanted them.

"*Farang*, come out," yelled one of the men in English. "We are Security. We take you down to safety." Broken English, broken promises.

Sure they will, thought Calvino.

Calvino crouched low, leaning forward, and watched as one of the men knocked over one of the tables and

stood only a couple feet away from Naylor. The next
move belonged to Calvino. For the moment, they had
the element of surprise on their side. The question was
how to use surprise and to keep alive.

Jess was thinking something along the same lines, only
his was tailored by his LAPD training. *Awareness. Balance.
Self-control. Skill. Timing.* The words went through Jess's
mind like a mantra. They were the core of his training on
the force. *Apply them and you live, forget them and you die.
They must become part of you. The way you think and feel. You
must dream them. You must live them every moment of every
day.* His instructor at the Academy said the elements were
New Age nonsense. Jess had told the instructor they had
come from an ancient age.

Mindfulness is what Buddhism teaches.

Naylor had stopped chewing and he wasn't showing
his Chinese Triad tattoos now. He curled up into a ball,
holding onto his fifteen-baht gold chain.

"You will not be harmed," said the same Thai voice.

Forget just one element, leave it out of your consciousness, and discover how unforgiving life can be. Being
forgetful of one's training was not forgiven, thought Jess.
The guy coming in their direction was only a couple of
feet away, standing erect, confident, holding his weapon
against his side, slowly observing an arc of 180 degrees
as he walked ahead. He was walking into the kitchen.
Calvino reached over and grabbed a coffee mug and
dipped it into the vat of oil. Two wire baskets holding raw
French fries were balanced above the oil. He waited until
the member of the squad was next to him. He stopped,
turned, and appeared to leave. Jess followed Calvino's
eyes and he nodded. Calvino crawled forward. Slowly
he edged himself around the end of the counter, holding his breath, watching the Thai. The man seemed to

have had second thoughts and doubled back through the kitchen and walked straight at Calvino without seeing him. The Thai male wore khaki trousers and a bulky vest under his brown shirt. Then he turned to his left, and Calvino threw the hot oil in the man's face. The man instinctively dropped his weapon, his hands covering his face. Off balance, he fell to his knees. Calvino had never seen anyone move as fast as Jess as he crawled out the other side of the counter with a kitchen knife, which he plunged deep in the fallen guy's throat. He pinned the guy down with his knees and waited until he was dead. Five, six seconds. Except in the movies, no one ever dies in an instant. Five seconds is enough time to kill another man. Jess never gave him that chance. He rolled off the inert body and behind a set of cupboards. Jess grabbed the dead man's CAR-15 from the floor.

The other two members of the team came running, firing their automatic weapons as they ran. Spraying rounds into the fast food restaurants. Muzzle flashes streaked across the fifth floor. This was undisciplined, undirected fire, showering broken glass and plastic everywhere. The huge plastic ice cream cone in front of the Dairy Queen exploded as it took several direct hits. Pieces of the overhead plastic signs rained down on top of Jess and Calvino. As they looked around, they discovered that Naylor had vanished. There was no time to look for him.

Calvino had dipped the coffee mug back into the oil and was waiting behind the counter. He saw the second Thai emerge, his black high-top boots catching a glimmer of light. He was shooting random bursts. More muzzle flash as glass exploded from the cinema ads above the elevator. Calvino crawled to his left side, slowly set the mug on the floor, rolled underneath the counter, edged out the other side, and, lying on his back, squeezed off three rounds. Two of the shots from the .38 hit the second member of the squad just above his right ear; the impact of the bullets sent him crashing over a table and chairs. He was dead before he hit the floor.

One to go, thought Calvino.

Jess had crawled out in time to see the last member of the team running to the other end where all the electronics, washing machines, fridges and TVs were sold. Calvino took the CAR-15 off the dead man he had shot and shouldered his .38. Jess fired several rounds at the fleeing man. None of the rounds connected.

"Naylor, he's coming in your direction," said Jess, who was now on his feet, running down the outer perimeter, past the automotive, the sheets, blankets, and towels near the elevator. Squeezing off rounds as he ran, Calvino ran the opposite side past all the glassware and expensive crystal. As they converged at the back, they had the third man trapped.

"How many more men came with you?" Jess said in Thai. Another member of the team rose into sight, his hands raised over his head. He was a *farang*. A sheepish grin on his face as he stepped forward. The question was whether he was the surviving member or whether there were others.

"Hey man, don't fucking shoot. I am American. Who were those guys? Jesus, first a blast and now those guys. Hey, what's going on?"

"How many others, asshole?" asked Calvino, who squatted low, looking around for other members of the commando team. But the floor was silent. He looked back at the *farang*.

This looked like the same guy who had hit Naylor in the face as they had walked out of the elevator. But in the low light it was difficult to tell. This *farang* was dressed in commando gear, which made it difficult to play the innocent tourist role.

"Put your hands against the back of your head," said Jess. "Do it now." He had the CAR-15 pointed at him. The blond-haired man stepped forward, his hip touching the metal railing that wrapped around the side of the atrium.

"Am I under arrest or something?"

"Don't move. Just stand very very still and everything will be okay."

Calvino had come around the opposite side past the kitchen appliances and mobile phones. The *farang*'s back was turned in his direction.

"Did you guys hear that bomb? Man, that was something."

"How did you know that it was a bomb?" asked Jess.

Calvino was close enough to see the *farang* was palming a small hand-gun at the base of his skull. Another two steps was all that separated him from the *farang*. As he had moved in closer, he was sure he was the same guy that Naylor had kicked in the balls. He was sorry now that he hadn't let Naylor kick him a couple of more times. Now he pressed the barrell of the CAR-15 in the *farang*'s back. "Drop it."

"You seen Naylor?" asked Jess.

"He's probably eating chicken at KFC," said Calvino.

The brief conversation was a distraction. A split second in which the *farang* had to make a decision. On one side was Calvino with a CAR-15 and on the other Jess, holding the same kind of weapon on him. He knew the other two members of the team were down. Was he running or was he looking for Naylor, thought Calvino. But where was Naylor? The question hung unanswered in the air.

The *farang* had committed himself to a course of action, and once the momentum of action started, one's fate was sealed. It didn't matter that this was absolutely the wrong course of action, much like his assault at the elevators, which had backfired. The man had learned nothing. At the first twitch of the *farang* lowering his gun from the base of his skull, Naylor rolled out of the cupboard where he had been hiding and put the full weight of his shoulder into the *farang*, striking him hard from behind, knocking him against the railing. The *farang* struggled to break free of Naylor as Jess and Calvino moved in. They were a couple of seconds too late. In superhuman feat of strength, Naylor had hit the *farang* from behind, pushing him forward, knocking him off balance; he raised him up. The *farang* was screaming as Naylor shoved him forward and the momentum carried him over the railing like a diver coming off a three-meter board. But it was more than three meters and there was no swimming pool at the other end. The *farang* dropped five floors, hitting the marble floor with a dull thud. A body hitting with such force ought to have made more noise. Flesh and bone smashing hard and splattering across the floor was barely audible. The three men stood at the railing and peered down. The *farang*, splayed out on the floor, was barely visible in the half-darkness. Naylor reached up and put his arm around Jess and Calvino's shoulder.

"Who's the bodyguard in this crowd?" he asked, wiping his hands together as if cleaning off dust. "Thought I had run away? You don't know me. I never run from a fight."

"We better check him out," said Calvino, looking over the railing. He had a strong feeling that the team hadn't been sent to kill Naylor.

"Forget it. We are getting the fuck out of Dodge City," said Naylor.

"Calvino's right. We check him out first," said Jess. "That was the same guy who attacked Naylor outside the elevator." This was more of a question than a certain observation.

"It looked like him," said Calvino.

"Of course it was him. Why do you think I threw his ass overboard?"

"What matters is finding out who was behind this hit," said Calvino looking directly at Jess. "And we might even find who they were sent to hit."

"They were after me," said Naylor. "Who do you think they were after?"

Calvino looked straight at Jess, who had the CAR-15 cradled in his arm. "Naylor, you are no doubt a really important guy. But I don't see any reason why or how a dysfunctional Chinese family would hire a commando team to make a military-type assault just because you came to buy their hotel. The expressway shooting, yeah, that I can buy. That is their level. A couple of *Isan* cowboys in a ten-wheeler who can't shoot straight. Now let's go."

"Then who were they trying to kill?" asked Naylor. "We don't know," said Jess.

Calvino nodded. "He's right. We don't know. That's why we need to check out the guy you shoved over the balcony."

"He ain't gonna be answering too many questions," said Naylor.

There was no need to say anything to Naylor about the drug case in LA. Jess already knew what he was saying and was grateful he was keeping his thoughts to himself. The last thing Jess needed was Naylor's big mouth broadcasting to the world that he was part of an undercover drug bust in Bangkok.

★★★★★★

NOI held the bloodied head of the dead *farang* in her arms. Sitting on the floor, she rocked back and forth, crying, tears streaming down her face. Calvino squatted beside her, put a hand on her shoulder. "You are mixed up with some very dangerous people."

"I didn't know. Danny never told me he was going to do this. Now he's dead. I don't understand why he used me. You have to believe me." Her sobbing continued.

"Noi, it would be safer for you if you came with us."

"I can't leave him like this."

"There's no time to argue. There's no time to mourn," said Calvino. It wouldn't take long for others to find out the three-man squad had gone down. Others would be dispatched. That's how these kinds of people worked.

"*They* wouldn't do anything. I did what they asked. I didn't know." She quickly lost her English and slipped into Thai, the natural storage bay of words to express her feelings. She didn't even realize she was speaking Thai, saying that she was afraid, as the full implication of what Calvino had said sunk in. She gently laid the *farang*'s head down on the marble floor.

Exactly who were *they*? If there were no other reason to pull her along it was to find the answer to that question.

"You are lucky to still be alive," said Jess in Thai. Her attention turned away from the dead man. She rose to her feet. "You won't let them hurt me?" Her eyes searched Calvino's, then she looked across to Jess. "You're going to have to help us," said Jess. "Tell us about your friend and his friends."

She nodded, fumbling with a cigarette and staring down at the dead *farang*.

McPhail came down the escalator clutching a Tower Records bag.

"Another fucking jumper, man." He looked down at the dead body. Then opened his bag. "I wonder if they would take these back. There's bound to be a big sale. Bomber special. Hey, Noi is still here. Now that's a miracle. First you couldn't find her, now you can't seem to get rid of her. That's true of all *yings*."

★★★★★★

ON level B2 of the parking lot, dozens of uniformed police and military personnel worked the crime scene. A large part of the lot had already been cordoned off and no civilians were allowed inside the taped-off area. Police and military vehicles blocked the exits. The wall of tall glass which wrapped around the lobby had been blown out. After the explosion, all the dust and fragments of metal, paint, fabric, and flesh had been pulled up the atrium like hot air shooting up one very large updraft ventilation shaft. To the side of the entrance the electrical unit housing the main power supply was shattered, sparking and spitting talons of fire from a melted core made up of the smouldered maze of broken wires and cables. Inside the immediate blast zone—several meters wide—the scene was one of complete destruction. Shards of glass and twisted pieces of plastic, metal, and rubber had ripped through cars, splattered against the pillars and walls. No question about it: someone had set off a large amount of explosive to cause this much damage. Even seventy meters away car windows had been shattered.

Calvino walked ahead looking for his car. Noi and McPhail walked together behind Naylor and Jess. Calvino couldn't remember exactly where he had parked. They had come out a different entrance in the parking lot from the one they had earlier taken into the shopping mall. Finally he spotted it. Calvino stopped and motioned for the others to stop. His Honda, or what was left of it, was ten feet ahead. Somewhere in the wreckage was his car. Emergency service personnel were removing bodies. And body parts. On the driver's side an intact head was still attached to the spinal column and shredded meat and organs clung to the outer edges of the spine and the femurs. The shoes and feet, like the head, were recognizable as human; but the parts of the body between the head and the feet didn't look like parts that belonged to a human being. On the passenger's side was a limp, damaged body—the left side had been sliced away from the force of the blast—but the second victim was at least in one large chunk. A headless torso with ragged flaps of flesh where the head had once rested. The torso was minced around the edges and scorched black from powder burns. An emergency unit with its members wearing protective clothing, masks, and gloves placed the pieces in large, black plastic bags. Uniformed police stood guard around the car waiting for the owner to return.

"Let's get out of here," said Jess.

Calvino nodded and a couple of minutes later they had blended into the crowd of shoppers, clerks, security guards—a great exodus of people—walking, half-dazed, taking the Soi 24 exit ramp which led out of the parking lot.

"Someone toasted your Honda," said McPhail.

"What the hell is this?" asked McPhail, kneeling down and picking up a round steel ball.

Jess looked at the steel ball rolling inside McPhail's cupped hand. "Claymore," said Jess. It looked like an ordinary steel ball-bearing.

"Heavy shit," said McPhail. "No way your insurance is gonna cover this. The war exception clause fucks you every time."

"I've seen enough," said Calvino.

"How are we getting to the Brandy?" asked Naylor. "I've got a meeting this afternoon. And I want to see Jep before we go back."

"The meeting has been cancelled," said Calvino.

"You can't do that, Calvino. I came to Bangkok for that meeting."

That was probably somewhere between a half and three-quarters of a lie. But it was no time or place to argue. "Jess, Noi goes with us. McPhail, take Wes to the Brandy, then go along with him to his meeting."

Naylor and McPhail looked each other up and down like a couple of *soi* dogs marking their territory. McPhail had that "fuck you" expression on his ultra thin upper lip, making it curl into a sneer as he clutched his Tower Records bag.

"When did I start working for you, Calvino?" asked McPhail.

"About fifteen minutes ago."

"You can't assign your bodyguard job like a maintenance contract on a crummy apartment," said Naylor, suddenly becoming lawyer-like.

"I just did."

"Then you've seen Vinee's apartment," said McPhail, smiling.

"You don't need a bodyguard. You need a business agent," said Calvino.

"Jess, you're not going along with this shit, are you?" Naylor looked frightened.

"Let me put you straight, Mr. Naylor. If those men were trying to kill you, it was for reasons undisclosed to me. If it is just the hotel deal, Calvino's right. If it is some other deal, then he's still right. You don't need us because nothing is going to save you."

Calvino opened the rear door of a taxi that had stopped. Others were banging on the door, trying to get in the cab. Holding a taxi was a New York City art form. Calvino stood in the way of several others who tried to push their way in front. Jess and Noi climbed inside. Calvino shut the door and got into the front, looking at the driver, a small, dark skinned Thai with a thick head of badly cut hair. "Rama IV Road," said Calvino.

"Meter broken," said the driver, grinning. "Five hundred baht."

Calvino agreed to pay the extortion money for the fare. "Go."

Rama IV Road was a vague, opened-ended destination that made it clear to the taxi driver that Calvino both knew where he was going and wasn't going to tell the exact destination until the last moment. Such contradictions were natural components of life on the street.

Calvino knew where he was going. He was heading for Klong Toey. A vast slum built under expressways, along canals, beside the Port of Bangkok.

Klong Toey was the last place he wanted this driver with the stupid grin and appetite to make money to know. The five hundred baht rip-off fee told Calvino all he needed to know: The driver would take the first opportunity to tell to anyone who asked and paid for the answer to exactly where he had taken them. And no doubt, there would be men with their hair cropped short, guns in their waistbands, making the rounds, asking taxi drivers, offering money, for information as to where a group of *farangs* had been taken.

TEN

CALVINO PRESSED THE cellphone against his ear, watching the traffic as he listened to Pratt. "If you had replaced your window, you would be dead now. The two men who tried to steal your car got the Claymore lucky draw meant for. . . ." said Pratt, his voice trailing off. Those were the first words out of his mouth. He already knew what had happened.

"All of us would be dead," said Calvino, finishing Pratt's sentence. Their taxi edged through the crowds spilling into the street around the Emporium. Their forward progress was painfully slow. Noi and Jess sat in the back listening to Calvino's end of the conversation with Pratt.

It was difficult to comprehend that such a large element in their survival had turned on Calvino's failure to replace the broken car window. Normally neglect was the demon that got people killed; this one time, against all odds, negligence had parlayed itself into the ultimate good fortune—forgetting his keys in the car had kept Vincent Calvino alive.

"You'll find two bodies on the fifth floor. Commando types. They can find two CAR-15s in the pool next to the restaurant. Not more than a couple of feet away from the dead *farang*. The third member of the team was a *farang.* He went over the railing without a parachute. Do you have any idea who those guys were working for?"

It had been Jess's idea to dump the CAR-15s in the shallow water so looters wouldn't take them. No way they were going outside with the place crawling with cops carrying automatic weapons.

"We're checking on that," said Pratt.

"Okay, so you know about that. Have you figured out who those two guys were who got blown up in the car?"

"We're running their fingerprints," said Pratt.

"I am not sure they had any fingers left. What you're saying is the police know it was my car." There was a sudden wall of silence at the other end of the phone. "Talk to me, Pratt."

"The investigators have a theory of what happened."

"No explanation ever gets organized that fast," said Calvino as the taxi turned right onto Rama IV, heading towards the Port of Klong Toey. Governments and police specialized in creating explanations. It was one thing they did well. They knew how to exploit the instinctive weakness of people who needed to feel that someone in authority knew what happened and could explain how and why it happened, and most of all they had faith—because there was no alternative—that these explanations were real.

"We are more efficient than you think, Vincent."

"What's the official version?" asked Calvino as the crowd thinned out, the taxi slowly working its way through the knot of emergency vehicles. People spilled into the street walking toward the shopping center. What was it that attracted people to a cause of violence?

Pratt gave a summary of what the professional spin doctors had already come up with; they had been working on the right shape to give the basic facts reported from the scene, assessing the best alternative explanations, and coming up with a story, the official version that would find its way onto the TV news and international wire services. Explanations were just words and most of the time words were enough to convince people that action had been taken. That everything was under control. This was the big lie because nothing was ever under control or even controllable.

Calvino guessed the official explanation would conform with the first operative principle: No one in authority was to blame or responsible.

What needed massaging was the raw material of the reality. A Claymore had been intended to kill either Calvino or LAPD officer Jessada. Either Calvino was getting too close to finding out tourists killers, or Jess had some bad people looking to settle with him for a covert drug bust. What they hadn't planned for was that a couple of car thieves would break into Calvino's Honda and take a one-way ride into the next life. The story on the news would be: Two dead commandos, heroes, had been killed on the fifth floor as they tried to capture two heavily armed bombers.

The second operative principle was to always turn the dead who fucked up a mission into the heroes. The official line would be the bombers killed them. It was no good having heroes slaughtered by looters; it reflected badly on the state of preparedness. Some minor loose ends remained, like the dead *farang*, not to mention the dead men in Calvino's car. The dog meat inside the Honda became the dead bombers who had accidentally detonated a Claymore mine.

Third operative principle: Use the violence against one's political enemies. The bombers—believed to have been behind earlier bombings in Bangkok—were part of a clique with a political agenda to destabilize the government. At the time of their discovery, the dead men were unable to plant the Claymore inside the shopping center and the dead soldiers had prevented a disaster from happening.

Everyone would be happy with the story.

"You left out the dead *farang*," said Calvino.

No, they had covered the *farang*. His death would appear in a sidebar. It was good to dispose of the dead *farang* in sidebars. It kept them out of the main story and that eliminated a potential complication.

Sidebar: In the aftermath of the explosion, there had been panic as shoppers tried to escape, and a *farang* had fallen to his death while seeking to leave the premises. The police believe the *farang* may have committed suicide. There were no further details about the identity or nationality of the *farang*. The sidebar or footnote would run as a related story to the blast.

Main story, sidebar. It all fit together as a package.

Calvino's Law: In the real world those with fascist tendencies succeed best in owning, managing and shaping the news. Of course, it helps to know how to make allies of the twin demons of uncertainty and irrationality.

It wasn't a particularly good spin, or even a very good story. But it didn't have to be. No one was going to confront the men who had spun the yarn. If that was the story they wanted, then that was the story that would be printed and shown on television. Who was going to send in an independent demolition expert who might ask hard questions as to how two car thieves had come into possession of a Claymore mine, or forensic experts to ask how the two bombers had managed to kill two ex-Border Police officers with a .38 police service revolver and a kitchen knife or why these ex-officers were carrying automatic weapons and dressed in bullet-proof vests after the bomb had gone off and then got back into their car to take the full force of the blast.

"Whoever pulled this off has some pretty big balls," said Calvino. "It's gonna be tough to control this, Pratt."

"It will be far easier than you can imagine." Pratt understood well how the system worked.

"So what's Plan A?" asked Calvino.

"Keeping Jess and you alive."

Calvino glanced around at Noi and Jess in the back. "Along with a material witness who knew the dead *farang*."

"You have such a witness?"

"That's right. Plan A calls for two outward tickets."

"Take them somewhere safe until I can work out some details," said Pratt

"Don't forget Plan B and Plan C." He was looking out the window. The traffic was terrible.

"You don't have much faith in Plan A working," said Pratt.

"That depends." Plans were like explanations; if there were too many inherent contradictions and faulty assumptions then they wouldn't work.

"On what?" asked Pratt.

"How secure the airport is. There have been some problems," said Calvino.

"We're back to your serial killer, are we? And he's gone from injecting heroin overdoses to blowing up shopping malls? There is no connection, Vincent."

"Bombers and a backup team commando squad in the same place and at the same time. I'd call that a connection."

"Connected to what?" asked Pratt.

That was the question. Exactly, connected to what.

He called Father Andrew. "I need help." He explained that Jess and Noi needed a place to stay for a couple of days; he wanted to blend the two of them into the slum community. Make them invisible.

He didn't need to explain or say any more. Father Andrew laid out his Plan A without Calvino ever asking. Jess had tapped Calvino on the shoulder and showed him that the red alert light was flashing; someone was tapping into the phone call. "Got to go," said Calvino, turning off his mobile phone.

★★★★★★

CALVINO asked the driver to pull into an abandoned service station. He stopped before a row of boarded-up gas pumps. Jess helped Noi out of the back as Calvino paid the driver with a five-hundred-baht note. All the emergency vehicles—fire trucks, police cars, body-snatcher vans—had caused a massive traffic jam; trucks, motorcycles, delivery vans, and buses came to a halt. Several drivers stood beside their vehicles, looking ahead, wondering if the traffic would ever move again. But with a blazing hot sun on the shadeless road, most of the stranded motorists stayed inside their air-conditioned cars, listening to the radio reports of the bombing.

Noi remained in a state of shock, using one hand to cover her eyes from the direct sunlight. She hadn't said much since they had left the Emporium. She started shivering, folding her arms together; she stood looking at the road, goose flesh covering her arms.

"She doesn't look so good," said Jess.

"We have to get off the road," said Calvino.

Calvino led them out of the abandoned service station and past a row of shop houses and an open lot filled with garbage. Jess held onto Noi's hand, which was ice cold.

"We split up here," Calvino explained. "Keep walking straight and turn left at the next *soi*, then at the bridge turn right and in another hundred yards you will see Father Andrew's offices. I'll meet you there in five minutes." It was important that they were not seen together. For sure someone outside the Emporium who had spotted them would have reported they were traveling together. The people who had sent the bombers and commando squad wouldn't give up; they would be looking for a *farang*, a Thai male and a Thai woman. Take the *farang* out of the equation and suddenly Jess and Noi fell into the deep background of thousands and thousands of other identical couples.

Jess listened to Calvino's instructions and then said, "For a *farang*, you know your way around."

"Hold her hand, Jess. Pretend you are a couple," said Calvino.

"I can't walk any further," said Noi.

"You have no choice, tilac. Jess will help you. There are no taxis. Look at the traffic. It's very close. You can walk. No problem," said Calvino. He was starting to sound like a Thai speaking English, Calvino thought as he hurriedly walked away.

★★★★★★

HEADQUARTERS for Father Andrew was located in a long, narrow, concrete building that was also home for fifty street kids, runaways, throwaways. A number of vehicles were parked inside the garage: several tuk-tuks with "Amazing Thailand" painted on the front, and a couple of vans. Along the far wall were storage shelves stacked with old computers, printers, and office equipment. Noi and Jess waited outside the garage entrance until Calvino showed up. Then they walked together through the garage and into the main building, passing the kitchen where a large brown and white dog slept under a long wooden table. Two cooks worked at the table, cutting up vegetables and chicken with knives. The large entryway with offices running off to one side was cluttered with school- books, tiny pairs of shoes, school uniforms, and comic books. Old photos of Father Andrew were hanging crooked on the wall. A photo history of the good Father receiving awards, with a group of slum kids, opening a school, shaking hands with wealthy patrons, and in his vestments.

They hadn't been inside more than a minute before Bun, a former street kid herself, greeted them with a *wai* and a smile.

"I take you to meet Father Andrew."

"Where is he?" asked Calvino. He was surprised that he wasn't waiting to meet them at his office. He had just talked with him on the phone and he had been in his office. Bun sensed Calvino's disappointment.

"He not forget you, Khun Vinee. But he has emergency. Last rites for a dying man. This man has AIDS. This is the second time he gives last rites. This time, I think he kreng jai Father Andrew and die. Make Father Andrew give last rites, three, four times. Crazy. I think no good. Even God bored with such a guy." She smiled with a big buck-toothed grin. Few men could move as fast as a priest dispatched to administer last rites. Even for one who was only thinking hard about dying.

Bun rattled her keys, pointing through the open door at a white van parked down the narrow lane outside the main building.

"How did Father Andrew get through the traffic?" asked Calvino.

"He uses the horn. Everyone let him go."

Calvino slammed the van door and Bun gunned the engine and pulled away from the curb. The sun had been beating down and the seat was hot. Calvino rocked from one side to the other as the heat passed through his pants and into his thighs, legs, and ass.

"I turn on air-con, Khun Vinee. And some good Thai music. Seems you want to dance, Khun Vinee," said Bun, as she gunned the van. "*Farang* get too hot in Thailand."

"Except Father Andrew," said Calvino. "And I am not dancing. I am being burnt at the stake." He liked to remind Bun that her hero was also a *farang*. Only this line of argument always ended the same. He could hear what she would say before she said it.

"Father Andrew isn't *farang*. He's khon Thai." She didn't disappoint. In Bun's eyes, and every Thai's at his center, Father Andrew had become a "Thai." A status granted for having lived more than thirty years in Klong Toey; not that he had gone native, but he understood native games, thinking, schemes, survival techniques. And he fought for them, saw they got food for their family and education for their children, buried their dead, bought medicine for their sick and dying. Even if they couldn't quite swallow Christianity, it didn't matter. They believed in Father Andrew. He was the only person in authority who had never abused his position for personal gain. That alone made him a living saint.

Bun turned the van onto Rama IV, hitting the horn, crossing over to the far lane as the traffic had started to edge forward. After turning off the main road, she drove over a narrow bridge; on the other side they entered the outer perimeter of Klong Toey slum. They drove past the slaughterhouse—which was a row of low buildings with stained, broken concrete floors and metal fences and gates—Bun made another right turn and slowed to a crawl. Calvino recognized Father Andrew's Toyota in the parking lot off the main road. Some slum kids played on a broken-down, rusty set of swings nearby. Bun steered the van into the nearly empty parking lot and turned off the ignition.

"There are clothes for you two in Father Andrew's car," she said, looking back at Jess and Noi.

"What kind of clothes?" asked Jess.

"They're hanging in the back of Father Andrew's car. Inside the plastic bag. You've just become a priest," she giggled. "And lady, you get to be a nun."

Noi just stared ahead without blinking, without responding.

"Better get changed," said Calvino. Turning around in his seat, he looked straight at Noi. A confused, uncertain expression crossed her face.

"I am a Buddhist," Noi said in almost a whisper.

"You've just been converted. You have been on stage. You know how to pretend a role. That's all you have to do for a couple of days. Pretend you are a nun," said Calvino.

"I don't know what a nun does," she said.

"She pretends to know the difference between right and wrong," said Calvino. "And is convinced she knows the dividing line between good and evil."

"It's okay, you can handle it," said Jess, gently squeezing her hand.

Calvino got out of the van and walked over to Father Andrew's car. Bun had already located the small magnetic key holder under the rear bumper to Father Andrew's Toyota, opened it and took out the key and unlocked the car.

"Here are your clothes," said Bun, handing a bundle to Jess. Then she leaned over the back and emerged with a plastic carry-on bag. "Yours are inside," she said, handing the bag to Noi.

"Jess, you go first," said Calvino, standing next to the opened van door. "It's time to ditch the earphones. We're no longer on bodyguard duty."

"We need to stay in communication."

"No Jesuit priest walks into the slums with an earphone. It will attract attention. People notice things like that. We don't want to be noticed."

Jess took out the earphone and removed the mic and the rest of the gear, handing them to Calvino. "Take care of this for me. That's five hundred dollars' worth of equipment."

Calvino nodded. "I'll see you get an official receipt."

"I better get changed."

"Good idea. Then Noi can have her turn. And we get our chance to see if this works."

"And if it doesn't?"

"We're in about the same situation as we are now."

"Why do I have the feeling you've done this before?" said Jess.

"Remember when we talked about how the movies get things wrong?" Calvino slammed the back door to Father Andrew's car. "Like how does Father Andrew know your size? In a movie you never ask that question. Because you never think about it. But in real life it is an issue."

"How does he know?"

"He doesn't. So the clothes won't look like they are tailored. You aren't going to look great but you're not supposed to look great. You're supposed to look like a slum priest and slum nun. This isn't a movie. If we get it wrong, there is no retake. So Jess's a priest. Noi's a nun.

You're here from America. And Noi's gotta pull herself together. Because a lot of people are taking a load of risks for her. She better be worth the investment."

Jess climbed into the van and closed the door. Calvino watched Noi leaning against the back of the van, holding her nun's habit in her arms.

"I can't believe Danny's dead," said Noi. The blood had come back into her face.

The loud drone of trucks on the road going towards the port nearly muffled out the word "dead." Calvino didn't need to hear it; he could read it on her lips. Dead. Danny's dead. "I'd stop thinking about Danny and start worrying how you are going to get out of this," said Calvino. "I don't want to scare you, but Danny's friends aren't going to be your best friends. You have a problem with the people you've been doing favors for, Noi. And you can either deal with your problem by doing what we say or you can find a taxi back to the city and do whatever you have to do."

Jess opened the door and looked out dressed in a clerical collar, black shirt and jacket.

"I am sorry . . ." she started to cry.

"How did you ever get involved with Danny and Gabe?" Calvino asked. "Did you know they were going to put a bomb in my car?" Then he regretted asking the question. She only wept more openly.

Jess had been listening to the exchange. He stepped down from the van looking very much like a priest.

"Khun Bun, would you help Noi get dressed?" asked Jess.

Bun helped Noi into the van and closed the door.

Jess pulled out his 9mm and checked the clip. "We can't stay here. I can't see this 'movie' of yours working, Calvino."

"You have a better script?" asked Calvino. Gabe had been his client and the sonofabitch had set him up, thought Calvino. He got Noi to pull a string, betting that Jess and Naylor would be on the same end of the rope. So who was he really trying to hang?

"As a matter of fact, I do. We go straight to the airport. And we board the first plane to LA."

"You got your passport? Has Noi got her passport? Of course not. So how do you get through Immigration?" Calvino stared at the gun. "Put the gun away. Father Ben." Jess frowned. Being called Father Ben threw him off, and he slipped the gun underneath his belt and pulled down the cleric's black vest. It was for a smaller man and crept up over his stomach. Not exactly a tank-top look but short enough for someone to notice and think the priest might pray for a new tailor.

"Father Ben?" asked Jess. "How did you come up with that?"

"Ben fits you. Even if the shirt doesn't. Besides, there are no Father Jessies, not even the Jesuits go that far. Ben, that's a name they can live with. It's a name you can stay alive with." The van door opened and Noi climbed out, dressed like a nun, her face dry of tears.

"You really think this is going to work?"

"With some help from Father Andrew and Pratt and a few of their friends, we might just manage to pull it off. Unless you want to organize things by yourself. After all you are Thai and I am just a stupid *farang* who doesn't know the story."

Jess shook his head and smiled. "Get rid of the *farang*-sized chip on your shoulder. You know the story, Vincent. That much I will grant you." He wouldn't know where to start but Calvino's irony wasn't lost on him. "A *farang* and a Thai cop having their people watching the airport to get me out of Thailand. It's a stretch. But you're right. I don't have a better plan." Calvino had started to like this LAPD cop.

"Who would have thought LAPD would get cast for the part of a Thai village priest?"

Noi stood awkwardly next to Jess, avoiding his glance. The nun's habit fit her perfectly.

"Sister Teresa, you are looking good," said Calvino.

The white habit transformed her entire being; softened her, brought out an innocence in the line of her mouth, and in her eyes. She looked as if the divine had touched her.

"Father Andrew's in the shop around the corner," said Bun. "I don't think the man die yet. I can't hear them crying."

★★★★★★

BUN led them along a narrow dirt path, passing empty stone benches and a stone table as the sun disappeared in the late afternoon haze. Under foot were layers of garbage bleached by the sun—discarded plastic bottles, paper cartons, wrap- pers. Dead leaves had been raked into piles under a bare tree; a rope hung down from one branch. Hundreds of flies buzzed over the garbage, filtering into the open entrance. The front door was decorated with faded Mickey Mouse decals peeling at the edges. They removed their shoes and placed them among the several rows of shoes and sandals near the door. As they stepped inside, they found sixteen or more people crowded into every corner of the small shop house. The dying man lay on a mat at the far end. Friends, family, and neighbors gathered for the deathwatch. Standing, sitting, squatting, leaning against the door frame, they had come running as Father Andrew's presence indicated the dying time had arrived.

The shelves were stocked with shampoo, Fab, cooking oil, toothpaste, noodles, eggs, and rice. Father Andrew knelt on a mattress, his back to the door; his eyes, closed, his lips moved as a faint sound of prayer filtered across the room. Quietly Jess and Bun joined him, standing at his side. He didn't acknowledge them immediately. Calvino stayed back, hunched near the door watching the LAPD cop and the Thai singer playing their roles as the other people in the room watched them. He glanced at his wristwatch, and checked his time with the shop clocks. What would the time of death be? Calvino wondered. There were three choices. One green and pink clock with a jumbo elephant had been hung upside-down on the wall. Another clock had a run-down battery causing the second hand to twitch, almost moving ahead but never mustering sufficient strength to move past the number seven. Only one clock functioned as a clock: it had Disney characters on the face, a child's clock. Calvino figured it belonged to whoever had put the decals on the door. The Mickey Mouse clock kept time right side up. The three clocks made him think about time-rats, the *yings*, but it was more than just *yings* who devoured time—a life fell away minute by minute in a thousand small ways like the grains of sand falling down the neck of an hour glass. He looked over at the dying man and wondered how he would account for the hours and minutes when it came to his time.

Behind the Mickey Mouse clock was a table with six Buddha images surrounded by flowers. Incense sticks had been burned down to the red stick base in the cups of sand. All of the images faced away from the dying man. Each Buddha image faced the door.

The dying man lay on his back, bare chest mopped by a relative. His ribs visible under the skin. Another relative wiped the sweat from his face. His eyes were closed, his head turned to the side. He was semi-conscious. He gave every appearance of following through this time and dying.

Father Andrew finished his prayer and sat up, nodding towards Jess. Then making a half turn, he nodded in Noi's direction. He had this funny, wan smile. It must have been seeing his priest and nun outfits on the two of them. Jess knelt with his hands folded in prayer and Noi, following Jess's lead, knelt beside him, her hands folded, the long painted nails touching. The red fingernails stood out like cockroaches on the side of a wedding cake. Calvino couldn't decide whether anyone in the room had noticed Noi's manicured nails. The three of them prayed over the dying man like the three clocks marking time.

The shop phone never stopped ringing. A thin *ying* in a white blouse with sweat dripping down from her brow answered the phone but no one was on the other end. She wore ankle high plastic boots; she had a middle-aged, defeated look, and the skin on her right arm was webbed as if the flesh had been melted. Each time the phone rang she reached for it with her damaged arm. Two Thai nuns stood together inside the back door, watching, rosaries draped over their hands folded in prayer. One of them stared at Noi, wondering who she was and why she was kneeling next to Father Andrew on the mattress. The middle-aged nun was stern looking; the other still young, innocent—she had not seen as much death and her face had a pale beauty, her eyes a clear deep brown. School children in white shirts and pressed shorts watched from a corner. The heat made the children listless. They sat quietly on their knees eating snacks from plastic bags.

Several relatives of the dying man hovered near the mattress where the man lay.

Father Andrew rocked forward on his knees, his stocking feet sticking over the edge of the mattress, muttering prayers and sprinkling water. The nuns crept into the room and joined him in praying. The dying man groaned, his eyes closed as he moved in and out of consciousness with the same random irregularity as the clocks in his shop; his bare chest heaved up and down as if he could not catch his breath like a drowning man. His thin legs stuck out of the blanket like they belonged to a cartoon character on the door to his shop. One relative fanned the dying man with a magazine, another relative on the opposite side fanned him with a piece of cardboard. A scent of death and sickness clung in the heavy, still air. The close, confined smell of the slums mingled with the smell of the dying man. The relatives tried to circulate the heavy, stale air. But their efforts were wasted, useless. Even the small fan at the foot of the mattress did not bring any relief from the heat or the smell.

The prayers and sprinkling of holy water came to an abrupt halt. Bun looked unhappy; Father Andrew had performed the last rites for the third time and still the man refused to die. As he slowly rose from the mattress, Father Andrew motioned for Jess and Noi to do the same. He introduced Father Ben and Sister Teresa to some of the man's relatives before turning around and walking towards the front door. He looked at the back of the shop house, picked out Calvino, and made his way back to greet him. Jess and Noi trailed behind, making a religious procession. Father Andrew waited until everyone was outside the shophouse before he said anything.

"Sorry I couldn't meet you at my offices. But this man's family requested I perform the last rites. No, he's not dead. He probably won't die today. With AIDS you can never know when a man will die. It's not like the movies where the priest arrives and the dying man obliges everyone and dies after ten minutes."

Outside the shop Father Andrew examined various plastic bottles of medicine that the woman with the damaged arm showed him. He shook his head. "They prescribe this stuff for AIDS? It's vitamins." He handed the bottles back to the woman, found his shoes, put them on, and walked back along the path. "Don't worry, it was good it worked out this way. Another priest and a nun coming to his last rites was a good thing. His family will get a lot of face from that. And you will get equally good cover from the community. Or at least that is the idea. But I have to warn you; the slum is the least anonymous place in Bangkok. No one disappears in a slum. You are assimilated or accepted but you can't hide. Everyone knows the movements of everyone else. No police state was ever as well organized or as efficient in intelligence gathering as the good citizens of Klong Toey slum."

They reached Father Andrew's car. It was a short ride to his house.

"You two look the part," said Father Andrew trying to find something positive to say. "But looking the part and playing the part are two different things. Jess, I remember thinking there is a fine young man when you came with Pratt to my house. I didn't think I would be seeing you again so soon." "Or that someone would like to make sure that I never return to LA."

"Or that I don't find the serial killer," said Calvino.

"I'm worried this could be dangerous for you," said Jess. Father Andrew smiled. "No doubt. I specialize in dangerous people."

Christopher G. Moore

"What he's saying is that someone tried to blow up my car and then sent a commando unit after us," said Calvino. "We still don't know who they want to kill. Except it's not Wes Naylor."

"But it could be Naylor," said Jess.

"You two don't seem to agree on much other than that these dangerous people will probably try to kill someone tomorrow or the next day, or the day after that. If you can all stay alive long enough, then Jess will go back to Los Angeles, and Vincent back to delivering birthday cards and then you both will have truly been blessed. I can't guarantee you anything. I can't control what will happen. Any more than I can tell you whether the man back there will die tonight or tomorrow. All I can tell you is that he will die."

Father Andrew pulled into a parking lot jammed with flatbed trucks loaded with containers. Not that many years ago the parking lot had been a slaughterhouse. Pigs squealed throughout the night as workers cut their throats and butchered them for their meat. Father Andrew stopped in front of a vendor's stand and left the engine running.

"So is someone going to tell me why someone is trying to kill you, Jess?"

"It's connected with a case in Los Angeles," said Jess. "A drug case involving Thais," said Calvino.

"Drugs," repeated Father Andrew. "I know something about that. What kind of drugs?"

"Heroin," said Jess.

Like the original Opium Wars, modern drug wars were waged by local Mafia who had learned history's lesson on how to successfully colonize the poor.

Dogs slept along the narrow concrete walkway leading to Father Andrew's house. Low corrugated roofs

235

sagged in places, causing them to bend their heads as they walked underneath. Below the foundation was bilge water as evil as the end of time. Not even the rains diluted the foul water. Smells of cooking drifted from some of the houses. In front a woman cooked fish in oil. The crackling sound of the oil filled the air. A shirtless old man with a gold chain and amulets suspended from it squatted on a stool, watching as they passed. The eyes of the slum watched Father Andrew and those with him. The word circulated as they walked together that he had a Thai priest and nun in tow that no one in the slum knew or had met before. But that was Father Andrew, who always had strange guests, foreign journalists, news crews, politicians, patrons, overseas visitors coming to his house deep inside the slum. Reaching his house, Father Andrew unlocked his door and let Noi and the others go in first. His house didn't look like a slum. A modern kitchen and redone living room with fans and electric lights and air-conditioning. He went to the fridge, took out a plastic water jug and filled several glasses, gesturing for everyone to find a chair.

"Make yourselves at home," he said.

Noi sat at the dining room table beneath a photo of a single Chinese man in a white shirt facing off against five Chinese tanks. It was the famous Tiananmen Square photograph of one man's defiance against the brute forces of repression. Noi was gradually coming out of her shock. She no longer stared straight ahead into the mid-distance. Some song was floating through her mind and she was humming the tune to herself. Somewhere in her mind she was on stage performing before an audience only she could see. She had sought refuge from a state of overwhelming fear, going to that place where she felt strong and in control. On stage. She had some men in the background who had been ordering her to do things she didn't want to do and for some reason, she could not resist. *Be lost until we tell you to be found. Be a whore. Be at the Emporium. Be a nun. Sing a song.*

Jess sat a few feet away in an armchair, hands folded on his lap. On the wall behind him was a framed vestment: red brocade. From the old Latin church, from the days when priests were run over by tanks during the Cold War.

Calvino stood in the entrance to the kitchen opening a bottle of wine left over from his birthday party and poured a glass for Father Andrew.

"Jess is collecting evidence for the trial in LA," said Calvino.

"And a big-time drug smuggler doesn't like that idea, am I right?" asked Father Andrew, sipping the wine and looking straight at Jess.

"It's looking that way, Father," said Jess.

Father Andrew swirled the wine around the glass, held it up to the light, and said nothing for a moment. "The overdose cases. The *farangs* had all been injected with heroin. That means you are helping Vincent solve this terrible airport serial killer case?"

Jess, looking confused, looked over at Calvino.

"Yes and no," said Calvino.

"That is a very Thai answer, Mr. Calvino," said Father Andrew.

"We are working together but not on the heroin overdose cases."

"I don't think the cases are related," said Jess.

"Interesting. So what I am hearing is that you two are working on two separate heroin cases but haven't bothered to tell each other about your cases," said Father Andrew. Setting the wine glass on the table, he sat down opposite Noi. "If I am going to help you, I need to know exactly who I am helping and why they need help. Those are the rules. They apply to the street kids. They apply to people after heroin dealers, and particularly to those whom heroin dealers are after. So we can't afford to be even a little confused. I believe, as you might expect, that confession is good not only for the soul but for keeping people alive and healthy."

Jess thought about this as he looked over at Calvino. "I had no idea that I was being set up. I never intended to drag Vincent into my heroin bust. I've done bodyguard assignments before. This was another job. Naylor seemed to warrant protection. He had received death threats. On the way from the airport, there was another attempt on Naylor."

"We thought it was on Naylor," said Calvino.

"What I am saying is this didn't start out as a covert operation. I had a chance to talk to Pratt about my heroin case. He had some ideas. We exchanged some information. He showed me some of his data."

"Why not follow up the leads?" asked Father Andrew. "That's what you were thinking."

Jess nodded, broke into a grin. "Exactly."

"Pratt has good contacts with a colonel in a special Narc unit. Pratt started looking into the possibility of a serial killer with access to heroin. He was using the stuff to overdose tourists. What he found was that the heroin came over the border with Burma and then vanished. As if the white powder had gone into thin air. There was too much product gone missing. Where had it gone? Was the disappearance linked to the five overdose cases Vincent had him worried about? He had all of these questions and no real answers. I told Pratt about the guy I had arrested in LA with a kilo of heroin from the Golden Triangle, and we started to work on establishing a possible connection between a pending drug case in LA and missing heroin coming in from Burma. Was it the same stuff? I said I didn't know. My problem was I had arrested a low-level dealer who, as I said before, only had a kilo on him. But that's a lot of money on the street. This guy looks like he will fall and do the hard time rather than tell us where he got it. His trial comes up in a couple of weeks."

"In sixteen days," said Noi.

The three men looked at her. "How do you know that?" asked Jess.

"Because he's my brother."

"Interesting," said Father Andrew, breaking the silence.

"It's funny that Gabe never mentioned your brother was in jail," said Calvino. "Now it seems you were never lost. Your job was to lead us to the bombers."

Looking at Noi dressed as a nun made it difficult to believe she had drawn them to the Emporium in order to have them killed.

She shook her head, "I told you before. I really didn't know. *Jing jing.* You have to believe me." She was pleading, searching the faces, looking for some glimmer that at least one of them believed her. *Yings* like to say *jing jing.* It's true, it's true. When most of the time it was an outright falsehood.

The assignment had started as innocently as the look on Noi's face. Why not make some money from a bodyguard assignment in Thailand? After all, asking Jess to go to Thailand made sense, he was an ethnic Thai, and so was Dr. Nat. They understood each other. Dr. Nat had been his doctor ever since he was fourteen years old. He never stopped and thought the full implications through. Now it was obvious. He had been stupid not to realize that putting Calvino and him on full expenses plus the cash was too good to be true. If he had been smart, he would have started on day one looking for what had to be another agenda. Even now, in Father Andrew's house, Jess wanted to believe—and continued to believe—that Dr. Nat didn't know about the real setup. Dr. Nat had been used. And if Dr. Nat didn't know, maybe Noi was telling the truth. Both of them had been used. In reality, whoever was afraid of Noi's brother testifying had to be busting his guts laughing; here was the arresting officer taking four grand for four days to arrange his own execution. A cheap price to fix a drug case. A Thai who happens to be on LAPD is a lot easier to whack out in Bangkok than in Los Angeles. In Bangkok, the masterminds knew the chances were in their favor that they would get away with the crime. They would be protected. No matter what was found, the case wouldn't go forward because of insufficient evidence. In Los Angeles, the evidence would be found and they would get the needle and the big sleep.

"Who is this Gabe Holerstone?" Jess asked.

"He's one of my clients. And he's from LA," said Calvino.

"He was my boss at Sisuda. A club on Vine Street in Hollywood," said Noi. "I worked there as a singer."

Sure you did, sweetheart, Calvino was thinking to himself.

"I know the place," said Jess. "Your brother worked there?"

Jess had driven past the bar—he never thought of it as a "club"—hundreds of times; he knew the bar mostly from the outside. Maybe a year, two years ago, he had gone inside for a look around. Unimpressed, he never went back. It was one of those *farang* places. The bar was next door to a liquor store and sometimes there would be gang members hanging around by the liquor store, smoking, drinking, indulging in low-level intimidation of customers, and sometimes a fight would break out on the street. But Jess had never any personal or professional reason to enter Sisuda's karaoke bar other than that one time. He remembered that the bar had a dozen or so *yings* working, dork tong—gold flowers—planted inside, getting customers to water them and talk to them for fifty bucks an hour. Lots of Korean and Japanese customers would go into private rooms and sing along with the *yings*. She called herself a singer, Jess thought. He looked at Noi in her nun's habit, trying to imagine her as just another one of the gold flowers.

"I thought Gabe promised you a singing career in LA," said Calvino.

"He lied to me. He lied to my brother. I hate him," she said.

"This is the first time a nun has openly professed hatred for a fellow human being," said Father Andrew. Calvino brought over the bottle, waited until Father Andrew finished his wine and then refilled his glass. It had been a long day for the slum priest. The AIDS patient who didn't die. A Thai ex-bar singer dressed as a nun sitting in his house, her eyes filled with hate.

In Father Andrew's sitting room, Calvino and Jess discovered an axis of interest, of interlocking friendship and of sleazy LA business deals. What was coming into sharp focus was the identity of the bomber's target. If Calvino were a betting man, he thought that with some serious digging—and Pratt would know where to start—they would probably find a connection between the disappearing heroin and Gabe Holerstone, a wise guy running a near-beer karaoke bar called Sisuda on Vine Street in Hollywood. Whoever the serial killer was, one thing was for certain in Calvino's mind: the murderer would not be using Gabe and Noi to draw him into the Emporium for a hit. All they had to do was walk into his apartment and shoot him. He was no more important, in the scheme of things, than Naylor. Unless, of course, there was some bad blood between LA bar owner and LA lawyer. In which case, Naylor was the target.

"Did you know Wes Naylor in LA?" Jess asked her.

A Thai woman wandered into the room and whispered in Father Andrew's ear about how the dying man was doing with his dying. He was doing well, but was still holding on to the edge of life.

"It was Kowit's idea to get Wes involved," said Noi. Bring the slightly overweight *yingzine*—the Cause-members' online magazine of beautiful women—lawyer into the mix. Why not lay off some of the risk on the *farang*? Calvino thought. If anyone was cruising for a major league setup it was Wes Naylor and his Cause-member boys.

Jess leaned over, his hand cupped, and softly said to Calvino, "Pratt showed me a list of big-time distributors and their associates. This guy Kowit made the list as an associate."

Whatever the fuck that means, thought Calvino.

"You think your brother got the heroin from Kowit?" asked Calvino.

"I don't know," she said. "He didn't tell me. I didn't ask. I don't want to know."

"We could get him an immunity deal," said Jess. "But he has to cooperate. Do you understand what I am saying? Not just say he will help. He has to get into a witness box and point the finger at the man."

"He's fucking scared." She looked over at the priest, "Sorry, Father."

"Just keep talking. Language isn't the issue. Staying alive is," said Father Andrew.

Noi nodded, looked back at Jess. "I am scared. What they tried to do to you makes me afraid. And you're a cop. And they can do this to you. You have no protection."

When someone like Noi spoke straight about the reality of the situation it sounded different than when they talked their way around the tight intellectual and emotional corners of their life. A lot of what Noi had been saying, to Calvino's ear, had the sound of skid marks of a life in a near collision with the wall of reality. She hadn't given some bullshit assessment. Noi knew the score. It was all summed up in four words: *You have no protection*. And she was right, and he knew why she did what they asked her to do. What real choice did she have?

One of the nuns who had been at the shop suddenly appeared in the room. Her presence stopped the conversation cold as she went over to Noi and handed her a glass of water. "Would you like to rest? We have finished preparing your room."

Noi looked up at Jess, drank from the glass of water and put it down on the table. "I can rest later," she said.

"Sister, if you could come back a little later, then I am certain Sister Teresa will be ready for a rest," said Father Andrew. "Right now we are deep in the discussion of a theological crisis."

After the sister left, Noi loosened up more. "We should hear the rest of it, Noi. There's no point keeping any secrets," said Calvino.

"Vincent is right," said Jess. "If we know who is behind what happened at the Emporium it can only help you and your brother. You've got nothing to lose."

It turned out that ever since Noi's brother, Charn, had been in jail waiting for his trial date, Kowit had steadily become more nervous. He was afraid that the kid would make a deal; he wasn't doing all that well in jail and the way things worked in America, Charn might lose his courage, turn state's evidence. That would be his best move. He had less to fear in California and that made Kowit uneasy. Without the ability to instill raw fear, he lost his home-court advantage. But if Charn's case never went to trial, then the police would have to release him. Kowit let Noi understand that she had a role to play to keep her brother healthy and happy and breathing; she had to help out. She got the idea fast that, unless she helped Kowit, her brother could have a pretty hard time in prison. In fact he might never get out of prison. She believed Kowit had that power.

"No one was to get hurt, they promised me," said Noi. "They said they wanted to scare you. Then the case would be dropped against my brother."

"You saw the car, Noi. These people weren't trying to scare someone. Why did you get involved in this?" asked Jess.

Tears welled in her eyes. "They lied to me. I am so sorry."

She was a narrative creature totally devoid of any power of analysis to allow her to know what her story meant. That was the reason she always started to repeat her story whenever Jess asked her a "why" question. She couldn't answer such a question. She could only narrate and hope the story would wear down the resistance of the why question-askers. "Kowit talked to me about my brother. I had no choice if I wanted to help my brother."

Jess shook his head and she stopped the narration.

Whether this was a good *ying* pitch or the truth or something in between a pitch and the truth was difficult to say; the nun's habit gave her an edge of credibility that a cocktail dress lacked. She had knowingly agreed to set up the trial cop in her brother's narcotics case. Without Jess, the State's case against Charn fell apart; his evidence was needed to convict or the brother walked. She did the Thai thing, she did whatever was necessary to save her older brother. Family always came first; everyone else and everything else was way down the obligation ladder. And within the family the younger yielded to the elder. Noi understood the overriding obligation: be there for her family. That was her operative principle. He had been there for her; now it was her turn to help him. She would not let him down.

"His name was Danny. The *farang* who died at the mall. Gabe and Kowit sent him to watch me."

"Or help you?" asked Jess.

She shrugged, looked down. "Gabe wanted to make certain I didn't screw up. I didn't know he was going to try and kill anyone."

"Right, he seemed like such a nice boy," said Calvino, catching Father Andrew's eye.

"He probably did, Vincent," said Father Andrew, whose years in the slums had not stripped him of a glimmer of hope that a small amount of goodness resided in all men and women. Or almost all.

"They said that Danny only wanted to talk to Jess. Nothing heavy, just to let him know that testifying against the brother wasn't a hot idea."

They used the brother to get at her. Or that was her story. Seems that brother Charn had found Noi the "singing" job in LA. Actually he got a commission from Gabe for recruiting her. It hadn't taken her long—one night working in the bar—to find out that her brother was mixed up with some bad actors. According to her version, she didn't ask and he didn't offer to tell her about his connection with Kowit. Also she knew that Kowit was a frequent visitor to the nightclub, one of those near-beer places that the ABC hate but can't bust down to the foundation. The place didn't serve alcohol. It didn't need to; the men came for the women.

"Kowit had a share in the business with Gabe," said Noi. "Who told you that?"

"Gabe did."

Enough of a piece to launder drug money, wondered Calvino. Noi's brother worked as a bouncer at the bar. She warned him not to disgrace their family name. He smiled, promised, gave oaths of walking the right path, and then did what he wanted.

"If you thought he wasn't involved in drugs, why warn him?" The cop in Jess was coming. For Jess her story had enough holes that the boat of credibility had started to list.

"He had too much money. I knew he wasn't getting that kind of money from his job at the bar."

"Then you weren't all that surprised when I arrested him?"

"Yes and no," she whispered. "On the job he was clean. I never saw him doing anything other than what he was supposed to do. But he was spending a lot of money."

"Sometimes he would disappear for an hour or two. This happened a couple of times a week." Jess had Charn under surveillance and the bust had been done three blocks away, at a hotel. He dealt drugs out of a room in a rundown hotel. He had been tacking back and forth between the bar and the hotel, selling smack.

She blamed herself for not convincing her brother that he had to return to Thailand. He had enough money for a good life in Bangkok. But he was coming into some minor fame in LA, he liked the freedom. People didn't look down on him, he was *someone*, and he wasn't about to leave. "Wes Naylor was also a customer who came in a lot."

"How much is a lot?" asked Jess.

"I saw him a couple of nights a week. He spoke a little bit of Thai. He had been to Thailand and was always talking about the Cause this, the Cause that. He had bar *yings* on the brain. He took photos of some of the *yings* for his *yingzine*. He said guys downloaded off his website. Paid him to do so. He thought everyone working at Sisuda was a whore."

She *waied* Father Andrew. "Sorry, father."

"Were they?" asked Jess. "Prostitutes?"

Her answer was a wan smile. After all he was a cop. He was going back to that neighborhood and she could see him working with Vice to throw her friends in jail, or worse, having them sent home.

"Did Kowit and Naylor know each other?" said Calvino.

Jess smiled, "Kowit saw the chance to help himself if he gave Naylor his big break." He told Calvino and Father Andrew about how Gabe had made the introduction. One night Naylor sat at the bar talking about getting laid on the Causeway and Kowit walked in. Wes had a photo layout ready to load onto the *yingzine* and was inspecting the pictures. Half an hour later Kowit told Naylor about a possible hotel venture with a couple of respectable doctors. They needed a lawyer. Kowit would convince them to cut Naylor in for five percent of the deal. What did Kowit want? He wanted Naylor's friendship. Naylor took the job as unofficial adviser in case things got complicated. In LA, Kowit thought he needed a *farang* lawyer in his pocket. Kowit's pitch was good, fast balls down the middle, knee level over the plate; no way that Naylor was going to do anything but strike out. Dr. Nat, LA brother of the doctor in Bangkok, let Kowit convince him that Naylor was the right *farang* to attract the *farang* trade. He agreed that Naylor should be cut in for five percent of the deal. Naylor would do all the legal work at a discounted rate. A week later, the death threats started. Wes Naylor met with Kowit who told him to fly to Bangkok and to take a bodyguard, someone with police experience, someone who was an ethnic Thai. Such a man could lay the right groundwork and put an end to the threats. There was an LAPD officer who was Thai. "Naylor contacted me," said Jess. "He asked me to write my own ticket. Naylor told me that a buddy of his named Gabe had recommended a private eye in Bangkok, an American to help out. 'Write your own ticket,' said Naylor."

"What did you say?" asked Father Andrew.

"I said yes," said Jess. "And I wrote my own ticket."

"So did I," said Calvino.

There was a lot of loud talking and wailing outside Father Andrew's house.

"I think it must be his time to die," Father Andrew said. He opened his door and watched as the relatives removed the dying man in a chair to his sister's house. Calvino rose from his chair and walked through the kitchen in time to see the man slumped forward in the chair pass by the door.

"He will die tonight. I can feel that. Then we will have the wake and the funeral. We don't keep the dead long. The bodies start to fall apart real fast." He turned back to his guests "You, Father Ben, and you Sister Teresa, are welcome to stay here. Until Vincent can find a way to get you to safety."

"Back to LA?" asked Noi.

"Whatever it takes, we will get you back," said Calvino.

"You still want to help us?" Jess asked Father Andrew. "Because I wouldn't blame you if you asked us to leave right now."

"I just saw a man on his way to die," said Father Andrew. "I've seen it many times. You know what? It doesn't really worry me."

Noi's head was bowed and she slowly raised it until she looked straight at the priest.

"And you, my child, need to help these two fine men," said Father Andrew.

She looked at him like the Chinese guy staring down the tanks. "Whatever it takes," she said, using Vincent Calvino's words as she rose and saw the relatives of the dying man filing past. He was going to die soon. She sensed the presence of Death lurking in the shadows of the narrow pathways. Death was a frequent visitor in the slums of Klong Toey. Tonight the man in the chair would leave with that visitor. As she felt the shadow pass, she thought of Danny, and a sudden chill went up her spine.

ELEVEN

THE WOMAN WITH the shrivelled arm from the shop house came into Father Andrew's living room, tears rolling down her cheeks.

"*Pee chai dtai laew,*" she said. She looked weary from the ordeal, her eyes, red-rimmed, expressing sadness and relief. "My older brother has died."

Father Andrew was on the phone, "I know that it's important," he said into the receiver. "But someone has just died next door and his sister is standing in front of me."

He didn't bother to cup the phone as he spoke. "Tell your family that I will be right over. Let me finish this call first," said Father Andrew. "And I will be with you as well." He looked at his three guests. The woman slipped out of the house. Calvino went to the door, looked in the walkway. The neighbors and family were gathering outside. Father Andrew returned to the phone. He did not miss a beat.

"Who told you we can't drive the piles for the school? That guy? He said no one would stand in our way. What do we do? I tell you what we do. We drive the piles tomorrow and I'll have 322 kids handwriting letters to the Governor, the Chief of Police, and the Prime

Minister. The kids write, 'Can you give us a chance? We want to do better. We want an education for a better life. Or would you rather us little ones do like our parents and live on drugs and commit crimes?' And we send all 322 letters to the English language newspapers. Tell him that. So don't worry, you just get the crew to show up for work tomorrow."

He put down the phone and smiled. "Someone is either scared or wants a pay-off. So we do what needs to be done. We are practical here. We let the kids make the officials' position a public issue. These bad guys hate negative publicity. Three hundred plus kids talking to the TV cameras will send them running for cover."

This time Father Andrew's mobile phone rang. "No, I can't. I have a special mass in twenty-five minutes. Why? Because it is my birthday, and I always hold a mass on my birthday. Yeah, at the slaughterhouse. I hold it for the Laotians who are hiding out," he said, looking at his wrist. "I'll have to call you back. But tell Henry we can meet with his Board of Directors next Tuesday and tell him about the lunch program for our kids."

Father Andrew looked over at his guests. "Now where were we?"

"The man died," said Noi.

"And I need to comfort his family," said Father Andrew. "But first I have to catch my breath."

"And see if you can work us into your schedule," said Calvino.

"That can be arranged," said Father Andrew, looking at his empty wineglass.

Jess leaned over and filled the glass. "I am learning about Thailand," said Jess.

"Vincent wouldn't have brought you here if he didn't think I could help. I am not saying that you aren't in for a hard time. But we can manage. The community already accepts you as a priest and what's-her-name as a nun."

"Sister Teresa," said Calvino.

Father Andrew crossed himself.

"I specialize in hard times," said Father Andrew "Or have your eyes and ears been shut the last hour or so?"

He knew the score and that, given who was on the other side, the odds of the game were always against him. He was also straight, had no time for nonsense, and lived in a world where there was never time to explain the details or for theory. Too many people dying, doing drugs, robbing, whoring, and giving up hope. Too many street kids who never knew the meaning of hope or love. Father Andrew applied his faith as a triage to stop that last of drop of hope from dripping out of his community. He reached over and touched Jess's shoulder.

"As long as you and Sister Teresa are staying with me in Klong Toey, no one, and I mean no one, is going to touch you."

Jess put his hand over Father Andrew's. "I believe you, Father."

LAPD Officer Jess, born in Bangkok, a Buddhist, understood how an entire community of Thais had put its full faith in this single man. He felt the power, the strength of the man. He believed this priest could do exactly what he said. Jess had acquired an Americanized sense of justice; he believed in equality of law enforcement, that no one was above the law. He had forgotten a few things about how things really worked—like the influence of the people who had set out to murder him—members of the hidden class with their access to privileged information and power. These people did not go around the center of power; they *were* the center, the core, the black hole that was so strong that it bent light, justice, fairness, and equality. No one betrayed a fellow member of the privileged club. Their motto—handed from one generation to the next—everything and everyone could be bought: business opportunities, seats in elite schools for their children, forest land in national reserves, promotions, concessions, and friend- ship. Normal laws did not apply to them and there was disdain for individual merit and transparency. Those who questioned or failed to play by their rules disappeared from the game. What made the network work so efficiently while it remained so well hidden was the halo of fear and silence surrounding the members, keeping this class out of sight (except at high society functions), out of the press (except the society page), and out of controversy (except the occasional son who was arrested for shooting or beating someone and then released, or a rigged set of examinations for school entrance that was exposed and quickly faded away). The release from jail, the fading away of the scandals—this was only part of their power. But that power didn't extend to LA. Jess could not be bought. He would testify in Charn's trial; he would do what he could to convince Charn to implicate others. And Charn might listen to Jess, who was older and thus had to be deferred to, and Jess was Thai, and Jess was persuasive.

He had attempted to persuade Charn to breach the code of silence. They wanted Jess dead. It was no more complicated than that. The complication had been caused by Jess's failure to believe justice prevailed; that would only happen if he could bust the big boss and so far Charn had not been co-operating. He was learning about justice in Klong Toey and Father Andrew had all the makings of a good teacher. It was as if he were learning kick-boxing again. Watching a master demonstrate the moves, flow through the drills, automatically anticipate the angle and velocity of the next punch.

Taking a bodyguard assignment at face value had been a mistake. But finding Noi had been that lucky bonus that a mistake sometimes pays. If he could return with her to LA, she would help him turn Charn against Kowit and Gabe Holerstone. Whether there would be sufficient evidence to charge Wes Naylor, he wasn't sure. He hadn't made up his mind about Naylor's role in all of this. Was he an innocent dupe or was he involved in the smuggling operation himself? Most of the time Jess had a gut feeling one way or another. Naylor, however, had thrown him off-balance. He simply did not know how to read his act.

Father Andrew led them outside the house and down the narrow concrete pathway to the house of dead man's sister. They went inside and Father Andrew said a prayer. Jess and Noi, following Father Andrew, heads bowed, eyes closed, hands folded, joined him. Calvino wasn't sure whether they were pretending or whether these were real prayers and were for the dead man who lay on a mattress in the corner—or whether the prayers were for themselves. After a few minutes, Father Andrew led them back to his house. He went upstairs and a few minutes later came back down dressed in his pure white vestments.

"Now, it's time for Mass."

The birthday cake girl who had caused him to lose his five hundred baht tagged along as they walked through the slum and out of the parking lot and across the road to the slaughterhouses. Halfway across the parking lot Father Andrew stopped to talk to a man who was using a hammer to pull nails out of a wooden door. The man had a pile of lumber under his feet. A woman in baggy jeans and a T-shirt held the door as the man extracted the nails with a hammer. It was hot and dark in the parking lot.

"Where'd you get the door?" asked Father Andrew, shining a flashlight on the man, then the door and the woman holding it.

There was no answer. The man looked up for a moment with no sense of recognition or concern that Father Andrew in his formal white robes had appeared out of the darkness. Father Andrew then addressed to her.

"Did he steal the door?"

"No, we paid for it," she said.

Father Andrew watched in silence as the man pulled out nails. He wouldn't talk to Father Andrew; he wouldn't even look at him. Jess couldn't stand the disrespect and kicked the door out of the woman's hands.

"Get out," said Jess.

The man held the hammer and took a step towards Father Andrew. Jess dropped him with a high kick that hit him square in the face. He was out cold.

"Let's go, Father Andrew," said Calvino.

So much for a low profile, Calvino thought. A singing nun and a kickboxing priest who lays out a man with one solid kick in the face.

"Good idea," said Jess.

"The man is a thief and a drug addict. I've been waiting for years for the cops to take some action. I guess I had to wait until the LAPD came to town," Father Andrew said as he pointed the flashlight into the dark.

"And the woman?" asked Jess.

"She's a whore who sells herself around Lumpini Park," said the straight talking priest. "That is as low as you can go in the whoring business. She has six kids. She's also on drugs. And now and again, she deals drugs. They've both tested HIV positive. They make a nice couple. You know, I look at a man like that, and it tests my faith. It's not like he's human. He would kill you . . . he would kill all of us in a minute and not think that he had done anything wrong. It would be like pulling nails out of the door."

As they continued to the slaughterhouse, Noi tripped and nearly fell; Calvino caught her by the arm, breaking her fall. She had stumbled over a young man who sat hunched on the pavement. The young man lifted his eyes and smiled as Father Andrew shined his flashlight on him.

"Why don't you come to Mass?"

The boy made no response, looking up blankly into the beam of the flashlight. He wore a short-sleeved green football jersey but he had no arms. A birth defect had left him with tiny claw-like appendages attached to the shoulder.

"Get off drugs and come and work for me at the center. You can be an artist."

Still no response but a sloppy drug-induced grin.

"At least get out of the road before a car runs over you." The boy got to his feet with no hands to help him and wandered off into the dark.

As they entered the slaughterhouse, Father Andrew explained that the kid was a first-rate artist; he used his feet to paint, and he had shown talent. But there was one rule for working for Father Andrew: no drugs. He had just finished his story when they rounded a corner where about thirty people sat on the floor in front of a small altar. Laotian workers with no papers. This was the place where they hid at night. Dozens of cheap fluorescent strips—the neon lights of the poor—hung from the ceiling illuminating the faces of mostly *yings* and children in the group. Father Andrew walked to the altar, raised his arms, his eyes closed, and he gave a blessing.

"Sisters and brothers, I am honored you have come to this mass. I know that you have suffered. I know that you live in fear. You feel abandoned, alone. I want to tell you the story about a small girl who is very much alone. Her name is Dew. And she's eight years old and her parents are both dead. She has two younger brothers and Dew is the head of the household. She finds food for her family. She goes to school. And when her brother was crying and wanted to go home, she went to his *hong* in the center and sat on his cot. She told him that he should close his eyes. That she was going for a taxi to take them home. Her brother closed his eyes and went to sleep. The next day was easier for him in the slum. And the next day easier than the day before. You see, it is people like Dew who teach us that even the most humble and weak can find strength, and they can give strength to others. I ask you to follow Dew's footsteps. Do not give up. Do not give in to defeat. Find the light that is in all of us, the one that can give you hope in the moment of darkness."

As he was speaking to the worshippers, a group of men started unloading pigs from a large truck parked ten feet behind the altar. Calvino touched Jess on the shoulder, pointing toward the truck.

"I don't like the look of this. This time try to keep out of it. You kick one more person in the head and we will have broadcast our location to everyone who wants to know."

Jess nodded. "You're right."

The half-dozen men spoke to each other in Khmer. That meant they had come into Bangkok from Si Sa Ket or Surin Province. The men worked with sharp, long-bladed knives. One of the men cut the throat of a pig. Other pigs waiting for the knife squealed with pure fear. Blood shot out, hitting the edge of Father Andrew's robe.

He turned to the men and spoke to them in Thai. "Please, leave us for fifteen minutes. We are giving prayers. In your religion you pray, don't you? Can't you spare us a few minutes?"

The Khmer workers ignored his plea. A large knife quickly flashed as the worker slit another pig's throat and more blood splattered Father Andrew's vestments. The spray of blood struck Noi's habit. She wiped a droplet of blood off her arm. Rubbed it between her fingers until it became sticky. Some of the kids in the makeshift congregation started to cry. One of the mothers lifted her child, her bamboo mat under one arm, and quietly left. The mood of the workers was turning ugly. They knew what they were doing and no one was going to stop them from hacking away at the dead pigs.

Calvino pulled Jess back. "Let Father Andrew handle it. He's a pro and he won't need to kick anyone."

"Please don't do this," said Father Andrew, bowing his head. "Let us pray."

The slaughtering of pigs continued. The Khmer worked efficiently together killing pigs, one after another, dozens of carcasses piled up, and in minutes Father Andrew's vestment was soaked in blood. His eyeglasses and forehead and cheeks dripped with pig's blood. His birthday special mass looked like a blood sacrifice gone wrong. It was time to leave. The Laotians had vanished. One by one the neon lights went out as if they could not bear to see the priest bloodied. Father Andrew stood at the altar, his arms extended. "There's nothing left to celebrate," Father Andrew whispered. "Let's go back." The only people left in the slaughterhouse were Jess, Noi and Calvino and the Khmer pig killers, who had their own lights rigged up and carried on with the blood letting. None of the men looked up as they worked carving up the pigs. Some of the men dragged a fresh-killed carcass over to the boiling vat of water, hoisted the dead pig, and dumped the body into the water where another worker scrubbed off the hair. The blood and gore flowed down the concrete drains in the pen. The Khmer laughed at Father Andrew; their arms covered with blood, they pointed and laughed at the priest. Fluorescent lights shining from a long row of shacks made of plywood and paper looked like swifts' nests at ceiling level where dozens of eyes peered down at the spectacle of blood and death as if watching a battlefield. Father Andrew looked up at them. He had come to preach hope and strength and courage and there he was covered in blood, covered in humiliation.

As he turned around he saw Calvino, hand under his jacket, holding his .38 police special. He couldn't stand the humiliation of his friend. The smug smiles on the Khmers' faces as if they were untouchable and these *farangs* could do absolutely nothing to stop them slaughtering pigs.

"I am not gonna let them do this," Calvino said.

It was Jess's turn to rein in Calvino, grabbing Calvino's arm. "It won't help."

Jess had been waiting, thinking at first that this was a setup. Someone had found out they were in Klong Toey and these men had been sent to finish the business that the bomb had left unfinished. But they had shown no interest in Calvino, Jess, or Noi. They were doing their job. They didn't care about anyone or anything else. Jess walked to the back of the slaughterhouse and talked with a vendor squatting near a boiling pot. The vendor told him that the pig killers were just another illegal crew of Khmer with no papers doing the dirty work of a Chinese merchant.

Jess was returning to the altar as Father Andrew and the others were leaving the slaughterhouse.

"I am at a loss for words," said Father Andrew. His voice was shallow, small, and distant. "I am sorry to have let you and your friends down."

"You haven't let us down," said Jess. "If anything we let you down. We should have done something."

Something hung in the air like a lover's excuse.

"This isn't your fight." The blood dripping off his chin. "This is my turf. Or it was mine. There is nothing you or anyone can do."

Noi was still on her knees, praying, as if somehow she could make the blood of today disappear. Father Andrew tapped her on the shoulder. She opened one eye. He motioned for her to rise. She raised her hand palms up, showing the blood caked on her fingers.

"It's time to go, my child. The damage is done."

No one spoke as they walked back through the parking lot, passing the drug addicts working through the pile of lumber, taking nails out of another door. A *Por Tek Tueng* van was parked next to Father Andrew's Toyota and two workers, or body-snatchers as the locals called them, loaded the dead man's remains for the final trip to a wat as his relatives and neighbors looked on. Everyone stopped as they saw Father Andrew covered in pig's blood. The word spread quickly through the community and soon a crowd stared at their defiled priest. It took some time for them to understand what had happened. At first they thought he had been in an accident. Everyone was talking at the same time. Father Andrew raised his hands to quiet them.

"I am going to have to leave you now. You can see what they've done to me. I have lived with you for thirty years. But I can live with you no longer. I must leave.

You can see what the Khmer slaughtering the pigs have done to me? I was holding Mass and they did this to me." He made each word separate with tiny pauses in between. There was a silence, and he raised his hands. "This defilement. I have lost my dignity. How can any priest without dignity serve you? He cannot. Without dignity, there is no respect, and without respect, faith and belief cannot exist. I have failed as a priest. I am going to the church and tomorrow I will leave. I will not come back here. I cannot come back here. Please understand me." He started to say something else, his lips moved, and he was giving a benediction, blessing them, his hand raised high in the darkness.

A dozen men quietly moved out of the crowd and started across the parking lot towards the slaughterhouse.

"Jess, take Noi back to Father Andrew's and *wait*."

He looked at Calvino. "You're not going back there."

"It's going to be worked out the Thai way," said Calvino. Another group of men from the slum who had been talking slipped away from the main crowd. Calvino found himself following them through the parking lot. The guy pulling nails out of the doors saw them coming; he dropped his hammer and ran. The woman with six kids stood her ground as several of the men picked up two-by-fours from the pile of stolen lumber.

They continued walking as a unit towards the lights in the slaughterhouse. Without any warning, they entered the pen where the Khmer were butchering pigs. The leader of the group walked forward, swung the piece of lumber as hard as he could, smashing one of the Khmers' legs. The man fell hard on the cement, howling with pain, his leg shattered. The femur was shattered; a shard of bone stuck out as if he had stepped on a landmine. The other men set to work quickly, felling the other Khmer.

It took less than a minute for the Khmer at the far end of the pen to realize what was going on but by then it was too late as the second group came in behind them and beat the last of the workers until the two by fours were splintered and bloodied. The eyes in the lofts above the slaughterhouse floor peered down at the shattered Khmer whose broken bodies lay among the slaughtered pigs on the bloodied floor. Moaning and screaming and shouting in Khmer. None of them could walk. They were dragging themselves through the blood, gore and slime, afraid the Thais would come in and finish them off. That had never been their intention. The Thais said nothing as they battered a couple of the Khmer unconscious. Calvino had never seen any group work with such precision, taking out each of the workers. Breaking an arm or a leg. The blows were not intended to kill but to maim. By the time they had finished, the slaughterhouse was silent. The Thais threw down the bloodied pieces of wood and walked out, lighting cigarettes and speaking in low voices about how the Khmer should stay in Cambodia and how the Thais had shown them mercy given the grave sin they had committed. They filed past Calvino. The leader, who had lingered a moment, stopped beside Calvino, taking a long suck on his cigarette, and said, "Tell Father Andrew that he has his dignity back. And we would like him to return to the community. We beg him not to leave us. Tell him he is respected and that he is needed."

"You should tell him yourself," said Calvino.

"Will he come back?" asked the Thai with a long, drawn face cut with harsh lines; the kind of face that looked mean or a face that mean things had been done to.

Calvino nodded. "Yeah, I think he will come back. Once he knows that he does belong here. And you showed he does belong." He leaned down and picked up one of the bloodied, discarded two by fours, turned it over in this hand, the men watching him. He walked alone through the dark and he was remembering his dream about the stranger who had come to the village to teach the art of fire, and how the villagers had turned on the man, thrown him into the fire that he had started, and how Calvino had done nothing. Like in the slaughterhouse, he had observed, passive, detached, knowing the outcome was fixed and determined. Revenge substituted for law. In a culture of revenge, getting even was the way—perhaps the only way—of curing a wound. A wound was healed by inflicting on another an equal or greater harm. If there couldn't be justice, there could be an equal proportion of pain inflicted to balance the cosmic scales of right and wrong. Father Andrew would understand these people had taken it upon themselves to avenge his harm, and how the message from the Old Testament was far stronger, powerful and accepted in a place where the seeds of the New Testament had yet to take root.

By the time Calvino entered Father Andrew's house, the priest had several people from the slum hovering around him with towels, washing his face, his arms, and his feet.

Calvino sat down at the table. "They want you to stay."

"How can I, Vincent?"

"It's like this," said Calvino, putting the bloodied two by four on the table. "The Khmer don't look so good. Seems about a dozen of the men in the slum weren't too happy at what they did to their priest. So they put things right. They did it the Thai way. They can't undo what those men did to you. But they did the next best thing. They showed everyone in this community that you belong here. That no one can insult their priest. But if anyone tries to do so, then those people have to answer to everyone in this slum. They made a statement. You aren't just a *farang* living here. You are one of them. You can't go. And it seems pretty clear they believe you have your dignity back. And they believe they have their own dignity back. The way I see it, there's no longer any reason for you to leave. They have put it right in the Thai way."

Father Andrew nodded.

The same reasoning definitely didn't apply to them. The whole community would be talking about it tonight. Authorities would come to the slum. Questions would be asked about the strange Thai priest who went with the men into the slaughterhouse. The Thai nun with blood on her hands. And the *farang* who came with them.

"We've got to go, Father Andrew," said Jess.

"He's right. We can't stay. The police will be coming around checking out the slaughterhouse."

They walked back to the *Por Tek Tueng* van. The stiff was loaded in the back and the two workers were squatting on plastic stools eating a bowl of noodles. Calvino whispered to Jess, "Let's go back to the Grand Rose Hotel."

"You've got to be crazy," said Jess.

"It's the last place they will be looking for us. Take Noi and check in. I'll see you there."

Jess said nothing as Calvino turned and walked off. There was doubt in his eyes but Calvino knew that Jess and Noi would go. He went to the table where the *Por Tek Tueng* workers were finishing up. "The priest and sister will go along with you. They need to say prayers. Otherwise the ghost will be angry. Do you understand?" He pressed a thousand-baht note against the hand of the one worker. The man looked at the note and nodded. A thousand baht and an angry ghost were powerful reasons.

The two men didn't bother finishing their noodles and headed straight back to the van.

Calvino walked back to Jess. "They will take you."

One of the men opened the *Por Tek Tueng* van doors and Jess climbed in first, then held out a hand for Sister Teresa who followed after him. The doors were shut and Noi folded her hands in prayer over the dead body. Even the *Por Tek Tueng* crew bought the performance. As the van pulled away, Calvino watched it wind through the ten-wheel trucks in the parking lot and then disappear.

★★★★★★

WAS going to the Grand Rose Hotel the right call, Calvino asked himself in the taxi ride back to Sukhumvit Road. Jess didn't think so and maybe he was right. The fact was that no place was safe. Going to Klong Toey to seek sanctuary with Father Andrew proved that nothing was ever predictable in Bangkok. As he sat in the taxi, Calvino thought about what Father Andrew had said about dignity and knew that the priest was right. Dignity was all a man had of any worth and when that was lost there was nothing else left of value to lose. The life was there, of course, but it was no longer a life with any consequence, any meaning, or a driving force for good. There were ways of losing dignity and there were ways of gaining it back. Killing was one of those ways. In most times, in most places, men killed other men because they lost their dignity and used murder to recover it. The men in the drug business—a business devoted to stealing another person's dignity—exercised their power in the cloud line above the reach of the law, and these robbers of dignity found their dignity was on the line because one LAPD cop might trace the line of powder to their door. They weren't about to let some low-ranking LAPD officer come onto their turf and throw pig's blood in their face. And the fact that Jess was Thai made the indignity all the more difficult to bear. Jess had forgotten a few things over the years of living in Los Angeles. That this powerful hidden class demanded without any exceptions honor, respect, and deference. He was like the Khmer killing pigs in front of a priest having no idea of the consequences of their act. What had started as a routine stakeout of a cheap Hollywood hotel had led to the arrest of Noi's brother, who had been caught with a suitcase of heroin in Ziploc bags. The chain reaction began at that moment and the consequences of the arrest were still playing themselves out in the streets of Bangkok. Where to hide? Where would they think to look for them?

Calvino paid the driver and got out of the taxi. The Grand Rose Hotel looked deserted. He went inside, walked through the empty lobby, and leaned on the reception counter, hitting the service bell with the palm of his hand.

An old woman's voice croaked out a "Hallo."

"*Hallo hallo hia, la ka,*" he called back. The lyrics to a song.

In the back he heard an ancient, hoarse laugh. The old woman had been sleeping on a mat behind the desk. She rose up, a tiny, frail figure of a woman with her gray hair sticking out. The same old half-blind woman who had been at the desk the first time he had arrived with Wes Naylor and Jess.

"You have a vacancy?" Calvino asked in Thai. He said this without any sense of irony. He wanted to see her reaction.

She smiled with her black teeth. "Single or double *hong*?"

"A single *hong*," Calvino said, sliding a five-hundred-baht note on the counter.

"You like Thai music?" she asked him in English.

The old woman could speak English all the time. He wondered if she hid this from not only the *farangs* but also her own family.

"I love Thai music."

"Fill this out." She slid a registration form across the counter.

He filled in the blanks—Smith, John, Student, New Zealand, born on 1 June 1964, and Nepal as the next destination—and handed back the form. The old woman didn't even look at the form, knowing whatever lies it contained didn't matter. She handed him a key attached to a long clear plastic handle with ornate roses inset.

"That is 495 baht a night," she said, rolling a five-baht coin over the counter. It fell onto the floor and rolled over the floor and into the darkness.

He knew the rate was 350 baht but said nothing. Calvino's Law: Knowing too much was never a good thing when one went into hiding as a *farang* in Thailand.

"I have a friend who checked in before," said Calvino. Yeah, that was right, *before*, nice and vague and Thai in its inability to describe what before meant.

"What's his name?" asked the old woman without blinking a blind eye.

"I met him on the plane. He's a member of the Cause. If I could see the register, I am certain I would remember it. That was three, four days ago. I am sure he came here. Can you help me?" he asked as he folded a five-hundred-baht into her old papery palm.

"Since you like Thai music, okay." She put the five-hundred-baht note inside her bra, then looked down under the counter, murmuring to herself. She might have been trying to make out the denomination of the note or she might have been looking for the registration cards from the last week. There were only six cards. She laid them out on the counter like a fortune teller with Tarot cards putting them in a semi-circle. Calvino looked at the cards. There were only five customers for the day. A man and woman. The man's name was Axel and the woman's name Joanne. The *hong* numbers were 419 and 420. He memorized the numbers. McPhail had registered under his own name as had Wes Naylor. They were on the fifth floor; *hongs* 527 and 512. And he saw another *farang* name that he did not recognize. He figured the hotel might actually have one real guest on board.

Calvino turned over his *hong* key. Thinking it takes a thief to catch one, or, in this case, to make theft difficult. Someone in the family had designed the large plastic handles so a guest couldn't argue he had simply forgot to return the key; the guest—or the person staying for a short time in the guest's room—had to make a conscious effort to steal the key. An anti-ying theft device. They obviously knew their guests and the guests of their guests as well.

The old near-blind woman had put him in *hong* 421.

Blind but not stupid.

TWELVE

CALVINO FELT WINDED as he walked up the stairs to the fourth floor. He stopped at the landing, thinking that Jess had to be a good fifteen years younger than he. He pushed the fire door open, turned right and, still catching his breath, walked down the corridor. And the guy was fast with his hands and his feet. A couple of the lights were burnt out in the corridor. Naylor was right about the place being a slum. It could have been in the middle of Klong Toey. A large rat ate off a plate left outside one of the *hongs* and showed no fear as Calvino passed by. The hallway had a closed-up attic-like smell of musty decay; the air thick like walking through a thin wet spider's web. Only junkies and backpackers would feel comfortable breathing such air. He got his breath back before he knocked on Noi's door. Nothing. He put his ear against the door. No answer. No sound. No movement inside. Then he knocked on Jess's door and again no one was inside the *hong*. So he tossed his *hong* key up, the ugly red plastic end spiralling down. He caught it—a one handed catch—and walked two doors down the corridor to his *hong*; he was nervous, thinking they should be in their *hong*, trying to decide if they were having dinner somewhere, or maybe they had run into Wes Naylor and had gone out with him, and other possible explanations started to build up in his mind. Such as that they were inside the *hong*. But they were dead. Calvino reached out to put his key into the lock and stopped cold. The door to *hong* 421 was ajar. The TV volume was on low and the flicker of light from the screen danced through the opening. Were Jess and Noi waiting inside and that was why they hadn't answered when he knocked? Or it might be that someone connected with the drug ring that Jess had struck was waiting inside to blow his brains out.

He reached inside his 199 baht jacket and in one clean, smooth motion pulled his .38 police special from his holster, kicked open the door, and went in, low, his arms extended, both hands around the handgun. Pratt, dressed in casual civilian clothes, sat with his back to the door watching television. Calvino let out a long sigh as he holstered his gun.

"Jesus, Pratt, don't do that to me."

Pratt raised his hand, slightly turned his head. "I had a bet with myself. He will pull his sidearm, I thought. Then, I thought, no, Vincent won't do that," said Pratt. He never called a gun a gun or handgun.

"Why not?"

"That's why I left the door open. Would someone who wanted to kill you leave on the TV and the door open?"

Calvino shook his head in disbelief. "Would someone put a Claymore in my car at the Emporium? Pratt, anything is possible".

Pratt watched him holster his .38. "You should be more careful with your sidearm. That's all I am saying."

Calvino, regaining his breath and composure, collapsed in a chair next to Pratt. The TV was tuned to the Discovery Channel and on the screen two great apes were at the foreplay stage of what promised to turn into a

Monster Fuck. The male ape circled the female who was obviously in heat. As he approached her, the male reached out his hand, touching a finger to the female ape's vagina. The male ran the finger under his nose, grimaced, backed away, smelled it again, and fled the scene. The female let out this loud wail of a whooping sound, her lips pursed into a perfect "O", the echo of that painful rejection in a long, pitiful scream coming from the back of her throat.

McPhail came out of the bathroom zipping up his fly, a cigarette dangling from the corner of his mouth. "Bombs blowing up. Now, guns, guns, the place is filthy with guns. And while I am at it, hey Calvino, we've been waiting for you. I mean, what took you so long? Did you go for a short-time?" McPhail did not wait for an answer. He pinched the cigarette between his forefinger and thumb and pointed it at the TV. "Man, I once fucked a nun short-time and missed a crucial business appointment. I didn't know she was a nun. This was in Burma. I had her in the bed, and grabbed her hair and it came off in my hand; I have this wig hanging limp in my hand, and my equipment immediately goes south. Her head is bald. Smooth, shaved clean so you can see every blue vein in her skin. She had just left her order and was getting a little nest egg together as she adjusted back into, should I say, lay life."

"Where's Naylor?" asked Calvino.

"Upstairs in his *hong* with his whore from the Plaza, nursing her mosquito-bitten ass back to its perfect un-blemished state. Where else would he be?" said McPhail.

"And Noi and Jess?"

"They're up on the fifth floor also," said Pratt, leaning forward and switching off the television. "Jess's been asking her some questions about people in Los Angeles. He's made some phone calls. I have made some calls."

"What's she told him?" asked Calvino. "He's still talking to her."

Calvino shifted in his chair. "Naylor's staying here with Jep?"

"Sure, Daddy-O, he closed the deal on this baby. The Brandy's history. He now owns the Grand Rose Hotel. Or at least five percent of it."

"How did he pull that off?" asked Calvino.

"While you and your friends were taking the Kong Toey scenic tour, we did some business. Let's say we offered a couple of reasons why they should do the deal."

"Like what?"

"I said to the head of the family, 'hey, that bomb that blew up at the Emporium is just the start. Who are these dark forces, these mysterious bombers? No one knows. But there are some nasty rumors, man. Right-wing Thais. Next thing, this group is gonna follow the script of those crowds in Indonesia, man, they're going straight for the Chinese. Remember all those raped Chinese *yings*? Terrible.' And I paused, let them stew for about a minute, thinking about their *yings* getting fucked, then I said, 'And all those burnt-out Chinese shops? And they also went after the Chinese hotels. Next week you might not be able to give this place away. Assuming someone doesn't burn it down. Now here's a guy with a million and a half dollar check on the table in a city with things being blown up by forces that probably don't like the Chinese. And given the unnatural way your father died in this hotel, I don't think the family karma is all that good. I don't want to rub it in about the old man dying from the bottom up, but that's how it happened.' Bull's eye. You never saw a family who hates each other's guts fall in line so fast. The blood drained out of their faces. They looked like ghosts. Next I tell them where they can put their funds to work. I told them about the Japanese guys I am doing business with. I showed them pictures of jade chops we made right there in a beautiful catalogue. And how we have this huge profit margin, and with my help, I could get them part of the action. That was it. I appealed to their worst fear, then hit them below the belt with a chance for excessive greed."

"And they went for your jade and Japanese connection."

"Went for it? They couldn't get enough of it. Seems the old man was a Burmese jade freak. Roses and Jade. A good name for a gay boarding house in San Francisco, don't you think? They signed every paper that Naylor gave them. Put their company seal on. You never saw a *hong* of Chinese sign up a deal so fast. No negotiations, no arguing over the fine print. Whoever did your car, Vincent, did Naylor a favor. That bomb and the old man's butt melting were two deal closers."

Calvino was out of the chair and moved towards the door.

"What do you mean the old man died from the bottom up. Where did you get that?" asked Calvino.

McPhail leaned closer. "You know the old woman at reception? I smoked a jay with her. Some of my best stuff, and the old man's story just slipped out of her lips before she knew what she was saying, the whole enchilada flew out the oven door. We were out in the back standing near weeds that came up to her shoulder and there was this big piece of pottery like they keep water in upcountry and she starts to laugh. She's turning blue from laughter, and I say, 'Hey, what's so funny?' And she tells me one of those family secrets you shouldn't ever tell a stranger and if she hadn't been really stoned I don't think I would have got it out of her. It turns out the old man had not been able to get it up for a number of years. He'd tried all the Chinese herbs and other bullshit remedies his buddies swore would give him a woody and nothing happened. Then Viagra came out on the black market and he got one of the bellboys to buy him some blue pills under the table at a drugstore in Patpong. The bellboy brought the pills back, the old boy pops two of them, and forty minutes later, that maid he'd been watching over several months walks past and he grabs her, pulls her into his *hong*. He hands her a couple of thousand baht, takes one of her hands and puts it down his pants. She's grabbing him and he's stripping off her clothes. He does the maid every which way but loose. The old man is suddenly sixteen again and he's not wasting a moment, Baby. This humping goes on all through the next day and he's popping more Viagra like it's candy. Poking the maid, who seems to be having a good time. After this forty-eight hours of debauchery, he collapses. I know you're thinking heart attack. So did I. But no, he passes out from all the exertion and sleeps straight through for about sixteen hours. The next day he drops a little boast to the old woman, who is his sister, saying how he had shagged the maid ten hours straight. The old woman said, 'Oh, yeah, her sister had come around, we looked everywhere for that poor girl. Her sister was worried about her. Thought she might be sick. The girl had gone in for one of those HIV tests and it came out positive.' His face, which had been full of pride and new-found youth, turned pale and aged about twenty years right before her. He ran off into the garden. When they found him about six hours later the damage had been done; it was irreversible and fatal damage. He had stripped off his pants and sat his butt in one of those large clay urns which he had filled with weed killer. The stuff you spread to keep the roses from getting choked out by the weeds. Anyway he sat in that shit long enough that it got into his rectum, discolored his balls, Daddy-O, fucking melted that man right down like he was a weird species of dandelion. They fished him out and got him to hospital but he was in toxic shock and died about three hours later. That's the story. The old bastard died slowly from the butt up."

"What you're saying is you blackmailed the family with the story."

"Hey, whatever it takes. And, don't forget that bomb worked as well. Besides, Wes got his deal done. No more death threats. I'd call that a success. I thought you'd be happy. So why do I get this distinct feeling that you're upset?"

"I am having a bad day, nothing personal, McPhail. What *hong* is Jess in?"

"509," said Pratt.

"One more thing, Pratt; how did you end up here?" asked Calvino.

Pratt smiled. "McPhail phoned and said that you had asked me for a favor."

"What favor was that?" asked Calvino looking over at McPhail, who was lighting another cigarette.

"You know, man, that the Colonel was to come around and tell the owner that he should be careful." McPhail blew out the smoke. "Nothing heavy, just to let them know things were dangerous with bombs killing people on Sukhumvit Road. And the police were thinking about reopening the case on the cause of death of the father."

"Remind me, why did I want Pratt to do this favor?"

"Because it would remove the threat to this guy you were hired to guard. The same guy you asked me to guard for you. If the deal closed, no more threat. Finished. Everyone's a happy camper."

"Naylor was never under any serious threat," said Calvino.

"No shit?" replied McPhail, his jaw open and smoke pouring out.

"What are our chances of getting Jess back to LA?" Calvino asked Pratt.

"*I sometimes do believe, and sometimes do not; As those that fear they hope, and know they fear.*" Pratt quoted Orlando's reply to the Duke who had asked, "*Dost thou believe, Orlando, that the boy can do all this that he hath promised.*"

"What is that you just said?" asked McPhail, looking confused and amused at the same time—a state of being that pot induced. "Shakespeare? Cool. Man, you are profound for a cop."

★★★★★★

NOI smoothed out her white nun's habit, brushed her long nails against the pig's bloodstain that had turned an ugly blotchy dull copper tone. She sat on the edge of the bed, legs crossed, absorbed in her cleaning ritual. Actually she was buying time as she collected her thoughts, deciding what to leave in, what to leave out, editing her story, taking her pitch to that ultimate level that all super-sales people desire to achieve just once in their lifetime. Across from her, Jess had been asking for her confession. The fact that he was dressed as a priest *and* was a real life cop *and* a real life LAPD cop was enough to make Noi scratch holes in the nun's habit as she tried to navigate in her own mind what she was going to say to him. She liked him. More than that, she was attracted to him; physically attracted to him ever since she saw how well he could kick someone in the face. That made her feel safe and happy all at the same time. When Calvino wheeled into the *hong*, she looked up at his tired, beat-up face, and took a sip of water from a glass. She was glad that a *farang* was in the *hong* because *farangs* always made it easier to tell stories. They so much wanted to believe and they were so fucking earnest. The terrible oppression of being alone with Jessada in that *hong*, knowing he could see right through her, drill straight through her core material, see that she was bullshitting. The interrogation was almost too much to bear, even though she wouldn't have minded fucking his brains out—that was different from having his brain sift through the stuff that had happened to her. So she decided to continue her story, pretending that Calvino was the guy listening and forgetting that Jessada was only three feet away making her horny. She continued repeating her story, the start of the story anyway, over and over again, like a broken record or like a *ying* in a bar putting the needle on the beginning of the record each time a new customer sat down and asked about her life. From the moment Calvino walked into the *hong*, he had sensed what was coming down, the way she repeated herself. He asked himself: Had she been on the scene long enough to have refined her pitch to such perfection that the polished surface of reality became the only reality? And this little stutter trick was to throw everyone off as if she was confused and just working through it the first time. Or was she the real thing?

Give her a break, he thought. The nun's habit worked in her favor; if she had been in a bikini, forget it; he would have been out the door. It all started over lunch at a restaurant off Silom Road.

"I was with my friends. There a group of us eating lunch. Maybe ten people. All from the same office. All of my friends were women. Silom office workers' Mafia. That's what we called ourselves. We talked about everything. We gossiped about the bosses, talked about films, soap operas, movie stars, getting married, getting rich, buying a condo. And no one was paying any attention when a *farang* came over to our table. I thought it was some kind of a mistake. He leaned forward and whispered loud enough for my friends to hear that he was madly in love with me. I pretended not to hear him. Only he repeated himself loud enough that everyone else stopped talking. I could have died. He had been at the next table. He said that he had been watching me ever since I had arrived. I thought he was joking. I told him that he had a sweet mouth like all *farangs*, and I thought he would go away. I go back to talking to my friends. But the *farang* doesn't leave. I giggle. But he doesn't under-stand this is my way to ask him to leave. Next he pulls up a chair and he says, 'Please give me your phone number.' 'Why should I do that?' I ask him. And he is ready for me. 'Because I want to marry you.' My friends are watching the whole thing. They hear him proposing. Maybe some are a little upset, jealous. This is a young, good-looking *farang* who is thirty-something. But I have no experience in someone doing this to me in public. I think he's not dtem baht. Slightly crazy but not in a bad, dangerous way. I try to ignore him. That doesn't work. He takes hold of my hand and drops on one knee. For whatever reason, maybe I am a crazy girl, I start to take him seriously; I am not from upcountry, I am not stupid. I went to university. I graduated from university too. My family is not rich but middle class and they are very strict with me. No way a *farang* would be my husband. What should I do? I am about to do something that will disappoint my family. Maybe I am selfish. Because what I do next I know is wrong and will hurt my family. I take out my pen and write down my phone number. Now I think he will go away. And I think he won't call me and I am a little sad. I wonder if anything he said was real or truth; I think that someone had put him up to saying all those things to me or he was born with less than 100 satang in the baht, Thai slang for moron.

All this happened on a Monday, and a week later, I went to bed with this foreigner. Three weeks later he gave me his grandmother's wedding ring. He told me his grandmother put it on for the first time in 1907. I was so proud to have the ring on my finger. I would have done anything for him. Two months later, I had a baby inside, and only then did I start to find out the truth. When I was six months pregnant, I told him I would spend the night at my mother's house. I missed him too much so I went back to the apartment. It was two in the morning and he's in our bed with two bar *yings* from Nana Plaza. He was bent over one of them spanking her. With his hand. Her ass had red handprints. You could see the shape of each finger on her skin. I asked him, 'What are you doing?' And he answered me, 'A root job. I am rooting her. Stick around and you might learn a thing or two.' Root job, I had no idea what he was talking about. Root canal, tree root, root beer, root as in Route 66. I really didn't know that *farang* used this to mean having sex and doing other things. Like spanking. A week later I caught him with another girl. He was using a belt this time. This was no accident. This was his secret way of life. He cannot leave bar *yings* alone. He cannot stop himself from spanking them. When he's not at work, he's on the Internet three, four hours a day, posting photos of *yings* he has spanked. Puts them out there for anyone to see. I saw the photos and I read what he wrote about the *yings*. Afterwards I vomited. I was seven months pregnant when I found out that he had a child by a bar *ying* in Chiang Mai. He doesn't send support payments, though sometimes he goes to see his baby. I know him now and know that he had no interest in his child. I know he will have no interest in my baby. A month after I had the baby, I found out he had given other women his "grandmother's wedding ring" dated 1907; either the grandmother was getting married lots of times in 1907 or her grandson was a liar. I knew in my heart that I made a big mistake marrying him and that I had better get out of his life." Noi drank from a glass of water, put her head back for a moment.

She had taken them on the grand tour through the emotional and psychological freak show she had lived with the father of her baby; a *farang* who was half computer nerd, with the rest divided between Romeo, bum, scam artist, dreamer, and user. This monster had deceived her. Her friends and family abandoned her. She had nowhere to turn, no place to go. She had given birth to a beautiful child and she worried that he would no doubt come infrequently to stare at this child like the one in Chiang Mai as if it reaffirmed that he was capable of reproduction, that his genetic material had been passed down the line one more time. It was too late for her to go back to her old life. Being middle class and Buddhist, an abortion had been out of the question; her life was set now. She learned to accept a fate that was without hope; a remorseless fate of one day after another in which no one she had ever known or loved would recognize that she existed.

"That was Danny. The *farang* who died at the Emporium?" Jess was asking her in a gentle way.

She shook her head. "No, I met Danny later. He was a 'jockey' or that is how he described taking *yings* from

Bangkok to the States. Sometimes to England or Japan. Like with my husband, I didn't know what Danny really did until much later. I am such a stupid girl," she said. "So when you ask me to trust you, I ask myself, 'how can I do that?' Each time I trust a guy before, I get hurt."

"Did Gabe Holerstone lie to you?" asked Calvino.

"To be honest, he didn't. I met Gabe at Renoir on Soi 33. I had just started the week he came into the bar. Only two months earlier I had the baby. The bar hired me as a hostess. No dancing. No see-through blouses or bikinis. No one forced you to go out with customers. The other *yings* said the tips were good. Then I met Gabe. I told him my story. After he listened, he said that he owned a Thai karaoke bar in Hollywood, and that a really good crowd came to his place. And that if I really wanted a fresh start, working in the bar wasn't the way to go; I should go to Los Angeles and he would help me with my singing career. That had been my secret dream. To sing. To get paid to go on stage and sing before a large audience. I am looking at this guy across the bar, and I am thinking of all the lies *farangs* have told me. Is this bullshit or is this the opportunity of a lifetime? God, I really don't trust my own judgement. I think to myself, what do I have to lose? Not much. My respectable life was ruined, my reputation destroyed, my respectable family and friends saying that I was nothing more than a *farang*'s whore. Gabe's offer was a chance to leave Thailand. I had no future in my own country. Why not leave? With my university education, I had no trouble getting a visa from the American Embassy. A month later I was in LA standing in front of Gabe's place. In my mind his club was a grand palace like in the movies. Glamorous people, expensive cars in front, waiters in black tie. Instead, it was a rundown bar that served near-beer and the customers were mainly second, third level Koreans and Japanese businessmen. They paid forty-three bucks an hour for me to sit and talk to them. We would go back to the karaoke room and sing together. It was cheaper than seeing a shrink and probably a whole lot less stressful, as the customer didn't have to say anything if he didn't want to. And if he did, then I laughed as if what he said was the most amusing thing I had ever heard. By the time tips and drinks were factored in, it was costing the customer a hundred bucks for an hour's conversation. And I didn't have to fuck them. No one I knew would ever believe men would pay a hundred dollars to talk to a girl and know that the money only bought an hour of conversation. Gabe had promised me a singing career. And I was singing every night. Before an audience of one, two, up to six customers. But this was not the career I had in my dreams. I got a percentage of what the bar took but Gabe was a smart businessman and he kept most of the money. I was a popular girl and very busy most nights; talking and singing five, six, seven hours. Multiply that by a week, then a month, and it was clear I was making some serious cash for Gabe.

"I moved into Gabe's apartment, showed up for work, and talked to Koreans all night, seven days a week. He had already hired my brother. After Charn got busted for drugs, I went to Gabe and asked for money to hire a lawyer. He gave me a couple thousand dollars. I owed him big; hiring my brother, paying for the lawyer, so when he asked me to go back to Thailand for a holiday, all expenses paid, to see my son, I felt it was my duty to help him. He explained how he had invented this game where he would hire a private eye to try and find me but I was to stay out of Bangkok until Gabe told me that it was okay to talk to the private eye. And once he gave me the all clear, then I was to pretend that I didn't want to talk to Gabe. When I asked why he wanted to play this crazy game, he put a forefinger to my lips, asking me to remember that he had helped me and Charn and that Charn was still in jail and would need a lot more help. A couple of days later I get a call from Danny, my ex-boyfriend, a *farang* I met after I left the father of my baby. We had a thing that lasted six weeks. We had fights over money, his cheating with other *yings*, his lying. When I saw him this time, he looked completely changed. He had a new job. He picked me up in a new 730 BMW. He had a new Rolex and wore an expensive French designer shirt with gold cuff links. He told me he had learned his lesson about how I had said he was irresponsible. He said that he had found a good job, and was in business with some really cool people. I asked him what kind of work and he said he had become a 'jockey.'

"I liked his change of attitude and even thought for twenty- five seconds that something like a second chance might be possible. He said that he had scored a DJ job and the money was good. So I asked him who his boss was. 'Gabe Holerstone,' he said and I nearly fell off my chair. Danny had a gun and showed it to me and I started to get scared. The next thing he's falling from the fifth floor of the Emporium."

He had taken the big jump. Actually, Naylor had thrown his ass over the side, looking down as Danny went splat on the marble floor. Blood pouring out his ears and mouth. Brain splashed out of his skull. Calvino remembered finding her holding his lifeless cracked skull leaking brains onto her lap. And now he was thinking about the holes in Noi's story. Stuff that she had left out. He didn't believe for a minute that she had suddenly run into Danny and found out that he was working for

Gabe. A jockey didn't make the kind of cash for toys Noi had described; either she was lying about the new BMW or Danny had other cash flows. And not a word about Kowit and how he figured in the trouble her brother had gotten himself into. She was fast, smart, knew the kind of things to dwell on, like the spanking fetish of her nameless husband; the kind of thing that would have brought Jess over to her side, set him up to hate the bad *farang* who abused the women. The whole time that she was talking Jess was writing down notes in his cop's notebook. He had hardly looked up. There had been no need to egg her on; Noi was in high gear with the brake off. By the time she started talking about what happened in the Emporium, Calvino decided it was time to get her talking about LA again.

"Gabe and Kowit were buddies, right?" asked Calvino.

She nodded. "Kowit came around to the bar. Gabe told me that Kowit was a silent partner." It was interesting how she had dropped the polite form of address, "Khun", which Thais always added before the name of the person they were talking about. Either she didn't respect him or she had become Americanized, where this form of respect would have seemed old-fashioned, not cool.

"What do you think that Gabe meant by that?" asked Jess.

"That Kowit put money into the business and let Gabe make all the decisions about how to run it. I guess that's how he meant it. I never saw Kowit ordering anyone around the bar."

"But Gabe gave Kowit a cut of the take?" asked Calvino. "Kowit would come in and bring in cash? And then take out cash? Is that how they worked?"

"I wasn't their accountant. I don't know about the money. Who got what, I don't know."

"You lived with Gabe. A woman living with a man knows his business," said Calvino, and he was walking around, getting pissed off that she was being evasive.

"Once, I asked Gabe about Kowit, and he told me to leave the fucking business side to him. He was angry when he said this. Like I overstepped the line. So I backed off. That side of it had nothing to do with me."

"But it had a lot to do with your brother. How did your brother get mixed up with Kowit?" asked Jess.

The question left her silent for a moment. "It sounds stupid."

"What does?" asked Calvino.

"They both like to gamble on cock fights. There was a group of Thais that met every Sunday at Wat Thai. Cock fights and betting on them was illegal but Kowit got my brother to help arrange the place, help with security, that kind of thing. He bought my brother a prize cock and my brother won money for him at the cock fights."

"Then Kowit moved your brother into another illegal business. Drugs," said Jess.

A look of hate crossed her face. "You already know that. You arrested him."

"Would he testify against Kowit if I could get him immunity?" asked Jess. "Trust me, I can make this happen."

Here was another man asking her to do something based on trust. She didn't trust anyone. How could she trust the cop who had busted her own brother? Then she remembered some basic reality—that she was alone. She had almost no choice. It didn't matter if she trusted this LAPD cop or not. She had nothing to lose. Her eyes clouded over with tears that spurted out and rolled down her checks.

"I don't know. I don't know anything. If I did, do you think I would have got involved in any of this? I am scared and I am sad. And I know you think that I am bad and that I helped them plant the bomb. I didn't. Please believe me."

Calvino sat in a chair near the door. "About Danny?"

"I don't know. Don't ask me about Danny. I am worried about my brother, myself, my son. What will happen to my son? What if they try to hurt him to get back at me and my brother?" She paused and looked at Jess and Calvino. "I don't want to go back to LA. I have to stay and protect my son. Please understand me."

"Where is your son?" asked Calvino. "Pratt will make certain nothing happens to him."

"Should I believe you?" she asked.

Jess looked at him.

"You have someone else in mind who is going to keep your kid safe?"

★★★★★★

AT Lovejoy, Naylor sat next to a member of the Cause. This was a weekly mini-convention that members had when in town. They bullshitted each other about their conquests, going into the details of how many *yings* they had taken, the price paid, the performance, the quality, rating the last issue of *yingzine*. They could have been a middle-aged group of dog breeders talking about the awards they had received from their last show. The bond of their membership was clear: it was *ying* bonding. And there was a guy, a retired professor, named Arnold (with one of those family names that was two vowels short of being pronounceable) from Spring Lake, New Jersey, who nursed a Kloster Beer firmly wedged inside one of those moulded foam coolers the *dek serve* called "condoms."

"The only *yings* I've ever sustained a long term relationship with are the ones that I never fucked," said Ted. "Once bodily fluids are exchanged, the die is cast; nothing can ever call back the balance, the fidelity, the trust that preceded that act of coupling. What replaces this is a monstrous deterioration as if a slow-working poison had been injected into the veins, and the imbalance, the improbable scenes, the irrational behavior are the by-product of sex for which there is no cure."

"Whatever the fuck that means," said Naylor.

"Sex with any woman changes the equation. Afterwards all the numbers cling together, the demands are not far behind, and marching side by side with the demands are strange fears and desires, an army of demands fully capable of committing the worst atrocities."

"All I know is that I've got the sickness," said Naylor, squeezing Jep's thigh. "An abnormal desire to spend all my money on drinking, bar fines, and paying for the medicine, food, housing and spending money for a woman I haven't even fucked."

"Live with her and in two years she will despise you. Guaranteed," said Roadster, a youngish guy with one of those huge shit-bag guts like someone had opened his belly and stuffed a large piece of luggage inside and sewn him back up. "Live with her for five years and you will despise yourself."

"Live with her for eight years and she will own everything you've got, including your pension," said Skeleton, a speed freak who had never been seen eating any solid food and weighed about 120 pounds.

A member nicknamed Kashmir was eating a leg of chicken with greasy fingers, making sucking noises as he used his teeth to tear off strips of flesh and chew. He belched. "I've done eighty *yings* this year. All this talk about living with a *ying* is a perversion. You can't live with a woman anymore than you can breathe carbon dioxide."

Wes stroked the hair of Jep who, straddled his knee, resting on her pelvic bone, and was talking to the whore who was giving Ted a neck massage while watching the TV above the bar.

"Kashmir, you're full of shit. Roadster, buy the future Mrs. Naylor a lady's drink."

"Is that *ying* Eric's?" asked Weasel, who was sitting in the back.

That accusation brought quiet to the bar. It was laid on the table. Had Naylor breached the YINGS? "She says they broke up."

"A *ying* is known to lie. What does Eric say?" asked Weasel, moving down the bar. He kept a close eye on the future Mrs. Naylor.

"I know what you are doing," said Naylor. "Since you fucked Mucus' *ying* you are trying to shift the blame. Am I right? I have not had sex with her. Not once. So I am clean. You understand that? Clean."

"Mucus isn't ever gonna show up, so it don't matter," said Kashmir.

Calvino walked into the bar and took the stool vacated by one of Jep's friends. He sat next to Naylor. "Well, well, Vincent Calvino. Welcome to our meeting. We were just talking about the problem of relationships."

"A relationship is like a massacre," said Kashmir.

"A war crime," said Roadster.

"A sickness," said Ted the Professor.

"A court case," said Weasel.

"I heard you closed the deal on the hotel," said Calvino, pointing at the bottle of Mekhong above the bar.

"That Chinese family finally listened to reason."

"You mean they listened to McPhail," said Calvino.

"This is one of my ex-bodyguards," Wes Naylor said to Ted. He was like a guy bragging about owning a sports team or race horse. "Where's Jess?"

"With our assignment finished, he's booking his return to LA."

"Tell him that I wish him luck," said Naylor.

"He needs some help getting back," said Calvino.

Naylor's brows knitted together and he looked mean. "What am I, his travel agent?"

Naylor's tiny pig-like eyes flashed with annoyance. He pushed back Jep's hair and kissed her neck. Calvino let him alone for a few moments. Sucking on Jep's earlobe seemed to calm down Naylor. "Let's go outside."

"I'm in a meeting," said Naylor. "I can't just go outside. Besides, last time I went outside with you it got very dangerous."

"Okay, remember the guy you pushed over the side at the Emporium?"

Naylor lifted off his stool. "Let's go outside."

Once they were outside, Naylor looked like he wanted to punch Calvino.

"Jesus, you can't go around broadcasting that I killed that guy. Are you totally nuts? There are guys in there who will post that on the Net."

"You just admitted it. You killed him. Threw him over the side."

"He was trying to kill you."

"I told Colonel Pratt that's your story. But there are reports to fill out. It's not like the movies, where the police just forget the paperwork when someone is killed. You have any idea how many forms the police have to fill out?"

"You told the Thai cops that I killed that scumbag?"

"I told Colonel Pratt I saw you throw Daniel over the railing. Of course, I have tried to put in a good word for you. I don't think you would have to serve any serious time. I am willing to say that you acted in self-defence. Sometimes things go in weird directions in Thailand. Not that long ago the police kept a German locked up for months, saying he was a drug dealer but never charging. The German said he was innocent. The police said he was dirty. A stalemate. Who do you think wins in that situation? The *farang* or the Thai police? It's like this, Wes: it's hard getting a *farang* the police don't like out of jail."

"But if they like me, then my problem disappears?" asked Naylor, who looked worried. He no longer was joking around with Jep. Calvino had his full attention.

"If you help us, I think the police are going to love you. No problem."

"Fuck, Calvino. What do I have to do?"

"First, we go down to the morgue at the Police Hospital. A duty officer from the American Embassy needs you to identify the body," said Calvino.

"Tell Jess and the cops to go fuck themselves. I ain't identifying any dead body."

"You look at the body and say, that's Daniel Ramsey," said Calvino.

"For all I know this is some kind of confession that I killed someone and they will fuck me over for money. That's what this is about, isn't it?"

"No, that's not what it's about. You are the dead man's lawyer."

"I don't do estate work."

"The Ramsey family has authorized you to arrange their son's return to Los Angeles."

"You are a sick fuck. You're threatening me. You're coercing me, Calvino." The full implication of falling off the Causeway into the void of the legal system in Thailand finally began to sink into Naylor's skull. And this vision, this new vision of prisons and dirty cells and leg irons, made his stomach churn, his skin go cold.

Calvino paused for a moment, his hands on the railing, looking down at the Plaza. He could sense that Naylor was slowly giving in. He wanted to make it easy for him. Let him keep his face because he had to go back into the bar and tell his friends and Jep that he couldn't stick around. "This will take about twenty minutes of your time. I think you owe Jess one, Wes," said Calvino. "He saved your ass."

Naylor clenched his jaw so the bone showed through the skin. He stared hard at Calvino.

"I need to see the papers."

"I have arranged for that," said Calvino.

"I am not sure I wanna get near any papers you arranged. They might be like your car."

Calvino nodded to the bar. "Let's go back inside. Finish your drink. Settle up with your friends. Trust me. This will be different. Calm down. Relax. You get too excited. You could have a heart attack from too much excitement."

They sat back at the bar and Calvino took a drink from his Mekhong and coke, and took out the papers and slid them across the bar to Naylor. "Just sign the power of attorney."

Roadster, Kashmir, and Ted watched as Naylor put on his glasses and read the paper.

Naylor leaned in close to Calvino and whispered, "This says I am appointed by the deceased's next of kin to act as their attorney. Is this a joke? I killed the cocksucker. I can't fucking sign these."

Naylor's fists lay on the document in the dimly lit bar.

"Why not? As you said, you killed the bastard. All this is about is returning the dead man's remains to the States.

Is that such a bad thing?"

Naylor glared at him, looked down at the paper. "Why is it I don't trust you, Calvino?"

"You would be dead if it hadn't been for Jess and me."

Naylor leaned over the bar and signed the power of attorney and other papers in fourteen different places. He shoved them back across to Calvino. "What else do you want?"

Calvino stood up from the stool and shoved a hundred-baht note in the chit cup. "Let's go to the morgue. Tomorrow we take the coffin to the airport and see that it gets loaded onto the right plane."

"Remember the last time on that airport road, someone shot at us?"

"I thought that didn't bother you."

"Well, it didn't. It didn't seem real."

"Not real? Every time someone has shot at me, it seemed real. I never confuse the real with the pretend, the dead with the living, a lie with the truth, or a bar *ying*'s pitch with what actually happened to fuck up her life." Calvino finished his drink, nodded at Jep, who leaned forward, her hands clasped around Naylor's thick neck. She was laughing; she was taking him for a ride and her mosquito bites were healing. Roadster was eyeing her the way a predator eyes a meal strolling down a jungle trail. If Wes Naylor could violate the YINGS, why couldn't everyone else?

"One more thing: I wouldn't bring Jep along to the morgue." Calvino pointed at an unopened bottle of Johnny Walker Black set against the mirror.

Roadster broke into a wide, shit-eating grin of a smile. About five thousand dollars worth of dental work might have made it a pretty smile.

The waitress thought Calvino wanted a drink from the Johnny Walker bottle and she started to open it.

"I want the bottle. Don't open it," Calvino said to her in Thai.

As he paid for the bottle, Naylor leaned over and said, "You are an odd sonofabitch. You drink Mekhong in the bar, and take Johnny Walker Black to your *hong* to drink alone."

Calvino paid for the bottle and asked the waitress to put it in a plastic bag.

"We have some business to finish," said Calvino.

"You have business. Mine is finished." Naylor liked to challenge him; there were men for whom this was part of their nature—they could never give any ground, it was deep in their nature to throw back whatever someone said to them like it was a tennis ball. It was a game to see who would give in first, who would lose his cool. Calvino knew Naylor's game and he declined to play, as the stakes were too high. He needed Naylor's help or none of the plans would work, so what he did was let Naylor have his victory in front of his friends. Guys like Naylor were made controllable by allowing them to win. It only had to be a surface win for them to do a victory dance. Winning was their way of life, their face, their way of seeing themselves in a world where everyone was ultimately a loser. Kashmir and Roadster watched from the bar. As Roadster's hand crept over and touched Jep, Naylor slapped it away.

As Calvino headed for the door, he turned back and said, "You're right, Wes. I am the one with a problem. And I need your help. I am asking you because I have no other choice. You hold the winning hand. A full house and I am holding crap. But I don't think you will hold that against me. I'll wait for you outside." He went outside and stood besides the railing opposite Lovejoy Bar. He leaned back and waited. After a couple of minutes, Naylor hadn't come out, so he went back into the bar and stood near the staircase leading up to the private living quarters. Naylor looked annoyed as he saw that Calvino had come back inside. He moaned, reached for his wallet and started to take out cash to pay the bill. "Okay, okay. *Chek bin.* Bring me the fucking bill." One floor up Jack and his wife were fighting about money and her relatives and her fucking around. Jack was calling her a whore, a slut, a liar. Something made of glass smashed against a wall.

Naylor slammed the money down and said to his friends. "Meeting's adjourned. Case against Weasel dismissed. Insufficient evidence and the complainant failed to show."

Calvino let Naylor walk past him and out the door. It had started to rain and down below people were scrambling for cover. Calvino followed, stepping into the heavy night air of the plaza. The wet air smelled of garlic and palm oil and hamburger meat. On the landing, Calvino looked inside the beauty parlor where several *yings* were having their hair done. Below, the Plaza was filled with punters wide-eyed, grinning, negotiating the narrow corridor between the tables and bar entrances on the second floor. The corridor and landings were thick with beggars, kids selling gum, men selling flowers, and bar *yings* smoking cigarettes. A couple of *katoeys* in tight short-shorts patrolled the far end of the Plaza, trapping a couple of tourists and trying to drag them into their bar. Clouds kept the moon and stars hidden. Bright neon lights reflected off the wet pavement. Pretty Girl. G-Spot. Rainbow. Spirit House. Spider's Web. Hollywood. There were no stars on the walkways. Only wannabe stars appearing in their own scripted world, lining up the next *farang* for an audition, pitching him the story of their life. Like Noi had pitched hers in the hotel *hong*. There was a dreary sameness to the pitch. It was as if it should be in capital letters: THE PITCH. Every night, rain or shine, the pretty ones would get chosen. And the plain ones would dance until two and go home alone until they learned that the new *farangs* who had never heard the pitch would take them. That made all the difference in the world.

THIRTEEN

THE FIRST THING that happened after they left for the car park was that a couple of men seized the opportunity to loot Danny's body, so by the time the police and body-snatchers had arrived at the Emporium, all they knew was they had a dead *farang* with no ID. As terrified shoppers fled outside, the looters stripped Danny's wallet, Rolex watch, two rings, his Italian shoes, and cash inside his trouser pockets. They left his designer sunglasses with the smashed lenses. The thing about looting a dead body was that it didn't take long, as there was no resistance and the only pressure was to finish before another looter came along or the authorities arrived. The police had no way of knowing who the dead man was or his address, nationality or any of the small details that go into identifying someone and notifying the next of kin.

The second thing that happened to Danny's lifeless body on the ground floor of the Emporium after the police arrived and confirmed that he was dead was that the sergeant called a cousin who worked for one of the body snatcher associations. Twenty minutes later, a white van showed up with two men dressed in what might pass as a North Korean mini-submarine team, each zipped into a one-piece jump suit. They parked the van outside the front entrance. Other body snatcher meat wagons had been dispatched to the underground parking lot to pick up the pieces of the two men who had been killed by the Claymore inside Calvino's Honda. No one was sure from the body fragments how many bodies had been blown up. Rumors bounced from the hospitals to police headquarters, with the body snatchers monitoring police frequencies and dispatching their men in the race to be first. In the old days there would have been fights and sometimes shots exchanged between rival body snatchers. On the day of the bombing, no one was fighting for the mess in the underground parking lot.

Two body snatchers rolled Danny's body onto a gurney and pushed the gurney along the marble floors to the main entrance and loaded it into the back of the van. They drove straight to the Police Hospital, passing the Erawan Shrine, and delivered the body to the police forensic lab. Danny's body was wheeled into the autopsy room with half a dozen polished metal tables with three men in lab coats, rubber gloves, and flip-flops bent over bodies with sharp instruments, performing autopsies. The air-conditioning was cranked up full blast. Thai pop music boomed from speakers near the bank of drawers where the bodies were stored. The frozen smell of chemicals was overpowering, like sticking one's head into a freezer sprayed with Listerine. All the doctors wore white paper masks. Danny's body was added to the list for an autopsy. When the police sergeant returned to his office, he phoned the American Embassy and said they had collected the body of a *farang* who might be an American. A duty officer went down to the Police Hospital and by the time he had arrived, the attendants had stripped the body. On the left shoulder was a tattoo: LA Home Boy. Los Angeles was a large city but there was no way the Embassy could track down the identity of the dead man based on a tattoo. He was one of the forty-two Americans who had died in Bangkok over the past year. Dwight Morgan, the duty officer who saw the body, sighed and thought that more than likely the American Citizens' Service staff would have to chip in and pay for the cremation. Unless by some miracle a relative would show up and make a positive ID. Morgan called Calvino's office and asked his secretary if Vincent might be able to help identify a young man who had died in the Emporium. Ratana passed this message to Calvino, who phoned Morgan. Calvino took down a description of the deceased.

"This one isn't a heroin overdose—he died at the Emporium in a fall—and all his valuables are missing. So he doesn't fit the profile. But I had a hunch you might be able to help." Morgan had been the only one in the Embassy who had thought that a serial killer might be injecting Americans with heroin.

Hunch my ass, thought Calvino. Morgan had found out that it had been Calvino's car that had taken the bomb at the Emporium. "Let me make some calls," Calvino said.

A couple of hours later Calvino phoned Morgan, "There is an American who was seeing a guy named Danny Ramsey. Wesley Naylor is his name. He's a lawyer. Danny's parents sent him to Bangkok because they were worried about their son. Danny had some problems getting over a broken relationship with a bar *ying* and threatened to kill himself."

"Naylor really said that?" "That's what he told me."

"Could you bring him to identify the body? Maybe it's the same guy."

"Can do. Maybe your dead guy is another victim of a broken heart."

"Phone me when you are on the way. I will meet you at the morgue. Let's see if the lawyer identifies the body," said Morgan. He paused as if waiting for some reassurance that this was going to happen. Calvino didn't say anything, and Morgan continued, "Prepare him before taking him inside the morgue. The last time I took a civilian in they were sawing off a leg, then opened the wrong drawer and there was bloated body that had been dead for over a week. The guy passed out. His legs buckled and he went down hard. They carried him out to the hallway for fresh air."

"I was at the Emporium when the bomb went off," said Calvino.

"So I heard," said Morgan.

Calvino suspected he had already heard a great deal of things, and calling him had something to do with that inside knowledge.

"Meet us at the morgue in an hour."

"You don't want to phone and confirm?"

"I'll be there. Guaranteed."

★★★★★★

THE Police Hospital staff working the morgue knew Calvino. He was one of the few living *farangs* they had seen more than once or twice. All the rest of the *farangs* were either dead, passing relatives, or Embassy staff who usually burnt out after six months of dead-American duty.

"What I have to do is identify the body of that guy I dropped?" asked Wes Naylor. He made it sound like a piece of crystal that had slipped out of his hands. Like it has been some kind of an accident. Naylor stank of stale beer as he sat in the back of the taxi next to Calvino. "But I don't know the guy. Never seen him before."

"His name is Daniel Ramsey. Thirty-four years old. Born in Los Angeles. His father's name is Bill and his mother's name is Patricia. You have just become their family lawyer. I have already phoned Ramsey's parents and explained the situation. I told them an American lawyer was making the arrangements for their son. You can bill them when you get back to LA."

"I dropped that cocksucker and now you want me to bill his parents?" Ever since they had left Roadster, Skeleton, and Kashmir back at Lovejoy, Naylor had gone sullen, mean-spirited. He didn't want to be doing this. He hated himself for caving in to Calvino. And now he simply wanted to get it over with as soon as possible and get back to the Plaza.

"Up to you," said Calvino.

"What do I have to say?" asked Naylor, working his jaw with his right hand.

"That's Daniel."

"What else?"

"And that you are the family lawyer. You came to Thailand on behalf of the parents to find Daniel and bring him back home. The American Embassy will have a duty officer and he might ask a few questions. His name is Dwight Morgan. I know him. Dwight might ask you about how does he contact Danny's parents or wife or next of kin."

"I don't know who they are or where they live."

"His parents live in the Valley. I have their phone number. Give the number to the duty officer."

"Who is the duty officer?"

"Dwight Morgan. You are going to handle this just fine."

"What if Dwight calls the parents? They don't know me. I'm fucked. Defrauding the US Government is a serious fucking offence."

"There's no fraud, Wes. I've already talked to Danny's mother. I explained the situation to Mrs. Ramsey, and that you are bringing her son back to Los Angeles."

"You didn't tell her that I killed the little bastard," said Naylor.

"I left that part out."

★★★★★★

DWIGHT Morgan was waiting outside the autopsy room. He sat in a chair, reading The *Asian Wall Street Journal* and sipping a diet coke. A career officer half-way through his second year at the Embassy in Bangkok, Dwight wondered why, after a distinguished record at Harvard, destiny had led him to morgue duty in Bangkok while his classmates were getting rich doing M&A work, buying into Internet IPOs, and starting up e-commerce companies. America was about commerce. And here he was shipping back dead Americans for a living and calling himself a diplomat. As Dwight spotted Calvino walking in with a Foodland plastic bag, he folded the newspaper and rose from the chair. Naylor was walking next to Calvino. Morgan thought Naylor didn't look much like a lawyer with his shirt unbuttoned to his navel with a fifteen-baht gold chain the size of a horse collar around his neck.

"Dwight, this is Wesley Naylor, the LA lawyer who represents the Ramsey family," said Calvino.

Dwight extended his hand. "Sorry to meet in such unfortunate circumstances and to put you through this ordeal, Mr. Naylor. But when is the last time you saw Mr. Ramsey?"

"Yesterday. The day he died," said Naylor without a moment's hesitation. The conviction of truth rang in his words.

This impressed the duty officer. Morgan took another sip from his diet coke. "Then you should be able to tell us whether the body of the man inside is that of Mr. Ramsey."

Naylor simply nodded.

"Let's get it over with," said Dwight Morgan.

As they walked inside the morgue, Dwight Morgan walked ahead and, speaking in fluent Thai, asked one of the attendants to open the drawer with the dead *farang* from the Emporium. The attendants led them to the far end of the room and opened a drawer. Naylor was gagging and coughing from the smell. It was ice cold from the air-conditioning set on high.

"You okay?" asked Calvino.

"How can you stand that stink?" His faced twisted in horror.

"Try breathing through your mouth," said Calvino.

"It doesn't taste any better than it smells," replied Naylor. Morgan stood to one side as the attendant opened the stainless steel drawer. Inside was the body of the one of the Thais who had been blown up inside Calvino's car. Several of the steel ball bearings bounced off the side of the drawer making the ping sound of a pinball machine. The balls must have fallen out when the staff placed the body inside the drawer, thought Calvino. There were about 700 ball bearings in a Claymore mine, and the ball bearings that didn't rip the body apart at close range had lodged in the flesh and bone. The mangled body inside didn't look human; a mistake in cloning, yes, but a human being that had been born of a *ying*, no, that wasn't what Naylor stared down at inside the drawer. He gasped, spun around on his heel, bent over and vomited. Calvino looked inside the drawer, then at Morgan and the attendant. Was this a setup?

"I don't think this *one* is an American," said Calvino, staring down at the blown up body. "We came to identify a *farang*."

The attendant checked his clipboard. Sure enough the number was one digit off Daniel Ramsey's number. The attendant and Morgan discussed the mistake in Thai. Morgan then explained that there had been a foul up and the attendant was sorry. Naylor, who was still half doubled over, was leaking beer from his nose and mouth onto the floor. "They have a number of bodies that came in from the Emporium," said Morgan. "It's been a busy day. The foreigner is in the next drawer."

The attendant pulled out another drawer and this one contained Daniel's body. "Do you recognize this man?" Dwight Morgan asked him.

Naylor stood straight, cupped his hand over his mouth and nodded. His breathing was labored, and he was sweating, dripping sweat on the floor. The sound of loud pop music and the flip-flops on the floor caused Naylor to spew again.

"For the record, could you tell me who this man is?"

"This man is Daniel Ramsey of Los Angeles, California." His voice was low and hoarse. The voice of a sick, defeated man.

"You are sure. It is important that we don't make a mistake," said Morgan.

"For fuck sakes, I am sure," said Naylor, stopping himself one impulse short of saying he had seen the fuck's face for an instant as he had gone over the fifth floor railing.

Morgan asked the attendant to close the drawer. "We can go now," Morgan said.

Once outside the morgue, Naylor retched in a waste-paper basket but nothing came out; he had the dry heaves. Naylor slumped back in a chair, his legs sprawled out, and wiped his mouth with the *Asian Wall Street Journal* Morgan had left behind.

"It's never easy doing this. Sometimes I have had people faint. You did very well, Mr. Naylor, given the circumstances."

"I could use a drink, Calvino," said Naylor, making a grab for the plastic bag.

Calvino pulled the bag back and Naylor was too weak to go after it. "I'll buy you a drink later."

"Now what do I have to do?" moaned Naylor, looking up at Morgan and then reaching for the Foodland bag, pulling out the bottle of Johnny Walker Black. Calvino grabbed the bottle away from him and put it back in the bag.

"We will handle everything." Morgan explained, watching the tug-of-war over the bottle of scotch. He told Naylor that the Embassy took the responsibility for making all of the necessary arrangements for the body to be returned for burial in the States. Most of the time the Embassy recommended a number of funeral homes, including one run and operated by a Thai-Chinese family. A father and three sons, two of whom had been educated in the States, understood that Americans expected a degree of decorum in funeral parlor operators. They had to dress and behave like American funeral parlor operators. The father and his sons wore dark tailored suits. They were well-groomed: no hair growing out of their ears or nose, or goatees; their nails manicured and haircuts conservative and they knew how to stand, walk, and be silent like preachers. These funeral men were efficient and knew they were in the business of selling compassion and kindness. They inspired trust. Nothing like a pair of plastic sandals, shorts, nose-picking, coughing up lungers and spitting to shatter trust or faith that the deceased would be accorded proper respect. Morgan explained how the Embassy had complete faith in this family; they let them arrange a new suit of clothes, a coffin and the embalming. Unless the body was to be cremated. Most relatives of the deceased preferred the cremation option. It was far cheaper. Morgan also remarked that the father and three sons always had a small rose in the lapel of their suits, giving the faint impression they had just come from a wedding. The Embassy liked the cut of their suits, best of all they liked that they used a new Nissan carryboy supercab—they had the windows tinted and there were no dents or scratches on the Nissan—Americans hated the thought of their dead being transported to the airport on a flat bed pick-up truck tied down with rope so it wouldn't bounce off.

"How much does this service cost?" asked Wes Naylor.

"With embalming, it comes to four thousand dollars," said Morgan. He seemed to like that Naylor wanted to talk about the money part. It made him trust that Naylor indeed was an American. "But if you go the cremation route, then it is six hundred dollars."

"Cremation," said Naylor. "We shouldn't burden Daniel's family."

"That's what most people choose. Shipping a eight pound box of ashes isn't all that expensive," said Morgan.

Their conversation about saving money began to annoy Calvino. The whole point was not to cremate the body. He had neglected to tell Naylor: go for the embalming. We need the body; we need the coffin. Before Naylor completely blew that option Calvino cleared his throat and stepped forward.

"Wes, remember, we talked about this earlier," Calvino said.

Naylor was about to contradict him and say they had never talked about the money when Calvino rammed on, cutting off the sputtering start of a reply. "You said that the Ramsey family wanted Daniel's *body* for a funeral. They have a religious thing against cremation. Remember? That means we pay the higher amount. They authorized you to advance the money. You asked me to keep the cash in my office safe because you didn't trust the security box at your hotel. Remember?"

Of course Naylor didn't remember a goddamn thing as he was hearing all of this for the first time.

"Yeah, sure," Naylor, smiling. "Embalming. Of course, we want the body embalmed."

"Do you have the four thousand?" asked Morgan.

Calvino nodded, looking straight at Naylor, wanting to knock the smirk off his bloated face. "How soon can the body be shipped back?" asked Calvino.

Morgan outlined the steps and the time needed for each one. "As soon as we have the death certificate, the body is embalmed, then a suit is bought, the body is dressed, a coffin ordered, arrangements made with an American airline, and finally the funeral parlor arranges for transportation of the body to the airport." He paused for a moment. "Minimum of say two or three days. That's super fast track. Usually it takes a week."

"The body goes to the airport?" asked Naylor, playing stupid—which wasn't a stretch for him. He blinked, looked at Calvino, then at Morgan, the way a child looks with his mouth open upon learning clouds travel at five hundred miles per hour.

"Not to the passenger terminal. The coffin goes as cargo."

"How about tomorrow?" asked Calvino.

"Yeah, tomorrow is what we need, his family is in deep mourning," said Naylor. "And the Ramseys, my clients, want to get this sad affair over as quickly as possible."

Calvino removed forty hundred-dollar bills from his wallet and counted them out. Four thousand dollars. He handed the money to Dwight Morgan. Naylor hadn't looked so happy since he had Jep bouncing on his knee. Watching Calvino hand over his entire bodyguarding fee made him positively glow with happiness. Calvino avoided looking at him as he began to re-count the money. Morgan seemed to have second thoughts as Calvino counted the notes for a second time. A couple of attendants in the corridor stopped to look at all that money. It made Morgan a little nervous; he being a public official taking all that cash in a public place from one *farang* with a beat-up face and another wearing a huge gold chain. A photograph of that moment circulated around the State Department would destroy his career.

"You should wait and bring it around to my office and I will issue a receipt."

"I don't think you are going to flee the scene for four grand, Dwight. Try to help us make a flight tomorrow."

Calvino folded up the notes, reached over and stuffed them in Dwight's jacket pocket.

"I can't promise that, Vincent. Don't pin me down. You know how time works here as well as anyone. Nothing ever gets done in a hurry. Transporting a body is hardly a priority. This man was found at the scene of a bombing. All we need is for somebody to link him with the bomb and then you have a major problem of getting the body released. We need the report the police sergeant at the scene of the death filed. In normal cases, this isn't a problem. But to ask a police sergeant to accept responsibility for the paperwork in this case, I just don't know. And then you need a death certificate signed and issued by the district office. There's the embalming, and you know, all the other details. All you need is one person who doesn't have time or who is afraid or whose relative just died to throw everything into the future."

Morgan was backtracking, laying out all the bureaucratic excuses to pin delays on someone else. It was time to lay down a little guilt.

"If I hadn't got Naylor to identify this man, then where would you be?" asked Calvino. He knew the answer already but wanted to make sure that Morgan knew Naylor's identification meant that Morgan owed Calvino. Not a big debt but enough to have Morgan do what was necessary to get the paperwork done.

Calvino knew perfectly well what the Embassy had to do if no one stepped forward to claimed a dead American, and none of them at the Embassy liked that possibility. But he wanted to hear Morgan explain the problem unidentified dead Americans caused everyone in his section. "We would take up a collection in American Citizen Services and arrange to have the body cremated. We would store the ashes just in case. Every year we must do this four, five times. It makes us all feel terrible."

"What you're saying is that Naylor just saved you six hundred bucks out of your own pocket." Calvino had no reason to rub Morgan the wrong way. But he needed the man to go out of his way to clear the paperwork.

"The main thing is the death certificate," said Morgan. "The doctor has to sign it. Getting a doctor to sign the certificate isn't all that easy."

"Hold on for a minute," said Calvino. He went back into the morgue with the Foodland plastic bag. Less than five minutes later he came out without his bag and the bottle of Johnny Walker Black and handed Dwight Morgan the signed death certificate with Daniel's name on it.

Morgan read the certificate and smiled. "Cause of death: heart and breathing stopped."

"That seems to cover it," said Calvino.

"Mr. Naylor, you do have a power of attorney. Vincent mentioned this on the phone."

Naylor nodded. Calvino reached in his jacket and took out the power of attorney Naylor had signed in the bar and handed it to Morgan. The duty officer read through it quickly and then looked up.

"Mind if I hold on to this?" Morgan asked.

"No problem," said Calvino.

"No problem," said Naylor.

He suddenly realized that he had tried to drink the bribe. Calvino knew how the system worked; so did Morgan. But Naylor was green. He played the role of the fish out of water so well he could have made a profession out of it.

Naylor rolled his eyes. The document with his signature on it had gone into the possession of the United States, and if anyone ever found out that he had signed that document filled with a recital of lies, the California Bar Association would pull his license to practice law.

"We will aim for tomorrow. Again, no promises. Mr. Naylor come to my office tomorrow and sign some documents."

"Mr. Naylor will be there," said Calvino. "Won't you, Wesley?"

Naylor decided he definitely hated having Calvino calling him Wesley.

"I wouldn't miss the appointment for the world," he said, hands in his pockets; his face still flushed from his fit of hyperventilation inside the morgue. He saw himself standing in front of the American flag, a large framed photo of the President on the wall, swearing an oath.

"It should be okay, Vincent," said Morgan.

But Morgan's tone, his emphasis was different, as if they were already going to the airport, as if they were already on their way to LA. Working the system, massaging it with nimble fingers and strong hands, that is all that it took, and patience, a great deal of grim patience, knocking down walls with bottles of Johnny Walker Black. No one in Scotland would have ever guessed that a premium whisky had knocked down more walls in Asia than all the bombs that had ever been dropped since World War II.

Morgan had his car with blue US Embassy plates with the number 86 parked right in front so everyone had to walk around it. He was already inside the car when he opened the door and got back out. He shouted at Calvino, who turned and walked back.

"I almost forgot. About those guys who all died of overdoses. I did get back something you might find of interest."

"What's that?"

"It seems they were all members of some Internet sex cult calling itself the Cause. They have a website www. causemember.com. Check it out. You know, it's hard to work up much sympathy for such slime buckets." Morgan's Harvard accent made the word "slime" sound horrible, like some evil-smelling effluvium of morgue fluids. His voice was filled with disgust. It was semi-official policy for US Embassy people to be totally disgusted about all sexual matters. At least if they wanted to climb up the State Department ladder. Morgan, holding onto his car, looked like a man balanced to make a charge for the summit.

Calvino was doing a little jig in his mind. Morgan wasn't telling him anything that he didn't already know. Calvino looked over and smiled at Naylor, "Yeah, I know exactly what you mean. Thanks for the information, Dwight."

★★★★★★

NAYLOR sulked in the taxi. He wouldn't even look at Calvino he was so pissed off with Morgan's parting shot. "You did well, Wes," said Calvino, trying to break the ice. Nothing. Naylor stared out the window, sitting ramrod straight, his head slightly turned. They were returning to Sukhumvit Road. The Causeway. Taxis, motorcycles, and buses cut in and out of the lanes, running red lights, racing each other, going against invisible forces, looking for a small advantage. Flashing brights, hitting the horn, the nightly intimidation of road warfare in Bangkok. The taxi driver took both hands off the wheel for an instant to *wai* the Erawan Shrine. Fingers splayed, he ran his hands through his hair, and once again was in contact with the steering wheel. Keep me alive, give me a passenger, give me luck. The mantra of taxi drivers and prostitutes who prayed to the spirit of that shrine to guide their destiny onto a path of comfort and money.

"Calvino, you are a sick fuck. And Dwight Morgan is an Ivy League stick-up-his-ass piece of shit. He's the one who's slime. And those goddamn ball bearings rattling inside that drawer. Christ, I will hear those ball bearings banging on steel until the day I die," said Naylor.

"If Dwight's right, a serial killer has been knocking off your members right under your nose. You are supposed to know that kind of thing, Wes. Think what kind of publicity that would be if all of your members knew five of their brothers had been killed in Bangkok and you had done nothing to warn them."

"You're blackmailing me, aren't you?"

"All that I am saying is you have a problem. Someone is killing your members. It's not about blackmail. It's about catching the person who's doing the killing."

Naylor scratched his tattoo and thought about this as he lit a cigarette. It was staggeringly hot and the taxi's air-conditioning only half worked. At the same time it looked like rain clouds were closing in and that would be another excuse Morgan could use if there was any delay in getting the paperwork done. Everything came to a halt in the rain.

"Tomorrow we go to the Embassy and you sign the paper," said Calvino. "Then we go over to the funeral home and arrange Danny's one-way cargo ticket."

"Why does Morgan hate us?" asked Naylor.

"He's a pretty conservative guy. Or he wouldn't be in the job."

"Why do conservatives hate sex? I don't get it."

"Maybe they feel that liberals are better breeders. And sex is used by ghetto mothers to stuff the ballot box."

Calvino frowned, looking out the window. He didn't like Naylor using "us" as if Morgan's disapproval applied to him. He did sprinkle baby powder on the floor of his apartment to track the movements of *yings* he brought back, and if Morgan knew about that strange quirk, he would have no problem fitting him in with Naylor, Weasel, Skeleton, Kashmir, and Roadster. "If I give you the names of the five guys I believe were killed by the same person, can you get me details from your data base?" asked Calvino.

"That information is confidential," said Naylor, all huffy.

"It might help find the killer. It might help save lives."

"I'll think about it, Calvino. But don't go fucking twisting things." It was as if the balance of power had shifted back; Naylor flicked the ash from his cigarette on the floor of the taxi. He smiled, then took a hit off his cigarette as the first drops of rain splashed off the windshield.

★★★★★★

AT the Grand Rose Hotel, Jep was sitting on the front steps, her face all stained with dried tears. After Naylor got out of the taxi, she came roaring down the steps two at a time and ploughed straight into Naylor, putting her shoulder and head hard into his gut. Hard enough to knock him off his feet and into some of the overgrown rose bushes. Thorns cut his hands as he broke his fall. Her fists were flying like a windmill with only about half the blows hitting him around the head. She kept it up until she wound down like a toy with the batteries gone dead. She kicked him in the knee and he howled.

"Why are you doing this?" he screamed.

Calvino walked up the stairs, turned and sat down. "Aren't you going to stop her?" Naylor yelled.

"Remember, I am no longer your bodyguard," said Calvino.

Jep stood over him with her hands on her narrow hips, breathing hard, trying to catch her breath. A couple of the noodle vendors were laughing as they watched from behind their stalls. She reached down, picked up a rock and threw it at one of the dogs laying in the shade of one of the carts. The vendors knew the next rock would be for them so they stopped laughing and returned to cooking noodles.

"Would you please tell me what all of this is about?"

"It's about Roadster," she screamed. "He wanted to fuck me. He said you told him that he could fuck me."

"That is a lie," protested Naylor, picking rose thorns out of his pants.

"He's your friend. And because of him I got fired."

Naylor's Cause buddy had asked her to go short-time. When she refused, he got nasty, called her a whore. Jack had to come downstairs. He took the side of the customer and fired Jep, saying it was her job to fuck customers, and if she didn't want to fuck customers, then she should go back to planting rice. He had seen Jep's photo on a *yingzine* wearing a tiny dancer's bikini just as Naylor had and had made exactly the same plan to buy her out even though under the YINGS she belonged to Eric. Only after the mosquito attack, Jep gave up drinking and decided that Naylor was as good as any other guy and suddenly decided that she was unavailable for going out to have sex with customers. It was immoral to become moral in a bar. It was against the creed, the religion of Lovejoy according to Jack.

Naylor at last started to climb back to his feet.

"That's terrible, *tilac.*"

"He said it was okay. He says, Wes takes me from Eric. So I take you from Wes. No problem. He says this to me. I scream at him? I not go with you."

She collapsed crying against his chest, which again sent him sprawling back towards the rose bushes. They did a clumsy little dance until he regained his balance. He lifted her up, raised her above his head and eased her down over his shoulders. "I will look after you, Jep. Don't you worry about that. What Roadster said was wrong. What Roadster did was wrong. I am going to fuck him up. You wait."

These were the magic words for Jep, the score for playing the harmonics of guilt. It didn't matter that Naylor had a couple of university degrees, weighed in at two hundred pounds, had a profession and a business. None of those accomplishments or his size mattered. He had surrendered himself to the total control of a bar *ying* with a sixth grade education. She knew how to play the guilt chords . . . she knew how to control him with his own guilt. It was as if he wanted her to tell him what to do. She had seen guys like Naylor before. After a year on the game she knew how to make a *farang* dance, to dance to the guilt tune that she played. But most of all she knew Calvino's Law of guilt: Weaning a *farang* away from a strong guilt urge was harder than getting him to kick a heroin habit.

Calvino watched as Naylor climbed the stairs and disappeared into the lobby. Naylor's distant voice echoed in the stairwell as Calvino walked to the front desk. The old woman, who was smoking a joint, smiled at him as she handed him a note that Pratt had left. The message read: "Meet me in the Board Room." By the time Calvino arrived in the board room, Pratt had been pacing back and forth for more than an hour. Pratt had various papers and computer print-outs scattered on the conference table.

"If Jess doesn't leave Thailand within the next forty-eighty hours, it could become complicated," said Pratt.

Whenever Pratt used the word "complicated," it meant someone was going to die. "Morgan says he can have the Embassy paperwork done by tomorrow. Or the next day. There is a police report he needs."

"I have already arranged it with the sergeant." Pratt picked up a folder and pulled out some papers and handed them to Calvino. "It's here. Take these with you to the Embassy tomorrow."

"We need transport to the funeral home," said Calvino. "But you've already taken care of that, right?"

"I'll have a van for you." Pratt pushed aside a pile of papers and found a key ring. He took one key off the ring and handed it to Calvino. "It belongs to Manee's brother." Manee was Pratt's wife, and his brother-in-law had lent the van as a favor. Pratt had told him that he needed it to pick up computer and office equipment.

"I will be careful."

Pratt looked right at him. "You were careful with your Honda, too."

"It was just a window, Pratt. The bomb doesn't count."

"Let's go through the plan one more time," said Pratt. He was sitting down, hands folded on the table. Calvino had rarely seen him so nervous. Part of this was the unknown identity of the highly influential forces trying to stop Jess. Or was it just Jess they were after? Taking out Calvino would also have ended the serial killer search, his asking questions, making waves. Was it possible that the sapper team and a hit team had been dispatched by separate forces to the shopping mall? Or were they part of the same unit, so after the monster fuckup by the sapper team, the hit team took over? Pratt didn't pretend to have the answers. Nor did he have any clue who the mastermind was, assuming there was only one, but he knew that these men backed into a corner would cause problems, for him, his department, maybe for his family. What he hadn't yet told Calvino was that an intelligence report on Daniel Ramsey said he had associations with people in the drug business. What it also disclosed were rumors of official involvement, including a rumor that someone inside the US Embassy might be involved. It was one thing to stand your ground against the narcotic big shots; it was another to be looking over your shoulder, waiting for someone on your own side to take you out. None of this was good news, none of this was encouraging.

"I'll drive Jess and Naylor to the funeral home. Jess stays dressed like a priest. We have an official police document allowing us to remove the body for further forensic testing, then a funeral service at a church, before taking the coffin out to the Cargo Department at Don Muang Airport. The funeral home director, Khun Panya, will take one look at the documents and immediately co-operate. He's afraid of the police like everyone else. Once we have the coffin, we remove Daniel's body, get it cremated later, Jess climbs inside, we make certain he can pop the lid from the inside, check the coffin with him inside as cargo and eighteen hours later his commanding officer is at LAX with a dozen men, opens the coffin and Jess pops out like a Jack-in-the-box. Straightforward. Slam, dunk. I don't see the problem. The cargo hold is pressurized and temperature-controlled."

Pratt saw a hundred problems. Ugly spiders and snakes crawling over and under and inside the details of the plan. Only he could not think of a better plan to secretly get Jess out of the country. Pratt had thought of taking Jess out through U-Tapao to Samui to Phuket and then to KL. Too many people were compromised and too many people would need to know to allow this to happen; it was impossible to trust such a chain in an operation like this. "They know that if Jess goes back to LA, someone very powerful will have a very big problem. Whatever happens, it won't be a slam, dunk.

For instance the girl. Noi. We don't know where she stands in all of this. She was sent here to set him up and she's here. In this hotel."

"Don't worry about her," said Calvino. "She's not going back to Gabe and Kowit. Not after what happened at the Emporium. She knows Kowit would have her killed. She's worried they might go after her son. I said you would send someone to protect the kid."

"They can control her through her brother. That's how she came here to start with. Are you sure she has a boy?"

"Why don't you send someone to find out?"

FOURTEEN

THE PEDESTRAIN-OPERATED traffic light outside the American Embassy complex on Wireless Road was a testimonial to democracy. It may have been the only fully functioning and observed pedestrian traffic light in all of Thailand. The light was pure democracy in action. The idea that any rice farmer dressed in a pair of nineteen-baht shoes could push a button that turned a red light green and could cause a row of Benzes and BMWs to screech to a halt was so alien that peasants and office workers sometimes came to Wireless Road to push the button and watch. Push the light, cross the road. Even taxis stopped as the light turned red. For some reason, cars did not run this red light. At least not very often. That itself was a unique feature. The added security since the bombings made drivers nervous around the Embassy. A small army of security guards and uniformed police stationed outside the main entrance carefully watched everyone on foot, everyone behind the wheel of a car or on a motorcycle. Maybe it wasn't democracy after all; maybe it was old fashioned fear that made them stop at the light.

Inside the main entrance was a security checkpoint where guards ran handheld detectors over people's clothes. Calvino let Naylor go ahead in the line, which moved slowly as officials checked documents and bags. When it was Naylor's turn, he pulled out his passport, "I am an American. Let me through," he said. "The only thing the Thais are gonna blow up is that fucking traffic light outside." He was talking to Calvino, joking around. Only no one jokes around American security people. The guard scanned Naylor half a dozen times and each time the scanner made a loud electronic noise. "That fucking thing can give you cancer. Will you stop doing that?" That just made them run the scanner over him all the more. Then the guards—there were two of them now—made him take out the keys and coins from his pockets and put them in one of those plastic trays; made him take off his belt. His hands were all scratched up from the fall into the rose bushes. Bomb maker's hands, thought Calvino.

Calvino flashed his passport. "Better to do what they say," he said to Naylor. Another guard was checking a woman's handbag. The search was more thorough than the casual shifting through contents of briefcases and handbags in more normal times. No one was sure who was behind the bombings, and the damage at the Emporium was a new, unexpected escalation, making the authorities nervous, suspecting that the dark forces behind the attacks might do almost anything now. There had been enough anti-American statements in the press to create a climate of distrust. The Americans just assumed they might be a possible target. American officials placed the security staff on alert, taking no chances. There was no friendliness in the questioning, in the searches. Thais had their ID cards out, showing them proudly like school children. The coolness of the checkpoint did not erase the smiles; they moved slowly towards the turnstile.

"Bastards," said Naylor as they finally were allowed inside.

The guard glared at him. Calvino pulled him by the shoulder. "Forget it. We are in. Let's do our business."

"You see the way he looked at me. I am an American."

"Keep it up and they will strip search you. Look inside you. Shove a little traffic light up your rectum."

That shut him up. Naylor didn't want any Thai looking inside his rectum for a hidden explosive device.

Calvino walked ahead a couple of steps with Naylor walking with his hands deep in his pockets. They followed the narrow walkway through a courtyard which led to a door with a sign: American Citizens' Service. The Thais and other foreigners had to use another door in the grand tradition of the Old American South. Ahead of them on the walkway was a *farang* and a young Thai woman who looked about twenty-one or twenty-two. She was wearing a short dress, showing off thin muscular legs, and around her thin neck and slender arms were gold chains. She had long, thick black hair that looked freshly washed, her dark skin had a perfumed scent, and she had a pair of tits that looked like some kind of anti- gravity device had been built inside the cones just behind the nipples. Naylor muscled past Calvino and went straight up to the man, and placed his hand, that looked like it had been stuck in a bag of mad cats, on the *farang's* shoulder.

"Lark, you seeking sanctuary in the Embassy?" asked Naylor.

The middle-aged *farang* with a two-day stubble of beard turned. His hair was almost totally white and the middle of his head was bald. The skin covering his skull was perfectly tanned. He wore sunglasses and never stopped smiling.

"Wes, you sonofabitch, what are you doing here?"

"Shipping out a dead body, what else?" said Naylor. Calvino looked at the girl, who smiled at him, trying to remember where he had seen her before. He guessed it was the Thermae. She looked younger than she was but she would never look younger than she looked today.

"I'm getting a visa for Toy," said Lark. "I am taking her to San Francisco. We are going to get married. Right, honey?"

Lark was not alone. Several other winter and spring couples passed by them on the walkway.

Naylor raised his fist above his head. "The Cause is behind you."

"Catch up with you later," said Calvino, taking Naylor by the arm.

But Naylor resisted, following his friend into the main room. "I'm networking," said Naylor. "Lark fixes cars. Reconditions cars and sells them cheap. To his friends, that is."

Inside, fifty or so grim-faced people sat uncomfortably on folding chairs, filling out forms, looking through their papers, waiting to be called for an interview. They looked like people waiting to see a parole officer. Guys like Lark came along with Toy thinking his presence would make a difference but it never did; it hurt more than it helped. An old auto mechanic trying to export a forty-kilo *ying* with a fifth grade education would not inspire confidence. Lark wore a Cause-member pin on his shirt lapel; the interviewing officer wouldn't miss that pin. Toy's chance of getting to the United States was about as great as Daniel Ramsey rising from the dead.

A side door led to a small room where advisories and advertisements had been posted on a bulletin board. In the corner was a service window with one of those metal drawers customers put things in that pops up on the other side like one of those windows in a self-service station in the heart of East Los Angeles. Special ammo might penetrate the glass in that window but nothing short of special ordnance was going to blow out the lights of the embassy official digging documents out of that drawer. Calvino waited his turn as a Protestant min- ister showed off his Thai with a local staffer—a middle-aged woman, who eyed him with an icy smile. Anyone speaking Thai that well and talking non-stop about God's salvation was like the traffic lights on Wireless Road; the Thais were aware that such things existed, having seen them in movies or on TV, but when actually confronted by such a thing did not know whether to laugh, run away, pay respect, or simply stare, smile, and think about nothing. The clerk had taken the latter option. Her head moved mechanically but reading her eyes, the way she looked at the bulletin board across the room—she must have seen the posting a thousand times—it was clear she had gone into drift time, far away to a place where the minister's words were like shadows in a forest. When it came to Calvino's turn she was still in that other dimension.

"Dwight Morgan left some papers for me," said Calvino, leaning down on one elbow, staring at the clerk through the window.

"We don't have any. Come back tomorrow," she said. Her reply made no sense. Calvino could see that she was reading some religious literature that the minister must have shoved into the drawer.

"The papers are for Daniel Ramsey," said Calvino. "The American who died yesterday."

"He's on the third floor."

Calvino switched into Thai, explaining that Ramsey was dead and definitely he wasn't on the third floor but in the morgue waiting to go back to the States. The preacher's cheap paperback had pictures. She was looking at the pictures, ignoring Calvino as he tried to explain that Ramsey was an American, and that Dwight Morgan had prepared the papers and all she had to do was give him the envelope and she could finish reading her book with the title *How Jesus Saves All True Believers*.

She used her finger to trace along the edges of a color drawing of the baby Jesus. It was difficult to know if she knew who the baby was supposed to be. There didn't seem to be anything religious in her movement. Calvino thought she might have simply been fond of baby pictures, and maybe it made her think of her own baby. Finally she put the book to one side. The preacher's sermon and the picture of baby Jesus were wearing off and she looked at Calvino for the first time. "Who did you say you were?"

"Vincent Calvino. And this is Mr. Naylor. We are helping the Ramsey family," said Calvino.

Naylor's patience had evaporated and he squeezed in next to Calvino. Leaning down with his elbows on the counter, he pushed his nose against the glass. "I am Wes Naylor, the family lawyer for the Ramseys. We need the papers to clear Daniel's body through customs. To buy his ticket. It has been all arranged. Just get the fucking papers," said Naylor.

"We don't allow such language at the window," she said.

"Since Mr. Ramsey's death, we've all been under stress. I am certain you understand," said Calvino.

She stared at Naylor "Do you have some identification?"

Naylor pressed his passport against the window. "A United States of America passport," he said. "This is the American Embassy or have I made a mistake?"

The way Naylor was acting, Calvino thought they might bring in the security guards and start scanning him all over again. Instead, an American duty officer sitting a couple of desks away pushed his chair back and walked down the aisle of desks until he reached the service window. He had been listening to the exchange. "It is standard to ask for an ID, okay," he said.

"It is also standard to get some service," said Naylor. "Here's my passport. What else do you want? My mother's maiden name? It was Whyte. That's with a 'y' and not an 'i'. She met my dad during World War II. I was born in New York City. I have lived in LA for twenty-seven and a half years. I practice law in LA and I have worked on the campaigns of two governors and one congressman. They were all elected. They all remember me. They all owe me."

"Mr. Naylor, may I have your passport?"

Naylor slipped it in the drawer and the official pulled it out on the other side of the bullet-proof glass. He opened Naylor's passport and looked at the photograph, then looked up at Naylor as if they were not necessarily the same person. He turned and went to the other end of the room where there was a photocopy machine. He picked up the telephone and dialed. A secretary made a photocopy of Naylor's passport.

"Ease up, Naylor," said Calvino. "The idea is not to be noticed. You are making enough of an impression that this guy will be telling this story over dinner for the rest of his career."

"He's an asshole," said Naylor.

"In that case, I am thinking you may be part of his family."

When the duty officer returned from the photocopy machine, the first thing that he did was return Naylor's passport. "Mr. Morgan is unavailable," he said. "He's in an emergency meeting. The Ramsey papers are in his office. So if you could come back tomorrow, I can make an appointment for you to meet with him."

"I pay your salary." Naylor's face had gone rigid with rage. His clenched fists pounded on the window counter.

About the same time Dwight Morgan's head appeared around the corner at the far end of the room. Someone must have slipped him a note that two *farangs* were making a scene at the window and demanding papers. He came quickly to the window, looking pissed off. All the friendliness from the morgue had washed off. "Sorry I wasn't here." But he didn't sound sorry. "I had an emergency meeting. Go through the door, down the corridor and I will let you in."

Once they had cleared the public area and entered the inner offices occupied by the Embassy officials and staff, Naylor seemed to loosen up. That rock grinding inside his bowels seemed to pass unnoticed. His humor came back. "That guy you got working at the window looked like a Mormon. But didn't act like one. Like he was looking to turn people away from his church. Hey, we have enough believers. Come back another day."

"He was just doing his job," said Morgan.

Dwight Morgan closed his office door and sat in the chair behind his desk. Calvino and Naylor pulled up chairs in front of his desk. He didn't offer them coffee or water. Instead he folded his hands on his desk and launched straight into business. Just like at the window, being inside his office hadn't improved his mood. This definitely wasn't the same guy from the Police Hospital. His expression was serious, concerned, and a little suspicious. "I just got out of a meeting with Thai military, police, and our own security people. The bombing yesterday has everyone running for cover." Morgan paused, stretching his hand back behind his head. A framed photo- graph of a white woman and two kids under ten years old was on a shelf behind him. He was a family man, someone sent here to do a tour of duty, gain experience. Calvino thought Dwight was suddenly feeling wobbly on the State Department ladder. "And there's something else, Vincent. The police have traced the car that blew up in the basement of the Emporium and it was registered to Vincent Calvino. The police are looking for you. God knows who else is looking for you, Vincent. But this has become a very serious matter."

"He's suddenly a popular guy," said Naylor.

Morgan leaned forward balanced on his elbows. "This isn't funny, Mr. Naylor. This is a shit-load of non-funny problems for me."

"What are you going to do?" Calvino asked him point blank.

"I should play it by the book. Pick up the phone, let the Thai police know that you are here and they will soon be on Wireless Road."

"I wish you wouldn't do that, Dwight," said Calvino.

"The assholes who tried to blow him up are working with the police," said Naylor.

"You don't know that," said Morgan.

"No, he doesn't know that," said Calvino.

"Can you tell me why I shouldn't go by the book?" asked Morgan.

"I can give you a lot of reasons. But one is enough. For the last few months I've been working on this serial killer case. Three months ago I told you my theory. A month ago, I let you know that I had been getting closer to convincing the Thai police that there is a pattern. I think maybe I have convinced someone there is something to link these murders. Your intelligence people told you about the link. Whoever planted that bomb in my car was a professional. They had access to Claymore mines. They knew exactly what they were doing. These people don't want the serial killer found. You've been in Thailand long enough to know exactly what that means. What kind of people do such things, and the protection they have. If you make that phone call, then no one in Washington or the Department is going to criticize you for doing your job. They will defend you like you defended that guy at the window. And in a day or two or a week, someone will show up here on behalf of my relatives asking for you to sign the papers to have what is left of me shipped back to New York. You might be a little sorry but you can always say I did my job and what happened to Vincent Calvino doesn't have anything to do with me. I see you have a family. A wife, a couple of kids. I am here alone. No kids, no wife, no family. No one is going to miss that I am not around."

"What do you want, Vincent?"

"Have I always been straight with you?" asked Calvino.

Dwight Morgan thought for a moment, then slowly nodded his head.

"Give me twenty-four hours."

"I've known you since I arrived in Bangkok. You've always been straight. I said that in the meeting. I said you had never caused any trouble for us. You had actually helped us several times identifying people. You are trying to help stop the murder of American citizens. I told them that."

"Let me have the Ramsey papers, and twenty-four hours from now I will be in your office, and you can pick up the phone and make that call. I will dial the number."

Civil servants aren't born risk takers. Morgan leaned back in his chair, balancing the pros and cons, trying to decide which way to go. "Okay," he said. Dwight Morgan was that rare individual who was willing to give another a chance, the chance that he himself would have wanted had he been sitting in Calvino's chair. He pulled a file out of his desk drawer and handed it to Calvino.

"Get out of here. I have work to do," said Dwight Morgan.

On the way out of Morgan's office, Calvino wondered whether Dwight Morgan had a heart of gold or whether he was the mole inside the US Embassy who knew how the heroin found its way to America and the last thing he wanted was for the Thai police to take him into custody.

★★★★★★

NOI had been drinking pretty heavily. She could stand but she swayed from side to side like she was hearing music and doing an on-stage routine. She had gone through half a bottle of Sang Thip, drinking it on ice. Leaving the cola bottle unopened. No mixer to dilute the drink. She had wanted to forget about Danny's body on the Emporium marble, about her brother in jail, about Gabe using her to walk Jess into a trap, about how fucked up life was, and how she was sitting around dressed like a nun getting drunk. Working in Gabe's club in LA, she knew how to drink and sing. She could keep up with the Koreans, out-drink them, out-sing them, leave them glassy-eyed like day-old fish in the market and that was saying something, but even the Koreans could drink the Japanese under the table. Most of the time a half of a bottle of rum, gin, whisky would not cause her to blink. This time was different. The booze went straight to that part of the brain where demons and anger and hate live like a live virus waiting for liquor to hatch them full-grown into the world. More than liquor was involved. The accumulation of grudges swelled up in the back of her throat, making her feel like she was being strangled by her own and other people's lies.

She had overheard Jess and Pratt talking about her. She was in the bathroom and they must have thought she could not hear them. But she heard every last spiteful, horrible word.

"She's a risk," said Pratt.

"So far she hasn't tried to use the phone," said Jess.

"But she hasn't been alone," said Pratt.

"I know this place where she worked. A near-beer joint. A front for prostitution. Only the ABC can't really close them down because they don't have a license for beer or alcohol, so there is no way to stop the *yings* from accepting drinks from customers. Or going with customers."

"She's drunk now," said Pratt. "We have a situation."

Noi had walked out of the bathroom, headed straight for the door, walked out and left the door wide open like she didn't give a shit, and staggered down the corridor trying all the doors until she found a maid coming out of a *hong*. She walked into the *hong*, slammed the door, hit the light switch with the palm of her hand, and started to cry. She had a lot of reasons to feel sorry for herself, to question who were her friends and who were her enemies, and to decide how she was going to play it out. It was confusing and she had been trying to break down who hated her the most and who could inflict the most damage by finding ways to direct that hate at her. In her mind, Jess, Pratt and the over-weight *farang* named Naylor and the weird guy at the Mall, McPhail, all hated her, and made her feel like she was a whore no matter how hard as she tried to tell them that she was a singer. A talented singer who didn't need to fuck for money. She became angry as she saw that look of doubt in their eyes, "Sure you were singing in LA. Sure you didn't fuck for money." It made her mad; it made her a little crazy that no matter what she said, she couldn't get through their barrier of preconceptions, a barrier built not with bricks made of straw but bricks made of hate and lies. She had gone along with them but they made her feel that she wasn't really one of them. These men just assumed that she was a danger to them. Everything had gone wrong and each time one of them thought about the bomb, they stared at her like she was a personal force of evil who had inserted herself in their midst and had to be contained. They forgot that it was their idea she go with them. She would have stayed. They insisted. Then all the time they had been comforting her—after all, she could have been killed as well—was just an excuse to watch her. No matter what anyone called it, these men had been taking turns guarding her. Holding her like a prisoner who they thought was stupid enough not to know that she was in prison. They were afraid of her and what she might do. It had never occurred to them that she had nowhere to go. Where would she have gone? Who would she have turned to?

By the time Jess found her, all these dark thoughts had made her hysterical, desperate. He stood outside knocking and asking to be let inside. She ran over to the telephone, picked it up, and the old lady on the switchboard told her that she could not connect her to an outside line. She slammed down the phone and sat down hard on the bed. The Thai rum made her face feel hot. The nun's habit made her sweat. She stripped it off and sat on the bed naked.

"Why are you playing God with my life?" she shouted through the door.

"No one is playing God with your life," Jess said.

"You think I am a whore because I worked at Gabe's club."

Jess knew now that she had overheard the conversation. He kicked himself.

"I said to Pratt that places like that can be a front for prostitution. That doesn't make you a whore. It means some of the *yings* might go with customers. It means some of the people you worked for might be bringing in *yings* from Thailand. And those *yings* might be forced to go with customers."

When she didn't have to look at him, Jess sounded so reasonable. She had never met a cop who talked as well as he did. Explained things the way they really were.

"It's these bad people who put the bomb in the car park. No one is judging you. No one has time for that. We are trying the best way we can to keep you, and me, and the *farang* alive. And that means we must consider all of the angles."

She stripped the sheet off the bed and wrapped it around her body and went to the door. He waited for a long pause, then heard her unlock the door.

"Why can't I use the telephone?" she asked standing at the door.

"Where are your clothes?"

"I got too hot. Besides, I am tired of being a nun."

He stepped past her and into the *hong*. The nun's habit was crumpled on a chair.

"No one is allowed to use the phone. Not only you. That includes me. It includes Naylor and Calvino. We must assume that anyone organized enough to plant that bomb might trace any phone call."

Noi stared at him, wondering if this might be true or just something he said to shut her up, calm her down, and stop her from being angry and upset. She grabbed her glass and sat back on the edge of the bed.

"You want to send my brother to prison," she said.

The sweat dripped off her chin and onto her white sheet. Her hair was matted from all the sweating. She looked like she had just finished getting out of a sauna.

"Only a judge can sentence your brother to prison. That part is not my job."

"If it hadn't been for those cock fights and working part-time for Kowit, then none of this would have ever happened. Or if it had happened, it wouldn't have involved Charn."

"You're right of course. But it happened the way it happened and there's nothing I can do or you can do to make it happen a different way now."

Suddenly Noi felt too tired to argue, exhausted enough to put down her glass and stretch out her arms. It was all catching up with her—being scared half to death, the violence, the half bottle of whisky, the insane laugh from the old woman telling her she couldn't call out of the hotel, her sprint out of the *hong* and down the corridor into this strange *hong*. As she dropped her arms, she saw Pratt standing framed in the open door, watching. He had said nothing, showed no expression one way or the other.

"You are wondering why I have no clothes on?" she yelled at him. "It's because you guys make me steam."

Before Pratt could say anything, Naylor and Calvino came running down the corridor.

"They nearly handed Vinee over to the Thai cops," said Naylor.

All heads turned. "Who is they?" asked Pratt.

"The American Embassy. The cops traced his

Honda. And Dwight fucking Morgan thinks the bomb was intended for Vincent because of this serial killer business."

Pratt stepped inside Noi's *hong* and Calvino and Naylor followed, closing the door.

"Then the bomb wasn't intended for me?" asked Jess, coming around to the foot of the bed.

"We still don't know if they wanted Vincent or you. Or maybe both of you," said Pratt. "Two for the price of one, as Vincent once said."

"I don't think anyone knows a goddamn thing," said Naylor. He stalked over to the corner and sat on the chair where Noi had left her nun's habit.

"What's with him?" asked Jess.

"They scanned him too many times at the Embassy. I think it's interfered with his brain activity," said Calvino.

"I fucking heard that, Calvino." He looked at Noi. "Jesus Christ, when did you get naked?"

She threw the bottle of Sang Thip at him. It missed his head by an inch and a half and smashed through the window and out of the hotel. "I hate you, *ai-farang*." It doesn't sound like much hearing it in Thai but it is about one of the most impolite things a Thai can say to a *farang*. Only in Naylor's case he had no idea what she meant. She stormed into the bathroom and slammed the door.

"We got the papers for Ramsey," said Calvino, looking at Naylor, who was looking out the broken window. "Next we go to the funeral home."

"You know I now own this hotel. She's gonna have to pay for the window. I am fucking sorry but that is the way it is. And what is this *ai-farang* shit anyway?"

"It means you are a dickhead," she shouted through the bathroom door. "And I am not paying for the window."

"Let's go," said Pratt.

The bathroom door opened and Noi stepped out.

"What about me? Aren't I leaving?" she asked.

"You are coming along," said Calvino. "Provided you put the nun's habit back on."

"I can't, fatso is sitting on it."

Naylor squirmed on the chair as if trying to wrinkle the habit.

"Give her the habit, Wes," said Calvino.

"Not until she pays for the window."

Calvino walked over and slammed Naylor across the face. "Now she's paid up. Give me the habit."

Naylor looked up at Calvino with Pratt and Jess slightly behind him. He lifted one enormous thigh and pulled out the habit and handed it to Calvino, who turned and walked over to where Noi was standing. "Get dressed quickly."

Calvino's mobile phone rang.

"Vincent, some cops were out here looking for you and your friends," said Father Andrew. "You remember the drug addict taking the nails out of the stolen doors?"

Calvino remembered the shifty bastard and how he had taken off when the men had helped themselves to his two-by-fours to beat the shit out of the Khmer. "I am listening, Father Andrew."

"The cops gave him and his girlfriend a few hundred baht. I don't know what they told the cops. They wouldn't have known where you were going. Anyway, cops don't normally pay money for nothing. I thought you ought to know."

Calvino snapped the case shut and slipped the phone into his pocket. "The cops know I am here." He looked at his mobile phone. "I hate technology."

"They traced your phone signal," said Pratt. "I'll check downstairs."

"There is a service entrance in the back," said Naylor. "We can go out that way."

"Stay here. I will phone from the counter downstairs," said Pratt.

Calvino closed the door. "How do you know about the service entrance?"

"That's where McPhail goes to smoke a joint. The rose bushes almost cover the driveway," said Naylor. "And if you ever hit me again . . ."

"Wes, don't be a dickhead. We have to go."

As Pratt reached the lobby, two uniformed policeman were waiting at the reception desk. Pratt headed straight at the two cops and they half turned, wondering who this Thai in civilian clothes was and what business he had with them. "I am Colonel Prachai. This hotel is under my jurisdiction. I am operating a stakeout and the standing order is no uniform. So explain what you are doing here." Pratt flashed his police ID.

One of the policemen was a lieutenant and the other a sergeant. Pratt outranked them, and was older than both of them, and on the basis of rank and age they had already taken two strikes. To refuse his implied request for them to leave would have led to exactly the kind of confrontation that they had been drilled to avoid from birth. "We have orders from . . ." the lieutenant began to explain.

Pratt cut him off. "Lieutenant, perhaps you did not hear me. This is my stakeout. And you and the sergeant are risking a major CID operation. Do you want me to phone your superior and explain that you and the sergeant are about to destroy an undercover drug bust that the CID and the American DEA have planned for months?"

"We are looking for an American named Vincent Calvino. We have information that he is here," said the Lieutenant.

"Who told you he was here?"

Jep walked out from behind a fridge sucking on a straw stuck in a can of coke.

"She did." He pointed at Jep who was sucking on a straw, her eyes as big a child frightened by a ghost.

"*Farangs* all look alike to bar *yings*," said Pratt. He picked up the photo of Calvino from the reception desk and turned to Jep, "Have you ever seen this man—well, have you?"

Her lips pressed against the straw as she tried to figure out from Pratt's face exactly what he wanted her to say. She knew the lieutenant wanted her to say yes. And she got the idea from hearing Pratt and the lieutenant talk that Pratt had wanted to say she had never seen him. The question in her mind was who was going to be the most pissed off? The lieutenant had bought her the coke. From the way the power balance was shifting, though, it looked like the lieutenant was on his way out the door, meaning that Pratt would still be standing here after that man left. And if she had said or done the wrong thing, then she could be in for some kind of pain that would make her mosquito-bitten ass not even a nice warm up. She eyed the Lieutenant, looked at Calvino's picture again, and eyed Pratt.

"Come on, yes or no?" asked Pratt. She knew he meant no.

Jep didn't bother to remove the straw as she shook her head. Pratt handed the photo back to the Lieutenant. The tension immediately left Pratt's face and that made Jep happy.

"I am afraid you've made a mistake," said Pratt.

The Lieutenant held the photo. It was his move. If he knew about Calvino he would have known that Pratt was someone close to him and that Pratt would do or say anything to protect him.

"I am looking for him myself. When I find him, I will let you know."

"We are trying to carry out our duty," said the lieutenant.

"And I am telling you that your duty is not to interfere with my operation. Is that understood?" He looked at his watch. "I have a special unit waiting inside my van. I am taking them inside now. So I would appreciate it if you and the sergeant would leave."

The lieutenant and sergeant backed away from the reception desk and headed for the entrance. But they waited a decent interval at the door so it didn't look like they were running away. As they opened the main door, Pratt asked the desk clerk what the cops had wanted. They had shown her a photograph of Calvino.

"What did you tell them?" asked Pratt.

"What you told me to tell anyone asking. Never saw him before."

"Give me the key to the service entrance," said Pratt. He slid a five-hundred-baht note over the counter, and the receptionist slid the key back, their fingers brushing against one another for split second of human contact. He could smell the grass on her breath; her eyes, red-rimmed, were watery and cold like she was fishing her brother out of the urn with his ass all eaten away.

Pratt picked up the house phone and dialed the *hong* Noi had fled to. Calvino picked up on the second ring. "I'll drive the van around to the service entrance," said Pratt. "Take the others down the back stairs. We don't have a lot of time."

Pratt stood at the back as Jess, Naylor, and Noi climbed inside. Calvino picked one of the roses, pressed it to his nose, looked up at the sky, then smiled at Pratt.

"It's going to work," said Calvino. "I have a good

feeling. And you know my instincts are always right about such things."

He handed the rose to Pratt, who closed and locked the doors. The back windows were tinted black.

On the way out of the hotel, Pratt stopped next to the squad car and rolled down the window of the van. "My men are inside. They will notify you if Calvino shows up at the hotel."

FIFTEEN

RACHADA PHISEK ROAD crossing through the Din Daeng intersection suddenly looked as if a squadron of B52s had dropped a load of Big Bettys, those *ying*-named explosives that chewed up everything on the ground. Heavy construction equipment, dump trucks, and workers in hard hats swarmed down the center of the road. It was unclear whether they were the cause of the damage or working to repair the damage done by others. Pratt drove the van very carefully like he was giving Calvino a lesson in how to keep a vehicle in good shape. Pratt hadn't said much since they left the hotel. The others sat in the back and Calvino could hear their muffled conversation as it drifted to the front. Mainly a monologue by Noi worrying about her kid and a separate monologue by Naylor bitching about the window she had broken. From Jess's silence it seemed they were both driving him nuts and he would be happy to get back to his life arresting drug dealers in LA. Pratt didn't need to say anything because Calvino knew what he was thinking, that if you concentrated on what you were doing when you were doing it—a basis of Buddhism—then things didn't get broken. Calvino's recent bad karma centered mainly on windows like the one that was busted in his car and the one in the hotel *hong*. After they drove through the Huay Kwang intersection, there was a string of karaoke bars, massage parlors, membership clubs, and pool halls lining both sides of the road like new and secondhand car dealerships in New Jersey. The huge sign of a smiling *ying* reminded Calvino of the woman at the window in the Embassy tracing the drawing of the baby Jesus with her finger. Then one *ying* sign after another. Lovely, alluring twenty-five-year old faces on both sides of the road, promising to let a man trace any outline he wanted around her body. Pratt stopped the van at the traffic lights and turned into Lard Phrao Road. The funeral home Dwight Morgan had recommended was located on a *soi* off Lard Phrao. Rarely did *farangs* on holiday venture into this part of Bangkok; there were no attractions pulling them in that direction. Like parts of Queens, thought Calvino. Tourists never went to parts of Queens; people who lived in Manhattan never ventured to Queens.

Search the database of www.causemember.com and no Cause-member ever filed a report on Lard Phrao Road. Pratt turned the van into the *soi*, and continued half a mile until he came to a compound surrounded by a concrete fence. He braked, stopping the van at the front of the gate. He sounded the horn. To the right was an unfinished building; there were cranes swinging from the fifteenth floor and trucks and workers coming in and out of the site. Most construction in Bangkok had come to a standstill since the baht collapsed in July of '97. But this condo showed no sign of being abandoned. As a security guard opened the gate, Calvino watched the construction crane hoisting a load of long steel girders. This condo was someone's dream that had kept on going forward when most developments had entered the nightmare phase of bankruptcy. A moment later, a guard appeared and opened the gate, swinging back one side of the large, tall metal gate, then walking back and opening the other half. Pratt drove the van inside and the guard closed the gate behind them.

The main house, a wooden house with screens on the windows, was set back from the road, leaving a long well-kept garden in front, with a clean swept driveway. Tall trees provided shade and there was a grove of banana trees near the fence. A servant ran in front of the van, directing Pratt to the side of the house and, as instructed, he turned right following the drive past the outbuildings, pulling to a stop just in front of several large wreaths of flowers stacked on wooden pallets. The flowers looked fresh and the name of the deceased was written in Thai on a black ribbon that had been strung across the wreath. They did funerals for more than just the dead *farangs*, thought Calvino.

As the van stopped, Naylor was first to climb out. He stretched as the others got out and joined him on the driveway. A servant opened Pratt's door and he stepped down.

"Doesn't look like a funeral home," said Naylor. "Except for those coffins. It looks like a regular house."

Calvino thought that once again Naylor was looking for the world to mirror his own warped vision. But Calvino knew that the world was so warped that it almost never matched anyone's vision. To him the house looked like the perfect location for a funeral home; discreet, remote, commercially neutral like so many buildings in Bangkok. Not only were the Thais pragmatic, so were the buildings constructed and used by them, never disclosing a specified use in case that might offend or in case the use might need to change quickly. Nestled at the back of the compound was a large, two story house with a veranda around the side. Smaller buildings appeared along the back. What looked like maids' quarters had been converted into a morgue where the owners embalmed bodies. Someone came through the door peeling off a pair of bloody rubber gloves. He looked embarrassed, grinned, and immediately darted across the driveway and into the main building. There was also a garage that looked like some kind of storage facility. Looking over all of the grounds, Calvino could not help but think that this was a large piece of land; even far away from the main hubs of Sukhumvit and Silom Roads single houses occupied a much smaller area. Someone had bought it years before the boom and held it or someone had bought late with a steamer trunk full of cash. Pratt had pulled the van tight next to the back entrance. Wooden coffins—the kind used for cremation—were neatly stacked to one side.

A smartly dressed man in his twenties in a dark western business suit appeared at the back entrance, walked down the steps, and *waied* Pratt. The man introduced himself as Chaiwat, one of the three sons of the undertaker, and asked how he might be of help. At the same time, he eyed the van, as if half-expecting there might be a body inside. Chaiwat had a toothy grin and spoke with a perfect American accent. A pair of gold-rimmed glasses rode forward on his nose.

"I am Colonel Prachai. These foreigners have come for the dead *farang*," said Pratt in Thai. "They want to remove the body of Danny Ramsey."

The young man smiled, his eyes on the *farangs*, and nodded. "You had better speak with my father."

Chaiwat led them down the corridor with large potted ferns, passing the viewing room. The double doors were closed and the panels of glass were curtained with transparent white gauze. They walked up a flight of heavily panelled stairs, down a corridor and into an office on the second floor of the house.

His father, Panya, was seated behind his desk doing some paperwork. The undertaker stood, bowed slightly and *waied* Pratt. His son filed in last and closed the door and then crossed over and whispered in his father's ear. Panya nodded and grinned one of those execution-days-on-the-football-field grins. He was tall and skinny as a rail and his short-cropped hair was mostly gray. His narrow jaw made his teeth appear too big for his mouth and his deep-sunk eyes blinked as he looked at Pratt. He wore a brown suit and the shoulder material bunched up as if someone had lifted him in the air and set him down again. Under his jacket he wore one of those cheesy golf theme ties: green with inserts of golf clubs, golf bags, putting greens. He didn't look like an undertaker.

"I am sorry, I just got back from playing golf," he said. "Please sit down."

They had caught him on his golf day unprepared for visitors. Several black ties hung on coat rack to the side of his desk. He immediately began to remove his golf tie and slipped on one of his solid black mourning ties. He was mid-loop as he motioned for everyone to sit down.

Panya appeared nervous as once again his son whispered that a policeman had accompanied the visitors who filed into his office. He *waied* Pratt for the second time and handed him a name card. The name card was printed in English. Unexpected visitors, who included a police colonel, a priest, a nun and two *farangs*, were unsettling him. He was so rattled that it took him three tries to get the knot in the black tie right.

"You have already met one of my sons, Chaiwat. But he is unable to tell me exactly how we can help you." He gave a nervous laugh as he fiddled with his tie. He nodded towards Chaiwat, who stood next to the door, his hands folded together as if attending a funeral service. "We run a family business." The office was furnished with two comfortable sofas covered in soft black leather. Orchids floated in a bowl on the coffee table. On the wall above his desk, several framed certificates and diplomas were on display as well as a large number of photos. Panya was in all of them, sometimes with high ranking army officers. Others were taken on the golf course. A couple of photos of golf foursomes outside a clubhouse with cute *Isan* caddies squatting in the background beside the golf bags. Photos inside various offices, including his own. In one framed photo, Calvino recognized one of the officer's faces from the newspapers. Such photo displays indicated that Panya had influential friends; that those who exercised substantial power over the lives of others protected him. These photos were there for a purpose; they were displayed as Panya's personal symbols that brought him safety. His umbrella protection system in case the dark clouds moved in and threatened him and his family.

"The condo next door, is that part of the family enterprise?" asked Pratt, scanning the photos, registering the faces, rank, and names. The message was not golf buddies having a good time. The message was here are the people I know who fix things when they need to be fixed. Pratt read the photographs the way Russians used to read the line-up in Red Square as the tanks rolled past. The problem had never been a Y2K, it has always been a Y0K issue: the year Zero where BC flipped over to AD, where the old protection system was jettisoned and reliance on the powerful, the influential, was to be replaced by a system where everyone had protection. These new symbols were nowhere to be seen in his office.

Panya smiled, his yellow teeth exposed through parted lips. "Like many people, we are having some problems. We are struggling but we still manage to keep the project alive." Had his military connection kept the bank from pulling the plug, Pratt wondered.

Calvino's law—the shallower the bank balance the deeper the trouble. And the reverse was equally true: the larger the bank balance, the smaller trouble became until it finally disappeared altogether. Panya looked like a man who lived comfortably in a world of small troubles.

A servant brought in a tray of glasses filled with drinking water.

"Your card is in English," said Pratt. "Unusual."

"Many of our clients are *farangs*, Colonel Prachai," said Panya.

Calvino stepped forward and spread the Report of American Citizen's Death papers on Panya's desk. "We have come on behalf of Daniel Ramsey's family. We want to take the body. If you check, you will find all of the papers are in order," Calvino said.

Panya stared at the papers, shuffled them like a deck of cards; a Chinese grimace suggested a true desire for the undertaker to flee the room. He clearly wished he were somewhere else other than the funeral director's main office.

"Colonel Prachai, may I inquire as to the nature of your business here?" He treated Calvino as if he did not exist.

Pratt nodded in Calvino's direction. "As Mr. Calvino said, he has come for the body and I am here to make certain the coffin is taken to the airport."

"That's quite unusual," said Panya. "In fact, I can't ever recall such a request."

"We plan a short church service. That's normal," said Calvino. "We have arranged for a priest and nun and that is normal," said Calvino, watching Panya shift through the papers as if looking for an error. "You can check with Dwight Morgan at the American Embassy. Khun Dwight did speak so highly of you and how you understood *farangs*."

"We want the fucking body. Is that so hard to understand?" asked Naylor.

Calvino wished he had smacked Naylor harder. It might have shut him up.

"That language shouldn't be used here," said Chaiwat.

Panya grinned and started to reply, but his voice was so faint that no one could hear what he had said. From the back of the room his son Chaiwat repeated what his father said. "The body is no longer here."

Pratt knitted his eyebrows together. "Where is the body?"

"Twenty minutes ago, Mr. Ramsey's representatives collected his body," said Panya.

"What representatives?" asked Calvino. "You have seen the papers. We have the authority. So who did you give the body to?" He was getting mad. Angry that Naylor had to open his big mouth and throw off the questioning, upset that Panya was clearly trying to hide something.

Panya pulled out a thick file from his desk. "They had all of the right documents," he said, placing a folder on the desk and taking out a Report of American Citizen's Death. The report had been filled out with all the details. A copy of the death certificate in Daniel Ramsey's name was attached with a paperclip. "And they were Khun Danny's friends."

"His friends?" asked Pratt. "Did they tell you that he was their friend?"

Panya shook his head, his face clouding up with emotion. "He was my friend, too."

"You knew him?" asked Pratt.

The undertaker leaned back in his chair, hands on the desk, one folded over the other. "Yes, he came here many times. I am very sad when we get his body from the Police Hospital. It was a very big shock for me. And for my sons. I think maybe his work was too much for him. He had too many young *farangs* friends die in Thailand. It depressed him. That's why he killed himself."

Silence swept across the room. Only the faint hum of the motor on the side of the fish tank filled the void. Calvino looked up from the papers—all Reports of American Citizen's Death. "Daniel knew all of these dead Americans?" There were about thirty reports in the folder.

"His friends," said Panya.

Calvino made a point of looking at the age and the time of death on the reports, the deceased—all white males—who ranged in age between twenty-one and forty-nine years old. The cause of death was always the same: heart and breathing stopped. "Did it ever occur to you that Daniel's friends were dying in substantial numbers?"

"*Farangs* come to Thailand and play hard. That's what Khun Danny said to me. They take drugs, they ride motorcycles, they do many stupid, dangerous things. And sometimes they kill themselves," said Panya.

Calvino handed the folder to Pratt. But he kept some of the papers. "The five OD's are in the folder," Calvino said. The five men who had died of heroin overdose and had not been robbed. Jess and Noi sat quietly in the back as if they were waiting for their part in a church service. Noi seemed resigned that it was going to take a long time to get Daniel's body, if they ever got it. Jess looked like someone had blind- sided him with a foot to his head;

he looked pained, lost, and hopeless. If they didn't have the body he wasn't going back to LA. His eyes focused on the fish tank. Naylor groaned as he listened to Panya's explanation. "How many *farangs* are we talking about?"

"Thirty-three," said Calvino. "Over two years."

"Since the economic crisis started," Pratt noted. He was still thinking about the unfinished condo next door and how Panya was the kind of Chinese who yearned for acceptance into Thai society, and would do whatever was necessary to achieve his goal. Mortality, success, status, standing—all were measured in number of stories in the family show-piece building.

"The documents say they were all embalmed," said Pratt. "Is that right? You embalmed all of the *farangs* and afterwards you cremated the bodies."

"It wasn't our idea to cremate them," said Chaiwat, who was standing off to one side in the back of the office.

Panya's eyes closed for a brief moment. "No, that wasn't our idea," he said softly.

"After they were embalmed, they were cremated? I don't understand. You don't embalm someone you cremate in Thailand, do you?" asked Calvino.

Panya raised both hands palms facing up as if lifting a huge weight. "We cremate because of the cost of shipping the bodies back to America."

"You were paid for the embalming and cremation, and a large coffin, and now you will tell us what other payments you received? You had better tell us exactly how this worked." No one in the photographs frightened Pratt.

Panya smiled. "I did nothing wrong, Colonel Prachai."

"No one says that you did. We are asking you to help us understand some strange practices, Khun Panya. You said you knew Daniel Ramsey. How was he involved in this cremation business?" asked Pratt.

From the expression of doom on the undertaker's face, there was every indication that his world was crashing in. He had to make a choice. Answer the questions for the colonel in a way most favorable to himself or stonewall and hope that his military friends would intervene and have the colonel taken off the case. The same old Y0K problem.

"No one wants to cause you a problem," added Pratt. That was the small nudge of comfort that Panya needed.

"Khun Danny always came with two or three friends to make the arrangements. He had all the right papers. The papers were in perfect order. Signed by the American Embassy. Everything was done properly."

"Did he have a friend at the Embassy?" asked Pratt.

"I never asked him," said Panya.

"Did he ever mention the name Dwight Morgan?" asked Calvino.

Panya shrugged his shoulder and looked down.

After a moment, Calvino shifted away from names to the issue of responsibility, knowing the answer before he asked the question. "It was Ramsey's idea to cremate embalmed bodies?" he asked.

"We just did what the relatives asked," said Panya.

Just following orders, thought Calvino. Only Ramsey wasn't any relative of the deceased and Panya knew this to be the case.

"And you arranged the coffin?"

"Khun Danny was particular about the coffin. He made that arrangement himself," said Panya.

"Particular? What does that mean?" asked Pratt, knowing that undertakers made a handsome profit on coffins. Why would Panya let a *farang* cut him out of this lucrative end of the transaction unless there was some other bigger reward involved?

"Let me get this straight: Danny bought the coffins himself and delivered them here? Is this normal practice, letting strangers bring in coffins and ask you to fill them up with a box of ashes?" asked Calvino, who was tracking Pratt's line of argument.

"I thought he was making a little profit and never mind."

If there were ever a hand-held device to pick up bullshit, the red light would have been flashing, thought Calvino. Panya was a lousy liar.

"Never mind that you helped Danny load and ship five pounds of ashes in a coffin built for a dead body. Sounds like fraud," said Calvino. It was becoming clear that some kind of a Trojan horse scam had been hatched between Danny—or at least Danny was point man—and Panya and his sons.

"Sound like fraud? Bullshit, this guy is a crook," said Naylor.

Calvino turned around and pushed Naylor out of the room and locked the door. He was a large man but only made half-hearted resistance. As Calvino stepped back inside, he glanced over at Noi and she looked like she suddenly wanted to kiss him. Throwing Naylor out of the hong had made everyone relax and made Calvino a hero for five seconds. They could see the outline of Naylor's big head through the frosted windowpane.

"Thank you," said Panya. "It's not true. I don't make a fraud. They always arrived with a coffin and took away the same coffin. I never resold any coffin if that is what you are thinking. Never. Ask Chaiwat. Did we ever do such a thing?" Panya was suddenly becoming emotional.

"Not ever, father," said Chaiwat.

"The other men who helped Khun Danny, were they Thai or *farangs*?" asked Pratt.

"Always Thai," said Panya.

"Where did they take bodies for cremation?"

"I don't know," said Panya, his head down.

Pratt knew that he was lying. "I can't help you if you don't co-operate. The people who have done this may try and blame you for everything. Do you want that?"

The Chinese fear of becoming the scapegoat prevailed. "They cremated the bodies at a *wat* a few kilometers from here. The *wat* is near a *klong* and on the way to the airport."

"All thirty-three were cremated at this *wat*?" asked Calvino.

Panya nodded and a barely audible reply came from his dry lips. "And that's where they have taken Danny?"

"We've got to go," said Calvino.

★★★★★★

WHENEVER his mind became overwhelmed with the debris of the day, of a situation, of a problem, Jess began to concentrate on his breathing. Noticing each inhale and exhale, soon his mind would start to clear, his thoughts would still, the bombardment of ideas stop until he reached a place of perfect peace inside himself. Or perhaps it wasn't his self, but the non-self that had been achieved. While watching his breath, he looked straight ahead at a fish tank. Then he noticed for the first time something that had been before him the entire time but that he had not seen. He plunged his arm up to the elbow into the water, scattering the fish inside the tank. The splash had caught the attention of everyone in the room.

They watched as Jess pulled out his arm, dripping water on the carpet, and walked over to Panya's desk where he opened his fist. Water dripped from his knuckles onto papers on the desk.

"Do you know what these are?"

In the palm of his hand lay a dozen or so small pins—small smooth porcelain blue "Cs" and on the back of the "C" was the clasp which fastened it to the member's lapel.

"What are they?" asked Pratt. He picked one out of Jess's hand, examined it, and then looked over at Panya. "Is this some kind of a club?"

Naylor had worn the same kind of pin on his jacket. "The Cause, Colonel. This is the pin members wear when they travel to Thailand, Cuba, the Philippines or wherever so that they can recognize each other," said Jess.

"What are they doing in the bottom of the fish tank?" asked Calvino.

By now everyone was huddled around Jess looking at his catch of "C" pins.

Panya looked perplexed. "I don't know."

Chaiwat reached into the fish tank and pulled out another handful of the "C" pins and stepped forward. "My father doesn't know about the pin. Going through the clothing of the *farangs*, I found them. I liked the color blue so I threw them in the fish tank. If you think we were stealing them, then you are wrong."

"The dead *farangs* were all members of the same club as you so rightly called it. Naylor's Cause-member club," Calvino said to Pratt. "And they all ended up here." Poached off the Causeway with their last stop being Panya's funeral home, where the undertaker's son helped himself to their membership identification.

"Naylor's club?" asked Pratt. "Bring him back inside."

Calvino opened the door and Naylor was leaning against the wall, smoking a cigarette.

"Wes, we need you to identify something," said Calvino.

"Another fucking body?"

He pushed his way to the desk. Panya sat back in his chair, eyes half-closed; he wasn't mediating, he was projecting himself into another time and place. Only all the sounds of this time and place continued to intervene. When he heard Naylor's voice, his eyes popped open.

"These Cause pins were taken off about thirty bodies."

That got Wes Naylor's attention. He lifted his foot and stubbed the cigarette out on the sole of his shoe and put the half-smoked butt back into the pack. Calvino could begin to understand how cheap the guy was, and how even one broken window would make him go postal if he thought that he had to pay for it out of his own pocket. Naylor looked at the pins.

"They're real all right," said Naylor. "Where did you get that many?"

"From the fish tank," said Jess. "Chaiwat kept them in the bottom of the fish tank."

"Goddamn. Stealing personal property off the dead. Looting. That's fucking terrible," said Naylor.

"Khun Panya, would you go with us to the *wat*?", said Calvino.

The undertaker looked like someone had driven a stake through his heart. He shook his head violently. "No, I have so much work. I cannot go. Impossible."

Pratt turned one of the Cause pins over in his hand. He looked up at the undertaker, who was still shaking his head. "You and your son will go to the *wat* with us." This wasn't a request but an order and Panya knew he was defeated. "We will need you to identify the people involved."

From the moment Panya had been phoned and asked to collect Daniel Ramsey's body, he felt this *farang*'s death was a bad omen. This was the first time in memory that he ever embalmed a *farang* whom he recognized, had joked with, had drunk with. Daniel had become his friend. He had been at the funeral home many times to make arrangements for the dead *farangs*. Now in death, Daniel was pulling Panya and his son Chaiwat to the one place they did not wish to go—the *wat* where the embalmed *farangs* had been taken for cremation. Whatever Daniel's game had been, Panya suspected that there was more to it than an ordinary religious service. How could all of these *farangs* be Buddhists? Why weren't at least some of the services in a church? *Why, why, why* kind of questions that had caused him to suffer more than one sleepless night. Chaiwat found a way of dealing with Daniel's mystery emotionally; he said it wasn't their business. What happened along the edges of another's life had nothing to do with him; he had no responsibility to go over to that edge and peer down. Chaiwat's other two brothers always went along with Daniel to the *wat* and they reported nothing strange. They had never said anything unusual ever happened.

Daniel always arrived at the funeral home with two or three Thai associates in attendance—gangsters, Panya had thought. From the way these associates acted and dressed, the roughness of their speech, he knew that inquiry into their background would produce hard looks, and lies. But he didn't have to ask. He knew who these men were who escorted the bodies to the airport. But the transportation and cremation end of matters was strictly speaking none of his business, Panya had told himself. He had done his job. After that, well, it was not his place to inspect the world for all the things that might be out of order. Mr.

Morgan knew that Panya always did a first class job. Never once had there been a complaint. Yes, Panya knew it was wrong to embalm a body that would be cremated. But, on the other hand, it was a small wrong. The *farangs* were rich and he was now a poor man with a fifteen-story building to finish.

Noi, who had sat in a fugue-like motionless state until she thought Jess was about to deliver a cross-over punch into her face as his arm whizzed past and then plunged into the fish tank, rose from her chair and walked over to a side table displaying many framed photographs. She picked one up. She looked closely at the framed photo of Panya with another Thai who looked like a businessman. Both were smiling into the camera. The other Thai had his arm wrapped around Panya's shoulder. Noi's hands were firm on the frame as she turned and looked straight at Jess, holding the photo up for him to see.

"Why is a photo of Khun Kowit here?"

The whole room of people stared at Noi holding the photo.

"That's Kowit?" asked Jess.

Noi nodded.

"I could have told you that," said Naylor. "He's the one who introduced me to Dr. Nat."

"That we understand," said Calvino. "What is less clear, is how Khun Panya knows Kowit. Maybe he would like to explain his friendship to us."

A drop of perspiration fell onto his black mourning tie. "Khun Kowit's my friend from LA. He's also in the funeral home business," said Panya. "Perhaps you know him?"

"We know Khun Kowit very well," said Jess. He still looked like parish priest with one wet arm dripping on the glass covering the photo as if he had just rushed out of a baptism.

"I didn't know pee Kowit was a Catholic," said Panya as he took the framed picture and wiped the water off with the sleeve of his jacket.

"There may be a few other businesses Kowit has that you don't know about. Or maybe you do know," said Jess. "Maybe Naylor might have some ideas as well."

Naylor's lip rose in a sneer. "Ideas? When was the last time an idea bit your ass?"

"Not a polite way to speak to a priest," said Pratt.

Noi, pressing the photo against her breasts, said in Thai, "You will go to hell." She was looking past Naylor and straight at Panya. The undertaker's knees seemed to buckle as he fell back into the chair behind his desk.

At the LAPD, the ballistics people call this moment of realization a "cold hit." The distinctive marks on the casings which come from one handgun used in a crime in LA matched up on the central computer network with the distinctive grooves and scratches that left on a casing found at a murder scene in Chicago. The process requires running a line from one known point to an infinity of possibilities, only to find a connection, a confirmation that the same gun had been used in both places. Grooves and scratches etched into metal link an LA homicide to a murder in Chicago and suddenly two unrelated murders can be traced to the same gun and, more likely than not, to the same gunman. Except no one ever knows that such a line can be drawn until the casings match. Matching bullet casings is like matching funeral directors. It requires some luck. Then out of the blue a funeral director in Los Angeles under suspicion of smuggling drugs appears in the same photo with another undertaker 10,000 miles away. And the point A to point

B link is transformed into a trail of thirty-three dead foreigners. A cold hit. Hugging the photograph, Noi looked happy for the first time since Calvino laid eyes on her. She had found the equivalent of the casing that linked LA and Bangkok, a new trail of evidence that did not involve her brother. She was smiling and humming lyrics to a Thai song. *Hello, hello, hia, la ka.* She knew that she had hit a bull's eye and that felt good.

Before Panya rose from his desk again, Calvino, holding onto the folder of records, noticed the funeral director's passport in the half-opened drawer. He leaned over and grabbed it.

"You shouldn't leave home without it," said Calvino, sliding Panya's Thai passport inside his jacket pocket.

"I don't intend to go that far," said Panya.

"This may be your lucky day," said Calvino.

★★★★★★

AS they drove to the *wat*, a rainstorm came down. The smoky white clouds turned black and opened with what was at first a light, almost gentle rain that swept from the East over the road; but the gentleness soon vanished, and a torrent came straight down like water poured out of a bucket. Pratt switched the windscreen wipers onto maximum. This wasn't the rainy season. Planes had been dispatched to salt the clouds with chemicals to force the rain to fall to relieve the drought upcountry. As the approaching hot season loomed there was fear that Bangkok might run out of water. After a couple of minutes, solid vertical sheets of rain fell. The wipers could not keep up with the volume of water. Calvino was thinking it was a bad day for a funeral. He was also thinking about the pilot who had tried to land the plane at Surat Thani Airport, a small airport in the south; the airport lights were not working, and there had been driving rain, like this now, and the pilot, having failed twice to put the plane down, made the fatal decision for a third go around. Air speed, the position of the stabilizers, the degree of ascent became scrambled and the plane stalled and crashed, killing more than a hundred people. Calvino had lost a friend in that crash. A good man who had worked to preserve the environment had gone down with the plane. Rain, errors, being in the wrong place at the wrong time. How many times can one miss the runway before one's luck runs out? Sitting next to Pratt, he wondered if their luck would hold. Luck may have been the wrong word; there was no luck, only a destiny that awaited each man.

The traffic slowed to a crawl along the wet streets. Calvino looked over at Pratt at the wheel and wondered how he intended to handle Panya. There was a small sliding panel between the cab and the back of the van. It was shut after Panya gave directions to the *wat*. The *wat* turned out to be a considerable distance from the funeral home. Panya had lied about the location of the *wat* in his office. Inside the van, he had a change of heart. He had intended to stay in his office and send them on a wild goose chase to the wrong *wat*. His plans and directions to the *wat* changed once he and his son were in the van. As Pratt strained for visibility of the cars in front of him, Calvino leafed through Panya's Thai passport.

"He's been to LA four times in the last year," said Calvino, reading the dates on the LAX chop inside Panya's passport.

"Maybe he has relatives in LA," said Pratt. The jazz on the cassette player had switched to a Coltrane album. "There are over two hundred thousand Thais in LA."

That made LA the third largest Thai City in the world. Bangkok, Chaing Mai and then LA. Only the latter was a Thai city inside America and different rules came into play.

"Panya has at least one good friend who is involved in the drug business."

"He's scared, Vincent," said Pratt.

"You would think a funeral home owner wouldn't be afraid if he were innocent." Calvino's law was that a court operated under the presumption that the accused was innocent until proven guilty, while cops in the street assumed a suspect sweating as much as Panya was guilty until he could square his fear by proving himself innocent.

Pratt didn't react to the issue of innocence. For him it wasn't innocence or guilt but the nature of how a man faced death. "A Buddhist is not afraid of dying. What he should be afraid of is that if he dies in torment, in anguish, then that is the condition to which he will be reborn. When you die you want your mind at peace, you want to be tranquil. The next life is always a condition of the last moment of the last life."

Calvino put the passport away in his jacket, wondering about Pratt's wisdom about the transition between lives. It didn't look all that good for Panya's rebirth at the moment. "Maybe it is some kind of an insurance scam. Daniel Ramsey and a couple of grifter friends were in it for the insurance, arranging death certificates, collecting the money. White-collar crime. Bad, but not too bad."

"I am not sure just how much he really knows," said Pratt.

"Every one of the heroin overdose cases ended up at Panya's house."

"You said yourself the Embassy recommends him."

"That's why I asked him if Ramsey ever mentioned Dwight Morgan," said Calvino.

A smile creased Pratt's face. "You think Morgan is the serial killer you've been looking for?"

Calvino returned the smile. "In matters of real politic there are no friends or enemies, only a convergence of interest. And, no, I don't think Morgan killed anyone."

"Vincent, it doesn't mean anything that the Embassy handled these routine papers. Or it doesn't prove anything that Panya handled the shipments to the States. That is his business. And he's got a good business. He doesn't need to ship a few more dead *farangs* to the States to keep his condo project on track." Pratt paused and exhaled. "But we both know Panya's guilty as hell. What we don't exactly know is the crime."

Calvino watched the rain striking the window. It pissed him off knowing what Pratt said was right on the money. There still was no reason established. Even if Panya was padding the bill, this was chump change compared with the money and valuables found on the dead *farangs* with needles stuck in their arms. It was as if he were submerged in a world from which reason had been sucked out.

"I'm working on the crime," said Calvino.

"You'll let me know when you come up with one."

"What matters is Panya doesn't have a lot of choices to make right now. And if he makes the wrong one, then that's it. He's reborn as a beggar. Give me some time and I'll have our motive."

After they lapsed into silence, Naylor's cursing from the back filled the void. "Fuck this" and "Fuck that" and "I want money for the fucking window." The Thais were deadly quiet.

"The original plan isn't going to work, Vincent."

"I know. But I have a couple of ideas."

"For instance?" asked Pratt.

"What if it turned out that Panya's testimony could send Kowit to prison?"

"I am glad Noi spotted that photo," said Pratt.

"And that she said something. She didn't have to. She could have sat on her hands."

"Still the photo doesn't prove anything," said Pratt. "Other than they know each other and are in the same business. That's not a crime, Vincent." Pratt checked his rearview mirror before changing lanes. He kept on talking to Calvino, "We still have the problem of getting Jess out of the country. And now we have the added problem of what to do with Panya. I can't see him voluntarily stepping onto a plane."

"We have his passport. So we need to give him an incentive to go to LA. He has to want to go," Calvino said.

"Why would he do that?"

"He's in a lose-lose situation. If he's dirty, then he's going to be afraid to stay in Thailand. If he's clean, he's still going to be afraid no one will believe that he went to a *wat* with a Thai police colonel and revealed nothing about the operation." The force of the rain lessened and the traffic was moving again as they headed towards Klong Toey. "Remember a few years ago, the Chinese drug dealer who begged that the Americans take him back to the States? He said he felt safer in an American prison. Here was a guy who had lived on a diet of fried bugs in the jungle, lived with constant danger, snakes and tigers, but when push came to shove, pleaded to be sent back to the States. Because he knew those he did business with would kill him if he stayed. Panya isn't a moron. If he's doing funny business with Kowit, they will whack him in five minutes once they know we've been to his place and he's helping us and we have the photo of him and Kowit."

The original plan had been simple and straightforward. They would make a switch on the way to the airport. Jess would trade places in the coffin with Daniel Ramsey's body. Later, at Don Muang Airport, they would check the coffin in at the cargo terminal. They had all the paperwork. This would be a routine transaction and Noi would be driven to the passenger terminal and put on a flight to Los Angeles. Pratt would walk her through the paperwork even without a passport. They would book her on the same flight that Jess would be riding cargo class inside the coffin. Jess would square her entry into the States at the other end. Once that flight was airborne, they'd take Danny's body to a *wat*, pay a small fee to have it cremated, and scatter the ashes in the *klong*. The following morning, Calvino would go with Pratt to police headquarters, and Calvino would file a complaint that someone had blown up his car. He would demand that those who committed the crime be arrested and punished. The best defense was always an in-your-face offence. He wouldn't give the cops a chance to say they had been looking for him. He'd say he had been looking for them. And when they got around to questioning him about his companions, including the Thai national with the American accent, he would say, "Oh, that guy, he's gone upcountry for a kick-boxing tournament." Pratt would stand tall beside him and the cops would get the picture, it didn't need to be framed and hung on a wall, there was nothing they could do but turn him loose and watch him, tap his home and office phones. And they could watch him forever because it wouldn't matter; once that plane set down at LAX, Jess's commanding officer and a dozen other LAPD would be taking delivery of the coffin, clearing Noi through customs and all would be right in the world.

That had been the plan, a pretty good plan at that. But like life, plans were impermanent, subject to change, and this plan needed some radical changes. For starters, they didn't have Daniel Ramsey's coffin. They might never have that coffin at the rate they were going. There was a duplicate set of paperwork floating around. Checking in a *farang* body with the same name and paperwork twice on the same day would cause more than one or two phone calls to be made at exactly the wrong time.

"But I haven't told you my best idea," said Calvino.

"I am not certain I am ready for this."

"I am going inside the *wat*," he waited a beat and then added, "Alone. As a tourist. You drop me off like you are a tour guide."

"That is the worst idea you ever had. No tourist ever goes to that *wat* along that klong. It's not on any tourist map. That hit team knew your face."

"But they're dead. I figure on a division of labor between the grunts who do the heavy lifting and the gunmen who do the killing. If I am wrong, I'll let you know. I'll do my Forrest Gump routine, 'You mean this isn't Wat Arun? First my guide takes me to buy jewelery and then he brings me here. Am I being cheated?' This approach always works magic."

Pratt turned down the jazz. "You're a natural. But these are drug smugglers and they don't use magic to make someone disappear. They would shoot Forrest Gump."

"Do you have a better plan?"

"I turn around and drive to the airport. Jess goes out on the next flight. I can walk him through using Panya's passport."

"But he's got nothing right now. The guys he's been chasing, the same ones you've been after, can shut down the entire smuggling operation. Just change routes. Kill Panya and what is there to prove any of this was a drug smuggling operation? They are still in business. And what have we accomplished?"

The uncertainty of the situation made any telephone call Pratt might make to the department a dangerous alternative. It was unclear who might be involved in the operation. Colonel Virat of the special narc unit was the only man he thought could be trusted. The amount of money involved over the past eighteen months was staggering. He wouldn't want to guess who might have been tempted. He drove in silence. Calvino's plan was to buy some time and to gather some solid evidence. There was a feeling of a cold hit being made; what was missing was the casing, the link between the heroin disappearing from Burma and ending up in a smuggling venture operated by Panya and Kowit.

"You come up with a reason for the serial killer yet?" asked Pratt.

"One thing, Pratt. How did Jess get you involved in this from the start?"

"Why?" asked Pratt.

"I am starting to think that whoever teamed me with Jess was a two-for-one deal. They weren't wanting to kill just Jess or just me. They wanted us both out. And there has to be a good reason for that, don't you think?"

Pratt glanced over at Calvino. "A guy named Gabe told him we were friends."

"Maybe these guys were going for three for the price of one, Pratt."

"Vincent, hand me the carphone. I need to make a call."

He didn't ask why Pratt didn't wish to use his own phone. Other ears would be listening, wired to that number. He already knew they had been tracking Calvino's number. His brother-in-law had had the vision to install a phone in the van, and now he would be drawing his sister's family into the vortex. Pratt had no choice but to take that risk.

SIXTEEN

TO MOST FOREIGNERS most wats looked fungible—the basic architectural design was nearly identical, as if built—like fast-food restaurants—from the same design bible. This was an illusion of epic magnitude. Thais immediately knew the differences in each wat like they knew the difference between forty different kinds of rice; the difference was in subtleties within the interior of a *sala*, trees growing on the grounds, the mixture of stray cats and dogs and clients who came to kneel and give offering under the sloping roofs with ornate carvings; mostly, it was the abbot, the monks, novices, and others who lived inside that gave the wat its personality. Most offered a cremation service. Panya had changed his story about the wat where the men had taken Daniel Ramsey's body. It was no longer the wat near the funeral home; the dead *farang* had, as it turned out, never been taken to such a neighborhood wat. Undertakers were trained to deal with others' sadness and loss but if Panya was any indication, undertakers had some trouble applying this training to their own woes. Perhaps Panya had never thought it would come down to this precise moment, that is, a moment of truth. He adhered to the belief there was always a way out. An escape hatch through the highest wall. His faith was being severely tested for as hard as he tried he couldn't find any wiggle room left. The options were bleak—either he kept on lying and getting himself deeper and deeper into trouble, or he just got on with it, got it over with quickly and hoped they would go away and leave him in peace. He hated making such decisions. It was better to do nothing than to decide, but living with nothing was living with the adverse nature of any decision.

Chaiwat tried to provide comfort to his father. "Dad, we take them there. No problem for us." The old man's face collapsed into deep thought, then he nodded. He sat in the back of the van as if in a dream, a half-stupor, his head bobbing back and forth like a puppet on a string, his eyes wide open, one hand on the knee of his son, pressing it hard, a touch of fear, a touch of regret in the way he inhaled and exhaled as if he were counting his breaths. His other hand clutched three amulets, which hung on a gold chain around his neck. Panya was mumbling to himself, either praying or he had gone over the edge into incoherent madness. Chaiwat sat next to him watching his father fall apart. Father and son sat opposite Jess and Noi. Her nun's habit with the patches of dried blood was a mass of wrinkles from Naylor's fat ass, and Jess's clerical collar had turned brown from sweat and was coming undone at one end. In his hand he fingered several of the blue Cause pins, turning them over and over in his hand. It was dark in the back of the van with tinted windows, the sky had clouded up and it was raining outside. No one felt like talking. Except Naylor who had a tune in his head and couldn't remember the words. It was driving him crazy watching Panya finger his amulets and talk gibberish. He hummed the song but he was flat, off-key. It could have been anything. "Come on, Noi. It's driving me fucking crazy. Help me." Noi ignored him, trying to smooth out the wrinkles in her habit. "It goes something like this, 'Why I can't meet your major wife? Why I can't meet your major wife?'" On and on he sang those words. Naylor was demented enough that the entire rant might have been nothing more than an ugly way to humiliate her further. Maybe he simply wanted to hear a singer dressed up like a nun. One of those Cause fetish things, debasing a woman, making her an object through any crazy scheme at hand, words, gestures, music. The way Naylor remembered the words made it a crazy tune. Naylor knew almost no Thai but the *luuk tung* song wouldn't leave him alone.

"*Hello, hello, hia, la ka?*" Hello, lover. She finally sang the words.

"That's it. Goddamit. That is it exactly."

"*Tammai mai phoot? Tammai mai phoot?*" sang Chaiwat. "Why don't you speak?" The words had an ironic meaning as they headed towards the wat.

Noi and Chaiwat shared a laugh and that seemed to ease some of the tension. They were going to a funeral after all. They might be going to their own funeral. No one knew.

Naylor clapped his hands and tried to sing the song in Thai. Of course he got the words all jumbled up so they made no sense, and so he reverted to singing, "Why I can't meet your major wife?" words which carried some general meaning from the song but weren't even close to an accurate translation. Finally Jess looked up from the blue pins in the palm of his hand and shot Naylor a long, evil look. "Shut the fuck up, Naylor."

It was the first time anyone had heard Jess curse. It was the first time Panya or Chaiwat had heard a priest curse. But they rarely spent much time in the company of priests.

Jess told Naylor that if he didn't shut up he would throw him out of the van and looked at him the way a cop looks at a homeless drunk in front of a 7/11 at Hollywood and Vine. Naylor doubted Jess would do that; after all, they still needed him to clear shit at the airport and if they threw his ass out of the van, it would make their own lives difficult. Still, from the expression on Jess' face, he decided to back down—he might not actually throw him out but he could definitely inflict some pain—and he continued a low-key humming of the tune to himself as a minor defiance. They were all in this together. Sitting in the back of a van, off to find, if not the Wizard of Oz, then at least Daniel Ramsey's body and the little cocksuckers who were burning it into a five pound bundle of ashes, thought Naylor. Besides, he wanted to be present when the smoke came out of the chimney signalling that Daniel's naked soul had been sent to hell.

As it turned out the wat where the Cause-members had been taken for cremation had never been a famous one, or even one widely known by the locals. In a crossword puzzle, very few Thais would have been able to fill in the right letters—except Father Andrew. He knew it. The wat was in his backyard. Too close to a slum, the wat was neither fashionable nor popular. It survived from a few donors and no-questions-asked cremations and the funds were just enough to prevent it from running to complete squalor. The location was rotten and no one who was important ever turned up unexpectedly so authorities left it alone as unworthy of their attention. Situ- ated next to a *klong* the color of melted iron, whose water carried a heavy stench of decay and chemicals, which lay like a mist above the *salas* and *kuti*—living quarters for the monks. The monks lived next to a *klong* totally devoid of any ability to sustain life—an illusion of existence. Except for the smell of garbage, dead animals, and toxins that drifted through the wat. Such a location was ideal to cremate unimportant people; nobodies, the destitute from the slums, victims of upheavals, and others whose presence was best reduced to a small box of ashes and would never be missed because they had never counted in the first place.

Pratt slowed the van over a narrow concrete bridge and reached over and turned down the volume of John Coltrane's "Ev'ry Time We Say Goodbye." Down below Calvino on the *klong* were several sand barges stretched out like portable beaches. The sand was still wet from the rain, though the hot sun had broken through the clouds and dried the streets. Calvino found a digital camera in the glove box of the van.

"That belongs to my brother-in-law." Pratt sounded alarmed.

"I am not going to break it if that is what you are worried about."

"I didn't say I was worried."

"You didn't have to."

Calvino rolled down the window and snapped several shots. He squinted one eye and with the other stared through the viewfinder, looking, looking. But there was no sign of life below the bridge; not on the barges or along the *klong* or in the central courtyard of the wat, as if this was a forsaken place, a place abandoned by others who once lived here and avoided by those going about their daily business. On the same side as the wat were a number of Shell Oil storage tanks. Mainly the landscape was dotted with squat, ugly industrial buildings and water bobbing with the debris of the industrial age—Styrofoam cups, plastic bottles, milk cartons that floated on the surface, still, lifeless, as if in a painting. Calvino snapped a photo of a spirit house on the edge of the dock; potted flowering plants lined the small dock as if someone either innocent or crazed had taken some pride in beauty in this ugly sea of squalor.

Pratt gunned the van through the main gates, made a hard right turn, kicking up gravel in parking lot. "Remember, it's your brother-in-law's van," said Calvino as a thin haze of post-rain freshly baked dust settled down on the windshield. A dozen cars and pickups were parked near the entrance. Pratt had pulled alongside a red Toyota pickup. Wooden railings formed a fence around the bed of the pickup. A few feet ahead, several food vendors worked under the shade of big umbrellas, and next to them was an old woman with small wooden cages with birds to be bought and released to make merit. No place in Thailand was ever empty, especially the parking lot of an obscure, isolated wat. Always someone was selling food and someone was eating the food being sold. Two monks walked on either side of an elderly man who slowly opened the pickup and crawled inside with a crablike movement of his thin old legs. The old man kept the door open as he started the engine. He looked over smiling at Pratt as if something funny had crossed his mind. But no doubt this was the old man's default smile, the expression he assumed when he saw a stranger looking at him. Pratt reached around and flipped back the small window panel and looked into the back.

"Jess, open the back door," said Pratt. "Just push it open. But stay inside for the moment."

Jess leaned forward and pushed the door open.

"Khun Panya, do you recognize that van?" asked Pratt.

"No. I don't. My boys wouldn't stop here. They would have gone down the side road and parked near the crematorium. It's too far to carry a coffin from the parking lot."

For someone who knew nothing about the wat, suddenly Panya had disclosed that he knew a great deal about the layout of the grounds. How would he know where the van they were looking for might be parked unless he had been here before? Chaiwat rolled his eyes as his father spoke. The son was obviously no one's fool but what could he do other than stick a rag in his old man's mouth and it was too late even for that.

All of Panya's explanations made sense: heavy lifting in the heat was to be avoided. The rain had brought some relief; the sun was out, and all the cars in the parking lot were bone dry. Not a drop of rainwater on any of them. The grounds dusty.

"Tell me again, how many men are involved?"

"Three or four."

Pratt showed a flash of anger. "Which is it? Three or four. Or four or five?"

"Four," said Chaiwat. The kid seemed to have a knack for details like knowing the exact number of the blue pins salvaged from the dead. And the number of men who had come to collect Daniel's body.

"Are they armed?"

"I didn't see a weapon," said Panya.

"And Khun Chaiwat, what about you, did you ever see any guns?"

"Not directly. But they could have been packing under their shirts. They wore them outside, loose fitting." Chaiwat, flashing a toothy grin, was smooth with his American accent.

"My son has seen too many gangster movies," said Panya. "He speaks perfect English. Why the fuck he's working as an undertaker is beyond anything I can understand. I would hire him in a minute for the Grand Rose. You want to change careers, Chaiwat? No more dead bodies? I will cut you a deal," said Naylor.

"My boys are very happy in our family business," said Panya. "And very lucky, too. They make big money in the stock market. Internet trading. Very smart, my boys. We finish our condo and maybe we all retire."

Calvino knitted his brow. "Big money?"

Calvino opened the door but before he could climb out, Pratt grabbed his arm.

"You don't need to prove anything about this serial killer. I want you to know that I was too hard on you. I think I was wrong. There may be something to this serial killer business."

Calvino grinned, and then he lowered his voice. "Who's proving anything? And you are right. There is still no reason. No motive. So let me take a few pictures of the wat. No big deal. I'll look around. Loosen up, Pratt. No one is going to stick a needle in my arm. Besides, Jess thinks that a *farang* would never cross the street to help a Thai. Let me show him that it ain't true."

★★★★★★

SEVERAL bony dogs growled as they scratched patchy areas of furless hide, drawing blood from scabby sores, eyeing Calvino as he walked down a path between a *sala* and another flat, low building with rows of chairs inside. One of the dogs limped away with one leg hiked up like a society lady's little finger as she raised the teacup to her lips. Calvino swung his arm back as if pretending to throw a rock, and the dogs—which would never call such a bluff—scattered back into the shade and resumed their scratching. A monk came up to Calvino. He *waied* the monk before he could stop himself. A tourist, he thought, wouldn't likely *wai* a monk unless they had memorized the cultural section out of the Lonely Planet Guide. Even then a tourist would likely deliver the wrong *wai*. Like varieties of rice, there were many kinds of *wais*; each appropriate to the person and the occasion. There were charts with dozens of photographs of Thai men and women demonstrating the various *wais* that hung in upcountry schools so the children of peasants could learn that respect was not absolute; there were fine degrees of paying respect.

Calvino surprised himself. Anyone who had lived in Thailand for a very long time found himself doing what he did: making a *wai* to a monk as if he were on automatic pilot, one of those unthinking reflex reactions. The young monk acknowledged Calvino's *wai* with a smile. Monks never returned a *wai* with a *wai*. It didn't matter who delivered the *wai*. This was a one-way street of respect. Besides, the *wai* was to the robe not to the man.

The monk was young, handsome; his freshly shaved head had a couple of small nicks that looked like hairline fractures on his head. As he turned, his head glistened in the sunlight. His robes appeared new; Calvino thought he was a novice who had only recently entered the monkhood. His new status was written all over his face, the small cuts on his head, and his robe. He smiled at Calvino and greeted him in English.

"Where are you from?" the monk asked him. There were rarely any foreigners who came to the wat, and the monk had no chance to practice his English. He was an upcountry Thai with blue tattoos on his neck and arms.

His English sounded self-taught. But he was curious and brave enough to approach a stranger and risk making a fool of himself in a foreign language.

"New York City," Calvino said. He wanted the monk to go away and increased his speed, shooting ahead of the monk.

The monk, who must have trained running across *Isan* rice fields, caught up immediately and stayed right at his shoulder. There was no losing him.

"New York Yankees are a great baseball team," said the monk. His English had a strange accent but otherwise he could make himself understood.

"Who taught you English?"

The monk smiled. "My friend from Finland."

Finns had occupied the ground floor of Calvino's building. After the real estate market went bust, they left. Calvino wondered what had happened to them. Could they have set up an English language school? Calvino rounded a corner, thinking he might be lost.

"Did you get caught in that rainstorm?" asked the monk. He rambled on like a lonely person who had been kept in a cellar and this was his first day above ground in about five years. "The government puts salt in the clouds. They send planes up with salt. There is no water in the north. The farmers are angry. Their rice crop is dying. Rain this time of year? It never happens."

Calvino let the monk rabbit on about the relation of rain and rural poverty and, at the first pause in his monologue, Calvino stopped and looked around.

"You mind if I take some pictures?"

"I will be your guide."

"How long have you been living in this wat?"

"Four months." The monk grinned; he had won a small victory, he felt. The foreigner had not told him to "hit the fucking road" like the one other foreigner who he had tried to strike up a conversation with the first day he arrived. This defeat was like a scar that hadn't healed. Calvino was going to put this right for him.

"Not many *farangs* come here," said Calvino.

"Father Andrew from the slum. But you can't say he's really a *farang*."

"Only one other *farang*?"

The monk stopped smiling. He was thinking, wondering whether he should mention the *farangs* who used the bad words. Maybe this *farang* would think he was the kind of Thai who didn't like *farangs*. The monk had taken a vow not to lie. There was that to consider. And there was the *farang* who came half an hour earlier. Rough and mean, a *farang* who had arrived with Thai nak leng tough guys. Not the kind of people this tourist *farang* would be interested in. So there was that to consider as well. The monk hadn't bothered to approach and speak English with this other *farang*; he could sense this would be pointless. These men and that *farang* had come to the wat on business. Tourists were his hope, his prayer.

Calvino stopped and looked at the monk. "Today you didn't happen to see another *farang*?"

The monk nodded, gathered his robes and began to walk. "Maybe your friend?" He sounded disappointed, hoping that this could not be the case.

"He came earlier with some other men. Thai men. They went to the crematorium. Am I too late for the cremation?" Calvino took another photograph of the monk.

"Not too late," said the monk. "Why didn't you say before?"

The monk turned and pointed. They had been going in the wrong direction.

"How many men did you see?"

"I didn't count," said the monk. "But not so many. Like before. Three or four with a *farang*. Twice a month. Sometimes more, sometimes less. Always to cremate a body."

"Strange. This wat cremates *farangs* two or three times a month," said Calvino.

"That's nothing. They bring the body in a wooden coffin. Cheap for burning. Then they put the ashes in a fancy metal coffin. *Farangs* are strange. Thai people don't put ashes in such a big coffin. There is no need."

"You saw these coffins?" asked Calvino.

"Big, metal coffins. Beautiful. Thai people are not rich. Can't pay so much for dying."

"Let me get this straight. These men come to the wat with two coffins. One is wooden with a dead *farang* inside. They burn the wooden one. And they put the ashes in the nice metal one and drive away." He wanted the monk to confirm what he suspected to be true.

He got what he wanted. "One hundred percent," said the monk. "Today we have several cremations. The past couple of days have been a good time for dying. So they are waiting their turn."

Bangkok traffic jams didn't stop even at the crematorium door.

"The same men that come every month?" asked Calvino, thinking the delay had bought them some time.

"You don't ask questions like a tourist," said the monk. He cocked his head to the side; he looked discouraged.

"You never talked to a tourist from New York before. You see any weapons? M-16s, handguns, shotguns? In New York we're always interested in guns. And the Yankees of course."

It had been such a strange day. The freak rain. Another novice knocking over a broom into the abbot's lap. One of the senior monks said that was a bad omen. A pickup truck with men in military-like clothing riding in the back with two coffins. One of the junior monks said this event was the worst omen. One empty; one with a body inside. Now this New Yorker strolling around the grounds in circles, obviously lost, asking about whether he had seen any guns.

"Buddhism forbids killing," said the monk. That seemed like a safe answer.

"I'm glad to hear that. What about guns? Not that these guy would want to kill anyone."

"I saw something."

"A gun?"

"I am not sure."

"It wasn't a baseball bat?"

This made the monk laugh. "No, it wasn't that for sure."

They walked between a row of motorcycles, then a car with a broken wheel, then an empty taxi. Further down on the right was a Toyota pickup. "They came in that pickup," said the monk, nodding at the Toyota. The pickup was an old, beat-up Toyota. The back bumper was bashed in. It had one of those homemade sheet metal cabs mounted on the back with two small metal doors that swung out and which had been padlocked with a fat Yale lock.

"Your English is very good. I need a favor. Do you think that you could help me?"

The monk came alive with hope of doing some good. "What?"

"Go back to the parking lot and tell my guide exactly what you just told me."

"You have a guide? Why isn't he with you? What should I tell him?" He looked confused.

"Just let him know about the men who come a couple of times a month, the two coffins, the military outfits, and the guns you're not sure they were carrying. Now, please excuse me, I want to take some pictures."

Calvino watched the monk disappear around the corner, and then he walked over to the Toyota and picked the padlock. It took him a couple of minutes before the lock snapped open and he swung back the rear doors. The pickup was parked behind a Benz. Seated behind the steering wheel of the Benz, a driver slumped with his head flopped to one side, his eyes closed, his mouth open, his chest rising up and down slowly. Dreamland. He wasn't going to be taking any notice of the break-in, thought Calvino.

Kowit had problems in Los Angeles, but in Bangkok everything had been under tight control, thought Calvino as he looked inside the pickup. Panya and Kowit had powerful enough friends. So why get too concerned? Go on, leave the pickup unattended. Let the guy in the Benz continue with his nap, *sabai, sabai*. Who was going to fuck with the boys? Whoever had driven the pickup was standing in some queue waiting for their turn at the furnace door. Calvino walked around to the Toyota, snapping photos of the registration plate and more shots through the open doors, he snapped more photos of an expensive American-style metal coffin resting on wooden pallets. The same kind of pallets he remembered seeing at the back of Panya's house. Calvino leaned inside the cab. It was dark but there was enough light that he could see his own reflection in the highly buffed surface of the metal.

Then Calvino climbed into the back and squatted down in the low light like he was hovering over an Asian-style shitter. Immediately the sweat poured out of him. It must have been 120 degrees inside. He was thinking they had just about enough heat to roast Danny but probably short of what was needed to cremate him. He ran his hand down the rim of the coffin until he found a latch. Coffins were built on the same principle as suitcases. He slowly raised the coffin lid; but it wouldn't open the whole way. The outer edge hit the interior of the roof. With the lid half raised, he could sort of see inside. It looked empty, unused, and had that fresh new car smell. He reached inside and felt around. Cool satin-like fabric neatly puckered to give it a textured look. It reminded him of a bathrobe his mother wore when he was four years old. He was half inside the coffin, keeping his balance by shoving one foot against the inside of the sheet metal cab. At what he decided must have been the head of the coffin—it could have been the bottom since there was no indication in which position the head went and to which end the feet pointed—a small rectangular wire frame holder had been fastened by bolts to the floor of the coffin. It was tall enough and wide enough to hold a live chicken. But Calvino figured whoever had gone to all this trouble wasn't smuggling fighting cocks back to LA for Noi's half-witted brother. Someone had gone to a lot of trouble to pull off a professional job. An urn holding five pounds of ground-up ashes would slide nicely into the holder and along the side were buckles like on ski boots to snap the urn in place so as to keep it from rattling around inside like one of those ball-bearings from the Claymore in the morgue drawer. These guys had thought of everything.

Calvino edged back out of the coffin. He was drenched with sweat; it was dripping off his chin, staining the satin inside the coffin. He looked around until he found a tire jack and then crawled back into the coffin, hitting his head on the coffin lid. Fuck, he said. He rubbed his head with his free hand before he used the tire jack to slit the satin finished fabric; he peeled it back revealing plywood panels along the side of the coffin. Someone had used expensive upholstery, he thought as he tore back the fabric. The fabric had been stapled to these sheets of plywood. Calvino searched for a seam in the plywood panel, it was dark and he relied on touch, and when he found a crack, he stuck in the jack and ripped back a piece of the plywood. It broke off and dropped onto the floor of the coffin without any sound; he stuck his arm in as far as he could, feeling around behind where the panel had been and his finger felt cool plastic. He got a firm grip and pulled, dragging a ziploc bag packed with something that had some heft out of the coffin and into the back of the cab. He sat back and looked at the bag, put it to the side and dived back in, pulling out bag after bag. He was out of breath, sitting there in sweaty clothes, feeling a cold damp go up the back of his spine. Each ziploc bag looked exactly the same, contained the same amount of white powder, as if filled by a pharmacist working off a prescription.

He hoisted the Ziploc bag in his right hand, shifted it to his left hand, guessing the weight to be about one pound. His mind ran through some rough numbers. He was holding onto what translated at street level to one large hunk of cash. Maybe he was dripping sweat on a hundred grand bag. He smiled, thinking how they had them by the balls now. That is if he didn't get his own balls shot off in the next ten minutes or ten days. It was like tracking down the nest where that bitch monster in *Aliens* had laid her eggs. The smugglers had created coffins that had every conceivable feature that money could buy. All that was missing were racing stripes. Tiny containers tailor-made to ship a big load of drugs and few pounds of ashes. It was brilliant: make up for the rest of the body weight with heroin. That would let them send out seventy-five kilo shipments. These guys would have been generating enough revenue to buy a personal army. He thought of the three men with the CAR-15s in the Emporium. And they had almost no risk or downside. Some guy in customs opens the coffin, sees the ashes in the holder. He doesn't even ask for a bribe. Besides, no one is really looking for contraband inside a coffin which is accompanied by all those US Embassy papers. Who wants a whiff of some unrefrigerated dead body being shipped out of the tropics. They would be happy enough to see that the US Embassy papers were in order. Leave it to the Embassy to deal with its own dead people. *Fuck this*, Calvino could hear even the most corrupt customs officer say to himself. And at the LA end, same, same, thought Calvino. Who at LAX would be heartless enough to question, let alone deny, an American his birthright of being shipped home in style? Anyone coming home in a two-grand metal coffin would deserve some respect. The smugglers had used the Embassy to aid and abet their operation. They had gone into business with Uncle Sam.

"Hey, asshole, what are you doing?" boomed a *farang* with an unmistakable American accent.

Calvino stuffed one of the Ziploc bags under his jacket and turned around. He thought he recognized this voice but couldn't quite put a face to it.

A young *farang* stepped forward; he was wearing a Chicago Bulls T-shirt that showed off a muscular chest. New designer tennis shoes, too, thought Calvino. The man came straight at Calvino. The guy didn't say another thing as he jumped onto the back gate of the pickup. He grabbed hold of Calvino's jacket and in one smooth, clean jerk, pulled him out of the pickup. Calvino hit the ground hard. Looking up at the assailant, he remembered that voice. Calvino sat dazed for a moment, one arm of his second-hand jacket had been torn and sagged down to his elbow.

"Not you again, you fucking asshole." TJ threw a hard right, missing, as Calvino got to his feet. The severed sleeve hung by a couple of threads. He shook his arm and the sleeve fell onto the ground along with the Ziploc bag full of heroin. TJ looked at the bag, then at Calvino. TJ had a way with words. Not a good way with words, but a way that let anyone know that what he lacked in formal education he made up with intentional violence and a twisted, distorted passion to inflict harm.

"I broke your fucking nose. That should have told you to stay away from this," said TJ. He was pointing at the bag.

"What's your name, again?" asked Calvino.

This took him back for a moment. "TJ and it's the last new name you're gonna hear in this world." He came slowly at Calvino, who was keeping the bag of heroin between TJ and himself on the theory that this would make TJ more cautious.

"Tell me something, TJ. Did you know I was going to deliver that birthday card?"

"You are a stupid fuck. Of course, I knew you were coming. My job was to hurt you, to take you out."

"You didn't do a very good job, did you?"

"You got real lucky. But your luck has fucking run out. And I am going to finish what I started," said TJ, pulling out a knife.

Calvino, hands out, slowly backed away keeping the bag of heroin between TJ and himself. "Careful, TJ you are going to bust open the bag and then you will be in the shit." He really didn't want to shoot TJ unless he had no other option. Even killing someone as worthless as TJ inside a wat was bound to bring on one very huge amount of bad karma. Coming back as a limping *soi* dog would be a great revenge if Calvino shot TJ. This had to be one of the most stupid guys on the planet. How could he forget that Calvino was carrying a gun?

TJ circled around the back of the pickup, jabbing at Calvino with a six-inch blade that caught flashes of bright sun, bouncing light over the grounds. That was some fucking knife, thought Calvino. The dope on the ground was making TJ watch his own feet as well as Calvino, who was dancing around the bag. Calvino was going over the birthday card delivery incident as he watched the knife play. Frank Hogan had hired him. Could Hogan have been the serial killer? Or had Hogan been working with the dopers and lent them a hand? That would have accounted for Hogan's role in having Calvino's face smashed up enough to put him out of action so when the LAPD came around asking him to take on a bodyguard assignment he would have to decline. None of it was adding up, the small numbers, the negative numbers, the new math of deceit and betrayal that was played on the abacus of Bangkok's underworld.

TJ started shouting a Thai nickname, "Lek, Lek, Lek."

It didn't take more than a couple of seconds before a chubby Thai came running, huffing and puffing, his eyes crazy from the heat of the crematorium, his fat hands clutched into hamhock fists as he pulled to a stop, standing next to TJ. This was, Calvino could see from the slack shape of the jaw, the crooked hairline, and the plum-shaped earlobes, one of Panya's sons. All that was missing was the golfer's tie. Lek didn't appear to be carrying a weapon. TJ looked at Lek. "Take him out," TJ said.

Lek stepped forward and made a couple of kickboxing moves, grunting heavily after each kick. Calvino ducked the kicks, slow, torpid shots that looked more like modern dance than kickboxing. Lek gave every indication of being incapable of hitting a stationary target let alone one that had any slight movement attached. This performance totally pissed off TJ.

"Kick his fucking head in," shouted TJ, little white gobs of spittle resting in the corners of his mouth. It wouldn't be long until his mouth had a real froth flowing.

"Lek, my main man. Your dad Khun Panya and your older brother Khun Chaiwat are gonna be sorry you helped this *farang*," said Calvino.

Lek stood with both feet firmly planted on the ground. He saw the bag of heroin on the ground for the first time. His jaw dropped and he said, "Oh, shit, look what the *farang* dropped on the wat grounds." He looked up at Calvino, squinting as he looked into the sun.

"How do you know my dad?"

Another perfect American accent, thought Calvino.

"Your dad's here. So is Chaiwat. They're in the parking lot waiting. I don't think he would be all that happy if he thought you were getting the family into trouble, more fucking trouble than it is in already. Unless, of course, you really think your good friend TJ is worth going to prison for life. Up to you, Lek."

"Shut the fuck up, asshole." TJ lunged forward and made a real effort to cut him. The blade sliced the remaining sleeve of Calvino's jacket, putting a three-inch gash just above the cuff line. Calvino looked at the damage. "What are you, a tailor on speed?" Calvino turned out of the way as the blade thrust at him again. As the knife missed, Calvino lost his balance and went down on the ground. He reached inside his jacket—what remained of his jacket—for his .38 police special.

"What are you going to do, fucking shoot someone who isn't armed? Is that what you are about? Why not just you and me finish it?"

Calvino shook his head. He had pulled his gun. "TJ, TJ I hate it when someone says something like that in a movie. Do you know how fucking stupid that line sounds? 'Why not just you and me finish it?' I am going to drop my gun to fight mano à mano with someone who says such stupid shit? I don't think so. Of course, if you take one more step I will happily shoot off your balls. No problem. In Darwinian terms I really don't think you have much of a future however this is gonna turn out."

At this moment, Panya's other son, who had emerged with an urn of ashes, came up behind Calvino and kicked the .38 out of his hand.

"*Pee*, this guy knows dad. And he says that dad's here with *Pee* Chaiwat," said Lek.

"Shit," said his older brother, who backed off, turned and started talking to Lek.

"What do you mean, shit?" asked TJ. "Hey, man, I am fucking talking to you, Pruet." Lek and his elder brother, Pruet, looked at TJ and they didn't look that happy. "This guy's bluffing. He doesn't know your father. Let's finish him off and get out of here."

"One moment, please," said the older brother who was a taller, more slender version of his fat little brother who had tried out his kickboxing skills. After a brief exchange in Thai, the brother with the urn put it on the ground, and both brothers disappeared around the corner, leaving TJ to do whatever he wanted to do to the *farang*—but as far they were concerned it no longer had anything to do with them. "Hey, get back here." TJ half ran after them, then stopped and walked back to the pickup.

"Your leadership skills could use some work, TJ," said Calvino. His .38 was about ten feet away under a car.

"And you are going inside the coffin." TJ, breathing heavily, stood with the knife clutched in his hand, waiting to make his move.

"Do you have any idea what you are involved in, TJ?" From the expression on TJ's face he either knew or he didn't care. "But guys who think the Chicago Bulls are still a team have shit for brains," said Calvino.

It would have been better to call TJ a motherfucker than go after his team. When he saw that Calvino could not get to his gun, he rushed him, knocked him over, and sat on top of Calvino. Calvino had his hands locked around TJ's hands, which had the six-inch blade. If he let up even a little, TJ would plunge the knife into his chest. And TJ was strong, one of those guys who worked out, lifted weights, not to mention that he was twenty years younger.

Two other Thais appeared. One was the driver of the Benz. They stood in the shade and watched the two *farangs* rolling on the ground. Monks, hearing the shouting, came running down the path, their sandals flip-flopping on the hot pavement. TJ was using all of his strength; no question he was going to kill Calvino if he had the chance; he was going to finish what he had likely been paid to do that night arrived with the birthday card. Calvino tried, doing one of those stunt man rolls, like this was the movies. But TJ was too strong. All Calvino managed to do was drag TJ's leg through some fresh dog shit.

"TJ, tell me you really don't want to go back in a box like Danny."

TJ was thinking with his balls, his manhood, his ego, and he rotated his right shoulder just as Jess came up behind him with his gun drawn.

"Drop the knife," Jess shouted.

TJ half looked around in time for Jess to hit him as hard as he could between the eyes with the butt end of a .9mm handgun. There was a loud, sickening thwack of metal against bone. Calvino's hand came up with dog shit that he smeared over TJ's face as the blood spurted out of the ragged gash left by the blow. TJ was out cold, face down in the dirt. Blood poured out of TJ's shattered nose. Pratt knelt down beside Calvino, helping him to his feet.

"I was about to put out his lights," said Calvino, trying to decide what to do with the dog shit between his fingers. He leaned down and picked up his severed sleeve and cleaned his hand.

Pratt turned TJ over on the ground and saw the soft yellowish wormy dog shit and blood covering what had once been a not unattractive face. "I'd say in another minute he would have knifed you," said Pratt.

Calvino touched his own nose with his index finger and shrugged his shoulders. "He is a busy little bastard, running drugs, beating people up. I doubt even his mother would recognize him." He got to his feet, and put a hand on Jess' shoulder. "And by the way, Jess, thanks. I had the situation under control but I appreciate the help."

"What happened to your jacket?" asked Pratt.

"I fell down. Don't give me that look. That's what happened. All right?"

The monk who had met Calvino ran over to TJ, knelt down, looking to find a pulse.

"He's not dead," said Calvino. "After a big meal of dog shit he's just sleeping a little."

"You could have killed him," said the monk, looking up, his face filled with confusion.

"Like I said, I am from New York. If I'd wanted to kill him, he'd be dead. Believe it."

Panya's other two sons, Lek and Pruet, had run back to the parking lot and raised the alarm; the undertaker's boys had saved Calvino's life. They had found, their father and brother Chaiwat in the parking lot just as Calvino said. The reunion of one fearful, crooked family took place next to the van.

Calvino leaned down and picked the bag of heroin off the ground and handed it to Pratt. Whether Panya and his boys had any idea about what really was inside the coffin or not, it was difficult to tell. What they had been doing was close enough to standard procedure, including some back handers and special incentives; on the surface all they were doing was processing dead *farangs*, picking up the forms from the Police Hospital, getting the Embassy to process the papers, embalming the body, taking it out for a cremation, double charging for coffins. Doing what businessmen do: maximize profit in life and in death.

Pratt looked at TJ, then walked over to Calvino. "Khun Panya's sons heard you talking to this *farang* as if you knew him."

"I have a nose for these things." He reached inside the pickup and threw Jess a Ziploc bag of drugs. "Take a look at this. The coffin is filled with heroin."

The flight on which Daniel Ramsey's body was scheduled would leave Don Muang at 5:00 a.m. That allowed some lead time before the smugglers found out things had not gone down the way they were supposed to and came like a mad pack of dogs to reclaim their drugs. They weren't going to be all that happy to lose a seventy-five-kilo shipment.

Jess and Pratt pulled the coffin out of the pickup and put it on the ground not far from where TJ lay in his unconscious dog-shit sleep. Pratt squatted down, taking close-ups of the coffin interior from every angle. It was leaking heroin from where Calvino had ripped off the plywood panel. Pratt paused for a minute and looked up from the camera.

"Let me have the camera," said Calvino. "I know it's your brother-in-law's. But I haven't broken it yet, have I?"

Pratt handed him the camera but didn't look all that happy doing so. Calvino turned the camera on TJ. He snapped one, two, then three shots.

"You are wasting film," said Pratt.

"It's digital. It doesn't use film. Besides, I want to post these shots on the Internet," said Calvino looking up from the camera.

"Yeah?" asked Jess "Why bother?"

TJ was still out cold.

"A Cause-member after a Monster Fuck," said Calvino. He handed the camera back to Pratt.

They had a coffin full of the best evidence in the world: seventy-five kilos of heroin. Death sentence amounts of dope for an entire gang of smugglers. At the least for the guys who did the heavy lifting. But was the cache sufficient evidence for the big guys? It was already late afternoon when Pratt made a second phone call to a colonel in a special Thai drug unit. Colonel Virat had been waiting for this call. He and his men were elite cops who worked with the DEA, trained in the States, straight, tough, no-bullshit cops. No one was going to slip them a white envelope of cash or threaten them or make them destroy the evidence or doctor the case.

When Pratt switched off the phone, he confirmed that Colonel Virat and his men were on their way to the wat. They would take over. Calvino stood off to the side, leaning against the Benz, nursing some bruised ribs in the shade. Pratt and Jess were talking about how they could get the heroin to LA and waiting for TJ to regain consciousness and for the narc police to arrive. A monk with a bowl of water knelt on the ground wiping the shit and blood off TJ's face.

"Help me get him out of the sun," said the monk.

Jess and Calvino grabbed TJ under his armpits and pulled him to the shady side of the pickup, his heels dragged along the pavement. They lowered TJ to the ground.

"What a sorry sonofabitch," said Calvino looking down at TJ. "He's gonna be hearing worms and tiny insects crawling inside his head."

The monk knelt down again and dug some wormy dog shit out of TJ's left ear.

Calvino had gone over and picked up his .38 police service revolver and put it back in his holster. "I came this close to shooting him." He held his forefinger and thumb about an inch apart. "About the same distance he came to sticking that knife in my chest."

"If you shot him, that wouldn't have helped anyone but the men smuggling this shit," said Jess. "They would like him dead."

"And if he had killed me, he would have done five years for murdering a *farang*," said Calvino.

"What sick fuck made this poor guy eat dog shit?" asked Naylor, who had suddenly appeared out of nowhere and stood just behind Pratt to shield himself in case Calvino decided to slam him around again.

"Wesley, my good man, that's a good question. Why don't you come over here and ask him yourself?" asked Calvino.

"Good man, my ass, you are a fucking sadist." Naylor's lower lip shot out and he shook his head the way a child does when he doesn't want to do something he's been asked to do. "No, I'll watch from here. Thank you very fucking much."

"You're gonna get heat stroke. Get out of the sun."

"If I pay you to be my bodyguard, will you stop hitting me?"

"I'll have to think about that," said Calvino. "There are certain satisfactions in life that money can't buy."

"I have a good feeling about this," said Naylor, hands in his pocket as he sat on the gate of the pickup truck, looking down into the open coffin, its guts spilling out kilos of white gold.

SEVENTEEN

PRUET AND LEK broke into a run as they spotted the van. Lek pulled ahead, hitting the back door with the flat of his hands, yelling, "Father." In the distance a temple bell rang, making a clear, distinctive sound like a fingernail ping against fine crystal. Chaiwat moved crablike to the back of the van and opened the door and found his two brothers out of breath, wide-eyed with fear.

"Pa, we must go. It is very bad," said Pruet. His Adam's apple looked like it had a spasm.

"We have a problem," said Chaiwat.

Pruet was looking past his brother at the priest and nun.

"Who are they?"

Chaiwat shrugged, half-turned in his seat, glanced back, and said, "I don't know."

Pratt had been talking with a monk. Jess's first reaction was to stay with the van and watch Panya and his sons. They were material witnesses and that status gave them every incentive to make a run for it. But the more he studied Panya's face, the more he saw that the old man was not going anywhere. He had no energy. He was used up, defeated, scared. Jess half-turned in his seat and found Noi's hand, giving it a firm squeeze.

"I never doubted you," said Jess.

"Thanks. I hope you are not sweet-mouthing me."

"It's not my nature. I am not a *farang*," he said, and he was about to say something else. "That song you sing about feeling the pain, feeling in love, and waiting for him to tell you he cares."

She saw this and put a finger to her lips. "Yeah, I like that song, too. Nice words," she said.

"Then you better go and sing that song."

He nodded for her to get out the back. She didn't need any more of an invitation.

"See you around," she said, climbing past him and out of the door and stepping between Pruet and Lek.

She turned and waved.

"Yeah, see you around. Maybe on MTV," said Jess.

He followed her out of the van. And Panya like a robot ambled out of the van and into the parking lot, looking like someone who wanted to run but had nowhere to run to.

A smile crossed her face. "You never know."

Panya hadn't even realized, as he embraced Pruet and Lek standing in the parking lot that Noi had slipped out of the van and had walked out to the main road where she caught a taxi. The nun had fled the scene but the priest had real staying power. Big tears splashed down Panya's cheeks as he hugged his boys.

"We go to America," he said.

They thought the old man had lost his mind. But he knew exactly what he was saying.

"The police know," said Chaiwat. "I think they know *everything*."

Jess knew it was time to check on Calvino inside the wat.

Noi's instinct had been right. She had said nothing to Panya or Chaiwat or to the other two sons whose name she never learned; leaving them in their fear and grief. Better to leave them with the impression of her as a nun on her way to church. She had been inside that church of fear, she knew that place and did not envy them for what was lying ahead. Their old way of life in Thailand was over, and that was a forever kind of over; and her new life was about to begin.

★★★★★★

DON Muang Airport. Pratt knew that the international airport was the only practical way out of Thailand; practical meaning, he had a plausible explanation—backed by Colonel Virat—as to why things happened the way they did and why those who stayed behind made that decision and why Panya and his three sons were flying to LA. An entirely new cast of actors would have their credits high up in the "crawl" of the script written by the drug enforcement people who had swarmed into the wat and taken over as if it had been their operation from day one.

Pruet, the eldest of Panya's sons, drove the pickup onto the ramp leading to the cargo terminal. Daniel Ramsey's coffin and his ashes had been placed inside, all of the heroin had been put back inside, and the satin stapled back to the plywood panel. No one would ever know that Calvino had ripped it out with a tire iron. The Toyota van was followed by a mini fleet of unmarked cars. Colonel Virat, accompanied by two of his men, had a car, the DEA had two cars, and Pratt drove his brother-in-law's van with Jess and Calvino riding up front. The best cover was always the same: stick to routine; vary it and everyone notices that something new, something different is going down. They make a mental note, they sense something isn't the same and that makes them suspicious and that was the last thing anyone wanted to happen at the cargo terminal. Panya's sons did what they had done many times before—they unloaded the coffin onto a trolley and pushed the trolley into a cargo bay. None of the officials or other people in the bay thought twice about their presence. They weren't doing anything strange. They were getting on with their usual business, in the usual way, and smiling the usual smile. An official sat behind a counter watching a soccer match on TV. He looked up long enough to take the papers from Pruet and the airline ticket for the cargo. He looked over the side at the trolley, stamped the papers, and waited until the goalie stopped a score before handing them back. Lek, the fat dopey-looking son, set a bottle of Johnny Walker Black wrapped in a brown bag on the counter. The official reached up, grabbed the bottle by the neck and lowered it below the counter. He didn't take his eye off the TV. They briefly talked about football. Pruet was a Manchester United fan, and they talked about betting and bookies. They talked about the weather, about food, and about the traffic. And how the clouds had been seeded with salt and the rain had flooded Sukhumvit Road. They talked about everything except the cargo: the coffin, the remains that were supposed to be inside. A hand with thick blue veins came over the counter and passed the papers, all neatly stamped, back to the Panya boys, who walked back to the van. The fleet, which hadn't killed their engines to keep the air-conditioning going full blast, followed the van as it headed out of the cargo terminal and crossed over to the international passenger terminal.

They parked inside the loading area next to the VIP building.

"We can handle it from here," said Dean, a woman about five-eight wearing a conservative gray pantsuit. She was one of two DEA agents who had gone to the wat. What Dean meant was that Pratt and Calvino and Naylor were no longer needed. But she didn't want to sound like a complete bitch so she left it a little vague, knowing that Colonel Virat had enough brains to pick up on what needed to be done.

Colonel Virat stepped up to Dean and whispered something. "Of course, Colonel Pratt will come along with us."

"I guess that leaves you and me," said Naylor.

"Calvino comes along," said Pratt to Colonel Virat in Thai. Dean puffed her cheeks up with air and blew hard; she was annoyed. She wore just enough lipstick to indicate that she had taken some care over her personal appearance. She had displayed just about the right amount of displeasure to indicate her attitude towards civilians. She was one of those cops who hated civilians. "But just don't open your mouth about anything," said Dean.

"But I signed all the fucking papers. And you are leaving me behind? Fucking white women."

Dean spun around and put a knee straight into Naylor's balls. "Fucking white men."

No one said anything to Naylor who leaned over, holding the side of the van, a sound coming out of his throat like the sound of the last dog barking after all of the others have stopped. A tiny, distant scared sound that gets half lost before it hits the air.

There was a slamming of doors, shuffling of feet and officials waiting to take them through Customs and Immigration. Passing through the various desks, not one of the officials showed any emotion. What they understood with absolute clarity was that some top brass had come to the airport. They knew that from a glance at Colonel Virat and the DEA agents. Bigwigs putting people through Customs was something they had witnessed before. The rest was none of their fucking business. Panya and his three sons were whisked through first without anyone asking them a single question. Jess waited behind for ten minutes—sufficient to give enough separation so as not to necessarily connect him with Panya—then the DEA agents walked him through. If there had been any representatives of the gangster contingent among those working the airport counters, and if they had been able to put together what was happening, they were powerless to do anything. There was no percentage in backing a horse that clearly had fallen. That race had been run. The winners were on their way to the States. The losers on their way to jail or exile. No allegiances survived once the horse stumbled, and before it hit the ground, the punters would be denying they had ever had a ticket on the loser. The odd official winced, or maybe it was only a normal pissed-off glance officials develop over years on the job, the way the neck muscles stiffened, the fixing of a lip, pressed down hard as Panya's passport was presented, and they were told that the boys didn't have passports but they had clearance. They didn't need passports. Okay. A few minutes later Jess slipped through by flashing a Thai police ID Pratt had given him.

The other DEA agent, a black guy from Detroit named Andrew, looked like a tunnel of ice ran like an expressway through his eyeholes. He was someone who could show his teeth without it looking like he was smiling; and when he did smile, he had a right incisor that when it caught the light shone a pure solid gold. In the parking lot, Andrew had let Dean do all the talking.

Calvino figured she out-ranked him. More than rank, Andrew was the ferret who Dean sent down the hole to chew off the face of whoever was hiding below decks. He had to be six four with a thick neck that seemed as wide as his shoulders. Andrew was huge and had a serious don't-even-think-about-fucking-with-me attitude. When TJ saw Andrew about one inch away from his face, sniffing the dog shit and wrinkling up his nose, TJ passed out again.

Andrew walked ahead of everyone else; he was like a guard on an American football team who had pulled, clearing bodies out of the path on a quarterback sweep. Just behind him were Pruet, Lek and Chaiwat; the three brothers stepped up like the three monkeys who spoke, heard and saw no evil. Andrew looked at the official with a dead-eye look, and said, "They are cleared at LAX." He flashed his DEA badge. Colonel Virat translated what Andrew had said, not that it needed any translation. A rule of thumb as wide as a kneecap was always avoid confrontation with those who were in a superior position of power. Whatever they wanted they got; they cannot ever be stopped from attaining their goal, and standing in their way was like trying to stand in front of tanks. Sooner or later that guy at Tiananmen Square moved out of the way and the tanks rolled on. Above all, the code was: be practical, don't draw attention, and don't talk too much. No one ever got transferred to an inactive post for following the unwritten code.

The two DEA agents walked Jess to the departure gate where Panya, his boys, and Colonel Virat and two of his men were waiting. Andrew pointed to chairs and nodded towards Panya and the three sons. He had clearly taken control of the situation and was giving orders. Jess sat off to the side between Calvino and Pratt. Panya and his three sons sat just in front in total silence except for this hiccup the old man would let out, or it could have been a sob. And right next to the Panya boys were Dean and Andrew. The boys glanced mainly at Andrew, who sat with his arms folded, showing his gold tooth, twisting his neck which made a cracking noise. This was the start of their new life. American law enforcement personnel with that dead-eye stare, part contempt, part hate, and part suspicion. As if to say, *Hey, motherfucker, we know you're dirty. That you have committed crimes. And you are gonna pay and pay and get a new asshole along the way.*

Most criminals like most whores come with a long rap sheet of priors. Later Colonel Virat told Colonel Pratt who told private eye Vincent Calvino that the DEA agents had more than babysitting duty; they had been assigned another mission—once the plane landed at LAX, Kowit would be waiting and he would claim the coffin. They wanted to be the first to find out how he did his business. Watch who he did his business with. The DEA had decided this was a Federal operation. Their baby. Dean and Andrew had patience and plans—for promotions, decorations, and public recognition—dreams of making this a high-profile bust that would justify the DEA Southeast Asia budget for the next two years. The main idea was for Kowit to hang himself with the piece of rope they had given him. Panya would turn up once Kowit had claimed the coffin and identify Kowit. Calvino imagined Kowit to be a small, slender man, looking up at Andrew; Kowit would drop like a puppet with the string cut. He would see the rope, then the drop, and then they would find out the story. Jess would be given a footnote reference in the DEA final report. Colonel Virat and his special forces unit—after all they had been trained by the DEA—would get just enough credit to make them heroes in Thailand and little enough to cast them in the also-starring role in the States. Pratt would not be mentioned. Naylor, Noi, Calvino—such people were like the best boy, the key grip, the foley artists; only insiders really knew what these people did, why they were needed in the movie, and besides, even in a movie, no one stuck around long enough except the cleaning crew to read that deep into the crawl as it scrolled down to the copyright notice.

★★★★★★

FOR Panya and his three sons, there had been no time to kiss a lover, to say goodbye to a friend, or to pack a case. Whatever they had, they had on them; but what they had most of all were their lives. They squirmed in their seats, looking out the tiny airplane windows at the tarmac.

The old man unbuckled his seat belt and started to get up.

"I can't leave everything. I won't. I am going home," said Panya.

Colonel Virat put his hand on Panya's shoulder and pushed him back into the seat.

"You can't force me to stay on this plane," said Panya.

Dean was already in the aisle, efficient, smart, deadly. She stood just behind Colonel Virat. She had the look of someone who knew how to put the boots in, heels first, hard and fast, stomping and kicking. A shit-kicking bitch. And there was that huge Andrew guy right behind her, his eyes bulging out, making his hands into fists like a professional wrestler.

"You won't live twenty-four hours, if you go back to your house," said Dean, in a drone of a DEA instruction video kind of voice. "The drug operators are the big boys. They will *kill* you."

Andrew leaned in close to Panya and said in a soft voice. "These men will cut you and your sons into pieces to fit the size of a rat's mouth. Is that what you want? Because if it is, then you and your boys get up and move your ass back to Bangkok and good luck to you."

No good cop/bad cop. These were both playing the same-in-your-face motherfucker role.

Panya looked at Dean, then at Andrew. Whatever resolve he had vanished. Dean leaned forward and buckled his seat belt. He got the message—good luck in the next life because if you get off this plane then you are totally fucked. You can't ever go back.

Panya sucked his teeth in a look of total defeat, the look of a generation of Chinese who had fled oppression with nothing but their lives, only to have their new life torn apart, their success stripped away, forced to flee once again. He was still wearing that terrible golf shirt and black undertaker's tie and it seemed strange to see tears fill the undertaker's eyes. Panya and his three boys stayed bolted to their seats on the plane. The main hatch was closed, and from the departure lounge Colonel Virat, Colonel Pratt, and Calvino watched the plane back away from the gate and taxi to the runway. The physical evidence was stored in the cargo hatch; oral evidence sat in first class. This was starting to look like a good international drug bust case in the making. Hands across the seas in unity; the kind of bullshit that politicians use to get themselves elected on.

★★★★★★

AFTER they returned to the VIP parking lot, Colonel Virat's men and a doctor were talking to TJ, who was wide awake, groaning, saying he was in great pain and screaming for a doctor, and then choking, spitting and demanding to see a lawyer. Calvino stood looking inside the back of the van.

"I hope they salvage the motherfucker," said Naylor. He was sitting up front and talking through the panel between the front cab and the back. This made him feel safe. Not even Calvino could touch him that far away.

"Salvage him," Naylor said again.

This was Cause lingo from someone in the Philippines who had posted to his buddies that murdering someone who had injured you or caused your manhood offence was to "salvage" the offender. Revenge talk.

"I don't think you know what the fuck you are talking about, Wes," said Calvino. "No one is going to hurt TJ. He is a valuable asset. And if you weren't such a dickhead you would understand that and not try to be cool using a word when you have no idea what it means."

After TJ had regained consciousness, he blinked his eyes, looked around and the light went on in his head; he was being held in custody in an underground airport parking lot. He had started screaming.

"Where is that big black guy?" His head jerked from side to side. He slurred his words.

"On his way to LA," said Colonel Virat.

"Are you sure?"

TJ blinked a couple of more times. "Very sure," said Colonel Virat. "Time for you to rest."

The doctor opened his bag, removed a needle and much to TJ's horror stuck it into his arm. The ultimate American cry of anguish died in his throat as the injection brought him to the edge of unconsciousness. He mouthed the words, "Get me a doctor; get me a lawyer." Neither was forthcoming. Then he made no more sound. No more protest or demands. He was out, his mind closed down, left with the sepia image of the monk who had cleaned the dog shit off his face. Otherwise his mind was empty. In the land of smiles there were no Miranda warnings, no right to a lawyer. No right to remain silent if he knew what was good for him.

★★★★★★

TJ opened his eyes, blinked a couple of times, and looked around. It took him about a minute before he realized that he was in a prison cell. His bloodied Chicago Bull's T-shirt was caked with dog shit. He sat up shivering and hungry. He looked out the window. It was dark outside and he was alone in the cell; except for a large rat and about a thousand cockroaches. He lay back down, his arm over his eyes and cried. He lay on a bamboo mat, knocking the cockroaches back, trying to think how to get out of the cell. TJ decided the best plan would be to call their bluff; what did the police really have? The pickup wasn't in his name. He hadn't actually been caught in possession of the drugs. He would tell them he had no fucking idea that heroin had been hidden in Daniel's coffin. He had gone to a fucking funeral service. What goddamn right did they have to throw him in a prison cell? Yeah, that worked for TJ.

The next morning Pao, his girlfriend, was allowed to visit him. She brought him cigarettes and told him to show the warders a little respect. And the police. He wanted to hit her. And what was worse was that he could see that she knew he wanted to belt her and there wasn't a goddamn thing he could do. She smiled at him. She was playing with him. Pao could say whatever she wanted and there wasn't a thing he could do about it. So she started about how the police wouldn't have him in prison unless he had done something wrong. She believed that he was guilty and she was the only person in the entire city he could trust. In her face, TJ could see that she had already given him up; he saw exactly how lost he was by the way she stared at him, as if he were dead. He tried to explain to her that the cops were holding him on an assault charge.

"I got in a fight with that guy who gave you that birthday card. It's no big deal," he said.

"I don't believe you," she said.

He found himself screaming that he had nothing to do with any drugs. Besides, the main witnesses were in Los Angeles. They would not be coming back to Bangkok to testify at his trial. Sure, the Panya's sons would blame him for the drugs in the coffin, and had they pointed the finger at him in person, in a Thai courtroom, he knew who the judge would believe. But they weren't going to be in the courtroom. They had no evidence.

"They can go fuck themselves," TJ shouted.

Taking a mirror out of her handbag, Pao, who was dressed like a real babe on the make, turned it so that he could see his face. From the pain every time his face moved he knew that it was going to be bad. But he had no idea what the real damage had been inflicted by that asshole Thai with the .9mm. Must have been a cop, he thought. TJ saw that blood had leaked into his right eye, the eye looked loose in the socket, like it might fucking fall out. His nose and face bloated, turning shades of black and blue; an infection had set in—it must have been the dog shit—and unless he received medical attention, he was going to have doctors cutting parts of his face off and throwing them into the hospital garbage for burning.

She might have been a whore but she knew the outcome, the end game, and that certainty of her knowledge rattled him. Whatever scheme, plan, hope he had been harboring had vanished as he put down the mirror.

"My brother go to jail. My uncle go to jail. My father was in jail three times," she said. "Now my *farang* boyfriend go to jail."

TJ spurted, his lips forming a large oval shaped 'O' like he was trying to blow bubbles, only he had no bubbles to blow; he blubbered that he loved Pao and he was going to fight, goddamit. Tears and snot splashing off his broken upper lip and onto the table. Somehow from the expression on Pao's face it seemed she probably had seen this performance from her brother, uncle, and father. It didn't move her.

After a minute or so, TJ calmed down a little. "They can't keep me here," he whined.

TJ was slowly coming apart. He had been tough enough to cuff her around when he wanted, and the guards would give him the same treatment. There was justice after all, she thought.

"I think you are in very big trouble, TJ. And they can keep you here for as *long* as they want." She hit the word "long" and stretched out the sound.

"But I didn't do anything." He blinked at her, his head cocked to the side as if maybe some more of the dog shit was about to purge.

"Don't worry, TJ. They will find something." Pao was proving to be a real comfort in his moment of crisis.

TJ remembered that he had either heard or read these words—*They will find something*—before, and now Pao was saying them, making him feel even more desperate. It was the matter-of-fact way she said those words that was disturbing, as if she had total faith in the system to frame his ass so he would spend years and years in some hell hole prison. Someone else had said them, but who? TJ was already losing his ability to concentrate, his ability to think. It didn't matter that he hadn't done anything? Well, anything they could pin on him. Logic, relevance, causation—since when did any such concepts ever explain why one guy ended up going to jail and another walked free? Caught up in the system like the pig in the mouth of a python, it would take a very long time for the Thai justice system to digest TJ and spit out his bones.

She leaned forward on her elbows and smiled at him, "Who do you think the court's going to believe? The *farang* or the Thai?"

A guard tapped TJ on the shoulder and he jumped like someone had strung electrical wires around his balls and hit the switch. His eyes bulged, and his mouth formed that terrible 'O' again. He hung his head and pleaded. "Please, five more minutes. Pleasssse."

The guard cuffed him on the ear. This made Pao laugh. "Go on, TJ. He's just playing with you. He didn't really hit you. You better go now. Bye."

Later that afternoon, TJ cut the best deal he could with the Thai cops. They had started to play the good cop/bad cop routine and he told them it wasn't necessary; they were all bad guys, and he wanted to make a deal. They promised him seven years if he helped them, and life if he didn't. It was that simple; if he wanted to avoid life inside a Thai prison, then it was up to him. TJ caved in, signed a confession as to his involvement, providing details of his relationship with

Daniel Ramsey and others inside the heroin smuggling operation. Fortunately for TJ, Ramsey was dead, so he could lay off all the blame onto Ramsey and claim he had only done the heavy lifting along with Panya's sons who, by the way, were up to their necks in the business. Firewalls had been built to insulate TJ from the higher levels of the smuggling operation. No, he didn't fucking know who made the deal in Burma. No, he had no fucking idea who brought the shit from the border area to Bangkok. No, he never saw anyone packing the shit in the coffins. That was Daniel's fucking job, and he didn't trust anyone else except Lek to touch the product. He, however, had a rich ore of details about getting the bodies, burning them, filling ashes into urns, driving coffins to the airport. TJ was more like an ordinary foot soldier who knew nothing of the larger war he was fighting, who had walked the trails assigned to him, and after he was ambushed and captured all he could do was babble about burning civilians and houses and so forth, making it clear to everyone who heard him that outside his small free-fire zone, TJ was as ignorant as any bar *ying* in a geography quiz. He really didn't know anyone other than Daniel, Chaiwat, Lek, and Pruet. Sure he had seen Panya but he didn't really know the undertaker. The DEA tried its hand on TJ, thinking the Thais had given in too soon. But the DEA found nothing more after a two-day interrogation. The DEA agents reported to Dean that in their view the crime scene (meaning the wat) had been contaminated by civilians (meaning Calvino and Naylor) who had no business being near the operation.

"What the fuck are these civilians doing here?" Andrew had asked at the wat. He was looking at Calvino and Naylor as if they were a couple of white guys on 125th Street in Harlem at two in the morning. "Take them in." Andrew had a personality rough enough to file down an elephant's toenails.

"This *asshole* thinks we are drug dealers," said Naylor in a loud voice. "Tell Tyrone, we ain't doin' any drugs. And how do we know he ain't a drug dealer?"

Of course Andrew took this the wrong way and started to slap a pair of handcuffs on Naylor, who darted around the side of the pickup. "Keep away from me. I am a lawyer, goddamit. You have no jurisdiction here."

Pratt said something to Colonel Virat who said something to Dean, the DEA agent, her line of lipstick growing thinner on her lips as she listened. She called Andrew over and said something to him and he looked even more pissed-off than she did.

"Get them the fuck out of my face," said Andrew, pointing over at Naylor, who was sticking his tongue out at him. "I swear to god I'll shoot your white ass if you don't get out of here."

That elephant's toenail of a personality was getting filed right to the flesh and bone.

Jess showed the DEA agents his LAPD badge. "This man has been working with me on this case. He's the one who found the drugs."

"LAPD," said Dean. "What are you doing here?"

"Working on assignment," said Jess. "And what have you been doing in the US Embassy the last year with tons of drugs going into LA?"

"That's the way you want to play it?" asked Dean.

"Jess is saying none of this could have happened without someone in the Embassy being involved," said Calvino. "How do we know we can trust you?"

"Because you have no other choice," said Dean.

It had started with that question that made Calvino an instant enemy. Jess had already rung the bell to begin a jurisdiction fight, like dogs kicking dirt and lifting their hind leg to piss against a wall in order to mark their turf and to guard their territory. If Darwin had studied cops rather than finches, he would have come to pretty much the same conclusions. Those who attacked aggressively accumulated the spoils, survived, prospered, had all the best *yings*, and got promoted and laid. Those who didn't, well, they got through life by taking the kind of illegal drugs that were shipped from Bangkok inside the lining of coffins.

★★★★★★

SOMETIMES things work out the way they are supposed to, or at least, on the surface a sense of order and success pops up like a bubble and floats towards the shore. Jess had phoned his commander from the plane, and briefed him on what was going down. His commander backed him all the way, even bringing him a uniform to the LAX. By the time Jess had changed into his police uniform, he still had time to observe as Kowit wandered into the cargo area wearing his dark undertaker's suit, claiming the coffin. One reporter from the *LA Times* and another from Channel 4 News, dressed like airport janitors, pretended to be picking up trash as Kowit came to the counter. Both reporters owed favors to Jess's commander, and this was going to be a big story. Thai LAPD officer Jessada Santisak was about to make news for organizing a major international drug bust.

Jess waited until Kowit took possession of the coffin before stepping out in the corridor to block his way. Panya and his three sons were one step behind him. When Kowit saw Panya with his sons surrounded by more than a dozen members of LAPD (who kept Dean and Andrew a few feet back), he turned a kind of hazel green color, and began wheezing as if he had an allergy attack. It was just his way of dealing with stress. Jess got his wish; he had been there to see Kowit take possession of the coffin, and he had been the arresting officer. He read Kowit his rights but Kowit wasn't listening; he couldn't take his eyes of Panya. Then Chaiwat came up to his father, then the other two brothers joined the old man. Kowit's chin dropped, his head bowed. Jess had to ask him two times if he had heard and understood his rights. Kowit understood all right. His rights meant nothing.

"What are you doing, man?" asked Andrew as he bulled his way forward.

"Making the arrest."

"He's not yours to arrest."

"Says who?" asked Jess's commander.

"I am agent Dean, DEA, and we have this man in federal custody, sir."

The Channel 4 cameras were rolling, cutting from Jess and Kowit to the Commander and Dean and Andrew.

"No, you have *this* man in federal custody," said the commander, pointing at Panya. "If you would like to speak to the press on how you have any jurisdiction here, please feel free." He walked away and left Dean and Andrew looking into the camera. Never had two DEA agents looked more uncomfortable as they turned away from the camera and pushed their way through the sea of LAPD and out of the cargo area. They had Panya and the sons cuffed and the camera caught them being marched away. The LA Times reporter already had his story and photographs.

The story was carried on page one.

Lax at LAX as Dead Mules smuggle drugs from Bangkok into LA

Dead body of alleged mastermind led to expose of drug ring

LAPD smashed an international drug ring in a dramatic arrest at LAX yesterday. LAPD narcotic undercover operation in Bangkok led to an expose of a Thai/American syndicate that has smuggled 40 million dollars worth of heroin into the United States in the past two years. Two and a half tons of heroin sailed through LAX in coffins of dead A m e r i c a nss h i p p e d h o m e f r o m Thailand. In a final twist, police caught the operation smuggling the white powders in the coffin of an alleged mastermind.

A Thai-born LAPD narcotic officer, Jessada "Jess" Santisak, arrested a Thai-American funeral home director, Kowit Piboonchaitham, as he claimed possession of a coffin containing over 150 pounds of heroin yesterday. The coffin was supposedly containing the body of Daniel Ramsey, a Los Angeles native and an alleged mastermind of the drug smuggling ring. Mr. Piboonchaitham was identified at the scene in the media spot light by

Panya Lerdsrisab, another funeral home director based in Bangkok, as a key player in the Bangkok-LA drug ring.

The recent sting operation followed Officer Santisak's arrest of Charn Pradit, a Thai national and a low-level drug dealer, in a hotel located on Hollywood and Vine in March last year. Mr. Pradit was later found to be linked with a larger drug smuggling network across the Pacific. The leads took Officer Santisak to Bangkok to investigate the route of large shipments of heroin, which authorities had failed to trace thus far.

Police found 150 pounds of heroin in Ziploc bags hidden in secret compartments constructed inside a luxury metal coffin, which also contained 8 pounds of Daniel

Ramsey's ashes. According to Officer Santisak, this shipment was just one of many "routine" coffin shipments through LAX over the past two years. This dead mules' scheme worked through a network of American nationals in Thailand operating with Thai nationals.

The Thai-American team reportedly took bodies of western men who were left unidentified and unclaimed in several Thai morgues. The team arranged to have the dead bodies identified by network of associates as those of American citizens and later shipped by air back to the US, using forged documents and false witnesses to obtain clearance papers from the US Embassy in Bangkok and the Thai Customs at the Bangkok International Airport. In each case, the deceased was cremated at a Thai temple in Bangkok and the body weight was made up in heroin. Each of the deceased went through Mr. Lerdsrisab's Bangkok-based funeral home and was claimed by Mr. Piboonchaitham at LAX.

As to why such smuggling operation of large magnitude,

involving multiple layers of security, could have gone on for over two years, Officer Santisak said "This was probably not all that difficult because no one could imagine that drug dealers would use dead Americans as a cover for heroin shipments."

An investigation has been launched by the Customs Department at LAX and other international airports to ensure all cargos, including remains of deceased Americans being returned for burial, have been searched for contraband.

In an exclusive interview with the LA Times, both funeral directors claimed being misled by the deceased LA native Daniel Ramsey, whom they insisted was the real mastermind behind the operation. Both also insisted that their respective funeral home runs a legitimate business. Mr. Lerdsrisab told the LA Times that neither he nor any of his three sons, two of whom are graduates of the University of San Francisco had any prior knowledge of the drug shipment. The father and sons, who arrived in Los

Angeles on the same flight from Bangkok as the LAPD officer's, are now in protective federal custody of the DEA.

Reliable sources in the Thai police confirmed that D aniel Ramsey was involved in the smuggling operation. The Thai authorities ruled Ramsey's death was a suicide but did not elaborate on the cause of his suicide. TJ Lopez, a Chicago native, is being held in a Thai prison on drug-related charges. According to the sources, Ramsey and Lopez s earched hos pital morgues in Bangkok and holiday resorts such as those in Phuket for bodies that could pass as Americans. An official at the State Department has said that the number of dead Americans in Thailand has increased in the past two years primarily through over-dose cases.

According to LAPD Officer Santisak, neither Ramsey nor Lopez would have been able to make all the arrangements without the knowledge and active participation of others with local influence. The scheme worked in part because the LA-based funeral director's name, Mr. Piboonchaitham, was on official papers stamped by the US Embassy in Bangkok. The Bangkok-based funeral director, Mr. Lerdsrisab, may have used local lawyers in Bangkok to walk the papers through the Embassy where officials had no suspicion of the smuggling operation.

LAPD Commander Saunders said LAPD was cooperating with the DEA in a full investigation of the smuggling operation.

EIGHTEEN

TRYING TO TELL the whole story in a newspaper article was like trying to give a summary of *War and Peace*. It wasn't one story; it was many related stories. The miracle was that the reporter managed to get some of the facts right. Jess was back home, and for the first time, he was calling Los Angeles his hometown. "This is where I belong. I love America," he said to the Channel 4 reporter. The papers talked about his kick-boxing trophies. And Jess looked the part: handsome, a winning smile and an ability to look straight into the camera and look totally sincere. That was the next day and by then the buffet had been laid out and the press dined like starved ship rats finding a bag of rice. One moment Jess had been just another cop and, a moment later, he was on his way to becoming a celebrity. What the *LA Times* reporter couldn't have predicted was that within three days of his return, Jess's life would change beyond recognition; his phone never stopped ringing. He got an unlisted number and he hired a secretary, a sister of his partner at Hollywood Division. Next thing he knew some producer for "Larry King Live" called and said they wanted him on the show: An all-American Buddhist hero. Cop extraordinaire. International Drug Buster. That was going to be the cutline on the TV screen throughout the show. A film producer, TV producer, literary agent, and two publishing houses left messages. The night of the Larry King show, Calvino watched it at Father Andrew's house in Klong Toey. Jess, wearing his pressed black LAPD uniform, sat across from King, looking like he had walked out of central casting's A list for leading men. Jess had looked straight in the camera and said, "If it hadn't been for Vincent Calvino and Colonel Prachai, I wouldn't be here. I would have been killed in Bangkok. I owe these two men my life."

"What did you do?" asked Father Andrew.

"Nothing. Not a damn thing," Calvino replied.

Jack Mellows was upstairs above Lovejoy, and he screamed downstairs.

"Lek, get your ass up here! The cop who came here with Calvino is on Larry."

Lek stood at the foot of the stair and shouted back, "Tell him to get off Larry, or at least to use a condom."

"Smart-ass bitch."

Jack had the kind of personality that would set off an airport metal detector.

★★★★★★

IT seemed like a mountain of time had accumulated since Jess had returned to Los Angeles; in reality, it had been five weeks. Jess had phoned Calvino and asked for a favor; he wanted Calvino to deliver a message to Noi. Not a phone call or a messenger. He wanted a personal, hand-delivered message.

"So long as it's not a birthday card," said Calvino.

"Or if it's a card, there better be some cash inside."

It was about midnight on a weekday night when Calvino walked into the Hollywood nightclub to deliver Jess's message. He had been in the Hollywood before, trailing a *mia noi*, a minor wife, who turned out to be less than faithful—she was on the payroll of at least two other men who were claiming *mia noi* rights. The nightclub hadn't changed much since his last visit. Midweek during a recession didn't stop it from filling up with a vast sea of people. A galaxy of lights swept the crowds, showering them in vivid colors—blue, yellow, and green. Spotlights. Strobe lights. On the main stage were three musicians: a guitar player, drummer, keyboard player. Half a dozen dancers moved to the music. The place was packed, juiced, rocking and rolling. Maybe two thousand people were *dancing* at their tables. Yeah, dancing. Little round tables on chrome pedestals. Not a single *farang* face in the crowd. This Hollywood was not on the Causeway; it was a Thai place. Calvino slid onto an empty stool to the side of the main stage and ordered a beer. On stage a katoey singer in hot pants, low cut pink sequinned top with those expensive, tailor-made breasts busting over the top, pranced around the guitar player who wore a boyscout shirt. Lace up black boots came up to her kneecaps and she belted out the theme song from *Titanic*. Little bits of silver paper sprinkled down from the ceiling onto the crowd. They loved it.

The *katoey* passed the mike to Noi who walked out on stage dressed in a white nun's habit, her head covered in a white hood. A single spotlight shone on her as she kept her head bowed, fingers touching as if in prayer. She made the audience wait, standing there, a stark figure in pure white, a symbol of chastity and obedience. The band worked the audience playing riffs of rock 'n roll, heavy metal, with some Blues thrown in. Three guitars, a drummer, a guy on an electrical keyboard were giving her a long lead-in. Slowly Noi slipped out of her nun's habit and slowly pulled off the hood covering her head. She had shaved her head. Underneath the dress was nothing ever seen on a nun: tight fitting black leather pants, a leather sequin tank top that showed her belly button.

Jade: this was Noi's new stage name. She had reinvented herself as an *Isan* singer. She looked up at the audience and started off with a joke: "How do you get to *Isan* from Bangkok?" She paused, then answered her own question,

"You go to *Saraburi* and turn right."

The music volume cranked up and she tore into the song, her voice taking over the audience as if no other sound could ever edge into that void, this place she was staking out as her own. She used the whole stage, shaking, bending forward, changing the mike from one hand to the other, then back. She sang, she pranced and danced, and she drove the crowd below into a frenzy. She owned them. They were going crazy, singing along and dancing at the tables. Two thousand people waving their arms, loving her, wanting her never to stop singing. She had always wanted control. Now she had found it in this place.

After it was all over and she walked away, Calvino tracked her down. He wanted some answers. And over a couple-of-days period, Noi had told him a different story from the one Jess and he had heard in the hotel hong. She had nothing to lose. Why not tell the truth? She pulled the *ying* fast one—she swore that this was the real story. That Hollywood, Taurus, Pegasus, RCA, to mention just a few of the places, were where there were always buyers. In the toilets and parking lots and inside parked cars. Ramsey had hatched the dead mule idea. It should have been the name of a band, thought Calvino. Danny Ramsey had worked the audiences in all the major clubs. Selling drugs; there was no better place to find a captive market than a hot night club. But the retail end was drying up, as most of the rich kids wanted to use speed. Ramsey had met Noi backstage, told her that she had a terrific voice and that he could see her with a major career in LA. She was singing English songs. She would be *the* break-through female lead singer for Asians. The Whitney Houston of Asia. His contact was a guy named Gabe Holerstone who had a club in LA. Her story about being discovered on Silom Road at a table eating lunch with her office co-workers had never happened. There had been no mystery guy. She had never been pregnant. These were all working elements of her pitch. Along with several lies. She had never worked in an office; had never been inside a university, had never lived with Gabe, and never had a kid. Not that any of that mattered. Danny did take her for a ride, pointed out that the real stars were made in the real Hollywood and not some bullshit nightclub in Bangkok. What she didn't know was that Danny had figured out that he could use her to seal his deal with Kowit and the boys. No reason not to branch out into *yings*. Especially talented ones. And at the same time, she could give him all the information he wanted on Kowit; he knew this guy was a sucker for singers, and would do just about anything for one. Including giving a job to a worthless brother. Who really knew what was in Danny's brain other than some hormones storming around each time Noi came on stage in one of her sexy costumes? He had (or so she wanted to believe) fallen a little in love with her and convinced himself that he was doing her a favour. TJ was some muscle that Danny liked having around, hanging out with, and let him do some low level selling. In return, Danny called in the debt, and arranged for TJ to put Calvino out of action. TJ was all mouth about his right crossover that was supposed to keep Calvino in the ICU for a couple of weeks. All he managed to do was break Calvino's nose. It just might have worked out had a little bit of luck been working for them. But their luck ran out when the punch caused some damage but not enough. That had marked the beginning of the end.

Calvino waited until she finished her first set, then paid a waiter to hand her a note. He nursed his bottle of Carlsberg as he watched the note being delivered. Her lips moved as she read the note, balancing the mike between the palms of her hands. He had written: "*Kowit pleaded guilty. Your brother walks in six months. Jess got him a deal.*" He also asked her for a song.

"This song is for Khun Vinee. Someone I would call my friend," she said.

A spotlight picked out Calvino on the side as two thousand Thais stared at the one solitary *farang*. Then she launched into the song. It was a great song. Halfway through, he lifted off the stool, he was watching her on stage. She flashed him a big smile. "Someone I would call my friend," he repeated to himself. The start of a very good pitch, he thought.

Sometimes just enough truth leaks through the cracks of the shell a person hides under to make them a human being. Noi had started to come out of that shell. She was doing okay now. She had come home.

There she was on stage singing, *Hello, hello, hia, la ka? Tammai mai phoot?*"

★★★★★★

ABOUT one week later Calvino turned up at the "Office" on Sukhumvit Road; not *his* office, no, this was another place that turned over tables three or four times a night. The eleven to one crowd. After they left— stragglers always stayed behind for the next shift—the big kick in trade happened after two in the morning. By 4 a.m. no one could move. Smoky, noisy, crowded. The six in the morning shift at the "Office" had freelancers going around whispering, "four hundred baht." That wasn't for taking out the trash or buying donuts for the secretarial pool. That was the last round, the last price for a short-time as the sun appeared over Sukhumvit Road and anyone who wanted some action before sleeping through the heat of the day would at last pick a *ying* and take her back to his hotel. The Office was the epicenter of the Causeway; the heart and soul of the Comfort Zone. The *yings* freelancing out of that basement used the term "Office" when telling their parents, husband, or boyfriend where they were heading at night. The legitimacy in that word made their departure that much easier. And the *yings* used the "Office" amongst themselves as an in-joke. "See you at the Office." Or "Did you see Jack at the Office last night?"

The old place, Thermae, had been called "Head-quarters" or just "HQ"; but, as a sign of the times, proof that globalization had seeped into every crevice of planet earth, the new Thermae opened fifty meters away was now the "Office." Metaphors, like the *yings*, were always changing, always following the money. The era of Vietnam had at last given way to peacetime, where the full-time preoccupation was making money. Swords into plows. The Berlin Wall had fallen. Vietnamese vets were grandfathers. The members of the Cause were looking not for adventure but to make a killing in the stock market. The Office was where they went to deal, to talk about CNBC stock analysis, to swap information about the currency markets.

Calvino arrived during the first shift. He had had a rotten day—a stake-out in Thonburi had blown a twelve-hour hole in his day trying to find a client's secretary who had gone into hiding. She had made a five-grand error—dollar mistake—on a purchase order and he had called her into his office to show her the mistake. He told her that she could learn by the mistake. She never came back to the office after lunch. It was possible to teach by example; but it was nearly impossible to teach by illustrating the consequences of a mistake. Mistakes were taboo. They were not to be mentioned. They certainly weren't the subject of any learning exercise. Pointing out a mistake was inflicting a wound, and Calvino knew the meaning of that. Wounds, however inflicted, had to be avenged. When he found her, she said, "I cannot go back. My health is no good. I must rest now." He passed that along to his client. "She's quit. Health reasons."

As a result of the long day, he hadn't returned any of his phone calls; he hadn't even had time to read the newspaper. At the table towards the back were a number of regulars he recognized. Guys who had been living on the Causeway before there had been a Cause or anyone had heard of the Internet. The table was divided into conversational factions. There was a small balding guy who smoked cigars and everyone called Cuba because he had gone to Havana nine times. He shouted at Calvino.

"Come over and look at this," Cuba said.

He sat on a wooden stool behind one of the long bar counters. Next to Cuba a woman, her hair tied in pig-tails with pink ribbon, concentrated on the keys of a laptop as if she were picking apples out of a bin.

Calvino walked over to the counter. Cuba was holding out a piece of paper.

"Nueng's making fewer mistakes," said Cuba. He waved the paper around and then put it back on the counter.

Calvino assumed he meant her typing, but he might have meant the strange men Nueng attracted in the Office for short-time assignments. Cuba was one of those My Fair Lady men who had faith in their ability to turn a flower girl into a lady, or in Nueng's case a butterfly into a larva, reversing the usual course of nature. He had phoned Calvino a month ago and asked if he might hire Nueng.

Calvino looked down at the paper. "How many mistakes?"

"Only eighteen," said Cuba.

One of Nueng's friends in a micro-dress with pudgy legs and scarred knees leaned forward, pulled on Cuba's sleeve. "Nueng shouldn't quit her night job. She very good at night work in this Office."

Cuba tried to ignore Nueng's friend, focusing on Calvino. "But there's hope," said Cuba. He nodded towards Nueng, who sat in the dim flickering light from the laptop screen typing about one word a minute, using her two index fingers.

"There's always hope. Otherwise we wouldn't be here."

Calvino pushed off and went to his usual table in the back. A number of people he knew were drinking together, talking and laughing. He sat down, catching the end of a conversation.

A mid-forties expat named Elroy shouted, "Another fucking wando theory." He stopped as he saw Calvino.

"Why don't you give Nueng a fucking break? Give her a job. So she types fellatio with only one fucking 'l,' big deal." Elroy had had too much to drink and slurred his words but this did not stop him from sounding belligerent, mean, spoiling for a fight. "Buy me a beer," he said to Calvino. "Come on, Calvino, you are fucking loaded. Buy me a goddamn beer." The table went quiet, then Elroy smiled. "After I take a piss, of course."

Elroy staggered as he rose from his chair, almost knocking it over. After he disappeared up the stairs to the washroom, George Snow started in on how maybe Elroy ought to be added to the "List." George's List was of the long-term expats who ought to be dead. Most of the time it was someone who was so violent, obnoxious, or suicidal that no one could understand how he had managed to piss off so many dangerous people and still remain alive. There would be some poor asshole on a holiday that got killed on a motorcycle or was hijacked from the airport and murdered. Guys who knew nothing, knew no one, but ended up dead.

"Of course he hates you, Vinee. He's been in Thailand twenty years, dreaming of becoming somebody. Only it didn't work out that way. Elroy's given it his best shot but he never made it to the Show. It eats him, man." Snow liked baseball metaphors.

"Minor league assholes just stay assholes; but major league assholes, they at least get respect." What Snow meant was the major league player got a shot at immortality—the ultimate home run.

But Calvino didn't catch this at first; he wondered what they were talking about—first Elroy's comment that he was loaded and then Snow's suggestion that he had been called up to the major league. He had been called a lot of things in his time but having money was not a slur anyone had ever hurled at him. "George, what are you talking about? And what was Elroy talking about me being loaded?"

George pursed his lips and rocked his head back and forth, staring at Calvino like the man was having him on and it was fifty-fifty whether George was going to add Calvino to the List. "You're playing coy, right? The old Sam Spade cool and laid back in his moment of glory."

"Coy about what?" He wasn't really paying attention to George. Across from the table a long-bodied *ying* in a black tank top and mini-skirt leaned against a table, her legs pumping to the music.

"Yeah, yeah. Cool. Play it out. You just gave Father Andrew twenty grand to finish the school in Klong Toey, and that is US dollars kind of grand, and you can't buy Elroy a beer? Elroy hates you. Christ, you're lucky I don't hate you."

Calvino's attention was drawn to the *ying*'s shoes— white eight-inch platforms—billboard size advertising space—news-print and headlines had been printed in newspaper columns on the shoes. The *ying* turned, displaying each foot. One shoe was themed for the Kennedys; a black and white photo of JFK Jr. stenciled on the back. The other shoe had an image of Lady Di.

"Who told you I gave Father Andrew twenty grand?"

"He did, man. I just got back from interviewing him this afternoon. I don't know what you get out of this. Sainthood? Your name over the entrance? First dibs on the babes in each year's graduating class? But I am certain you have it figured out."

As the *ying* turned around, he saw the silhouette of a small plane on one shoe and on the other a Benz. The toy plane and Benz were made to scale. The plane had tiny flashing landing lights on the wings. The headlights of the tiny Benz flashed. Instruments of luxury and wealth and death and loss.

Calvino glanced down at his mobile phone and saw Father Andrew had phoned; his number was left like a footprint on the tiny digital screen, but he hadn't phoned back. Now he knew why Father Andrew had wanted to speak to him. To thank him for a gift that he hadn't made.

"You see the *Bangkok Post* article about how the police say Ramsey was the serial killer," said another regular at the Office.

Calvino's head dropped and he let out a long sigh. "Daniel Ramsey."

"That wando who got killed at the Emporium," said Snow. "Who would have thunk it?" George liked to say "thunk" for "thought" especially around the Office girls, hoping they would pick up these words and use them to confuse the tourists.

Calvino put down a five-hundred-baht note. "See that Elroy doesn't go without what he needs."

"You're not going, man?" said George Snow. "You just got here. Did you see that the police figured out Ramsey was the serial killer? Great story. What do you think, Vinee, you were there? Did Ramsey off those five guys?"

What Calvino thought was that the money to Father Andrew and the newspaper story had a special message for him. He was being bought off. They knew how to get to him.

Calvino glanced at his watch. "Got to go and count my money."

He walked over to girl with the bad-news shoes. The flashing lights from the toy plane and Benz danced off the chrome of the jukebox. She had seen him staring at her.

"You wanna spend the night?"

The answer was always a given: yes, of course, I want to spend the night.

He hadn't asked her name. Not that it mattered. She stepped out with the Benz leading the way, followed by the plane, one step after another. They left the Office together and Calvino was thinking he had taken all the bad news with him.

★★★★★★

BY the time Calvino had managed to get Jess on the phone, he had dialed three times, and then had been put on hold for ten minutes. He sat in the dark. The flashing lights on the Benz and plane were like fireflies. The *ying* sat legs crossed, naked on the edge of his desk. She kept her shoes on. He had asked her not to take them off. Only the street lights outside his office cast enough illumination for him to see the dim outline of the *Bangkok Post* on his desk. The five *farangs* who police have theorized were killed by Daniel Ramsey of Los Angeles, said the article. He didn't want to see such lies in the light. In the dark they didn't look any better.

Finally Jess came onto the phone. "Hey, Jess, how you doin'? I got a couple of questions about twenty grand getting into Father Andrew's bank account and the word going out that I am the donor. We know that ain't the way it happened. There's something else we know didn't happen."

"What do you mean?"

"You know who the serial killer was?" Calvino asked him.

The *ying* was flicking her tongue in his ear.

"Danny Ramsey." Jess's voice was distinct and firm.

"Wrong. It wasn't Ramsey. That's what is printed in the newspaper. But we know they got some bad information. Chaiwat is the serial killer. You know he majored in computer science at the University of San Francisco. After you returned to LA, Pratt and I went back to their house and I checked out his computer. I even know the nickname Chaiwat used with other members of the Cause. Moondance. One word."

"Good name."

She was moaning slowly, unbuttoning his shirt.

"He had built a massive data base of the Cause-members. He also knew what Ramsey and Kowit were doing. He helped himself to the supply of heroin and ran the five bodies of the men he murdered into San Francisco. Check it out. A funeral parlor run by a Chinese family on Russian Hill handled the arrangements. One of his own university buddies is a member of the Russian Hill family. You want me to go on?"

"Pratt already told me what you found in the computer. It seems the hard disk crashed so all the information got lost."

Calvino's voice was cracking up. She had his shirt off and threw it across the office. He saw a dim blur of JFK Jr.'s face on the back of her shoe.

"You are saying that the information got lost, is that it? But I read the information. So did Pratt. Our hard disks didn't crash. So why are you quoted in the *Bangkok Post* as saying Danny Ramsey was the serial killer? Why did you let the bullshit story go out?"

"Because that is the deal we made. Chaiwat, his two brothers, and his father have gone into the federal witness protection program. They are going to put Kowit and about six other bad guys in prison. We have destroyed a major smuggling operation. And one more thing. You were right. There was someone in the Embassy. A local hire who had an extra twenty million baht in his wife's bank account that he couldn't explain."

Anyone could have put the money in the account to frame him.

"Remember that movie where they framed the cop with the transfers into his account?" asked Calvino. "Are you sure it wasn't Morgan?"

"All the evidence points to a local staff at the Embassy. But this has been a major embarrassment for Morgan. I mean the guy did work for him."

"So that's it. Morgan is clean and the local guy gets collared and everyone has agreed to Plan A. We're saving face and saving ass, big time. And no Thai image is tarnished if the *farang* was the killer, right? And no American image is hurt if a Thai who worked at the US Embassy takes the fall. A trade-off, right, Jess?" He couldn't help but feel bitter.

"Sometimes to do a higher right, you have to compromise with some smaller wrongs. If we go after Chaiwat no jury is going to believe any member of that family's testimony. We lose, Vincent. And we can't lose this case. We must shut these people down. No matter how we play it, nothing is going to bring back the five dead guys. Chaiwat will pay for what he's done. The Embassy will make certain nothing like this happens again. What's the point of ruining careers and reputations?"

She was unbuttoning Calvino's trousers.

"Next life is when all of this comes right."

"There is that."

Calvino didn't say anything as he put down the phone. He pulled the *ying* up and sat her on the desk. She seemed startled.

"It's okay. I want to read your shoes."

He lifted her right foot and read—gossip, scandal, stock exchange numbers, and cartoons. Calvino translated her shoes to her in Thai and she started to laugh. She had no idea the shoes had any meaning. She laughed so hard she had to pee. Calvino gave her directions and she staggered down the corridor to the restroom.

Calvino sat alone, thinking about Jess, the all-American hero, who had become very Thai on the phone. He told Calvino since returning to Los Angeles he had learned a lot, and that his life had changed a great deal but that along the way he had both lost and found something. What he found was that life was like a professional wrestling match, all show, posture, growls, no real punches or kicks thrown that are intended to land. What he had lost was the reality of what had happened. That Calvino had paid out the four grand from his own pocket because he thought this was going to be the only way to get him out of the country alive. He had also made himself lose the memory of the dead bodies in the Emporium; the men they had killed. That had not been professional wrestling; that had been the real, lethal thing. Or the men in Calvino's car who had been killed by the bomb. He had thought how to make this equation of what had been found equal, what had been lost. Jess wired Father Andrew the money. He would like to believe it had nothing to do with the compromise over the destruction of the evidence showing Chaiwat had been the killer. The money had another purpose—an atonement for allowing evil to compromise good. Somehow in a world where things were at strange angles, this had put things level. Jess had tried to put things right. But could this kind of atonement ever really make things right?

He reached for the phone to call Pratt. His hand lay on the receiver for a couple of minutes. He didn't make the call. He would wait and let Pratt phone him in his own time, and, in his own way, explain that when one dances in the shadows of a big city, truth is eclipsed daily. In this theatre of darkness the expectation is to try and do right without stumbling in the process. Because those who fell hit the ground hard. He pulled open his desk drawer and took out the baby powder and sprinkled it all around his office. He would sleep in the office tonight. He wanted to track the *ying's* movements in the morning. He wanted to know where those bad-news shoes had gone during the night.

He threw down a mat in front of the desk and, after they made love, he let her remove her shoes. By the time Calvino had drifted off to sleep he was back in that village . . . and stood passively by as he watched one more time the stranger in black being thrown into the flames.

ABOUT AUTHOR

Christopher G. Moore is a Canadian writer who once taught law at the University of British Columbia. After his first book His Lordship' Arsenal was published in New York to a critical acclaim in 1985, Moore became a full-time writer and has so far written 23 novels and one collection of interlocked short stories.

Moore is best known by his international award-winning Vincent Calvino Private Eye series and his cult classics Land of Smiles Trilogy, a behind-the-smiles study of his adopted country, Thailand. His novels have been translated into eleven languages. His Vincent Calvino novels are published in the United States by Atlantic Monthly Press and in Great Britain and the Commonwealth by Atlantic Books.

He lives with his wife in Bangkok. For more information about the author and his work, visit his official website: www.cgmoore.com. He also blogs regularly with other cirme authors at www.internationalcrimeauthors.com

THE VINCENT CALVINO P.I. SERIES

CHRISTOPHER G. MOORE's Vincent Calvino P.I. series began with *Spirit House* in 1992. The latest, eleventh, in the series is *The Corruptionist* first released in Thailand in 2010

Moore's protagonist, Vincent Calvino is an Italian-Jewish former lawyer from New York who left his practice to turn P.I. in Southeast Asia. Calvino's assignments take him inside the labyrinth of local politics, double-dealing and fleeting relationships. Unlike typical tough-guy sleuths, Calvino admits he would never survive without his guardian angel, his Shakespeare-quoting and saxophone-playing buddy, Colonel Pratt, an honest and well-connected Thai cop who helps him find hidden forces, secret traps and ways to keep him alive in a foreign land.

The twelves novels in the Vincent Calvino P.I. series are: *Spirit House, Asia Hand, Zero Hour in Phnom Penh, Comfort Zone, The Big Weird, Cold Hit, Minor Wife, Pattaya 24/7, The Risk of Infidelity Index, Paying Back Jack, The Corruptionist,* and *9 Gold Bullets.* The novels are published in Thailand by Heaven Lake Press, in the United States by Grove/Atlantic and in Great Britain by Atlantic Books.

The third installment in the series *Zero Hour in Phnom Penh* won the German Critics Award for Crime Fiction (Deutscher Krimi Preis) for best international crime fiction in 2004 and the Premier Special Director's Award Semana Negra (Spain) in 2007 or the author's website: www.cgmoore.com.

SPIRIT HOUSE
First in the series

The Bangkok police already have a confession by a nineteen-year-old drug addict who has admitted to the murder of a British computer wizard, Ben Hoadly. From the bruises on his face shown at the press conference, it is clear that the young suspect had some help from the police in the making of his confession. The case is wrapped up. Only there are some loose ends that the police and just about everyone else are happy to overlook.

The search for the killer of Ben Hoadley plunges Calvino into the dark side of Bangkok, where professional hit men have orders to stop him. From the world of thinner addicts, dope dealers, fortunetellers, and high-class call girls, Calvino peels away the mystery surrounding the death of the English ex-public schoolboy who had a lot of dubious friends.

"Well-written, tough and bloody."
—Bernard Knight, *Tangled Web* (UK)

"A worthy example of a serial character, Vincent Calvino is human and convincing. [He] is an incarnate of the composite of the many expatriate characters who have burned the bridge to their pasts."
— *Thriller Magazine* (Italy)

"A thinking man's Philip Marlowe, Calvino is a cynic on the surface but a romantic at heart. Calvino ... found himself in Bangkok—the end of the world for a whole host of bizarre foreigners unwilling, unable, or uninterested in going home."
— *The Daily Yomiuri*

ASIA HAND
Second in the series

Bangkok—the Year of the Monkey. Calvino's Chinese New Year celebration is interrupted by a call to Lumpini Park Lake, where Thai cops have just fished the body of a *farang* cameraman. CNN is running dramatic footage of several Burmese soldiers on the Thai border executing students.

Calvino follows the trail of the dead man to a feature film crew where he hits the wall of silence. On the other side of that wall, Calvino and Colonel Pratt discover and elite film unit of old Asia hands with connections to influential people in Southeast Asia. They find themselves matched against a set of *farangs* conditioned for urban survival and willing to go for a knock-out punch.

"Moore's Vinny Calvino is a worthy successor to Raymond Chandler's Philip Marlowe and Mickey Spillane's Mike Hammer."
—*The Nation*

"The top foreign author focusing on the Land of Smiles, Canadian Christopher G. Moore clearly has a first-hand understanding of the expat milieu ... Moore is perspicacious."
—*Bangkok Post*

ZERO HOUR IN PHNOM PENH
Third in the series

Winner of 2004 German Critics Award for Crime Fiction (Deutscher Krimi Preis) for best international crime fiction and 2007 Premier Special Director's Award Semana Negra (Spain)

In the early 1990s, at the end of Cambodia's devastating civil war, UN peacekeeping forces try to keep the lid on the violence. Gunfire can still be heard nightly in Phnom Penh, where Vietnamese prostitutes try to hook UN peacekeepers from the balcony of the Lido Bar.

Calvino traces leads on a missing *farang* from Bangkok to war-torn Cambodia, through the Russian market, hospitals, nightclubs, news briefings, and UNTAC headquarters. Calvino's buddy, Colonel Pratt, knows something that Calvino does not: The missing man is connected with the jewels stolen from the Saudi royal family. Calvino quickly finds out that he is not the only one looking for the missing *farang*.

"Political, courageous and perhaps Moore's most important work."
—*CrimiCouch.de*

"Fast-paced and entertaining. Even outside of his Bangkok comfort zone, Moore shows he is one of the best chroniclers of the expat diaspora."
—*The Daily Yomiuri*

"A brilliant detective story that portrays—with no illusion—Cambodia's adventurous transition from genocide and civil war to a free-market economy and democratic normality. A rare stroke of luck and a work of art."
—*Deutsche Well Buchtipp*, Bonn

COMFORT ZONE
Fourth in the series

Twenty years after the end of the Vietnam War, Vietnam is opening to the outside world. There is a smell of fast money in the air and poverty in the streets. Business is booming and in austere Ho Chi Minh City a new generation of foreigners have arrived to make money and not war. Against the backdrop of Vietnam's economic miracle, Comfort Zone reveals a divided people still not reconciled with their past and unsure of their future.

Calvino is hired by an ex-special forces vet, whose younger brother uncovers corruption and fraud in the emerging business world in which his clients are dealing. But before Calvino even leaves Bangkok, there have already been two murders, one in Saigon and one in Bangkok

"Moore hits home with more of everything in Comfort Zone. There is a balanced mix of story-line, narrative, wisdom, knowledge as well as love, sex, and murder."
—*Thailand Times*

"Like a Japanese gardener who captures the land and the sky and recreates it in the backyard, Moore's genius is in portraying the Southeast Asian heartscape behind the tourist industry hotel gloss.
—*The Daily Yomiuri*

"In Comfort Zone, our Bangkok-based P.I. digs, discovering layers of intrigue. He's stalked by hired killers and falls in love with a Hanoi girl. Can he trust her? The reader is hooked."
—*NTUC Lifestyle* (Singapore)

THE BIG WEIRD
Fifth in the series

A beautiful American blond is found dead with a large bullet hole in her head in the house of her ex-boyfriend. A famous Hollywood screenwriter hires Calvino to investigate her death. Everyone except Calvino's client believes Samantha McNeal has committed suicide.

In the early days of the Internet, Sam ran with a young and wild expat crowd in Bangkok. As Calvino slides into a world where people are dead serious about sex, money and fame, he unearths a hedonistic community where the ritual of death is the ultimate high.

"An excellent read, charming, amusing, insightful, complex, localised yet startlingly universal in its themes."
  —*Guide of Bangkok*

"Highly entertaining."
  —*Bangkok Post*

"Like a noisy, late-night Thai restaurant, Moore serves up tongue-burning spices that swallow up the literature of Generation X and Cyberspace as if they were merely sticky rice."
  —*The Daily Yomiuri*

"A good read, fast-paced and laced with so many of the locales so familiar to the expat denizens of Bangkok."
  —*Art of Living* (Thailand)

COLD HIT
Sixth in the series

Five foreigners have died in Bangkok. Were they drug overdose victims or victims of a serial killer? Calvino believes the evidence points to a serial killer who stalks tourists in Bangkok. The Thai police, including Colonel Pratt, don't buy his theory.

Calvino teams up with an LAPD officer on a bodyguard assignment. Hidden forces pull them through swank shopping malls, run-down hotels, the Klong Toey slum, and bars in the red light district as they try to keep their man and themselves alive. As Calvino learns more about the bodies being shipped back to America, the secret of the serial killer is revealed.

"The story is plausible and riveting to the end."
 —*The Japan Times*

"Tight, intricate plotting, wickedly astute ... Cold Hit will have you variously gasping, chuckling, nodding, tut-tutting, oh-yesing, and grinding your teeth throughout its 330 pages."
 —*Guide of Bangkok*

"City jungle, sex, drugs, power, but also good-hearted people: a complete crime."
 —*Zwanzig Minuten Zürich*

"Calvino is a wonderful private detective figure! Consistent action, masterful language ... and Anglo-Saxon humour at its best."
 —Lutz Bunk, *DeutschlandRadio,* Berlin

MINOR WIFE
Seventh in the series

A contemporary murder set in Bangkok—a neighbor and friend, a young ex-hooker turned artist, is found dead by an American millionaire's minor wife. Her rich expat husband hires Calvino to investigate.

While searching for the killer in exclusive clubs and not-so-exclusive bars of Bangkok, Calvino discovers that a minor wife—mia noi—has everything to do with a woman's status. From illegal cock fighting matches to elite Bangkok golf clubs, Calvino finds himself caught in the crossfire as he closes in on the murderer.

"What distinguishes Christopher G. Moore from other foreign authors setting their stories in the Land of Smiles is how much more he understands its mystique, the psyche of its populace and the futility of its round residents trying to fit into its square holes."
—*Bangkok Post*

"Moore pursues in even greater detail in Minor Wife the changing social roles of Thai women (changing, but not always quickly or for the better) and their relations among themselves and across class lines and other barriers."
—*Vancouver Sun*

"The thriller moves in those convoluted circles within which Thai life and society takes place. Moore's knowledge of these gives insights into many aspects of the cultural mores. Many of these are unknown to the expat population. ... Great writing, great story and a great read."
—*Pattaya Mail*

PATTAYA 24/7
Eighth in the series

Inside a secluded, lush estate located on the edge of Pattaya, an eccentric Englishman's gardener is found hanged. Calvino has been hired to investigate. He finds himself pulled deep into the shadows of the war against drugs, into the empire of a local warlord with the trail leading to a terrorist who has caused Code Orange alerts to flash across the screen of American intelligence.

In a story packed with twists and turns, Calvino traces the links from the gardener's past to the doors of men with power and influence who have everything to lose if the mystery of the gardener's death is solved.

"Calvino does it again ... well-developed characters, and the pace keeps you reading well after you should have turned out the light."
—*Farang Magazine* (Thailand)

"A compelling, atmospheric and multi-layered murder investigation set in modern-day Thailand. The detective, Calvino, is a complex and engaging hero."
—Garry Disher, award-winning author of *The Wyatt Novels*

"We enjoy the spicy taste of hard-boiled fiction reinvented in an exotic but realistic place—in fact, not realistic, but real!"
—*Thriller Magazine* (Italy)

"A cast of memorably eccentric figures in an exotic Southeast Asian backdrop"
—*The Japan Times*

THE RISK OF INFIDELITY INDEX
Ninth in the series

Major political demonstrations are rocking Bangkok. Chaos and fear sweep through the Thai and expatriate communities. Calvino steps into the political firestorm as he investigates a drug piracy operation. The piracy is traced to a powerful business interest protected by important political connections. A nineteen-year-old Thai woman and a middle-aged lawyer end up dead on the same evening. Both are connected to Calvino's investigation.

The dead lawyer's law firm denies any knowledge of the case. Calvino is left in the cold. Approached by a group of expat housewives—rattled by the "Risk of Infidelity Index" that ranks Bangkok number one for available sexual temptations—to investigate their husbands, Calvino discovers the alliance of forces blocking his effort to disclose the secret pirate drug investigation.

"Moore's flashy style successfully captures the dizzying contradictions in [Bangkok's] vertiginous landscape."
    —Marilyn Stasio, *The New York Times Book Review*

"A hard-boiled, street-smart, often hilarious pursuit of a double murderer."
    —*San Francisco Chronicle*

"Humorous and intelligent ... a great introduction to the seamy side of Bangkok."
    —Carla Mckay, *The Daily Mail*

"Taut, spooky, intelligent, and beautifully written."
    —T. Jefferson Parker, author of *L.A. Outlaws*

PAYING BACK JACK
Tenth in the series

In *Paying Back Jack*, Calvino agrees to follow the 'minor wife' of a Thai politician and report on her movements. His client is Rick Casey, a shady American whose life has been darkened by the unsolved murder of his idealistic son. It seems to be a simple surveillance job, but soon Calvino is entangled in a dangerous web of political allegiance and a reckless quest for revenge.

And, unknown to our man in Bangkok, in an anonymous tower in the center of the city, a two-man sniper team awaits its shot, a shot that will change everything. Paying Back Jack is classic Christopher G. Moore: densely-woven, eye-opening, and riveting.

"[*Paying Back Jack*] might be Moore's finest novel yet."
　—Barry Eisler, author of *Fault Line*

"*Paying Back Jack* is so tightly woven and entertaining it is hopeless to try to put it down. Not only was it new and fresh, but I feel like I have taken a trip to the underbelly of Thailand. It is impossible not to love this book."
　—Carolyn Lanier, *I Love a Mystery*

"A vivid sense of place ... the city of Bangkok, with its chaos and mystery, is almost another character. Recommended."
　—*Library Journal*

"Moore clearly has no fear that his gloriously corrupt Bangkok will ever run dry."
　—*Kirkus Review*

THE CORRUTIONIST
Eleventh in the series

Set during the recent turbulent times in Thailand, the 11th novel in the Calvino series centers around the street demonstrations and occupation of Government House in Bangkok.

Hired by an American businessman, Calvino finds himself caught in the middle of a family conflict over a Chinese corporate takeover. This is no ordinary deal. Calvino and his client are up against powerful forces set to seize much more than a family business. As the bodies accumulate while he navigates Thailand's business-political landmines, Calvino becomes increasingly entangled in a secret deal made by men who will stop at nothing—and no one—standing in their way. But Calvino refuses to step aside.

The Corruptionist captures with precision the undercurrents enveloping Bangkok, revealing multiple layers of betrayal and deception.

"Moore's understanding of the dynamics of Thai society has always impressed, but considering current events, the timing of his latest [The Corruptionist] is absolutely amazing."
—Mark Schreiber, *The Japan Times*

"Politics . . . has a role in the series, more so now than earlier. What with corruption during elections and coups afterwards, the denizens watch with bemusement the unlikelihood of those in office serving their terms. Moore captures this in his books. Thought-provoking columnists don't do it better. . . . Moore is putting Thailand on the map."
—Bernard Trink, *Bangkok Post*

"An achievement . . . interpreting modern, fast changing Thailand with its violent political power struggles. . . . [T]he levels and depths of observation and insight reach an epic nature in [The Corruptionist]. . . . The new characters are stunning. . . . The ending is superb."
    —Richard Ravensdale, *Pattaya Trader*

"Very believable . . . A 'brave' book . . . Another riveting read from Christopher G. Moore and one you should not miss."
    —Lang Reid, *Pattaya Mail*

9 GOLD BULLETS
Twelfth in the series

A priceless collection of 9 gold bullet coins issued during the Reign of Rama V has gone missing along with a Thai coin collector. Local police find a link between the missing Thai coins and Calvino's childhood friend, Josh Stein, who happens to be in Bangkok on an errand for his new Russian client. This old friend and his personal and business entanglements with the Russian underworld take Calvino back to New York, along with Pratt.

The gritty, dark vision of 9 Gold Bullets is tracked through the eyes of a Thai cop operating on a foreign turf, and a private eye expatriated long enough to find himself a stranger in his hometown. As the intrigue behind the missing coins moves between New York andBangkok, and the levels of deception increase, Calvino discovers the true nature of friendship and where he belongs.

CPSIA information can be obtained at www.ICGtesting.com
Printed in the USA
LVOW121405220212

269931LV00002B/51/P